HEROIC REPUTATIONS AND EXE

Blackb

MANCHESTER
UNIVERSITY PRESS

YORK STUDIES IN CULTURAL HISTORY

edited by Geoffrey Cubitt and Allen Warren

HEROIC REPUTATIONS AND EXEMPLARY LIVES

MANCHESTER UNIVERSITY PRESS

MANCHESTER AND NEW YORK

distributed exclusively in the USA by St. Martin's Press

Copyright © Manchester University Press 2000

While copyright in the volume as a whole is vested in Manchester University Press, copyright in individual chapters belongs to their respective authors, and no chapter may be reproduced wholly or in part without the express permission in writing of both author and publisher.

Published by Manchester University Press
Oxford Road, Manchester M13 9NR, UK
and Room 400, 175 Fifth Avenue, New York, NY 10010, USA
http://www.manchesteruniversitypress.co.uk

Distributed exclusively in the USA by
St. Martin's Press, Inc., 175 Fifth Avenue, New York,
NY 10010, USA

Distributed exclusively in Canada by
UBC Press, University of British Columbia, 2029 West Mall,
Vancouver, BC, Canada V6T 1Z2

British Library Cataloguing-in-Publication Data
A catalogue record for this book is available from the British Library

Library of Congress Cataloging-in-Publication Data applied for

ISBN 0 7190 5780 9 *hardback*
 0 7190 5781 7 *paperback*

First published 2000

07 06 05 04 03 02 01 00   10 9 8 7 6 5 4 3 2 1

Typeset
by Florence Production Ltd, Stoodleigh, Devon
Printed in Great Britain
by Biddles Limited, Guildford and King's Lynn

CONTENTS

List of illustrations

Notes on contributors

DINAH BIRCH is a Fellow of Trinity College, Oxford. Her publications include *Ruskin's Myths* (1988) and *Ruskin on Turner* (1990). She has edited *Ruskin and the Dawn of the Modern* (1999), and is presently completing a selected edition of Ruskin's *Fors Clavigera*.

CHRISTOPHER CLARK is Professor of North American History at the University of Warwick. He is author of *The Roots of Capitalism: Western Massachusetts, 1780–1860* (1990) and *The Communitarian Moment: The Radical Challenge of the Northampton Association* (1995), and is co-author of *Who Built America?* (2000). He is currently writing a brief history of the United States from the Revolution to the Civil War.

KRISTA COWMAN is Senior Lecturer in History in the School of Cultural Studies, Leeds Metropolitan University. Her main research interests are in suffrage, women and socialism, and she is currently completing a book on women's political activities on Merseyside from the late Victorian period until the end of the First World War.

GEOFFREY CUBITT is Senior Lecturer in History at the University of York. He is the author of *The Jesuit Myth: Conspiracy Theory and Politics in Nineteenth-Century France* (1993), and of various articles on French political, religious and cultural history, and was the editor of the previous volume of York Studies in Cultural History, *Imagining Nations* (1998).

PATRICIA FARA is a Fellow of Clare College, Cambridge. Her most recent book is *Sympathetic Attractions: Magnetic Practices, Beliefs and Symbolism in Eighteenth Century England* (1996), and she is currently studying how Isaac Newton has been constructed as a scientific and national hero, and how meanings of genius have changed.

RICHARD HOLT is a Research Professor at the International Centre for Sports History and Culture, De Montfort University. He is author of *Sport and the British* (1989) amongst other works on British and European sport. He wrote the catalogue essay for *The Book of British Sporting Heroes* (National Portrait Gallery, 1998), and is currently writing a book on Sport and the English Hero.

MAX JONES is a Fellow and Director of Studies in History at Christ's College, Cambridge. He has recently completed his Ph.D. thesis on 'The Royal Geographical Society and the Commemoration of Captain Scott's Last Antarctic Expedition'.

TOM LODGE is Professor of Political Studies at the University of Witswatersrand in Johannesburg. He is the author of *Black Politics in South Africa since 1945* (1983), *All Here and Now: Black Politics in South Africa during the 1980s* (1991), *South African Politics since 1994* (1999), and *Consolidating Democracy: South Africa's Second Popular Election* (1999).

JOHN M. MACKENZIE is Professor of Imperial History at Lancaster University. He was the editor of the National Portrait Gallery Catalogue 'David Livingstone and the Victorian Encounter with Africa' (1996) and is co-curator (and editor of the accompanying book) for an exhibition, 'The Victorians', at the Victoria and Albert Museum in 2001.

ROSEMARY MITCHELL is Lecturer in History at Trinity and All Saints College, Leeds, and has worked as a Research Editor for the New Dictionary of National Biography. She has written *Picturing the Past: English History in Text and Image* (1999), and is now researching Victorian women intellectuals and scholars.

ADAM SUTCLIFFE is the Chaim Lopata Assistant Professor of European Jewish History at the University of Illinois at Urbana-Champaign. He has recently written on Voltaire and on Judaism and toleration, and is currently completing a book on the significance of Judaism in the European Early Enlightenment.

CHRISTIAN TURNER completed his D.Phil. in the Department of English at the University of York. His research interests focus on the transmission of classical traditions in Middle English poetry, particularly Chaucer. He has researched and written historical documentaries for Channel 4 television, and currently works in the Cabinet Office.

NORMAN VANCE is Professor of English and Director of the Humanities Graduate Research Centre at the University of Sussex. His books include *The Victorians and Ancient Rome* (1997) and *Irish Literature, a Social History* (2nd ed., 1999). He is currently working on a study of politics and Irish writing since 1800.

ALLEN WARREN is Head of the History Department and Provost of Vanbrugh College at the University of York. His most recent publications have been studies of Disraeli and Ireland, and Disraeli and the Church of England, both in *Parliamentary History* (1999 and 2000).

Acknowledgements

Apart from the introduction and the essay by Rosemary Mitchell, the essays in this volume originated as contributions to the second York Conference in Cultural History, held under the title 'Exemplary Lives' at the University of York in April 1997. Those principally involved in the organisation of that conference, besides the present editors, were Chris Clark, John Arnold, Joanna de Groot, Jane Rendall, Katy Cubitt and Mark Ormrod. Thanks are due, both to them and to all the other contributors to the conference, for their part in making the present volume possible, and to Vanessa Graham of Manchester University Press for support and encouragement throughout the process of the book's preparation.

Geoffrey Cubitt

Introduction: heroic reputations and exemplary lives

'We have undertaken to discourse here for a little on Great Men, their manner of appearance in our world's business, how they have shaped themselves in the world's history, what ideas men formed of them, what work they did; – on Heroes, namely, and on their reception and performance; what I call Hero-worship and the Heroic in human affairs.' The opening words of Thomas Carlyle's lectures *On Heroes, Hero-Worship and the Heroic in History* (1841) may, with the addition of women to men in the wording, serve as a makeshift opening to the present book. His next sentence – 'Too evidently this is a large topic; deserving quite other treatment than we can expect to give it at present' – could no doubt prudently be added.[1] To mitigate the largeness of the topic, and to demarcate the agenda of this volume and of this introductory chapter from Carlyle's own (which was to promote the idea that heroes were the sole creative influences in human history and that hero-worship was the life-blood of human societies), two clarifications, both implicit in the book's title, are necessary.

First, this is not a book that deals, for the most part, with some raw reality of heroic existence. It is a book that deals with heroic reputations – with the ways in which heroes have been represented, the ways in which their heroic status has been established and sustained, the ways in which their lives and personalities have been imaginatively constructed and embellished, both during and after their own lifetimes. In short, this is a book about heroic images, and about the cultural and political uses of those images, rather than about the direct influence of genuinely heroic actions and personalities in human history. The chapters seek to make a contribution to what is now a well-established and growing literature on the politics and culture of the heroic. As well as casting light from new angles on such well-established topics as Christian sanctity and hagiography,[2] the heroic culture of chivalry,[3] and concepts of genius in science and the arts,[4] recent studies (both by historians and by scholars with backgrounds in fields such as sociology, art history or literary studies) have explored the evolving reputations, shifting images and varied uses of a succession of heroic historical figures, from Joan of Arc to George Washington, Columbus to Pocahontas, Mary Queen of Scots to General Custer.[5] Others have examined the heroic cultures and ideologies of, for example, the American and French Revolutions, British imperialism, Nazism and Communism,[6] or have explored the gender dimensions of heroic reputations.[7] The present volume draws on such literature and seeks to develop some of its insights.

Secondly, however, this is a book which seeks to develop, within this general study of heroic reputations, a specific interest in that element in such reputations which tends to assign to the hero's existence the status of an 'exemplary life'. Such a life is one valued and admired not merely (or even necessarily) for its practical achievements, but for the moral or ethical or social truths or values which it is perceived both to embody and, through force of example, to impress on the minds of others. Discourses of exemplarity intersect and overlap with discourses of the heroic, but are not co-terminous with them; while the majority of chapters in this volume address the area of overlap, some (those of Clark (Chapter 11) and Cowman (Chapter 12) for example) are concerned with broader applications of exemplarity, resulting in less explicitly heroic kinds of reputation. One purpose of this introductory chapter will be to explore at a more general level some of the ways in which notions of exemplarity have helped to shape the cultural uses of heroic figures. To do this will involve juxtaposing the moral discourse of exemplarity with other ways of defining heroic status – essentially with those that celebrate (as Carlyle did) the role of Great Men (or more rarely Women) as historical agents. Studying the tensions and interactions between the moral and the historical in the development and elaboration of heroic reputations is one way of charting their ideological fluctuations.

These two points of focus – the cultural construction of heroic reputations, and the relationships within and around them of moral and historical discourses – supply the agenda for this chapter. The next section of the chapter will offer some general remarks on the processes of construction; the later sections will delve further into the detailed meanings of exemplarity and into its relationships to historical narrative. The chapters that follow have been arranged under four headings. The first two offer contrasting sets of thematically linked case studies, the first dealing with the cult of exemplary intellectuals in Europe between the later middle ages and the eighteenth century, the second with that of British heroes of empire and overseas adventure in the nineteenth and twentieth centuries. The chapters in these two sections permit comparisons to be made between two different periods and cultural contexts and between two ostensibly very different kinds of heroic image, the one focused on the life of the mind, the other on the physical as well as moral strenuousness of the imperial endeavour. The chapters in the third section explore some of the varied uses made in nineteenth-century culture of heroes or exemplary figures drawn from the historical (or even legendary) past: these range from their deployment in discourses on empire or on femininity to their use in the complex intellectual self-fashioning of Victorian intellectuals. The chapters in the fourth section look at what might be called the fashioning of exemplary 'types' – figures possessed of generic as well as individual characteristics: exemplary businessmen or sportsmen or female socialists, again drawn from the nineteenth and early twentieth centuries. The book concludes with a detailed study of a contemporary heroic example: that of Nelson Mandela. Between them, then, the chapters in this book – drawn chiefly though not exclusively from British history – offer a diversity of heroic specimens and a variety of approaches to their analysis. The present chapter seeks to place their detailed contributions within a wider framework of discussion.

For the purposes of this chapter, a hero is any man or woman whose existence, whether in his or her own lifetime or later, is endowed by others, not just with a high degree of fame and honour, but with a special allocation of imputed meaning and symbolic significance – that not only raises them above others in public esteem but makes them the object of some kind of collective emotional investment. (Such figures sometimes, of course, go by other descriptions – saints, geniuses, cultural icons, men or women of destiny – but the term hero will here be used as shorthand to cover these variations.) The concept of reputation is thus central to the understanding of the heroic that this chapter will develop, and reputations are understood here not as the vapour trails of natural glory that the great and the good leave behind them, but as cultural constructions reflecting the values and ideologies of the societies in which they are produced. The assumption here is not, of course, that the real actions and personalities of individuals are irrelevant to their reputations, but that any reputation that proves durable necessarily involves a translation of the individual existence into imaginative terms which resonate with the structures of meaning and value that compose a given culture. What resonates is not the life as lived, but the life as made sense of, the life imaginatively reconstructed and rendered significant. The lives of heroes become playgrounds of the imagination, richly inviting terrains for ideological projection and mythical speculation. Whatever relationship they may bear to the details of an individual life, heroic reputations are products of the imaginative labour through which societies and groups define and articulate their values and assumptions, and through which individuals within those societies or groups establish their participation in larger social or cultural identities.

Any analysis of the making of heroic reputations must have a social and institutional dimension. Human societies have developed a range of more or less formalised procedures and practices both for the general regulation of fame and honour and for the selection, promotion and celebration of heroic figures. Honours systems, decorations and citations, canonisation procedures,[8] state funerals and pantheonisations,[9] centenary celebrations,[10] erections of public statuary,[11] namings of streets and cities, imagery on stamps and banknotes,[12] as well as more obvious forms of official propaganda, are common elements in the apparatus. Control over these elements can be a powerful instrument in the hands of an assertive political or religious authority or of a hegemonic social elite, as any study of the politics of Catholic sanctity at certain periods or of the heroic cultures of modern Communist regimes will confirm. Even in such cases, however, the rigid frameworks of an official heroic culture may disguise a more complex political reality, with different groups seeking to turn the conventional forms of the heroic to their own political advantage, or to practise a kind of symbolic resistance through the promotion of rival heroic candidatures or the reinterpretation of existing ones.[13] And, as Patricia Fara (Chapter 4) and Max Jones (Chapter 6) both show in their contributions to this volume, formal commemorative practices, both monumental and ceremonial, can provide, under other circumstances, the means by which a range of individuals or of corporate bodies or of local communities invest in heroic reputation and shape it to their own purposes, elaborating their own understandings of the hero's significance within the capacious frameworks of a broader cult. Formal rituals and official procedures constitute, anyway, only the most explicit part of a society's hero-worshipping and hero-producing activity. Equally important are the ways in which heroic reputations are developed through the generally less formal practices of social, cultural and economic life – through story-telling and entertainment, through gossip and news reporting, and through the circulation of literature, visual images and artefacts under the influence either of propagandistic or of commercial motives. Attention has often been drawn to the tremendous impetus given to the generation and circulation of heroic stories and images through the dramatic expansion both of the news media and of the general apparatus of commercial production and exchange between the eighteenth century and the twentieth.[14] Patricia Fara supplies further evidence here of the eighteenth-century commercialisation of heroic reputations such as that of Isaac Newton, while Norman Vance (Chapter 8) indicates some of the ways in which heroic references were developed in nineteenth-century theatrical entertainment.

Within these frameworks of institutional and social practice are carried out the rhetorical and intellectual manoeuvres that convert individuals into bearers of heroic status and significance. Some of these manoeuvres are stylistic or linguistic: a person becomes a hero, at least in part, by having his or her life and actions and character described in the conventional terms which govern the acclamation and celebration of the heroic within a particular society or culture. The application of the style is part of the attribution of the status. Each version of the heroic style – and different versions may co-exist in a given society – will tend, through the imposition of a common rhetoric and vocabulary, to standardise perceptions of excellence in the field over which it has application. But such versions are also composed of flexible elements: heroic imagery or terminology originally developed in connection with one branch of human activity can be imaginatively extended to others. The language of military heroism – battles won, enemies vanquished – can come to apply to scientific endeavour ('the conquests of science') or to agriculture or to motherhood ('the battle for grain', 'the battle for births'); images of martyrdom can migrate from religion to secular politics or to science (including, as Max Jones reminds us in Chapter 6, to polar exploration); concepts of destiny or genius can spread from art or science into other realms. The heroic is not a realm of fixed and timeless meanings, but one of changing definitions and shifting constructions, operating within and through the apparent regularities of heroic style and language.

One common feature of heroic styles is the rhetorical linking or assimilating or comparing of new to old. When Joseph Warren fell in the struggle for America's independence, his eulogist Perez Morton constructed his heroic persona in terms which simultaneously bound together the different elements (civil as well as military, classical as well as modern) in the eighteenth-century republican lexicon of patriotic accomplishment: 'like HARRINGTON he wrote, like CICERO he spoke, like HAMPDEN he lived, and like WOLFE he died'.[15] When Camões acclaimed the explorers and kings of Portugal as hardy innovators in the heroic ('The heroes and poets of old have had their day; another and loftier conception of valour has arisen'), he did so still through comparisons with Ulysses and Aeneas, Alexander and Trajan, Caesar and Charlemagne.[16] Such habits of cross-reference run persistently through the heroic mode, sometimes connecting present heroes to the legendary heroic histories of their own communities,[17] sometimes transmitting what Huizinga called 'historical ideals of life' – models of conduct imaginatively rooted in perceptions of a former golden age of virtue or valour.[18] Classical antiquity, the days of the early church, the age of chivalry, and the heroic heyday of the French Revolution have all, in their turn, supplied such standards against which to measure the heroic achievements or shortcomings of later ages, turning subalterns on the Western Front into Galahads, eighteenth-century revolutionaries into representations of Brutus or Cato, and nineteenth-century ones into repetitions of Robespierre or Marat. The framing of modern candidatures for heroic standing in terms of their relationship to such earlier models or patterns of excellence or achievement is one of the principal means by which discourses of the heroic serve as vehicles for the articulation of larger ideologies.

The social construction of heroic reputations involves the imaginative construction of heroic lives – lives, in short, that are not just heroic in isolated detail, but that constitute, in some sense, a heroic totality. Heroes may be celebrated for particular actions or traits of character, but they are celebrated in a way that implies the essential consistency of action with character, and the dramatic unity of the successive stages in individual existence. Heroes do what they have to do, in the nature of their being; they become what they have to become, in the nature of their destiny. Their existences are narratively fashioned as mythical drama or edifying process, marked by moments of heroic resolution or decisive action. Tales of destiny and self-realisation, of quest and discovery, of conversion and redemption, convert the life-course of the individual into an unfolding dramatic revelation of existential truths and heroic dilemmas.

Texts and images and formalised oral productions give a kind of tentative stability to such narrative constructions. Studies of epic poetry, songs and ballads, sermons and funeral oratory can all shed light on this fashioning and codifying of heroic lives, as can studies of portraiture and memorial sculpture, of history painting, of stained glass, lantern lectures, *images d'Épinal* and strip cartoons, murals, film and television. (Patricia Fara in Chapter 4 and John M. MacKenzie in Chapter 5 draw particular attention in this volume to the importance of a diversity of visual media in developing the public images and reputations of Newton and of Livingstone.) It is in written literature, however, and above all in the different forms of 'life-writing' (running from Plutarch and medieval saints' lives to Boswell and the *Dictionary of National Biography*), that the narrative practices involved in the construction of heroic reputations have been most fully and influentially developed.[19] It is hard to overestimate the significance of texts such as Plutarch's *Lives* of notable Greeks and Romans, Boswell's *Life of Johnson* or Southey's *Life of Nelson* in structuring perceptions of their subjects. Equally important, of course, are the complex histories of textual interaction and of cross-fertilisation between text and image and oral tradition, through which the evolution of particular reputations may often be traced. The film *Braveheart*, for example, which has been the principal promoter of William Wallace's standing as a nationalist icon (for Scots and others) at the end of the twentieth century, is based on a twentieth-century novel itself heavily influenced by an eighteenth-century loose translation into English of a sixteenth-century Scots epic poem (whose author, indeed, claimed to be basing his own account on a probably non-existent biographical work in Latin by one of Wallace's contemporaries).[20] At each stage in the chain, different political and cultural influences have affected the transmission and rearrangement of images and data.

The chapters in this volume shed light from various angles on these complex relationships between lives lived, lives imagined and lives textually reproduced. Christian Turner, for example, shows in Chapter 2 how a heroic or at least an exemplary persona was constructed for Plato in the later Middle Ages out of fluid combinations of anecdotal materials, in the absence of any coherent surviving narrative of his life as a whole. Adam Sutcliffe in Chapter 3 shows how an idealised image of Spinoza's character was developed in a succession of writings after his death (including some by writers hostile to his ideas). Though faithful in some ways to the detail of his actual existence, this image of him as a wholly secular kind of moral paragon was then used to validate the more extreme ideas of the radical Enlightenment, in ways which tended to substitute a celebration of the alleged 'spirit' of his life for a direct engagement with his own philosophical positions. Allen Warren, in exploring the career and public image of Baden-Powell in Chapter 7, focuses on a central issue in biographical understandings of him – that of how to relate his life as soldier, culminating in acclamation as the heroic defender of Mafeking, to his later life as founder and leader of the Scout and Guide movement and 'world citizen'. Different ways of imposing coherence on this existence have different implications for the way Baden-Powell's heroic personality is described and evaluated.

To move from this brief discussion of the social and cultural mechanisms by which heroic reputations are produced and sustained to a consideration of their cultural and ideological functions requires the development of a more differentiated conception of the heroic mode – one which permits us to explore its internal tensions and to map its shifting relationships to other fields of cultural practice or production. One starting-point here is a recognition of some fundamental – or at least deep-seated – ambiguities and tensions in traditional conceptions of the heroic. The original heroes – those of Greek mythology and epic poetry – occupied a position intermediate between that of gods and that of ordinary human beings. Distinguished from ordinary men by an indefeasible superiority in strength and valour, 'godlike' indeed in many of their qualities, they yet lacked the defining characteristic of divinity, exemption from ageing and death. Indeed the ability courageously to confront the perpetual possibility of violent death was a vital ingredient in their heroic standing, and gave their existence a kind of moral grandeur that the gods themselves did not possess.[21] Definite though it was, their superiority to other humans was a superiority bounded by the common limits of the human condition. Something of this ambiguity has remained in later heroic conceptions: heroes appear sometimes as figures of radiant excellence, effortlessly superior to other mortals; sometimes as common men or women writ large, with whose struggles and triumphs others can identify. The promotion of them is sometimes an incitation to servile admiration, sometimes an intended inspiration to popular energy or enthusiastic emulation.

This ambiguity in the heroic may well have been deepened, in societies influenced by Christianity, by the way the central mysteries of the faith present the relationship of God and Man. Not only does Christianity propose the vision of a fallen humanity that is destined eventually to return to its original harmony with the divinity. It also prefigures this recaptured unity in the person of its redeeming hero: in Christ, for a moment that resonates through eternity, God incurs the risks and limitations of human existence – becomes a historical actor, faces death upon the cross. Christ becomes the supreme heroic reference.[22] The ambiguities of the heroic are concentrated on this single point of miraculous conjunction between divine and human natures. Christ stands at once as the embodiment of divine perfection and as the supreme inspiration of human moral striving: imitation of him becomes the path of righteousness, open in principle to all believers. The reflections of this ambiguity then pervade the whole Christian notion of sanctity or spiritual heroism. The spiritual hero of the Christian vision is always in progress towards an image of perfection that is never (at least in this life) fully realised. The highest excellence that he or she may achieve is still an excellence in striving, not that of final arrival; it is always an example to others labouring in the same path. Yet it is also a reflection of the divine glory towards which it aspires, and as such a source of wonder and admiration. The saint is a figure at once of higher excellence and of common aspiration; he or she invites a mixture of adoration and emulation. Insofar as Christianity has exerted an influence on broader conceptions of the heroic, that influence has probably tended to sustain the ambiguities of the heroic and to facilitate its conceptual oscillations.

The question of the hero's relationship (in terms of superior or common identity) to ordinary unheroic mortals also raises that of his or her relationship (in terms of conformity or non-conformity) to social normality. Here similar ambiguities and variations arise. On the one hand, heroes are often presented as elite representatives of the values on which society is or ought to be based; on the other, as figures of a barely controllable dynamic energy and personal magnetism, geniuses or charismatic leaders whose power has little to do with established social norms and structures of authority. Such a tension is well captured in David B. Edwards's account of the heroes of the Afghan frontier:

> On the one hand, they embody through their deeds the axiomatic truths by which societies define themselves. On the other, they strain the limits of what societies can tolerate in order to survive. The hero rarely knows his place; he creates his own space at the expense of others and in doing so almost invariably transgresses the limits and agreements around which the normal commerce of daily life takes shape.

Though 'praiseworthy' and 'noble', such heroes 'stand outside the normal orbit of human interaction and are never entirely fit for ordinary society'.[23] (One is reminded of Hegel's remarks on the 'almost animal' instinctiveness of great men.)[24] Heroes, then, may be both admirable and disruptive, both representative (in the sense of embodying truths or values with which others can identify) and exceptional (in the sense of living outside the normal rules and conventions). In practice, of course, heroic reputations often arrange themselves along a spectrum, with paragons of virtuous normality at one end and wild romantic geniuses at the other. Some co-existence of normative and disruptive tendencies remains, however, a common feature of heroic personas.

Latent in traditional conceptions of heroic personality, the ambiguities that have just been considered find a kind of articulation in the interplay between 'moral' and 'historical' conceptions of heroic significance – between notions of the hero as exemplar on the one hand, and notions of the hero as a historically significant 'Great Man' (or occasionally Woman) on the other. At the risk of over-schematising, the outline may be sketched here of two incommensurable (rather than incompatible) discourses on the heroic. The significance of Great Men (taking the term in a loosely Carlylean sense) lies in their perceived prominence and effectiveness as historical agents: it is a dynamic rather than a passive significance, a significance less of what they are than of what they bring about. Above all, it is a significance that presupposes, and reinforces, the narrative patterning of history. By contrast, exemplarity – the relationship that pertains when one human existence is taken as a model or as a bearer of significant truths for the moulding of others – has nothing necessarily to do with instrumental effectiveness, and no necessary relationship to historical narrative. To cast heroes as exemplars is to establish their heroic status by reference to moral and ethical standards rather than to historical processes; it is to glorify character rather than achievement, qualities embodied rather than effects produced, present educational usefulness rather than historical services rendered. These two radically different ways of establishing heroic status and significance are often, of course, applied to the same existences, producing heroic reputations that slither between moral and historical layers of meaning. It is with the variants of these different systems of significance, and with some of these slitherings, that the rest of this chapter will be concerned.

'True biography', wrote the second editor of the *Dictionary of National Biography*, Sir Sidney Lee, 'is no handmaid of ethical instruction.'[25] The dictum expresses a twentieth-century wisdom that is at odds with much of the thought and practice of preceding centuries. Since the time of Plutarch, the contrary assumption – that the represented lives of individuals are both an appropriate and an especially efficacious vehicle of moral instruction – has been one of the principal determinants of biographical composition. Writers as diverse as St Augustine and Samuel Smiles have believed in the capacity of personal examples to remedy the deficiencies of more abstract forms of instruction: 'what in words we are not able to understand, in the deeds of the saints we gather how it is to be understood'; 'Good rules may do much, but good models far more, for in the latter we have instruction in action – wisdom at work.'[26] According to Plutarch, virtuous action had a tendency to generate an active impulse to imitation in the beholder; originating as a spontaneous reaction of admiration, this could be deepened through reflection to become the basis of principled moral action.[27] Oliver Goldsmith framed a similar thought in the more sentimental language of the eighteenth century: the specimens of noble and generous conduct that could be gathered from history and ancient literature had the power to awaken 'the most pathetic emotions' in hearts 'entendered by the practice of virtue', making them 'enamoured of moral beauty' and enlisting their passions 'on the side of humanity'.[28] For all of these writers, virtuous behaviour had an edifying force, which writing merely served to spread to a wider audience. Dryden, in presenting his translation of Plutarch, went further, attributing to life-writing – the presentation not of isolated actions and episodes, but of individual lives in their entirety – a special capacity to intensify this moral effect: just as an optical lens could concentrate the force of the sun's rays, 'so the virtues and actions of one man, drawn together into a single story, strike upon our minds a stronger and more lively impression, than the scattered relations of many men, and many actions . . .'.[29]

Beliefs like these shaped the notions and practices of exemplarity, applied to lives and actions and characters, that have run through Western and other societies over many centuries. Exemplarity involves a belief in the transmissibility of moral or ethical qualities from one existence to another, not through abstraction and theorisation but through the pedagogic force of practical example. Faith in this possibility of 'continuity through replication' was central to classical concepts of education and of moral character, and Peter Brown has shown how it was reworked rather than abandoned to meet the practical and theoretical needs of early Christianity. Christian holy men became links in a chain of embodied Christliness that attached each Christian believer to Christ's own supreme example.[30] Despite what some have seen as a 'crisis of exemplarity' consequent on the development of new modes of historical consciousness during the Renaissance,[31] there can be little doubting the persistent influence which notions of exemplarity have continued to exert both in secular and in religious culture in later centuries. We find it in the traditions of children's literature, from James Janeway's compendium of the 'holy and exemplary lives, and joyful deaths' of pious children in the seventeenth century to Charlotte Yonge's *Book of Golden Deeds* and Mary Pilkington's collection of 'characteristic histories: calculated to impress the youthful mind with an admiration of virtuous principles, and a detestation of vicious ones' in the nineteenth.[32] We see it in the French Revolutionaries' enthusiasm for models from classical antiquity and in the late twentieth century's appetite for 'positive role models' in sundry walks of life. Nor, of course, have strategies of exemplarity and emulation been confined to the ethical systems of the West, as studies of China and Mongolia, for example, make clear.[33]

Exemplarity involves a perception not just of excellence, but also of relevance – and thus, in a sense, of similarity. Those whom we take as exemplars may be better than we are, but not than we might in principle become – not better in some absolute way that implies a difference of kind, but better relative to some common standard against which we hope to improve. Sometimes, this perception of similarity is framed restrictively, as when a range of exemplary figures are used to map separate and specific behavioural models for particular groups – rulers, soldiers, gentlemen, artisans, women, children, masters, servants, party workers. Exemplarity serves here either to reinforce the static divisions of a rigidly structured society, by showing people their duties in the social position to which they are consigned, or to regulate the conditions of social mobility or flexibility, by teaching them the approved ways of acquiring and enacting new social roles. Several chapters in this volume explore aspects of this socially specific kind of exemplarity. Rosemary Mitchell, for example, in Chapter 9 shows how the lives of medieval queens were used in the nineteenth century to generate both positive and negative models of 'queenly' conduct fit to guide the women of the Victorian middle classes in the extension of their domestic virtues into new realms of public activity. Krista Cowman in Chapter 12 shows how contemporary women who achieved a certain prominence in a particular field – in this case, socialist activism – could themselves be pressed into service as exemplary figures, whose public personas were crafted, more by others than by themselves, into living images of particular ways of acceptably combining femininity with socialist commitment, often at the expense of a fuller recognition of the diversity of their interests and contributions to the cause. Richard Holt in Chapter 13 examines the complex social and cultural dynamics of English cricket in the first half of the twentieth century, and shows how the leading batsmen of the era came to serve as icons of a gentlemanly style now transposed from the level of the upper-class amateur to that of the suburban and professional middle classes: their status as exemplary figures preserved a delicate balance between the continued acceptance of social differentiation and the emerging culture of social mobility. Finally, Christopher Clark in Chapter 11 reveals the powerful influence of exemplary forms in the commercial culture of the nineteenth-century United States. In all of these cases, exemplarity performs a fairly specific social as well as a broader moral function: it speaks to the perceived needs of specific classes of people at specific historical junctures.

But, while exemplarity frequently performs such functions, its pretensions are often not limited by them; the perception of similarity that underpins it is often expressed as a larger sense of human community or common destiny. Dr Johnson believed that the narrative of almost any life might serve a useful didactic purpose, not merely for the narrow reason that 'every man has, in the mighty mass of the world, great numbers in the same condition as himself, to whom his mistakes and miscarriages, escapes and expedients, would be of immediate and apparent use', but also for the broader one that 'there is such a uniformity in the state of man, considered apart from adventitious and separable decorations and disguises, that there is scarce any possibility of good or ill, but is common to human kind'.[34] Christianity, for its part, has long maintained a belief in the essential unity of human ethical experience, all merit in human actions stemming from God, through the central mediating influence of Christ's example. Such universalising tendencies of thought permit the development of exemplary reputations that cut across the obvious social divisions (between classes, sexes, races, nations or occupations), proposing images of heroic virtue that are capable of bearing a range of meanings and of sustaining the pretension to a larger and more enduring kind of ethical validity.

At its simplest, exemplarity is transparent and one-dimensional: exemplary figures stand as simple illustrations of moral qualities or codes of conduct, inviting imitation without much interpretation. Such, for example, were many of those promoted to exemplary status by the propaganda apparatus of Communist China in the 1960s. Anita Chan has shown how the exhortation to 'Learn from Comrade Lei Feng' and others like him formed part of a process of political socialisation which 'created competitive aspirations to prove personal devotion' and 'instilled exaggerated needs to conform to political orthodoxy'; youthful imitators of Lei Feng struggled to outstrip each other in the performance of ostentatiously humble good deeds and in zealous docility to Mao's teachings. (They were discouraged from following the more dangerous example of Mao's own insubordinate youth.)[35] Somewhat different from the case of Lei Feng (in which exemplarity is attached to a certain repetitiveness of moral performance) are those cases where the essential message to be derived from a life is encapsulated in a particular dramatic moment – Brutus's decision to order the death of his sons, the French Revolutionary child hero Bara's defiant cry of 'Vive la République' in the face of his murderous captors,[36] Grace Darling's selfless act of rescue. Virtue, in such cases, is dramatised as well as illustrated: the structures of narrative give a heroic status to the exemplary individual, and by imaginative extension also to those who might read a meaning for their own lives in what is narrated. Exemplarity and emulation serve here less as the means of circulating 'best practice' among a particular class of persons than as the promoters of a heroic attitude to moral and existential questions.

The cult of exemplary figures has often served as a powerful means of moral indoctrination in the service of an established social and political order. The habits of emulation to which it can give rise can also, however, play an important part in processes of self-fashioning and in the construction of personal identities. By selecting exemplars, people make choices, not just of moral precepts, but of character, of existential attitude, of presumptive destiny. It is important to remember that notions of exemplarity have often developed historically as an extension and formalisation of educational arrangements that placed a strong reliance on close personal relationships between teacher and pupil, casting the former not as a mere purveyor of abstract knowledge to the latter, but as a guide in the business of living, a mentor with whose practical example the pupil would enter into a kind of active sympathetic communion.[37] Even when exemplarity has been detached from such intimate pedagogic contexts, the belief that one can best learn how to live by meditating and following the practical examples of carefully selected others has remained strong. Attention here has often focused less on the individual manifestations of virtuous character than on the processes of its formation and the means of sustaining it through life's vicissitudes. In the nineteenth century, for example, the historian James Froude made an impassioned plea for the kind of exemplary literature that could be handed to young men with the words 'Read that: there is a man – such a man as you ought to be; read it, meditate on it; see what he was, and how he made himself what he was, and try and be yourself like him.' Life, in Froude's opinion, was a perilous journey, for which practical guidance was needed: 'It is the *track*, which these others, these pioneers of godliness, have beaten in, that we cry to have shown us; not a mythic "Pilgrim's Progress", but a real path trodden in by real men.'[38]

In its more developed forms, then, exemplarity is not transparent: it is not a mere device for making particular moral precepts imaginatively appealing, but rather an invitation imaginatively to rework one's own existence through investment in another. As Caroline Humphrey argues in relation to Mongolian examples, an ethical system based on such notions of exemplarity can function very differently from one based on the primacy of abstract moral rules.[39] In the West, where elements of the two have usually been combined, the function of the more developed forms of exemplarity has often been to provide 'scripts' with which people may identify and which they may use to give imaginative structure and ethical direction to their own existences either in retrospect or in prospect. Such 'scripts' may be especially important at times of social or cultural uncertainty, when more abstract forms of moral guidance seem insufficient or unworkable. Christopher Clark shows in Chapter 12 how, in the unstable financial conditions of mid-nineteenth-century America, narratives describing an exemplary recovery from business failure through honest industry and perseverance, culminating in the successful paying off of creditors, played an important part not just in the establishment of business as a morally respectable activity, but also in the development of self-images. In a different context, Iurii Lotman has drawn attention to the significance of exemplary constructions in the reforging of personal identities among the Russian elite that followed the cultural dislocations of the reign of Peter the Great. According to Lotman, this reforging passed through several phases, from an initial ritualisation or theatricalisation of behaviour to the development of specific styles of behaviour for particular social settings or conditions, and from that to an adoption of individual behavioural roles, modelled on stock figures from history or literature or folklore. The final transition was one from roles to plots – from the projection of such a modelled persona to the understanding of one's own life as a drama shaped to the same script as the heroic existence by which it was inspired. Russia's young aristocratic radicals looked to the exemplary figures of history and literature – to Addison's heroically suicidal *Cato* especially – not merely for imitable specimens of heroic conduct, but for existential plot-lines which would supply the key to their own heroic and possibly tragic destiny.[40]

Exemplarity need not necessarily involve a heavy emphasis on direct imitation or emulation by one individual of another; it may involve a more oblique taking to heart of the ethical or existential truths that the exemplary existence is supposed to embody. There are obvious tensions, especially in modern societies, between moral arguments based on the possibility of replicating one human existence in another, and philosophical conceptions that attribute a kind of irreducible uniqueness to the individual human spirit. These tensions were well brought out by Ralph Waldo Emerson in his lecture on the 'Uses of Great Men' (1845):

> There is indeed a speedy limit to the use of heroes. Every genius is defended from approach by quantities of unavailableness. They are very attractive, and seem at a distance our own: but we are hindered on all sides from approach. [. . .] It seems as if the Deity dressed each soul which he sends into nature in certain virtues and powers not communicable to other men, and, sending it to perform one more turn through the circle of beings, wrote 'Not Transferable', and 'Good for this trip only', on the garments of the soul. There is somewhat deceptive about the intercourse of minds. The boundaries are invisible, but they are never crossed.[41]

Heroic existences, in short, were not in the end convertible into models on which others could found their own development. This did not, however, for Emerson, deprive heroes or great men of all exemplary value. Their value, however, was not as models to be imitated, but as 'representative men' – men whose existences were impressive illustrations (though always partial ones) of the capacities which mankind collectively possessed. In contemplating such figures, one caught a reflection of one's own human potential: one gained a tool for self-understanding, rather than a model for living. Emerson's lectures are one example of the ways in which the nine-teenth century opened exemplarity to new critical uses. Dinah Birch, in Chapter 10, offers another, showing how Ruskin's intellectual engagement with and artistic deployment of a variety of exemplary lives, treated some-times in a sympathetic but sometimes in a more sceptical and critical spirit, formed part of his efforts both to reach an understanding of his own diffi-cult and in some ways frustrated existence and to develop critical reflections on contemporary society. Here again, the images and reputations of exem-plary figures appear no longer as simple models to be emulated, but as symbolic references to be invoked in the imaginative analysis both of self and of society.

Though exemplary figures need not, in all circumstances, be heroic, there is no doubting the powerful contribution that discourses of exemplarity have made to many heroic reputations. In constructing heroes as exem-plary figures – as role models or bearers of essential moral insights – these discourses necessarily interact with the historical narratives in which many of these heroes also hold a prominent place. These interactions are not necessarily easy. Forms of ethical discourse that imply the possibility of drawing moral inspiration for the present from ancient examples do not, for example, sit easily with forms of historical consciousness that stress the inexorably distancing effects of historical change, and the fundamental differences between past and present conditions. In practice, of course, historical narratives themselves have often forged symbolic connections between past and present experience, and endowed selected heroic individuals – founding fathers, heroic liberators, successful revolutionaries – with a status that transcends their immediate historical location, by virtue of the magnitude or significance of their historical achievements. Only under certain kinds of narrative condition, however, do such historical heroes become promising candidates for the projections of moral relevance that would make them exemplary figures. A brief examination of how heroes have been presented in some of the more sweeping metaphysical visions of human history may help to clarify this point. Here, three different modes of connection between the existence and action of heroic individuals and the general patterns of history may be identified, each in its way posing obstacles to the easy incorporation of historical heroes in discourses of exemplarity.

In the first mode, heroes are seen as functionally important agents of an ineluctable historical process. This is best exemplified in the Hegelian vision of history. For Hegel, it was the progress of the universal spirit towards realisation in human consciousness that was the central dynamic of history. Each substantial stage in that movement was marked by a moment of creative disruption – the collision between an established social and moral system, whose possibilities of development were now exhausted, and new possibilities of development requiring new social and cultural forms for their realisation. It was at such moments that heroes (or 'world-historical individuals' as Hegel called them) exerted an influence. The greatness of these individuals lay in their intuitive attunement to the needs of the moment, their capacity to will and to pursue with the full force of their being that which was objectively necessary for the march of the spirit to continue. Their influence over others lay in the fact that, in the unconscious depths of their 'inner soul', all were already tending in the same direction; the role of the hero was simply to give the awakening spark of leadership to this latent inclination. For Hegel, in short, 'world-historical individuals' were not autonomous actors, but executors of a higher historical purpose – catalysts of an essentially collective historical process, the basic impulses of which lay not in the spontaneous power of individual genius, but in the unfolding of humanity's rational destiny. Their role accomplished, they generally, in Hegel's view, fell aside 'like empty husks'.[42] This absorption of the heroic personality in the discharge of a strictly momentary and purely instrumental historical role offered little scope for seeing the hero as an exemplary figure.

The second mode of connection again places the Great Men or Women of History in relation to some overall scheme of historical development, but sees them this time less as decisive instruments of that development than as illustrious markers of the different stages of human progression – 'worthies' whose existence has benefited humanity and contributed to an accumulating fund of wisdom or civilisation. A highly structured example of such a presentation is the calendar which Auguste Comte proposed as part of his nineteenth-century Positivist religion of Humanity. Comte's conception of historical change differed fundamentally from Hegel's in placing the emphasis on gradual intellectual and cultural evolutions rather than on moments of revolutionary advance. The historical figures selected for inclusion in the calendar were taken to have contributed collectively to these evolutions by their achievements in different fields (and indeed the seven whom Comte chose to stand for the days of the week were described as the 'seven principal organs' of the West's 'transition from Theocracy to Sociocracy'), but their real significance in the calendar is as representative 'types', each illustrating the achievements of the human spirit in a particular field at a particular stage of its development.[43] Here again, the scope for notions of exemplarity is limited: Comte's heroes are examples of past achievement, but they are there to be honoured commemoratively as part of a larger cult of humanity, not to be received as models by the present generation.

The heroes of Hegel and Comte are restricted by their place in a preconceived pattern of history. The third mode of connection stresses instead the hero's autonomous creative energy. In its more expanded versions, it turns history itself – the whole process of humanity's creative development – into the product of heroic initiative. Carlyle was the most famous exponent of this view that 'Universal History, the history of what man has accomplished in this world, is at bottom the History of the Great Men who have worked here'. Great Men, for him, were the essential movers of history, 'the modellers, patterns, and in a wide sense creators, of whatsoever the general mass of men contrived to do or to attain'.[44] Each was like 'lightning out of Heaven' to the 'dry, dead fuel' of the age into which he was born; each was 'the saviour of his epoch', impressing his vision on others through the force of his unflinching sincerity and the instinctive 'originality' of his insight into what was 'True, Divine and Eternal' in the human condition.[45] Carlyle's heroes were not fettered by their historical roles as Hegel's or Comte's were, and the language he used to describe them sometimes resembled the language of exemplarity (as when the hero is described as a fountain not just of 'native original insight', but also 'of manhood and heroic nobleness'),[46] but they are shapers of humanity much more through the inspiring power of thought than through the edifying force of personal example. The natural elite of humanity, they are there to be worshipped and followed rather than to be emulated. Here again, discourses of exemplarity find little purchase.

It is when we move away from these grand philosophical or synthetic conceptions of history, and concentrate on more restricted kinds of historical vision, that larger opportunities for the cross-fertilisation of historical and moral discourses, through the medium of heroic images or reputations, can be observed. Recent centuries, in Western culture especially, have witnessed a proliferation of 'heroic histories', focusing either on particular social formations or movements (nations, churches, political movements, etc.) or on particular branches of human activity (art, science, exploration, etc.). It is through their imaginative connection to these sometimes formally stated but often implicit historical narratives that the lives of heroes most commonly take on a historical kind of significance. Two things happen here. First, heroes become associated with historical conceptions or narrative lines in which particular groups have a kind of emotional investment, as part of their collective sense of identity. Narratives of national history are an obvious example. As the concepts of nationhood and nationality have broadened their cultural range in recent centuries – to apply to fields such as science and literature and sport as well as to more traditional matters of political and military organisation – so an increasing range of heroic reputations have been converted into national assets.[47] (Patricia Fara reminds us, for example, in Chapter 4 of Newton's reputation not just as a great natural philosopher but as a great Englishman.) The celebration of heroes as influential historical individuals becomes increasingly closely connected with the maintenance of a sense of national community. People, in short, are encouraged to develop a sense of kinship or imaginative identification with the heroes of history, and thus, potentially at least, to see the existences of the latter as bearers of ethical meanings relevant to their own lives.

Secondly, the points of intersection between individual existences and the larger narratives (of progress or liberation or dramatic conflict) to which they are connected become promising material for imaginative development. The moments of the hero's heroic action are moments that link the story of his or her personal development (the story of how the hero became a hero) to the collective story of historical change (the story of how the nation became a nation, of how a group won its liberty, of how religion was brought to the heathen).[48] History sheds new light on the meanings of individual existence, and the moral glories of individual existence give an added splendour to its historical contributions. Heroes carry their potential as exemplars into the arenas of their historical engagement. Thus, for example, as John M. MacKenzie reminds us in Chapter 5, Livingstone's multiple reputation as scientist, explorer, missionary and humanitarian was reinforced by his status as one of the exemplars of Self-Help actively promoted by Samuel Smiles: the exemplary nature of his life and personality helped to legitimate the imperial endeavour to which he contributed.

Both history and exemplarity emerge transformed from such exchanges. 'The narrative of his troubled life', wrote Washington Irving of Columbus, 'is the link which connects the history of the old world with that of the new.' This was true not only in the banal sense that the narrative of Columbus's life was bound to include the discovery of America. What mattered was the element of heroic character in the story – the drama of vision and striving, in which Columbus, 'by his hardy genius, his inflexible constancy, and his heroic courage', had 'brought the ends of the earth into communication with each other'. The historical achievement was inseparable from the qualities which had made it possible; it was the combination of the two that allowed the life of Columbus to serve 'one of the most salutory purposes of history, that of furnishing examples of what human genius and laudable enterprise may accomplish'.[49] History serves here, not as a backdrop against which edifying displays of virtuous or noble conduct are periodically enacted, but as a drama into whose dynamic action such displays are integrally woven. It becomes at once a record of heroic achievement and a revelation of human potential.

Exemplary images, for their part, take on new and often complex ideological functions. The construction of George Washington as America's primary model of morality is an instance of this. Mason Weems, whose popular biography was the source of many of the questionable anecdotes that contributed to this construction, deliberately subordinated the presentation of Washington's heroic achievements as soldier and statesman to that of his private virtues, on the grounds both of causality (for these virtues were 'the food of the great actions in him') and of utility: it was in these details of private rather than of public life that ordinary American children would find the messages that were relevant to their own condition.[50] But this emphasis on Washington's virtue, by Weems and many others, was also a way of affirming the virtuous foundations of the Republic itself, and of indicating the kinds of patriotic and civic virtue that were required for its development. The frequent comparisons of Washington to Cincinnatus (the Roman statesman who left his farm to save the Republic and returned to it when the task was accomplished) not only glorified Washington's own resistance of any temptation to play the contrary role of Caesar; they also placed a powerful image of disinterested leadership, and of public office envisaged not as a political career but as a patriotic duty to be balanced and underpinned by the domestic virtue of the private gentleman, at the core of the nation's foundational mythology. Washington's exemplary life, in this sense, became a central part of his heroic political legacy. Henceforth, as Aaron Bancroft claimed, all civic and political instruction might 'be comprised in one sentence, GO, IMITATE OUR WASHINGTON'.[51]

Such ideologically coloured interweavings of moral and historical significance can take shape not only around the successful heroes of history,
but also around its heroic failures. Figures such as Robert E. Lee in the
United States and Saigō Takamori in Japan stand, on one level, for defeated
military and political causes. Their reputations as exemplars of noble virtue,
however, reach beyond the ranks of those nostalgic for those causes. Even
more important than this is the way in which the dramatic narrative of
their individual lives has become the site of a fusion of moral and
historical readings which permits them to be regarded as figures somehow
encapsulating elements of heroic tragedy lying at the heart of the nation's
history. Saigō's personal tragedy – one of the initial leaders of the progressive Meiji Restoration, yet dying in rebellion against the government he
had helped to create – came to symbolise the tensions between modernity
and tradition that were often regarded as central not just to Japan's modern
history but to the Japanese character.[52] The dramatic moment of Lee's decision, at the outbreak of the Civil War, to place his loyalty to Virginia over
his sentiments for the Union, serves at once to display his own virtuous
qualities and to expose the tragic nature of the national conflict. The tragic
heroism with which his decision is invested is magnified by its place in the
national narrative, whose epic and tragic qualities are themselves heightened by this heroic inclusion; his self-sacrificing spirit of duty acquires a
national rather than a purely personal significance.[53] In a somewhat similar
way, as Max Jones reminds us in Chapter 6, the deaths of Captain Scott
and his companions were turned, despite their defeat in the race to the
South Pole, into heroic evidence of the nation's moral potential, to coun-
terbalance the prevailing narratives of decadence and decline. In a rather
more oblique way, the nobly defeated figure of Caractacus could, as Norman
Vance shows in Chapter 8, perform a complex emotional and ideological
service for the British imperialism of the nineteenth century: if the image
of his resistance reminded Britons of their past as a courageous and
resourceful island people, the story of his later reconciliation with Roman
imperialism could help to reconcile them to their own imperial present.

Complex fusions and combinations of moral and historical meaning
give the images and reputations of heroes their often potent (and sometimes unstable) ideological significance. History is converted into images of
heroic virtue; moral values are projected through narratives of heroic action
and historical achievement. The lives of heroes assist in the imaginative
construction of social and political identity, and provide reassurance of the
moral basis of existence amid the uncertainties of historical change. The
chapters in this volume illustrate the diversity of their cultural and political uses. They show how the celebration of heroes has served as a means
of articulating and legitimating social values in a wide variety of historical

contexts. These functions of heroic reputation are often, of course, controversial; the meanings that attach to heroes are often contested, and the political implications of the emotional investments that are made in those meanings are often ambiguous. This is so especially, of course, when heroes are not figures drawn from the past, but living ones whose lives and reputations uncoil together and in unstable relation to each other, and when the implicit historical narratives to which they may be imaginatively connected are not ones matured and settled over centuries, but ones still disputed, open for development, beset with unfulfilled hopes and uncertain expectations. Tom Lodge's chapter on Nelson Mandela, with which this book closes, amply illustrates these points. It permits us to gauge at once the flexibility of Mandela's reputation – the openness of his life and personality to multiple readings, each defining his significance in relation to a different implicit historical narrative (that of the new South Africa, that of the ANC and the struggle against apartheid, that of the civil rights struggle in America, etc.) – and the centrality of his symbolic figure to the processes by which the moral and political basis of post-apartheid South African nationhood has been improvised. In Mandela's own autobiographical statements, as in the writings of his admirers, his personality remains at once powerful and elusive, oscillating between the magisterial and the emotional, between the publicly heroic and the privately reflective, between the image of the leader rooted in African tradition and that of the dynamic guiding hand of a pathbreaking democracy. Here again, we find the ambiguities of the heroic encountered earlier in this chapter: the hero is at once human yet superhuman, at once exemplary yet exceptional; his charisma appears at once indispensable to the construction of order yet by the same token imbued with a latent authoritarian capacity potentially at odds with the order it serves to establish. In Mandela's case, as Lodge suggests, these ambiguities are no doubt to be related to the inherent fragilities of a liberal democracy perilously established in an unequal and tension-ridden society. They tell us something also about the terms on which heroic reputations, present or past, are commonly established – the conversion of lives lived into narratively structured interweavings of moral and historical meaning, capable under certain circumstances of conveying ideals and forging identities through majestic and inspiring images of human dignity, striving and accomplishment, and under others of miring these same ideals and identities in a potentially dangerous dependence on the moral or historical grandeur attributed to selected individuals. In either case, the politics of reputation – the means and methods by which heroic lives and exemplary existences are imaginatively constructed and politically sustained – call for the kind of scholarly investigation that the chapters in this book seek in their various ways to offer.

Notes

1   T. Carlyle, *On Heroes, Hero-Worship, and the Heroic in History* (World's Classics edn., Oxford, 1904), p. 1.
2   The literature here is massive; among recent works, see D. Weinstein and R. M. Bell, *Saints and Society: the Two Worlds of Western Christendom, 1000–1700* (Chicago, 1982); S. Wilson (ed.), *Saints and their Cults: Studies in Religious Sociology, Folklore and History* (Cambridge, 1983); T. J. Heffernan, *Sacred Biography: Saints and their Biographers in the Middle Ages* (New York, 1988); A. Vauchez, *Sainthood in the Later Middle Ages* (Cambridge, 1997). Among older works on hagiography, H. Delehaye, *The Legends of the Saints* (London, 1962), originally published in 1905, remains fundamental.
3   See, for example, M. Keen, *Chivalry* (New Haven, 1984), ch. 6: 'The historical mythology of chivalry'; N. T. Burns and C. T. Reagan (eds), *Concepts of the Hero in the Middle Ages and the Renaissance* (Albany, 1975). On nineteenth-century reworkings of chivalry, see M. Girouard, *The Return to Camelot: Chivalry and the English Gentleman* (New Haven, 1981).
4   See, for example, P. Murray (ed.), *Genius: the History of an Idea* (Oxford, 1989); C. Battersby, *Gender and Genius: Towards a Feminist Aesthetics* (London, 1989).
5   See, for example, M. Peterson, *The Jefferson Image in the American Mind* (New York, 1960); W. F. Sater, *The Heroic Image in Chile: Arturo Prat, Secular Saint* (Berkeley, 1973); T. L. Connelly, *The Marble Man: Robert E. Lee and his Image in American Society* (Baton Rouge, 1977); M. Warner, *Joan of Arc: the Image of Female Heroism* (New York, 1981); B. Schwarz, *George Washington: the Making of an American Myth* (Ithaca, NY, 1987); C. L. Bushman, *America Discovers Columbus: How an Italian Explorer Became an American Hero* (Hanover, NH, 1992); M. Peterson, *Lincoln in American Memory* (Oxford, 1994); B. Dippie, *Custer's Last Stand: the Anatomy of an American Myth* (Lincoln, Neb., 1994); R. S. Tilton, *Pocahontas: the Evolution of an American Narrative* (Cambridge, 1994); N. Heinich, *The Glory of Van Gogh: an Anthropology of Admiration* (Princeton, 1996); C. Hamilton, *Terrific Majesty: the Powers of Shaka Zulu and the Limits of the Historical Imagination* (Cambridge, Mass., 1998); J. E. Lewis, *Mary Queen of Scots: Romance and Nation* (London, 1998). Studies primarily concerned with the shorter-term heroic reputations of particular individuals include R. Armstrong, *Grace Darling: Maid and Myth* (London, 1965); B. Worden, 'The republican kidney of Algernon Sidney', *Journal of British Studies*, 24 (1985); L. G. Schwoerer, 'William, Lord Russell: the making of a martyr, 1682–1983', *Journal of British Studies*, 24 (1985); K. Wilson, 'Empire, trade and popular politics in mid-Hanoverian England', *Past and Present*, 121 (1988); M. Poovey, 'A housewifely woman: the social construction of Florence Nightingale', in her *Uneven Developments: the Ideological Work of Gender in Mid-Victorian England* (Chicago, 1988); John M. MacKenzie, 'David Livingstone: the construction of the myth', in G. Walker and J. Gallagher (eds), *Sermons and Battle Hymns: Protestant Popular Culture in Modern Scotland* (Edinburgh, 1990); I. Germani, *Jean-Paul Marat: Hero and Anti-Hero of the French Revolution* (Lewiston, NY, 1992); Y. Druzhnikov, *Informer 001: the Myth of Pavlik Morozov* (New Brunswick, NJ, 1997); J. Bergman, 'Valerii Chkalov: Soviet pilot as new Soviet man', *Journal of Contemporary History*, 33:1 (1998); L. Riall, 'Hero, saint or revolutionary? Nineteenth-century politics and the cult of Garibaldi', *Modern Italy*, 3:2 (1998).
6   On these, see, among others, D. Adair, 'Fame and the Founding Fathers', in his *Fame and the Founding Fathers* (New York, 1974); M. T. Gilmore, 'Eulogy as symbolic biography: the iconography of revolutionary leadership, 1776–1826', in D. Aaron (ed.), *Studies in Biography* (Cambridge, Mass., 1978); H. T. Parker, *The Cult of Antiquity and the French Revolutionaries: a Study in the Development of the Revolutionary*

Spirit (Chicago, 1937), esp. pp. 23–33, 116–18, 139–77; A. Soboul, 'Religious feeling and popular cults during the French Revolution: "patriot saints" and martyrs for liberty', in Wilson (ed.), *Saints and their Cults*; A. Jourdan, 'Robespierre and revolutionary heroism', in C. Haydon and W. Doyle (eds), *Robespierre* (Cambridge, 1999); A. Potts, 'Beautiful bodies and dying heroes', *History Workshop*, 30 (1990); H.-J. Lüsebrink and R. Reichardt, *The Bastille: a History of a Symbol of Despotism and Freedom* (Durham, NC, 1997), esp. pp. 86–106; G. Dawson, *Soldier Heroes: British Adventure, Empire and the Imagining of Masculinities* (London, 1994); John M. MacKenzie, 'Heroic myths of empire', in John M. MacKenzie (ed.), *Popular Imperialism and the Military, 1850–1950* (Manchester, 1992); M. Lieven, 'Heroism, heroics and the making of heroes: the Anglo-Zulu War of 1879', *Albion*, 30:3 (1998); C. I. Hamilton, 'Naval hagiography and the Victorian hero', *Historical Journal*, 23: 2 (1980); J. Baird, *To Die for Germany: Heroes in the Nazi Pantheon* (Bloomington, 1992); J. McCannon, *Red Arctic: Polar Exploration and the Myth of the North in the Soviet Union, 1932–1939* (New York, 1998), chs. 4–5; V. Bonnell, *Iconography of Power: Soviet Political Posters under Lenin and Stalin* (Berkeley, 1997); M. Sheridan, 'The emulation of heroes', *China Quarterly*, 33 (1968); P. Stranahan, 'Labor Heroines of Yan'an', *Modern China*, 9:2 (1983); U. Bulag, 'Models and moralities: the parable of the "heroic little sisters of the grassland"', *The China Journal*, 42 (1999); A. Chan, *Children of Mao: Personality Development and Political Activism in the Red Guard Generation* (London, 1985), pp. 60–9. Relevant works on other heroic cultures include P. Karsten, *Patriot-Heroes in England and America: Political Symbolism and Changing Values over Three Centuries* (Madison, 1978); W. E. Houghton, *The Victorian Frame of Mind, 1830–1870* (New Haven, 1957), ch. 12: 'Hero worship'; B. Riffenburgh, *The Myth of the Explorer: the Press, Sensationalism, and Geographical Discovery* (Oxford, 1994); K. L. Steckmesser, *The Western Hero in History and Legend* (Norman, 1965); C. Amalvi, *De l'art et de la manière d'accommoder les héros de l'histoire de France* (Paris, 1988); D. B. Edwards, *Heroes of the Age: Moral Fault Lines on the Afghan Frontier* (Berkeley, 1996).

7 See, for example, Dawson, *Soldier Heroes*; Warner, *Joan of Arc*; Poovey, 'A housewifely woman'. Discussions of gender and the heroic may be said to go back at least to Christine de Pizan in the fifteenth century: see her *The Book of the City of Ladies*, tr. E. J. Richards (New York, 1982). See also E. M. Waith, 'Heywood's Women Worthies', in Burns and Reagan (eds), *Concepts of the Hero*.

8 See E. W. Kemp, *Canonization and Authority in the Western Church* (Oxford, 1948); P. Delooz, 'The social function of the canonization of saints', *Concilium*, 129 (1979); K. Woodward, *Making Saints. Inside the Vatican: Who Become Saints, Who do Not, and Why?* (London, 1991); P. Peeters, 'La canonisation des saints dans l'Eglise russe', *Analecta Bollandiana*, 33/4 (1914).

9 See A. Ben-Amos, 'The sacred centre of power: Paris and Republican state funerals', *Journal of Interdisciplinary History*, 32:1 (1991); M. Ozouf, 'The Pantheon: the École Normale of the dead', in P. Nora (ed.), *Realms of Memory: the Construction of the French Past*, 3 vols. (New York, 1996–98), III.

10 See, for example, K. A. Marling, *George Washington Slept Here: Colonial Revivals and American Culture 1876–1986* (Cambridge, Mass., 1988), chs. 5 and 11; Bushman, *America Discovers Columbus*, ch. 5; J.-M. Goulemot and E. Walter, 'Les centenaires de Voltaire et de Rousseau', in P. Nora (ed.), *Les Lieux de mémoire*, 6 vols in 3 sections (Paris, 1984–92), I.

11 See A. Yarrington, *The Commemoration of the Hero 1800–1864: Monuments to the British Victors of the Napoleonic Wars* (New York, 1988); M. Agulhon, 'La "statuomanie" et l'histoire', *Ethnologie française*, 8:1 (1978).

12 See M. Pointon, 'Money and nationalism', in G. Cubitt (ed.), *Imagining Nations* (Manchester, 1998).

13   For a good example of this, see Bulag, 'Models and moralities'.
14   On commercial exploitation see, for example, Marling, *George Washington Slept Here*, esp. chs. 5–7; Armstrong, *Grace Darling*, pp. 1–4; on the press, Riffenburgh, *The Myth of the Explorer*; Dawson, *Soldier Heroes*, esp. pp. 145–47.
15   Quoted in Gilmore, 'Eulogy as symbolic biography', pp. 134–35.
16   L. Vaz de Camões, *The Lusiads* (Penguin edn., Harmondsworth, 1952), pp. 39–41.
17   A good recent example is the comparison of modern Israeli heroes to those of ancient Israel in a volume originally published under the auspices of the Israeli Ministry of Defence in celebration of the fiftieth anniversary of the state of Israel: M. Bar-Zohar (ed.), *Lionhearts: Heroes of Israel* (New York, 1998), p. xiv.
18   J. Huizinga, 'Historical ideals of life', in his *Men and Ideas: History, the Middle Ages, the Renaissance* (London, 1960).
19   The historical and critical literature on life-writing is, of course, too massive to be accounted for here; the following, however, have seemed helpful in thinking about issues relevant to this chapter: I. B. Nadel, *Biography: fiction, fact and form* (London, 1984); W. H. Epstein, *Recognizing Biography* (Philadelphia, 1987); L. Marcus, *Auto/biographical Discourses: Theory, Criticism, Practice* (Manchester, 1994); L. Stanley, *The Auto/Biographical I* (Manchester, 1992). See also, for a useful anthology of earlier writings on the subject, J. L. Clifford (ed.), *Biography as an art: selected criticism, 1560–1960* (Oxford, 1962). On aspects of the earlier history of 'biographical' writing, see A. Momigliano, *The Development of Greek Biography* (Cambridge, Mass., 1971); T. A. Dorey (ed.), *Latin Biography* (London, 1967); and the works on Christian hagiography cited in n. 2 above.
20   See E. King's 'Introduction' to the recent edition of William Hamilton of Gilbertfield's 1722 version of Blind Harry's poem, published as *Blind Harry's Wallace* (Edinburgh, 1998).
21   On the mortality (in both senses) of the Greek heroes, and the nature of their heroic standing more generally, see J. Griffin, *Homer on Life and Death* (Oxford, 1980), especially ch. 3 ('Death and the god-like hero'); also S. L. Schein, *The Mortal Hero: an Introduction to Homer's Iliad* (Berkeley, 1984).
22   See Weinstein and Bell, *Saints and Society*, p. 240; also Brown, 'The saint as exemplar in late antiquity', *Representations*, 1:2 (1983) p. 6.
23   Edwards, *Heroes of the Age*, p. 21.
24   G. W. F. Hegel, *Lectures on the Philosophy of World History (Introduction: Reason in History)*, ed. D. Forbes (Cambridge, 1975), p. 86.
25   S. Lee, *Principles of Biography* (Cambridge, 1911), p. 18.
26   Saint Augustine, 'De mendacio', Bk 1, ch. xv, quoted in Heffernan, *Sacred Biography*, p. 28; S. Smiles, *Self-Help: with Illustrations of Conduct and Perseverance* (new edn., London, 1890 [original edn. 1859]), p. 368.
27   Plutarch, 'Pericles', in *Plutarch's Lives*, tr. B. Perrin, 11 vols. (Cambridge, Mass., 1914–26), III, p. 7.
28   O. Goldsmith, 'Cultivation of taste', in *The Complete Works of Oliver Goldsmith, Comprising his Essays, Plays, and Practical Works* (revd. edn., Edinburgh, n.d.), pp. 377–78.
29   J. Dryden, 'Life of Plutarch', quoted in Clifford, *Biography as an Art*, p. 18.
30   P. Brown, 'The saint as exemplar', quoted passage p. 5.
31   See the articles in the special section 'The crisis of exemplarity' in *Journal of the History of Ideas*, 59:4 (1998), for discussion of such a crisis, in relation not simply to the use of exemplary models of human conduct, but to the employment of *exempla* in thought and rhetoric more generally.
32   J. Janeway, *A Token for Children, being an Exact Account of the Conversion, Holy and Exemplary Lives, and Joyful Deaths of Several Young Children* (London, 1671);

C. M. Yonge, *A Book of Golden Deeds of All Times and All Lands* (London, 1864); M. Pilkington, *Biography for Boys; or Characteristic Histories: Calculated to Impress the Youthful Mind with an Admiration of Virtuous Principles and a Detestation of Vicious Ones* (London, 1800). For a useful brief survey of such literature, see S. Hannabuss, 'Historical biography for children', in S. Hannabuss and R. Marcella, *Biography and Children: a Study of Biography for Children and Childhood in Biography* (London, 1993).

33 C. Humphrey, 'Exemplars and rules: aspects of the discourse of moralities in Mongolia', in S. Howell (ed.), *The Ethnography of Moralities* (London, 1997); Sheridan, 'The emulation of heroes', p. 47.

34 S. Johnson, 'The dignity and usefulness of biography', *The Rambler* 60 (13 Oct. 1750), in *The Works of Samuel Johnson LL D.*, ed. R. Lynam, 6 vols. (London, 1825), I, pp. 282–3.

35 Chan, *Children of Mao*, pp. 1–2, 60–69, quotation p. 2.

36 On Bara, see *Joseph Bara (1779–1793): pour la deuxième centenaire de sa naissance* (Paris, 1981).

37 See Brown, 'The saint as exemplar', pp. 2–3; Humphrey, 'Exemplars and rules', pp. 36–38.

38 J. A. Froude, 'Representative men' (1850), in his *Short Studies on Great Subjects* (2nd edn., London, 1867), pp. 389–90.

39 Humphrey, 'Exemplars and rules', pp. 34–43. Humphrey argues (p. 43) that the availability of a range of different exemplars supplies 'not only alternative conceptions of how one ought to conduct oneself, but a discursive space for deliberation about ideals. This enables people to transform themselves and gradually to commit themselves to certain ethnic modes of being.'

40 I. Lotman, 'The poetics of everyday behavior in eighteenth-century Russian culture', in I. Lotman, L. I. Ginsburg and B. A. Uspenskii, *The Semiotics of Russian Cultural History* (Ithaca, NY, 1985). One of the effects of this, according to Lotman, was to focus the minds of men like Alexander Radishchev on the prospects of a suitably heroic death: Radishchev's suicide is interpreted by Lotman as a deliberately Catonian gesture (pp. 86–91).

41 R. W. Emerson, 'Representative men' (lecture 1: 'Uses of great men'), in *The Collected Works of Ralph Waldo Emerson*, 4 vols. (Cambridge, Mass., 1971–1987), IV, p. 16.

42 Hegel, *Lectures on the Philosophy of World History*, pp. 82–6, quotation p. 85. For a Marxist development of such ideas, in which the necessities of material development replace the necessary advances of the spirit as the historical driving force served by the far-sighted action of heroic individuals, see G. Plekhanov, *The Role of the Individual in History* (London 1940 [originally published 1898]). Efforts to establish the possibilities and limitations of heroic action as part of the historical process from other philosophical standpoints include William James's 'Great men and their environment' (1880), in his *Selected Papers on Philosophy* (London, 1917), and S. Hook, *The Hero in History: a Study in Limitation and Possibility* (New York, 1943).

43 A. Comte, *System of Positive Polity, or Treatise on Sociology Instituting the Religion of Humanity*, 4 vols. (New York, 1966, repr. of London 1875–77), IV, pp. 116–37, 346–51 (quotation p. 120). The main features of the calendar are conveniently depicted facing p. 348. (The original French publication of the *Système de politique positive* was in 1851–54.)

44 Carlyle, *On Heroes*, p. 1.

45 *Ibid.*, pp. 13, 45–46, 126–27, 156–57.

46 *Ibid.*, p. 2.

47 For the application of this to scientific heroes, see L. Jordanova, 'Science and nation-
    hood: cultures of imagined communities', in Cubitt (ed.), *Imagining Nations*,
    pp. 202–6; for brief general remarks on the cultural broadening of nationhood and
    nationality, see Cubitt, 'Introduction' in the same volume, pp. 14–16. For interesting
    insights into the connections between the names or images of individuals and
    national histories, see M. Frisch, 'American history: a modest exercise in empirical
    iconography', *Journal of American History*, 75:4 (1989).

48 See, for example, the dovetailing of Bismarck's personal development with his histor-
    ical role in Emil Ludwig's *Genius and Character* (London, 1930), p. 52: 'His own
    personal struggle, a restless oscillation between sentiment and realism, duty and
    power, renunciation and action, loyalty and vengeance, had its parallel for him in
    the condition of Germany; and this almost mystical, yet natural, kinship gave him
    both the desire and the courage to battle for national integration.'

49 W. Irving, *A History of the Life and Voyages of Christopher Columbus*, 4 vols. (London,
    1828), I, p. 4. Irving's view of Columbus is discussed in Bushman, *America Discovers
    Columbus*, pp. 107–26.

50 M. L. Weems, *The Life of George Washington*, ed. M. Cunliffe (Cambridge, Mass.,
    1962, following the 1809 edn.), pp. 4–5.

51 Quoted in Gilmore, 'Eulogy as symbolic biography', p. 147.

52 See C. L. Yates, *Saigō Takamori: the Man Behind the Myth* (New York, 1995); also
    I. Morris, 'The apotheosis of Saigō the Great', in his *The Nobility of Failure: Tragic
    Heroes in the History of Japan* (Harmondsworth, 1980).

53 See Connelly, *The Marble Man*, esp. pp. 194–202; on Lee's decision to secede, see
    also A. T. Nolan, *Lee Considered: General Robert E. Lee and Civil War History*
    (Chapel Hill, 1991), pp. 30–58.

PART I

THE INTELLECTUAL AS HERO

Getting a life: reconstructing the late medieval exemplarity of Plato

Every person has many potential biographies – psychological, professional, political, familial, economic – each of which would select some aspects of the life history and discard others. But in order to understand the way in which exemplary biographies are produced as desirable models in a society, we must of course recognise that biography is culturally constructed. Exemplarity is an identity endowed with culturally specific meanings, constantly classified and reclassified into culturally constituted categories.[1] This recognition raises questions such as: what is a biography and where does it come from? Who fashions it? What are the cultural markers for exemplarity and how do they develop over a period of time? In particular, this chapter is concerned with the way in which exemplarity is constructed through transmission and reception, with how it is culturally re-defined and put to use in multiform ways. This will be explored by looking specifically at the reception of an exemplary life in a culture far removed from that in which its subject lived; that is the fashioning of Plato in the later Middle Ages.[2]

Statements about medieval perceptions of Plato tend to be based upon our understanding of how his philosophy was received during the Middle Ages. Modern scholars thus predominantly identify his medieval exemplarity with the only one of his works widely available to the Middle Ages, a section of the *Timaeus*.[3] Yet medieval Neoplatonists and commentators on the *Timaeus* said hardly anything about the persona of Plato in their treatises, and usually only remarked that he was a reverential disciple of Socrates. This meant that while philosophical treatises gave evidence for Plato's status as an exemplary philosopher, they concentrated in the main on expounding or developing his philosophy. It is therefore necessary, for a fuller under- standing of the cultural associations which Plato assumed, to search beyond the evidence offered by university courses and philosophy. Richard Southern has argued that the late medieval knowledge of Plato shows that 'Plato was valued as a doorway to knowledge, and not as a personality, philosopher or guide.'[4] However, this chapter will demonstrate that the philosophical exemplarity of Plato was in many ways the least accessible part of his medieval construct, and that there was indeed an extensive understanding of him as an exemplary personality.

There are six ancient lives of Plato extant which supply the original sources for much of the material about his exemplary life.[5] However, no scholar has addressed the late medieval variations of this tradition, and the diversity of sources upon which it draws. Isolated biographical particulars were circulated in varied sources, for example the report that Plato's body had been found in a tomb with a golden tablet on his breast declaring belief in Christ. Versions of this story were referred to by Diogenes Laertius in the early third century AD, by Olympiodorus in the sixth century, by Richard of Cluny in the twelfth century, and by both William Wheatly and John Ridevall in the fourteenth century. They said that Plato merited a pre-revelation of Christ, and that a medal on his corpse's breast was inscribed with the motto (in Ridevall's words), 'I believe in Christ, Son of God, to be born of the Virgin, to die on the Cross, and to rise again on the third day.'[6] This meant that in the context of the late medieval controversy about the salvation of 'just pagans', Plato was placed in the select category of *majores*. These were an especially enlightened group who were singled out by God for divine pre-revelation of Christ, in contrast to the *minores* who arrived at a belief in a just God, but did not possess explicit faith. Plato was thus particularly elevated, present in the ranks which normally contained only Old Testament prophets and the Sybil, privileged to achieve eternal salvation without the help of the institutionalised Church.[7] This aspect of his status was also referred to in several Latin and vernacular versions of the *Life of St Katherine,* as well as in the iconography of a statue of Plato on the west facade of Siena Cathedral.[8]

To further reconstruct such examples of Plato's medieval exemplarity, four sources can be examined in detail. These are John of Salisbury's *Policraticus* (a treatise for the education of princes), Vincent of Beauvais' *Speculum historiale* (an encyclopaedia), John of Wales' *Compendiloquium* (a preacher's manual) and Walter Burley's *De vita et moribus philosophorum* (a history of philosophers).[9] There are a total of thirty-one anecdotes which run (with variation) through these sources, and they provide details about Plato's birth, family, travels, schooling, character and death. They begin by outlining his origins, saying that his name (which means 'breadth' in Greek) signified the width of his knowledge (or alternatively his shoulders), and give details of his family and birth date. A consistent feature was that he was associated with Apollo, principally because he was reported as being born of a virgin. His mother was said to have had a 'liaison' with the spirit of Apollo,

and this was taken to symbolise Plato's future wisdom, as well as the role
of the Holy Spirit in Christ's virgin birth. His future eloquence was also
symbolised in a report that bees, a symbol of the Muses (who were closely
linked to Apollo), had dripped honey on his lips as a sleeping infant. The
sources go on to explain that Plato attributed his dialogues to his master
Socrates out of humility, and that the night before he met Plato, Socrates
had dreamed that a cygnet (i.e. Plato) settled into his lap before developing
into a sweetly singing swan and flying away. It was also reported that Plato
was successful at gymnastics (he had been victor in wrestling at the Pythian
games), and that he had a talent for painting. The accounts also say that
he excelled as a poet, and single him out as an exemplar of eloquence.

Plato's exemplary ability was thus constantly emphasised in these
accounts. John of Salisbury makes comments such as:

> He attained such eminence in philosophy by the vigor of his genius, his
> zeal for study, his personal charm, and the sweetness and fluency of his
> diction that, as though seated on philosophy's throne, he seemed to dictate
> by a sort of authority precepts not only to the philosophers who succeeded
> him but even to those who had preceded him.[10]

Such comments indicate that the late medieval representation of Plato was
an almost entirely positive one, enhancing his personal status and ignoring
the negative side of the tradition which had flourished among those writers
who had opposed Plato's philosophy in antiquity.[11] These sources also
presented Plato as well-travelled in his youth, and say that he went to Egypt
and parts of Italy in order to acquire knowledge, humbly having decided
that 'his own ability was not enough to bring philosophy to perfection'. In
addition, it was reported that Plato had made three journeys to Sicily. This
story developed from a tradition that had been highly critical of Plato,
accusing him of being a parasite at Dionysius's court, but by the later
Middle Ages such insinuations became indistinct. Another anecdote reports
that he had foreseen in a dream his capture and enslavement by pirates,
so further constructing the idea of his divine pedigree and protection.

With regard to his status as teacher, Plato was closely linked to the
foundation of the Academy. The sources say that after Diogenes the Cynic
had trampled on Plato's couches with muddy feet, Plato set up the Academy
in an unhealthy and diseased location, so that students of philosophy would
withdraw from worldly temptation, and specifically from lust. The motives
of Diogenes are not made clear, but the inference is that he was opposed
to pride and angered by the wealth of Plato's furnishings. However, any
arrogance on Plato's part was not elaborated upon, so leaving an overall
impression of his exemplary asceticism. This austerity is reflected in another
anecdote that some of Plato's students plucked out their eyes to avoid being

distracted from their philosophical endeavours. As to what Plato actually taught in the Academy, the anecdotes make diverse references to certain of his doctrines, but do not discuss them as a comprehensive whole. This shows how fragmentary late medieval knowledge was about Plato's actual teachings as we know them today, and the seemingly obvious fact that Plato was not a Christian was asserted relatively little, any such censure being rare compared to the many accounts of his Apollonian wisdom and consequent near-divinity.

More prominent than any material on the teachings of Plato are sections which list various gnomic sayings attributed to him. Rather than being directly linked to Plato, these might have been ascribed to any exemplar, being offers of advice on any or all aspects of life and philosophy. They contain such exemplary maxims as 'the most true justice is that which is shown to those of the lowest class', or 'the strength of all philosophy is patience', or 'the triumph of innocence is not to transgress when it is able to'.[12] Likewise, anecdotes which depict aspects of Plato's character are varied in content, and help to build a picture of an exemplary persona with a prophet-like status of *gravitas* and authority. He was portrayed as having a dignified and serious nature, always ready to deal with any situation in a wise and morally suitable fashion, and there are many references to the self-discipline that led him to avoid sensuality and alcohol. There were related reports that Plato had shown restraint when angered by a slave, and had refused to punish him personally. As a result of such anecdotes, John of Wales presented Plato as withdrawing from the world, living in poverty and occupying a smaller room in the Academy than any of his contemporaries, conducting a life of learning and peace and modesty. This gives him an almost monk-like existence, contrary to the evidence of his desire for travel to broaden his learning.

There are various other miscellaneous episodes of which the most intriguing is the allusion that Plato had died of confusion when he could not answer a riddle put to him by some fishermen. According to John of Wales, this story came from a tract by Gregorius Nazianzenus which said that when Plato had asked the sailors what they had caught they replied 'what we have caught, we have not; what we have not caught we have'. Plato, his mind fixed on fish, was so puzzled that he could not eat or drink, and so died. (The answer was . . . that they were catching lice in their clothes!) Once again, the anecdote refers to an older, negative tradition, which John of Salisbury discredited by pointing out that the story had also been told of Homer. He explained that the confusion with Plato was because both had a perfection of wisdom, a charm of style, and broad shoulders. The prince of philosophers was thus removed from a potentially negative encounter, and freed from any blame.

Therefore, overall, it is particularly notable that while the anecdotes of Antiquity and the early Middle Ages contained stories which both praised and vilified Plato, all four of these later medieval accounts left the negative tradition behind and portrayed him in a highly positive light. There were popular legends which portrayed some pagan sages in a negative light, most notably by employing the topos of the wise fool, in which disgraced sages served as moral *exempla*.[13] The figure of Plato avoided such abuse, partly because the transmitters of his exemplary life removed any such negative stories. So complimentary is the tradition in places that Plato achieves an almost Christ-like status, being a pagan of virgin birth, with a divine nature, prophetic vision, gnomic wisdom, humble asceticism and meritorious of a visit by Magi. These parallels must have placed him on the highest level of exemplarity, as a philosopher of great personal standing, whose thought was acknowledged to be the closest to the tenets of Christianity. The easy availability of such an extensive corpus of knowledge about Plato (which may well have been far more directly familiar and accessible than any detailed knowledge of his works) must have provided positive context in which his philosophy could have been discussed.

How then does this presentation of Plato help us to understand medieval constructions of exemplarity? The most familiar form of exemplary medieval narrative is the saint's life, but unlike most hagiography, the anecdotes about Plato do not amount to a complete 'life'. Therefore, to present Plato's exemplarity as a fairly homogenous biography is somewhat misleading. None of the four sources which narrated Plato's exemplarity were written solely about him, and they included him only as a part of much wider schemes. The individual anecdotes retain some detachment from each other, often appearing to be out of any context, and the episodes are presented in differing ways by each source (see table 1). The four texts drew from each other as well as from common material, and this tends to obscure their original sources. Such 'borrowing' should not be seen in a negative light, for it demonstrates how this vibrant tradition was developed and passed on from the twelfth to the fourteenth century. Plato was represented as the paragon of an ancient sage, and his distant pagan identity was re-crafted to meet the demands of different texts or authors.

Each text therefore provides a slightly different perspective on the material, moulding Plato to its own needs. John of Salisbury is the most adulatory, seeing him as the most faultless of pagans yet also as very human, an 'historical' sage as well as a philosophical *auctor*. On the other hand, Vincent's account, being that of a master compiler, is more factual and less emotive. Plato's status remains high in the *Speculum*, despite a lack of explication, but his great *auctoritas* is stressed rather than details of his

Anecdote	POL	SpecH	ComP	VEMP	HIGD
1 Name	*	*	*	*	*
2 Family	*	*	*	*	*
3 Apollonian Birth	*	*	*		
4 Birth date	*				
5 Bees dripping honey on lips	*	*	*	*	*
6 Socrates Swan dream	*	*	*	*	*
7 Tutors	*		*		*
8 Pre-eminence among disciples of Socrates			*	*	*
9 Travels to Egypt and Italy	*	*	*	*	*
10 Three trips to Sicily			*	*	*
11 Dionysius of Sicily and bodyguards	*	*		*	
12 Capture by Pirates	*	*		*	
13 Academy founded on unhealthy site	*	*		*	*
14 Students plucking out eyes		*		*	
15 Teachings close to Scripture	*	*	*	*	*
16 Theobrosus Ambraciensis suicide		*			*
17 Plato not a Christian		*	*		
18 Names of Plato's books		*		*	
19 Plato's moderation	*		*	*	
20 Plato's asceticism			*		
21 Plato's possessions	*				
22 Use of mirror to examine facial changes	*			*	
23 Rebuke of ferryman		*	*		
24 Refusal to personally punish a slave		*		*	*
25 Disbelief of Xenocrates slander		*		*	*
26 Student reproaches father			*		
27 Death by confusion over fish riddle	*		*		*
28 Death date		*		*	
29 Death age	*			*	*
30 Magi visit				*	
31 Aristotle and Plato	*	*	*	*	*
TOTAL	18	19	16	21	16

TABLE 1   POL – *Policraticus*; SpecH – *Speculum historiale*; ComP – *Compendiloquium*;
VEMP – *De vita et moribus philosophorum*; HIGD – Ranulph Higden, *Polychronicon*

life and nature. John of Wales seems to portray Plato as friar-like and
Christian, drawing implicit parallels between the friars and philosophers.
For him both must possess great learning and humility, be enthusiastic
about teaching, and lead by example. Walter Burley presents the most
composite account of Plato, drawing on the laudatory sentiment of
Salisbury's 'human' Plato, and the more factual reporting of Vincent, as

well as the moralised Plato portrayed by John of Wales. Thus, what is most
interesting about the exemplarity of Plato is that, unlike medieval hagiography, his identity was built up without having a unified text, or 'life',
written about him. I have therefore used the label 'anecdote' deliberately,
because even when read in its entirety, Plato's exemplarity lacks cohesion,
and cannot be associated with any single complete life history.

However, while Plato's anecdotal life differs markedly from medieval
hagiography in this way, these types of medieval exemplary narrative share
a fundamental similarity. That is, rather than purporting to render faithfully the historical record of an individual life, both aimed to represent the
Divine Truths which that life represented. In this way medieval exemplary
lives differ from some modern understandings of the term 'biography'. Where
'biography' tends to be associated with an empiricist approach to factual
truths, the medieval approach to the self (seipsum) was in general terms
non-empiricist, for it saw the subject as a reflection of the mystery of the
transcendent deity. The growth of empirical biography since the end of
the eighteenth century has meant that hagiography has often been patronised and regarded as being of little worth because it fails to describe
accurate historical life-histories.[14] However, rather than claiming to portray
exact historical 'truth', medieval exemplary narratives were concerned more
with the Divine Truths which an exemplar represented. Therefore medieval
exemplarity represented not so much the uniqueness of an individual, as
that individual's exaltation as a vessel of God's universal providence. As a
result, any judgmental notions of historical accuracy should be treated with
suspicion when applied to medieval exemplarity. In the words of Thomas
Heffernan:

> Medieval authors, especially sacred biographers, saw that little need be
> contradictory between the worlds of fact and fantasy; both fact and fantasy
> were signs to the acute observer of the nature of things, different signs to
> be sure, but nonetheless signs revelatory of truth.[15]

Perhaps surprisingly to a modern audience, this meant that Plato, even
though he was a pagan, could still be held up as an exemplar, as long as
his anecdotes contained 'signs revelatory of truth'. As a pagan he had no
'official' cult or life-cycle, yet his anecdotes were transmitted in a treatise
for the education of princes, an encyclopaedia, a friars' sermon manual,
and a history of philosophers, all of which incited their intended audiences
to follow his worthy example. Pagan narratives such as the Plato anecdotes
could thus operate as part of a didactic scheme whereby a Christian audience was encouraged towards the goal of salvation, by being shown what
pagans could achieve by reason without revelation.[16] For example the stated
intention of John of Wales in the Compendiloquium was

to stimulate and incite the young, to instruct them, to induce among those who wish to imitate the said philosophers a salutary shame that leads to glory, to repress the elation of the arrogant heart, and to encourage humility in perfect men ... when they hear and read of the Gentiles doing perfect things (in so far as they can be perfect without faith working through love) and bearing much for honour and human glory.[17]

John's attitude thus reveals that even a pagan such as Plato, who had not (historically speaking) lived a Christian life, could still offer exemplary precedents for the moral exposition of preachers. A pagan exemplary life could thus demonstrate that moral order was possible even in unregenerate history, and could thus become a textual site for the appropriation of the past by the present. This was even more the case with Plato because of reports of his foreknowledge of Christ. Irrespective of the actual historical facts of their lives, exemplary pagan *auctores* could provide the basis for profitable teaching, so long as the interpreter of their life records was in line with orthodox Christian Truth.

What, though, is the evidence for the use and transmission of Plato's exemplary anecdotes in this way? The Christian moralisation and redeployment of classical themes and *exempla* became an increasingly common practice. It was an approach that was promoted by John of Salisbury, who called for readers to be like bees, carefully selecting then accurately reading the pagan writers.[18] Texts such as the four sources which this chapter has used (as well as those in the genres of compilation, *florilegia* and encyclopaedia) made inherited material available in a more condensed and convenient form, for easy use by future readers, vernacular poets, commentators and preachers. These compilations then often acted as collections of source material for the *exemplum*.[19] This narrative device was valued by the Church because its persuasive narratives gave doctrine an ideological power. As modern readers we tend to react negatively to didactic forms such as the *exemplum*, seeing them as entirely dependent upon established authority. However, medieval authority should not be treated as entirely static and unquestioned, or as standing in opposition to (vernacular) narrative complexity. The authority carried in exemplarity is not pure or given, but is an ideological structure that must be produced and maintained. Therefore exemplary lives not only confirmed but *reproduced* moral authority, and were re-used to establish cultural authority in vernacular traditions. The use of exemplarity thus enacts cultural authority as a narrative, but it is a narrative which constantly needed renewing and re-enacting.

This may be demonstrated by giving some examples of how fragments of Plato's anecdotal life were transmitted through vernacular poetry. That the anecdotes might have been accessible in such spheres is made probable by translations such as Stephen Scrope's fifteenth-century *Dicts and Sayings of the Philosophers* or John Trevisa's 1387 translation of Ralph Higden's *Polychronicon*. Higden (and thus Trevisa) closely followed John of Wales's *Compendiloquium* in his section on Plato, presenting as comprehensive a coverage of the Plato anecdotes as exists in any text of the late Middle Ages. It is from texts such as these, as well as the four sources which this chapter has used, that vernacular poets could have gained knowledge of Plato as exemplar.[20]

There are at least two occasions when Middle English writers directly refer to Plato anecdotes. The first is in Thomas Usk's *Testament of Love*, when Lady Love cites Plato's restraint in punishing a slave as an example of how anger should not influence judgement. In Chaucer's *Parson's Tale* a similar story is told of a 'philosophre upon a tyme' who had his disciple beat him for impatience after he had been about to whip the child in anger. The Parson's *exemplum*, though different in detail, might have been influenced by the Plato anecdote. The second illustration of direct use of a Plato anecdote in vernacular poetry is in John Lydgate's *Fall of Princes*. Lydgate compares Cicero to Plato, and describes Plato as the superlative example of eloquence, citing the bees story as his example:

> Among Grekis [at] Athenys the cite
> He was so gret of reputacioun
> So famous holde of auctorit[t]e,
> To be comparid bi ther oppynyoun
> To the philisophre that callid was Platoun,
> To whos cradel bees dede abraide
> And hony soote thei on his lippes laide.
> A pronostik[e], lik as bookis tell,
> Plato sholde bi famous excellence,
> Of rhetorik be verray sours & well,
> For his langage, merour off elloquence.
> Yet the Grekis recorden in sentence,
> How Tullius in parti and in all
> Was onto Plato in rethorik egall.

This focuses on Plato's excellence in rhetoric, an exemplary characteristic which is reflected in the anecdotes by accounts of Plato's youthful love of poetry and Apollonian nature.[21]

The most noticeable point about the references to Plato in William Langland's *Piers Plowman* is that he is described on all but one occasion as a 'poet'.[22] Editors have been unanimous in their analysis of these lines, arguing that the use of the label 'poet' has a general meaning of any 'writer,' and that Langland employs it largely because of alliteration, as an arbitrary 'authority' for proverbial sayings. It may be suggested, however, that this loose definition of 'poet' is in fact tenuous, and that Langland calls Plato a poet because he had access to the anecdotal tradition which clearly discussed Plato's exemplary love of poetry. To be sure, the alliteration of Plato and poet is a vital factor, but to claim that this is only 'random citation' or 'rhetorical amplification', and that these labels 'were probably little more than names to Langland'[23] is uninformed, because the repeated mention of Plato as poet is confirmed by the evidence of the anecdotal tradition. In the words of Stephen Scrope: 'the saide Plato lernede first the science of poetrie, and it pleased him much to lerne it'.[24]

Likewise, the most detailed use of the figure Plato by Chaucer also contains echoes of his anecdotal construct. This is in a dialogue which contains the rudimentary elements of alchemical knowledge, occurring at the end of *The Canon's Yeoman's Tale*.[25] This dialogue is based on a Latin translation of a tenth-century Arabic alchemical treatise, which labels two debating figures as Solomon and an unidentified wise man. Chaucer changes this so that the alchemical discussion is between Plato and one of his disciples. Yet the debate is not to be found in any of Plato's philosophical works, or indeed in any of the anecdotes, and a satisfactory explanation for why Chaucer changes Solomon to Plato in his version of the dialogue has not been made. However, the exemplary construct of Plato offers ample support for making him (instead of Solomon) an alchemical master. Alchemical works were often attributed to wise holy men or saints, and it was claimed that ancient sages were by their alchemical knowledge granted an insight into Christian mysteries, including the Incarnation and Virgin Birth. The alchemical process was thus made analogous to the Christian mysteries, and a knowledge of one could imply an awareness of the other.[26] Therefore, it is wholly appropriate that exemplary Plato should be associated with this alchemical revelation, not only because of the tradition of his Apollonian nature and virgin birth, but also because of his own special position among the *majores*, who received revelation of the Christian mysteries.

In conclusion, it can be seen that the exemplary persona of Plato which was built up in anecdotal lives was accessible in the vernacular, and that this material was occasionally drawn on by vernacular writers. There is no need to imply that the anecdotal part of Plato's construct is in some way culturally 'inferior' to his philosophy, for his medieval anecdotal life could have operated alongside his thought, having been drawn upon by medieval scholars who had little access to his doctrines.[27] Cut off from the iterative authority of the texts which he had written, Plato was reinvented and reinscribed during the Middle Ages. His prophet-like status was perpetuated so that he came to have a multi-functional exemplary identity which could operate in a variety of discourses and contexts, often in spheres far removed from the academic study of his philosophy. In general, it might be asserted that exemplary biographies can either homogenise values on the one hand, or at the other extreme present life patterns as utterly singularised. However, in this instance, Plato's exemplary life can be understood not as a static image of individuality but as a dynamic series of signs, because his identity was a synthesis of various voices, with assorted anecdotes coinciding in fluid combinations. Accordingly, just as there is no 'perfect biography' there can be no single exemplary life. Therefore, in the Middle Ages, Plato not only had a life; he had many lives.

Notes

1   Cf. the comments of I. Kopytoff, 'The cultural biography of things: commoditiza-tion as process', in A. Appadurai (ed.), *The Social Life of Things: Commodities in Cultural Perspective* (Cambridge, 1986), pp. 64–84.

2   Parts of this chapter are reproduced from my doctoral thesis, 'The Reception of Plato and Neoplatonisms in Late Medieval English Literature', University of York, 1998, in particular pp. 31–86.

3   Sections 17A-53B (as translated by Calcidius), *Timaeus a Calcidio translatus commen-tarioque instructus*, ed. J. H. Waszink, *Plato Latinus IV* (London, 1962). On the survival of Plato's texts see Turner, 'Reception', pp. 5–13.

4   R. W. Southern, 'Platonism, scholastic method, and the School of Chartres', *The Stenton Lecture* 1978 (Reading, 1979), p. 10.

5   See A. S. Riginos, *Platonica, The Anecdotes Concerning the Life and Writings of Plato*, Columbia Studies in the Classical Tradition III (Leiden, 1976).

6   'Credo in Christum, Filium Dei, nasciturum de Virgine, moriturum in Cruce, resur-rectum tertia die', quoted by B. Smalley, *English Friars and Antiquity in the Early Fourteenth Century* (Oxford, 1960), p. 313. See also Turner, 'Reception', pp. 34–36.

7   On 'just pagans' see A. J. Minnis, *Chaucer and Pagan Antiquity* (Cambridge, 1982), pp. 31–60; T. G. Hahn, 'God's Friends: Virtuous Heathen in Later Medieval Thought and Literature', Ph.D. dissertation, University of California L.A., 1974.

8   See Turner, 'Reception', pp. 70–71, 77.

9   John of Salisbury (Joannes Saresberiensis), 1115–1180; *Policraticus* VII.5.644a ff., ed. C. C. J. Webb (Oxford, 1909) and trans. J. E. Pike (Minnesota, 1938). Vincent of Beauvais (Vincentius Bellovacensis), *c.* 1190–1264; *Speculum historiale* III.40–74, Graz, Akademische Druck- und Verlaganstalt, facsimile reprint of Baltazar Belleri, Douai, 1624. John of Wales (also Joannes Gallensis, Wallensis, Waleys and Vallensis), d. 1285; *Compendiloquium* III.iii.4, ed. Guilielmus Astensis (Venice, 1496). Walter Burley (Gualterus Burlaeus), *c.* 1275–1345; *De vita et moribus philosophorum* LII, ed. Herman Knust, Bibliothek des Litterarischen Verenis in Stuttgart CLXXVII (Tübingen, 1886).

10 'in tantum eminentiam philosophiae et uigore ingenii et studii exercitio et omni morum uenustate eloquii quoque suauitate et copia subuectus est ut quasi in trono sapientiae residens praecepta quadam auctoritate uisus sit tam antecessoribus quam successoribus philosophis imperare', *Policraticus* VII.5.644a, trans. Pike, p. 227.

11 See Riginos, *Platonica*, pp. 199–201, for a summary of this negative tradition.

12 'illa est verissima iusticia, quae erga inferiores servatur'; 'tocius philosophie robur est paciencia'; 'triumphus innocencie est, non peccare, ubi licat posse', Burley, *Lives*, LII, 67a and 68b.

13 e.g. Aristotle, who was duped by a courtesan to let her ride on his back; and Virgil, who was left stranded in a basket halfway up the wall of a tower by a lady whom he had been (unsuccessfully) wooing. See Turner, 'Reception', p. 76.

14 See T. J. Heffernan, *Sacred Biography: Saints and their Biographies in the Middle Ages* (New York, 1988), pp. 38–71.

15 Heffernan, *Sacred Biography*, pp. 70–71.

16 See also the discussion of R. H. and M. A. Rouse, *Preachers, Florilegia and Sermons: Studies on the Manipulus Florum of Thomas of Ireland* (Toronto, 1979), pp. 43–64, and Turner, 'Reception', pp. 36–38.

17 'ad iuniorum tamen stimulationem et incitationem, ad eorum informationem et ad utilis erubescentie ducentis ad gloriam inductionem in minus habentibus volentibus predictos philosophos imitari et ad elationis cordis arrogantie repressionem ac humilitatis in viris perfectis exhortationem ... cum audiunt et legunt gentiles exercere opera perfecta, prout possunt esse perfecta sine fide operante per dilectionem, et multa sustinere propter honestatem vel gloriam humanam', Prologue to *Compendiloquium*, trans. W. A. Pantin in 'John of Wales and medieval humanism', in J. Watt et al. (eds), *Medieval Studies: Presented to Aubrey Gwynn* (Dublin, 1961), p. 309.

18 *Policraticus* VII.10.660. On this use of pagan texts see Minnis, *Pagan Antiquity*, pp. 31 ff.; and Minnis, 'Late medieval discussions of *Compilatio* and the role of the *Compilator*', *Beiträge zur Geschichte der Deutschen Sprache und Literatur*, 101 (1979), 385–421.

19 See L. Scanlon, *Narrative, Authority and Power: the Medieval Exemplum and the Chaucerian Tradition* (Cambridge, 1994).

20 Stephen Scrope and William Worcester, *The Dicts and Sayings of the Philosophers*, ed. C. F. Bühler, Early English Text Society o.s. 211 (1941); Ralph Higden, *Polychronicon*, ed. C. Babington and J. R. Lumby, 9 volumes, Rolls Series 41 (London, 1865–86), III, 23. See Turner, 'Reception', pp. 61–63.

21 *Testament of Love* II.xi, lines 92–97, ed. W. W. Skeat in *The Complete Works of Geoffrey Chaucer*, 7 (Oxford, 1897); Parson's Tale X, lines 669–72, ed. L. D. Benson in *The Riverside Chaucer* (Oxford, 1987); Fall of Princes VI, lines 3116, ed. H. Bergen, Early English Text Society extra series vol. 123 (1924), p. 758.

22 See Langland, *Piers Plowman B-Text*, ed. A. V. C. Schmidt (London, 1984), X, 175–76; XI, 37, XX, 275–76. In the *C-Text*, ed. D. Pearsall (London, 1978), these references correspond to XI, 121, XI, 306 and XXII, 275–76.

23 As Derek Pearsall does in his edition of the *C-Text*, p. 129. For detailed discussion see Turner, 'Reception', pp. 73–74.

24 Scrope, *Dicts and Sayings* 42b, p. 110.

25 *The Riverside Chaucer*, VIII, lines 1448–1471, ed. Benson. See Turner, 'Reception' pp. 68–70.

26 See D. Finklestein, 'The code of Chaucer's "Secree of Secrees": Arabic alchemical terminology in The Canon Yeoman's Tale', *Archiv für das Studium der Neueren Sprachen und Literaturen*, 207 (1971), 260–76.

27 Cf. N. G. Round, 'The shadow of a philosopher: medieval Castilian images of Plato', *Journal of Hispanic Philology*, 3 (1978), 1–36, who concludes that Plato was a marginal figure of limited appeal.

The spirit of Spinoza and the Enlightenment image of the pure philosopher

Philosophers are not generally thought of as a particularly likeable breed. Standard accounts tell us that Kant was an obsessive, Marx a scrounger, Leibniz a sycophant, Hegel an egomaniac and Rousseau a paranoid neurotic. In the collective mythology of modern philosophy, there is only one prominent counter-example of an apparently thoroughly contented and inspiringly virtuous thinker: Baruch, later Benedict, Spinoza. This humble lens-grinder, we are told, devoted himself solely to his honest craft and to the disinterested, systematic search for truth, without any concern for money, fame or public approval. When for his independence of mind he was expelled and hounded into exile by the Jewish community into which he was born, he accepted his fate calmly and without bitterness. Impervious to the religious dogmatism and bigotry that surrounded him, he quietly devoted the rest of his life to developing his humane, rational philosophy of tolerance, and of freedom through self-mastery.

This traditional account of Spinoza's life, which remains deeply lodged in the popular historical imagination, differs very little in essence from the narratives and anecdotes that began to circulate almost immediately after the philosopher's death in 1677. Over the past three centuries, striking continuities have marked the enduring iconic status of Spinoza's life, despite the wide diversity of interpretations of his philosophy. Whether he has been regarded as an atheist or a pantheist, a dangerous heretic or an inspired genius, a wayward Jew or a true universalist, Spinoza's life, both during the Early Enlightenment and since, has almost always been framed as a distilled, exemplary narrative of serene, virtuous philosophical detachment.

These admiring assessments of Spinoza's life and character may to a considerable degree simply reflect the truth. A perusal of Spinoza's surviving correspondence unquestionably conveys the impression of a scrupulously polite, modest, even-tempered and honest man.[1] No human life, though, is utterly uncorrupted by the complexities of interpersonal interaction; and recent historical research makes possible the construction of a less hagiographical account of Spinoza's careful management of his scholarly relationships and of his philosophical reputation and impact.[2] However, whatever the relationship between myth and reality, the idealisation of Spinoza's life remains a remarkably intense and enduring phenomenon. During the Early Enlightenment – approximately the half-century centred around 1700 – his image was deeply embedded in the formation of the identity of anti-establishment philosophy. Spinoza's importance in this process was not simply his intellectual contribution, but also his unique status as arguably the first thoroughly secular individual in European history. In choosing to remain without even a nominal religious affiliation after the rabbis of Amsterdam imposed the communal ban on him in 1656, Spinoza placed himself radically outside conventional social categories. Because of this independence, he readily stood as representative of the universalism of philosophy in its purest form. This universalistic philosophical aspiration – and his imputed embodiment of it – was, though, troubled and uncertain. The ambiguities of Spinoza's cultural status, and particularly the ineradicability of his Jewish origins, have ever since the Early Enlightenment remained a key prism through which the philosophical difficulties of negotiating both identity and universalism are brought into focus.

The oldest known biography of Spinoza, and the source of many enduring hagiographical anecdotes, was almost certainly written within a year of his death. Its author, Jean Maximilien Lucas, was a French Huguenot resident in the Netherlands, and an admiring member of Spinoza's circle. His account of his hero's life is devoted and at times hyperbolic in tone, portraying Spinoza as a tireless seeker after truth: 'He was so ardent in the search for Truth that, although his health was very poor and required rest, he nevertheless took so little rest that once he did not go outside his lodgings during three whole months.'[3] Lucas's Spinoza is a paragon of virtue. He is utterly modest: when dying, we are told, he requested that his name not be credited on the title-page of his *Ethics*, 'saying that such affectations were unworthy of a philosopher'.[4] He had no desire for riches, and no fear of poverty; 'His virtue raised him above all these things.'[5] Lucas is careful, though, to humanise his hero. He tells us that Spinoza 'was no enemy of innocent pleasures', recounting how he happily chatted with the common people for relaxation, delighting everybody he encountered with his unpretentious, clear, and genial conversation. He tells us that Spinoza had excellent manners, and notes that he 'had a quality which I esteem all the more because it is rare in a philosopher. He was extremely tidy.'[6]

Lucas emphasises Spinoza's equanimity and lack of rancour, reporting his calm, patient response to the many bitter and defamatory attacks on him personally and against his *Tractatus Theologico-Politicus*.[7] He presents the advocacy of Spinoza's ideas as inseparable from the attempt to emulate his life: the virtue of Spinoza's philosophy merges with the virtue of the philosopher. This elevation of Spinoza to the status of a philosophical saint is expressed most clearly in the concluding paragraphs of the biography, in Lucas's lamentation of his hero's death:

> But since he could not escape the lot of all of us that has life, let us strive to walk in his footsteps, or at least to revere him with admiration and with praise, if we cannot imitate him. This is what I counsel to steadfast souls: to follow his maxims and his lights in such a way as to have them always before their eyes to serve as a rule for their actions. That which we love and revere in great men lives still and will live through all the ages ... BARUCH DE SPINOZA will live in the remembrance of true scholars and in their writings, which are the temple of Immortality.[8]

The only other full-length early biography of Spinoza was written by Johann Colerus, a German minister of the Lutheran Church at The Hague. Colerus moved to this city several years after Spinoza's death, and it seems that he was originally prompted to explore his life when he discovered the coincidence that his own home had earlier housed the infamous philosopher himself. His *Life of Benedict de Spinosa* first appeared in Dutch in 1705; French and English translations were published in the following year.[9] Unlike Lucas, Colerus was a declared opponent of Spinoza's views, which he regarded as dangerously atheistic: 'This is the true opinion of Spinoza, whatever he might say. He takes the liberty to use the word God, and to take it in a sense unknown to all Christianity.'[10] However, he deals only cursorily with what he describes as Spinoza's 'impious and absur'd Doctrines'. For further information, he refers his readers to the many published refutations of Spinoza's philosophy, explaining that he has touched briefly on some of his key ideas 'only to inspire the Christian Reader with the aversion and horror he ought to have for such pernicious Opinions'.[11] Colerus's interest is drawn to more elusive questions regarding Spinoza's life and identity. Although he portrays Spinoza's character in a markedly less star-struck fashion than does Lucas, he nonetheless essentially corroborates the image of a serious-minded and modest man. 'He was sober, and very frugal', Colerus tells us, elaborating that although he had numerous friends, had a good sense of humour, and enjoyed conversation 'even about trifles', he was nonetheless profoundly serious, spending most of his time 'quietly in his own chamber; troublesome to no Body'.[12]

Two moments in Spinoza's life particularly fascinate Colerus: first his excommunication from the Jewish community, of which he gives a detailed account, and secondly his death, an analysis of which occupies more than ten pages in a text of barely one hundred. This is a subject, Colerus writes, on which there have been 'so many various and false reports' that it is necessary to attempt finally to establish the truth.[13] Amongst the stories he recounts is the belief that Spinoza refused to allow people to visit him while he was dying, 'that he spoke once and even several times these words "O God have mercy upon me miserable sinner"', and that on the point of imminent death he poisoned himself with 'some Juice of Mandrake' which he had kept by him for this purpose.[14] After detailed research, including an interview with Spinoza's former landlord and landlady, Colerus scotches all these rumours. He takes particular care in refuting the final suggestion, providing us with full details of Spinoza's apothecary bill: 'I find in it some Tincture of Saffron, some Balsam, some Powder, etc., but there is no Opium nor Mandrake mentioned therein.'[15] Colerus thus establishes that the mask of Spinoza's fearless atheism did not slip at the point of imminent death. Despite maintaining allegiance to the orthodox belief that final reconciliation with God is amongst the deepest of human imperatives, Colerus meticulously marshals evidence to demonstrate that the case of Spinoza suggests the possibility of a death that is both dignified and godless.

Notwithstanding the theological and philosophical differences between Colerus and Lucas, they are both similarly mesmerised by a mythic quality in their subject. For both biographers, Spinoza is exceptional in his fearless transcendence of all the worldly attachments and comforts that for normal folk are so essential. He has no need for material possessions, strong emotional or community ties, or the reassurances of religious belief. For Colerus, as for Lucas, Spinoza represents the epitome of detachment, which both biographers regard as the mark of the true philosopher. While from a theological perspective this detachment is inextricable from Spinoza's alleged 'atheism', to which Colerus is so implacably opposed, he is nonetheless clearly deeply impressed by the exemplarity of Spinoza's noble equanimity. This ideal, so powerfully crystallised in Spinoza, to a considerable extent transcended the philosophical and theological divisions of the period. From the outset, Spinoza's philosophy inspired intense polemic: in Germany alone, more than thirty writers engaged substantially with his philosophy between 1670 and 1700, and only three of these offered an even partially positive assessment.[16] Nonetheless, even the most trenchant refutations of Spinoza's philosophy typically acknowledged the virtuousness of his character, which appears nowhere to have been called into question. Acceptance of Spinoza's exceptional virtue sat in odd compatibility with the demonisation of him as the arch-systematiser of atheism.

Questions of conduct and virtue were a major preoccupation of the Early Enlightenment Republic of Letters.[17] The construction of non-theological codes of behaviour and ethics was a key dimension of the cultural practice of scientific and intellectual circles in this period. The nature of this ethical distinctiveness, however, was understood in widely differing ways. The conventional argument that only religious faith made true virtue possible had first been sustainedly attacked by the sceptic philosopher François de la Mothe le Vayer, in his *De la vertu des païens* (1642).[18] Pierre Bayle, in his *Pensées diverses sur la comète* (1683), further developed this theme, in which he argued that 'atheism does not necessarily lead to the corruption of morals'.[19] He here offers various ancient philosophers as evidence that 'Atheists are not distinctively immoral', but the only modern example he discusses in any detail is Lucilio Vanini, burnt in Toulouse in 1619 for alleged atheism.[20] It seems likely that when writing the *Pensées diverses* Bayle was not yet familiar with the recent hagiographical biographies of Spinoza. In his later *Dictionnaire historique et critique* (1697), however, the article on Spinoza is the longest in the entire work.[21] Most of this essay is devoted to a vigorous refutation of Spinoza's philosophy, and in particular of the arguments of the *Tractatus Theologico-Politicus*, which Bayle describes as 'a pernicious and detestable work' containing 'the seeds of atheism'.[22] Nonetheless, he also provides a detailed and flattering account of Spinoza's life, drawing heavily on Lucas as well as other sources. Because of the great success of Bayle's *Dictionnaire*, it was largely via this conduit that the image of Spinoza as the quintessential virtuous atheist became powerfully fixed in the mainstream European mind of the eighteenth century. As in so many other articles in the Dictionary, Bayle highlights with relish what he sees as a paradoxical dissonance between beliefs and actions:

> Those who were acquainted with him [Spinoza], and the peasants of the villages where he had lived in retirement for some time, all agree in saying that he was sociable, affable, honest, obliging, and of a well-ordered morality. This is strange; but, after all, we should not be more surprised by this than to see people who live very bad lives even though they are completely convinced of the Gospel.[23]

For Bayle, Spinoza's exemplary life starkly demonstrated the disjuncture between virtuous living and religious devotion. For more outspoken critics of conventional religion, it was important not only to expose the ethical inadequacy of piety, but also to develop an alternative, secular notion of virtue. Spinoza's philosophy was a key inspiration for these radicals in their search for a new, more rationalist ethic. Traces of the impact of Spinoza abound in the French clandestine philosophical literature of the first few decades of the eighteenth century. The manuscript texts that were produced and circulated in this philosophical underground reveal an intense concern not only to challenge religious orthodoxy, but also to define and reflect a new culture of fearless inquiry and secular virtue.[24] One such clandestine manuscript – a brief, anonymous essay titled *L'Idée d'un philosophe* – presents virtue as the path to true happiness. Expounding an argument that closely echoes Spinoza's *Ethics*, the author states that the philosopher must devote himself to the mastery of his passions, through the use of his natural reason. The ideal philosopher, the text asserts, is 'a man who has perfected his natural reason to the highest possible degree'.[25] He must not be excessively bookish: 'he reflects not only on what he reads, but on everything that happens to him'.[26] He is careful to control his passions, and lives to the best of his abilities in accordance with reason, as is appropriate for philosophical 'lovers of wisdom'.[27]

A similar argument, emphasising the fact that reason alone is adequate as a guide for virtue, is advocated in another anonymous clandestine manuscript, *De la conduite qu'un honnête homme doit garder pendant sa vie*. In the search for virtue, this text argues, 'we need reason alone; and when reason speaks we must listen and be silent'.[28] The text offers a list of several exemplary virtuous atheists, including several ancient philosophers as well as Thomas Hobbes. Pride of place, however, is given to Spinoza, whose numerous virtues are celebrated in full: 'Benedict Spinoza lived an irreproachable life, teaching reason alone and demonstrating admirable maxims on the duty of the honest man'.[29] For early eighteenth-century radicals, Spinoza's life was thus sanctified as the epitome of philosophical perfection. His virtue was represented as undiluted by any distracting commitments or interests: his romantic unattachment, although never directly highlighted, reinforced the impact of his communal neutrality. As the supreme philosopher, all mundane foibles and peculiarities were expunged from his identity. Spinoza's uniquely isolated and autonomous social status made him an ideal exemplar of detachment and neutrality. Whereas all of his disciples remained at least to some extent bounded in their thinking by their specific national, cultural and religious allegiances, Spinoza alone appeared totally free of such attachments. His life could thus readily be universalised as one of total liberation from all social roots and bonds.

This exemplary universalisation of Spinoza's life intersected problematically, however, with one particular biographical fact: his Jewish origins. Spinoza's ethnicity is invariably obscured in idealised representations of him, but the mechanisms of this occlusion are varied and intricate. Spinoza's biographers appear unequivocally certain that on renouncing Judaism Spinoza no longer remained in any sense a Jew. Bayle presents the stages of Spinoza's life in linear sequence: Spinoza was 'a Jew by birth, and afterwards a deserter from Judaism, and lastly an atheist'.[30] Colerus similarly seems to be in no doubt about the totality of this transformation. Spinoza, he tells us, was 'originally a Jew' but 'after he had forsaken Judaism he changed his Name, and call'd himself Benedict in his Writings, and in the Letters which he subscribed'.[31] However, Spinoza's status as a Jew who had rejected Judaism placed him in a uniquely indeterminate category. The

ambiguity of his identity was an issue which his admirers handled with
considerable delicacy. Lucas makes only one substantive reference to
Spinoza's Jewishness. However, this isolated statement makes it clear that
he sees this fact as highly significant:

> But what I esteem most in him is that, although he was born and bred in
> the midst of a gross people who are the source of superstition, he had
> imbibed no bitterness whatever, and that he had purged his soul of those
> false maxims with which so many are infatuated . . . He was entirely cured
> of those silly and ridiculous opinions which the Jews have of God.[32]

Spinoza is here implicitly represented as something almost miraculous: a
Jew who has utterly transcended the mark of his origin. A powerful echo
resonates of the life of an earlier Jew who, it was believed, rejected the
narrow dogmas of his people. This echo is reinforced by Lucas's explicit
assimilation of Spinoza into his own brand of enlightened Christianity: 'The
Law of Jesus Christ leads us to the love of God and of our neighbour,
which is precisely what reason inspires us to do, according to the opinion
of Mr. de Spinoza.'[33]

This portrayal of Spinoza as the Jesus Christ of Reason reflects the
powerful associations for Lucas and others of Spinoza's exit from Judaism.
Millenarian expectancy, so intense amongst radicals in the mid-seventeenth
century, remained a potent strand in the thinking of many minority Christian
groups throughout the Early Enlightenment and beyond. These expectations were intimately connected to hopes for the mass conversion of the
Jews to Christianity.[34] Henry Oldenberg, the secretary of the London Royal
Society and an admiring and enthusiastic correspondent with Spinoza, was
an avid millenarian, and saw Spinoza's abandonment of Judaism as extremely
significant in this schema.[35] It seems likely that similar expectations
animated many more of Spinoza's Christian friends, for whom his 'conversion' could not but have appeared to be meaningful.[36] Evoking submerged
but powerful Christian imagery, Lucas uses Spinoza to cast the heralding
of the new insights of natural, rational religion as truths laid bare by a
prophetic Jew. Once again, a Jewish outcast upholds the deepest spiritual
truths of Judaeo-Christianity, in rebellion against the primitive group that
first, and most drastically, corrupted this message. The dawn of
Enlightenment is thus given a subliminally millenarian tinge, with Spinoza
performing the key messianic role as its necessarily originally, and then no
longer, Jewish harbinger.

From the late 1670s onwards, Spinoza's iconic status penetrated rapidly
into the various subcultures of the Radical Enlightenment. Almost as
soon as they appeared, his works were banned virtually everywhere; even
in the liberal climate of the United Provinces, pre-existing anti-Socinian

censorship legislation was used to drive underground the circulation and sale of the *Tractatus Theologico-Politicus*. Nowhere could Spinoza's ideas be publicly discussed or referred to approvingly.[37] Published refutations of his ideas – most prominently Bayle's *Dictionnaire* article and Christopher Wittich's *Anti-Spinoza* (1690) – became the main conduit by which knowledge of the actual content of Spinoza's thought was made accessible to an educated readership. The transgressive nature of Spinoza's ideas heightened his attractiveness to groups of freethinkers and religious radicals, particularly in the Dutch Republic, where they were a significant presence. These *Chrétiens sans Église*, to use Leszek Kolakowski's phrase, were in various ways attempting to redefine the relationship between private faith, reason, and the organised church, and were often powerfully drawn both to Spinoza's ideas and to his own 'sans église' status.[38]

In some cases, for example that of the Collegiant Johannes Bredenburg, Spinoza's ideas were influential mainly through the process of their rejection.[39] Other Dutch radicals, such as Frederick van Leenhof and the heterodox Zeeland preacher, Pontiaan Van Hattem, show clearer signs of a positive Spinozian influence. All these thinkers, in varying ways, absorbed elements of Spinoza's ideas into a loose radical theology of popular Christian irenicism.[40] Amongst the opponents of these religious radicals, the term 'Spinozist' rapidly came into widespread use as a hostile, broad-brush synonym for atheist. Dutch theological conservatives commonly used the term to brand their opponents; even Christopher Wittich, whose refutation of Spinoza had attempted to argue from a Cartesian perspective that he had falsely applied the Cartesian method, found himself accused by Voetian anti-Cartesians of Spinozism.[41] To self-conscious radicals, allegiance to Spinoza became in itself a transgressive gesture. Because of the danger of expressing open sympathy with the philosopher's ideas, celebration of the exemplarity of his life could stand as a coded implication of Spinozist sympathies. By the 1690s, materialist ideas to some extent influenced by Spinoza, and strongly associated with him, were being propagated and popularised in the Dutch Republic with increasing boldness. Two decades later, Spinoza's reputation as the most seductively dangerous modern philosopher was firmly established across continental Western Europe.

The text that most powerfully linked the name and the reputation of Spinoza to the materialist philosophical underground of the Early Enlightenment was the most infamous treatise of the early modern age: the anonymous *Traité des Trois Imposteurs*. The origins of this polemical tract are still extremely uncertain and mysterious. Its central thesis has extremely long antecedents: Moses, Jesus and Mohammed, the three great religious leaders, are presented as cynical impostors, who invented the details of their respective creeds in order to gain political mastery over the gullible masses. This notion was traditionally associated with Machiavelli, but can be traced back much further. The allegation that Jesus was an impostor appears in the *Toledot Yeshu*, an early Jewish satire the existence of which was known to Christians by the ninth century.[42] Claims of the existence of a prototype *Three Impostors* text extend back to the thirteenth century: a common putatative author was the Emperor Frederick II, who was excommunicated by Pope Gregory IX in 1239 allegedly for this heresy.[43] The specific blasphemy was also widely attributed to Averroës, who was another, even earlier candidate for the original authorship of the text. Although there were many reported sightings of the manuscript during the early modern period, we have no safe evidence of the existence of any such text until around the end of the seventeenth century, when various slightly differing versions began to circulate clandestinely, often under an intriguing alternative title: *L'Esprit de Spinosa*.

In the form in which it then surfaced, the treatise largely consisted of a composite of various unattributed extracts, sometimes tendentiously translated, from Vanini, La Mothe le Vayer, Naudé, Charron, Hobbes and Spinoza, including a large extract from the *Ethics*. The authorship and dating of the original composition of the manuscript is unclear, but according to the recent scholarship of Silvia Berti, it seems probable that the individual responsible was Jan Vroesen, a diplomatic representative of Brabant at The Hague, and the most likely date around 1700.[44] In a sense, though, the identification of a definitive author is here not of central importance. As Miguel Benítez has pointed out, clandestine manuscripts are by their nature 'open texts', and this applies particularly strongly to the highly slippery and shifting *Traité des Trois Imposteurs*.[45] Both authorship and meaning are highly ambiguous in this text, which still resists the attempts of historians to ascertain its precise developmental chronology. Particularly unclear is the relationship between those versions circulating under the standard *Trois Imposteurs* title, and the many manuscripts entitled *L'Esprit de Spinosa*. It is unknown how or exactly when this title first came into use, but as almost all copies of the *Esprit* are preceded by a version of Lucas's biography of Spinoza, it seems that a decision to link these two texts together was the stimulus for the introduction of the new title. By 1716, much the same text was circulating both as *Le Fameux livre des Trois Imposteurs* and as the latter part of *La Vie et l'Esprit de M. Benoît de Spinosa*.[46]

In 1719, the *Vie et l'Esprit* was finally published, by Charles Levier, a Huguenot bookseller in The Hague. This was the first time that a major clandestine manuscript had been printed, and therefore was a significant publishing event. The printed volume is extremely rare, and clearly did not

circulate at all widely, but it should not be concluded from this that the
publishing venture was a failure. Rather, as John Christian Laursen has
argued, the small print-run was part of a deliberate price-maintenance
strategy. This proved to be a effective commercial decision, enabling the
volume to circulate at very high prices of up to fifty florins, only ten florins
less than the price for the massive bulk of Bayle's four-volume *Dictionnaire*.[47]
It was also important within the culture of radical thought that libertine
philosophising should remain a minority pursuit, shrouded in a certain level
of mystique and exclusiveness. Had the market been flooded with the treatise, this would potentially have been politically dangerous, even in the
relatively tolerant atmosphere of the Dutch Republic. It would also have
jarred with a key element of the self-identity of radical readers: that these
ideas were only accessible to the select few who were capable of true philosophical thinking and of realising the deception of organised religion.

The relationship between Spinoza's own philosophy and the overall
argument of the *Esprit de Spinosa* is somewhat tenuous. Richard Popkin
has suggested that Spinoza may even have participated in the composition
of a very early edition of the *Three Impostors* treatise, but the highly selective use of his *Ethics* in the text makes this seem extremely unlikely.[48] As
Françoise Charles-Daubert has argued, the *Esprit de Spinosa* did not diffuse
a faithful account of Spinoza's own ideas, but selectively assimilated them
into an older tradition of 'libertinage érudit', heavily laced with materi-
alism.[49] Silvia Berti has pointed out that the definition of God in the treatise
as 'an absolutely infinite Being, amongst whose attributes is to be an eternal,
infinite Substance' is a distorted translation from the *Ethics*.[50] In making
the claim that substance itself is a divine attribute, in contrast to Spinoza's
own definition of God as 'a substance consisting of infinite attributes', his
metaphysics is given a more unambiguously materialist gloss.[51] Not only is
the tone of the text generally much more polemical and impassioned than
Spinoza's own writings – the Bible is swiftly dismissed as a product of
'rabbinic fantasy'[52] – but its philosophical preoccupations diverge from his
own. This is particularly stark in the exposition of a totally materialist philosophy with which the *Esprit* culminates. The materiality of the soul, described
as 'a very nimble substance, continuously in movement',[53] is here discussed
in great detail, whereas no such argument is even touched on by Spinoza.

Why, then, was this only very loosely Spinozist text given its secondary
title? And what was the perceived relationship between Spinoza's hagiographical *Life* and his impassioned, impatient *Spirit*? The mild, temperate
tone of Lucas's *Life* contrasts markedly with the philosophical and political vigour of the *Spirit*. This poses a paradoxical disjuncture between the
two texts: the fiery *Spirit* does not at all seem to be in the spirit of Spinoza
as he is portrayed in the *Life*. It is on a different, less literal level that the

Esprit de Spinosa is worthy of its name. The two texts share a common theme of outsiderness, and of the rejection at the most fundamental level of religious tradition. Because Spinoza's adult life was lived outside the structures of organised religion, his 'spirit' could be claimed as that of the repudiation of all religious authority, which is the central theme of the Three Impostors thesis. The radical appropriation and selective rewriting of Spinoza's philosophy extends into the intellectual domain the iconic sanctification of his life. His own metaphysics is displaced by a new representation of his ideas as imbued with a generalised spirit of anti-religious subversion. In these combined texts, the libertarian ideals of the Radical Enlightenment find their fullest expression. Together, the *Life* and the *Spirit* present Spinoza as the embodiment of the most total escape from all dogma and constraining traditions, to the ideal of absolute philosophical freedom and wisdom.

The idealisation of Spinoza was problematised, however, by the fact of the philosopher's Jewish roots. Not only did this ethnic particularity jar with the universalisation of his image, but Judaism itself was widely regarded as the epitome of unenlightened superstition and legalism: the very opposite of the values symbolised by Spinoza within the Radical Enlightenment. Claiming Spinoza fully for radical philosophy thus required the overcoming of his Jewishness. In Levier's 1719 publication, the moves by which this was attempted are particularly revealing. Levier interpolated into Lucas's *Life* a physical description of Spinoza, based on the information given by Colerus in his biography. Colerus, however, explicitly describes Spinoza as characteristically Jewish:

> He was of a middle size, he had good features in his face, his skin somewhat black. black curl'd Hair, long Eyebrows, and of the same Colour, so that one might easily know him by his Looks that he was descended from Portuguese Jews.[54]

In Levier's version, Colerus' words are subtly amended:

> He was of slight stature, with well-proportioned facial features, very dark skin, black curled hair, eyebrows of the same colour, small, black, lively eyes, a pleasant physiognomy, and a Portuguese air.[55]

This description, and the vagueness of its concluding 'Portuguese' reference, cleanses Spinoza of any explicit trace of his Jewish ethnicity.[56]

This conscious erasure is more explicit in the choice of image and words on the frontispiece of Levier's edition (See figure 1). Opposite the title page, a portrait of Spinoza appears that is immediately striking in its total lack of resemblance to any other surviving portrait of the philosopher.[57] A print of an engraving by Étienne-Jahandier Desrochers, later

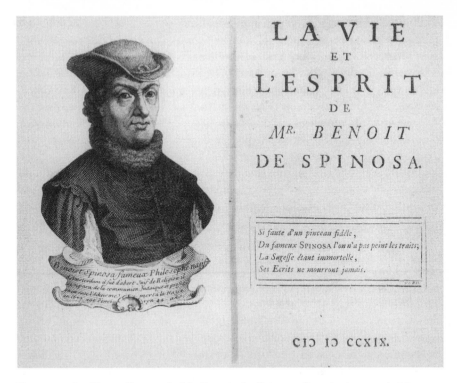

Figure 1 *La Vie et l'esprit de Mr Benoit de Spinosa*, frontispiece and title page (The Hague, 1719)

appointed 'graveur du roi' at the French court, it was identified by Ernst Altkirch more than eighty years ago as a representation not of Spinoza at all, but of René 'the Good', Duke of Anjou and King of Naples in the fifteenth century.[58] Silvia Berti has recently confirmed that the costume was copied directly from an engraving of King René in Desrochers' collection, and has suggested that the visage was intended elegantly to depict the physical features attributed to Spinoza in the text.[59] Significantly, the rhyme that appears opposite the image amounts to an admission that the portrait is not a genuine one:

> Although, for the lack of a faithful brush,
> We have not shown the features of the famous SPINOZA,
> As Wisdom is immortal
> His writings will never die.[60]

Together, the poem and the portrait seem implicitly to make the claim that the transcendental immortality of his wisdom render irrelevant the precise details of Spinoza's personal appearance. As representative of the quintessence of philosophical goodness, it matters little if his individual looks are blurred with those of another semi-mythical archetype of goodness, René of Anjou, who reputedly retired from kingship to a life devoted to Provençal poetry and agriculture. As Silvia Berti has argued, the editors of the volume were clearly particularly concerned to de-judaise Spinoza, by representing him with an abstract image that carried no hint of Jewishness.[61] A conscious decision was made not to use any of the portraits of Spinoza painted during his life, which typically depict him with much more characteristically Jewish features.[62]

However, it is not simply the case that Desrochers' image is intended to erase all awareness of Spinoza's Jewish origins. The cartouche beneath the bust indeed specifically mentions this fact:

> Benedict Spinoza, famous Philosopher of Amsterdam. He was first a Jew by religion, then separated himself from the Jewish communion and professed Atheism. Died in the Hague in 1677, at the age of about 44.[63]

Bizarrely, this strikingly un-Jewish portrait attracts attention in its own caption to the fact that it is of a Jewish subject. Spinoza's Jewish origins are not concealed, but actually highlighted, in order then to be transcended. Spinoza's separation from 'la communion Judaique' is presented not only as significant, but as absolute to the extent that even all visual traces of his Jewishness are overcome by it. The insistence on Spinoza's universality is here revealed as in a sense dependent on his original Jewishness. This ethnic specificity represents the photographic negative of his philosophical idealisation: it must not to be forgotten, so that it can be deliberately inverted, and thus erased. Paradoxically, though, the need to maintain the visibility of this act also guarantees its inconclusiveness. The attempt to obliterate all remnants of Spinoza the Jew in Spinoza the philosopher cannot, ultimately, succeed, particularly when the strained artificiality of this process is rendered so explicit. Spinoza's ineradicable Jewishness thus lingers as a powerful destabilising fault-line in the narrative of universal philosophical exemplarity constructed around him.

The image of Spinoza was a central site of contestation in the formation of the modern identity of philosophy, as a distinctive perspective and cultural practice. Universalism was fundamental to the identity of the Enlightenment: in contrast with the culturally and textually specific truth claims of religion, philosophy in its purest form was defined by its rejection of these horizons of thought. Both for the detractors and the proponents of this emergent intellectual culture, Spinoza stood as the archetypal philosopher, epitomising pure detachment and abstraction. However, he also represented the limits of this vision. Taking their lead from Bayle, those who saw Spinoza as a dangerous atheist typically set his mild-mannered life and pernicious philosophy in stark juxtaposition with each other, thus underlining the danger of the deceptive charms of secular philosophising. For radicals, identification with Spinoza permitted symbolic identification with an internally contradictory self-image that was simultaneously respectably virtuous and fearlessly radical, and both abstractedly universal and concretely individual. Although these paradoxes were almost always concealed, the deployment of Spinoza in Early Enlightenment radicalism nonetheless exposes a notable fissure within its thought.

Over the middle decades of the eighteenth century, interest in Spinoza declined across Europe. In the salon culture of Paris at the height of the Enlightenment, philosophy seemed to merge easily with cultured sociability. The identity of the philosopher was no longer a focus of tension, and there was therefore less need to invoke Spinoza as an exemplary model. However, with the emergence of Romanticism the nature of philosophy once again became a focus of attention, and with this came renewed interest in Spinoza. The German 'Spinoza Renaissance' of the 1780s centred around the controversy between Moses Mendelssohn and Friedrich Jacobi over the interpretation of Spinoza's philosophy. This debate had wide cultural and intellectual resonances, not least for Mendelssohn's own negotiation of his identity as a Jewish philosopher.[64] Both Herder and Goethe deeply admired Spinoza, as a philosopher and as a person. In his *Dichtung und Wahrheit*, Goethe lauded him as the perfect model of a temperate thinker, praising 'the boundless unselfishness that shone forth from every sentence'.[65] Herder's creative engagement with Spinoza was central to his attempts to reconcile a personal metaphysics with a scientific physics.[66] By the end of the eighteenth century, the appropriate nature and role of philosophy no longer seemed as self-evident as it had been to Voltaire and Diderot. In attempting to rethink the relationship between personal ethics and belief and objective truth, the problematics of Spinoza's universal exemplarity were for these thinkers a key point of reference and focus of debate.

More than three hundred years after his death, the figure of Spinoza still retains a particular inspirational power. Exactly what Spinoza represents remains highly contested: in recent decades, he has been claimed as a proto-Marxist, a proto-Zionist, and a bulwark against the excesses of postmodernism.[67] Spinoza's spirit thus still stands in a very uncertain relationship with his historical, embodied life. Echoing Derrida's evocation of Marx as a spectral presence that perpetually and inescapably haunts the political conscience of the capitalist world,[68] we should perhaps also identify the presence of Spinoza's spirit as another philosophical apparition who refuses to be exorcised. Spinoza's spectrality is that of the ideal of a pure philosophy, embracing both personal wisdom and universal reason. In the radical Early Enlightenment, this aspiration was powerfully alive, and its envisioned realisation was encapsulated in an image of Spinoza simultaneously as an exemplary individual and as the universal voice of philosophical truth. However, this universalisation was destabilised by the particular specificity of which it was an inversion: Spinoza's ineradicable Jewish origins. In the ultimately unwinnable battle to escape the confines of cultural particularism, the biblical *Urkultur* of Judaism was widely positioned by Early Enlightenment radicals as a proxy enemy, standing metonymically for the much more nebulous target of the inescapable constraints of their own cultural horizons. The universalisation of Spinoza represented the enactment of this strategy, but the inevitable inconclusiveness of the eclipsing of his Jewishness discreetly undermined it from within. The creation and endurance of this exemplary life highlights the enduring problematics and ambiguities inherent in the universalistic aspiration of the Enlightenment.

Notes

1   B. Spinoza, *Correspondence*, ed. and trans. A. Wolf (London, 1928).
2   See W. N. A. Klever, 'Spinoza's life and works', pp. 13–60 in D. Garrett (ed.), *The Cambridge Companion to Spinoza* (Cambridge, 1996).
3   J. M. Lucas, 'The life of the late Mr. de Spinosa', in A. Wolf, *The Oldest Biography of Spinoza* (London, 1927), p. 60.
4   *Ibid.*, p. 62.
5   *Ibid.*, p. 64.
6   *Ibid.*, pp. 63–44, 71.
7   *Ibid.*, p. 71.
8   *Ibid.*, p. 75.
9   A. J. Siebrand, *Spinoza and the Netherlanders* (Assen, Netherlands, and Wolfeboro, NH, 1988), p. 120.
10 J. Colerus, *The Life of Benedict de Spinosa* (The Hague, [1706] 1906), p. 63.
11 *Ibid.*, p. 71.
12 *Ibid.*, pp. 36, 41–42.
13 *Ibid.*, p. 89.
14 *Ibid.*, pp. 93–94.
15 *Ibid.*, pp. 97–98.
16 M. Walther, '*Machina Civilis* oder *Von Deutscher Freiheit*: Formen, Inhalte und Trägergeschichten der Reaktion auf den Politiktheoretischen Gehalt von Spinoza's *Tractatus Theologico-Politicus* in Deutschland, bis 1700', pp. 184–221 in P. Christofolini (ed.), *The Spinozistic Heresy: The Debate on the Tractatus Theologico-Politicus, 1670–1677, and the Immediate Reception of Spinozism* (Amsterdam and Maarssen, 1995), p. 184.
17 See A. Goldgar, *Impolite Learning: Culture and Community in the Republic of Letters* (New Haven and London, 1995).
18 See J. S. Spink, *French Free-Thought from Gassendi to Voltaire* (London, 1960), pp. 17–18.
19 P. Bayle, *Pensées diverses sur la comète* (Paris, [1683] 1939), 2 vols., vol. 2, pp. 5–8.
20 Bayle, *Pensées*, pp. 107–14.
21 G. Brykman, 'La "Réfutation" de Spinoza dans le *Dictionnaire* de Bayle', pp. 17–28 in O. Bloch (ed.), *Spinoza au XVIIIe siècle* (Paris, 1990), pp. 17–18.

22 P. Bayle, *Historical and Critical Dictionary*, ed. and trans. Richard H. Popkin (Indianapolis, [1697] 1991), p. 293.

23 *Ibid.*, p. 295.

24 See O. Bloch, ed., *Le Matérialisme du XVIII siècle et la littérature clandestine* (Paris, 1982); F. Moreau, ed, *De bonne main: la communication manuscrite au XVIIIe siècle* (Paris, 1993); M. Benítez, *La Face cachée des lumières: recherches sur les manuscrits philosophiques de l'age classique* (Paris, 1996).

25 *L'Idée d'un philosophe*, MS Aix 814, p. 1.

26 *Ibid.*, p. 2.

27 *Ibid.*, p. 5.

28 *De la conduite qu'un honnête homme doit garder pendant sa vie*, MS Bibliothèque Mazarine 1194, p. 113.

29 *Ibid.*, p. 127.

30 Bayle, *Historical and Critical Dictionary*, p. 288.

31 Colerus, *Life*, p. 1.

32 Lucas, 'The life of the late Mr. de Spinosa', p. 69.

33 *Ibid.*

34 See C. Hill, 'Till the conversion of the Jews', in *The Collected Essays of Christopher Hill* (Brighton, 1986), II, pp. 269–300.

35 S. Hutton, 'Henry Oldenburg and Spinoza', in Christofolini (ed.), *The Spinozistic Heresy*, pp. 106–19.

36 R. H. Popkin, 'The convertible Jew', in Christofolini (ed.), *The Spinozistic Heresy*, pp. 119–22.

37 J. Israel, 'The banning of Spinoza's works in the Dutch Republic', in W. van Bunge and W. Klever (eds), *Disguised and Overt Spinozism around 1700* (Leiden, 1996), pp. 3–14 (esp. p. 8).

38 Leszek Kolakowski, *Chrétiens sans Église: la conscience religieuse et le lieu confessionnel au XVIIe siècle* (Paris, 1969), pp. 206–17.

39 See Emanuela Scribano, 'Johannes Bredenburg (1643–1691): confutatore di Spinoza?', in Christofolini (ed.), *The Spinozistic Heresy*, pp. 66–76.

40 See F. van Leenhof, *Den Hemel op Aarden* (Amsterdam, 1704); M. Wielema, 'Spinoza in Zeeland: the growth and supression of "popular Spinozism"', in Van Bunge and Klever (eds), *Disguised and Overt Spinozism*, pp. 103–15.

41 Siebrand, *Spinoza*, pp. 100–07.

42 B. E. Schwarzbach and W. Fairbairn, 'History and structure of our *Traité des Trois Imposteurs*', in S. Berti, F. Charles-Daubert and R. H. Popkin (eds), *Heterodoxy, Spinozism and Free Thought in Early-Eighteenth-Century Europe: Studies on the 'Traité des Trois Imposteurs'* (Dordrecht, 1996), pp. 75–129, esp. pp. 81–90; S. Krauss and W. Horbury, *The Jewish-Christian Controversy: Volume 1 – History* (Tübingen, 1995), pp. 12–13.

43 See H. S. Nisbet, '*De Tribus Impostoribus*: on the genesis of Lessing's *Nathan the Wise*', *Euphorion*, 73 (1979), 365–87, esp. p. 368.

44 S. Berti, 'L'Esprit de Spinosa: ses origines et sa première édition dans leur contexte Spinozien', in Berti et al., *Heterodoxy*, pp. 3–50; S. Berti, 'Jan Vroesen, autore del *Traité des Trois Imposteurs*?', *Rivista di Storica Italiana*, 103 (1991), 528–43.

45 M. Benítez, 'Une histoire interminable: origines et développement du *Traité des Trois Imposteurs*' in Berti et al., *Heterodoxy*, pp. 53–74, esp. p. 53.

46 See F. Charles-Daubert, '*Les Traités des Trois Imposteurs* et *l'Esprit de Spinosa*', *Nouvelles de la République des Lettres*, 1 (1988), 21–50; F. Charles-Daubert, '*L'Esprit de Spinosa* et les *Traités des Trois Imposteurs*: rappel des différentes familles et de leurs principales caractéristiques', in Berti et al., *Heterodoxy*, pp. 131–89.

47 J. C. Laursen, 'The politics of a publishing event: the Marchand millieu and *The Life and Spirit of Spinoza* of 1719', in Berti et al., *Heterodoxy*, pp. 273–96, esp. pp. 293–95.

48 R. H. Popkin, 'Spinoza and the Three Impostors', in Edwin Curley and P.-F. Moreau (eds), *Spinoza: Issues and Directions* (Leiden, 1990), pp. 347–58.

49 F. Charles-Daubert, 'L'image de Spinoza dans la littérature clandestine et l'*Esprit de Spinoza*', in Bloch, *Spinoza*, pp. 51–74, esp. pp. 64–65.

50 *Traité des Trois Imposteurs*, ed. S. Berti (Turin, [1719] 1994), p. 92; compare B. Spinoza, *Ethics*, ed. and trans. G. H. R. Parkinson (London, [1677] 1989), p. 3.

51 *Ibid.*, p. 270.

52 *Ibid.*, p. 96.

53 *Ibid.*, p. 228.

54 Colerus, *Life*, p. 39.

55 *Trois Imposteurs*, ed. Berti, p. 56.

56 *Ibid.*, pp. xxxvii–xl.

57 *Ibid.*, p. xxxvii.

58 E. Altkirch, *Spinoza im Porträt* (Jena, 1913), pp. 70–71.

59 *Trois Imposteurs*, ed. Berti, pp. xxxvii–xxxix.

60 *Ibid.*, title page. [See illustration]

61 *Ibid.*, p. xl.

62 See Altkirch, *Spinoza im Porträt*; S. L. Millner, *The Face of Benedictus Spinoza* (New York, 1946).

63 *Trois Imposteurs*, ed. Berti, frontispiece. [See figure 1.]

64 See S. Zac, *Spinoza en Allemagne: Mendelssohn, Lessing et Jacobi* (Paris, 1989); A. Altmann, *Moses Mendelssohn: A Biographical Study* (University, AL, 1973), pp. 593–637.

65 Cited in D. Bell, *Spinoza in Germany from 1670 to the Age of Goethe* (London, 1984), p. 151.

66 Bell, *Spinoza*, pp. 97–146.

67 A. Negri, *The Savage Anomaly: The Power of Spinoza's Metaphysics and Politics* (Minneapolis and Oxford, 1991); Y. Yovel, *Spinoza and Other Heretics: The Marrano of Reason* (Princeton, 1989), p. 190; C. Norris, *Spinoza and the Origins of Modern Critical Theory* (Oxford, 1991), pp. 251–74.

68 J. Derrida, *Specters of Marx* (New York, 1994), p. 1 ff.

Faces of genius: images of Isaac Newton
in eighteenth-century England

In the 1790s, collectors keen to advertise their cultural affiliations but with only a couple of shillings to spare could decorate their homes with a Staffordshire statuette of an English hero such as Milton, Shakespeare or Newton. In contrast with elite representations with which we are now more familiar, this earthenware Newton was a robust young man dressed in brightly coloured clothes.[1] Godfrey Kneller's expensive oil-painting (figure 2) presents a more recognisable image of the reclusive genius who cared little for his health and appearance as he plunged in and out of insanity. Newton commissioned it in 1689, two years after publishing the *Principia*, when he was cultivating his role as a private Cambridge scholar. The thin pale face and unkempt natural hair conform with traditional imagery of the melancholic philosopher.[2] But although this picture is often reproduced in modern texts, very few eighteenth-century people were aware of it: like many other aspects of eighteenth-century natural philosophy, its current prevalence perpetuates Victorian ideologies. Both the original versions were privately owned and virtually unknown until the mid-nineteenth century, when the one illustrated here was rediscovered and engraved for public distribution.[3] It contributed to the extensive debates about genius and insanity, a link which had not yet been forged in the eighteenth century.[4]

Thirteen years later, Newton occupied a position of metropolitan prominence as Master of the Mint, and he chose to be portrayed very differently, swathed in crimson and wearing an elegant wig. Victorians preoccupied with finding an authentic likeness of a creative genius condemned this depiction of Newton as a 'dandy, and ... prosperous man of the world'. But, produced in an earlier period when portraits were valued as role models of ideal types, it matched Enlightenment accounts of an equable, sociable gentleman.[5] Through engravings and other derivations, it became well known to a broad public (figure 3).[6]

Figure 2 'Isaacus Newtonus', mezzotint by Thomas Oldham Barlow (1868) of Godfrey Kneller's 1689 portrait. Reproduced by kind permission of the Wellcome Institute Library, London

Figure 3 'Sr Isaac Newton', engraving by Jakob Houbraken (1743) after Godfrey Kneller's 1702 portrait. Reproduced by kind permission of the Wellcome Institute Library, London

This portrait and the pottery figurine, originally designed for very different audiences, were just two amongst many Newtonian images purveyed during the eighteenth century. As a hagiographer observed in 1782, 'Various are the effigies of Sir Isaac, both in frontispieces, medallions, busts, seals, and other engravings, but most of them are dissimilar from his monument and from each other.'[7] Many historians of science have described the verbal tactics employed by Newton's supporters to consolidate his reputation as England's greatest national philosopher, while literary critics have demonstrated the influence of Newtonian philosophy on eighteenth-century poetry. This paper will supplement these studies by exploring how he was presented visually, so that he became a familiar national icon for many people who knew little about optics or gravity.

Particularly for intellectual figures such as Newton, historians are more accustomed to study texts than pictures, but material artefacts are invaluable for exploring popular cultural perceptions. In addition to around twenty major oil paintings, Newton and his friends commissioned several busts, engravings and plaques before he died.[8] Rather than focusing exclusively on these expensive originals seen only by restricted circles, the present essay will examine the statues, engravings, and other media which reached wider audiences and played a significant role in constructing his public image as a British scientific hero. Unlike in our post-Freudian era, eighteenth-century portraits were not valued primarily for exposing individual idiosyncracies, but were expected to carry moral messages of improvement. They simultaneously revealed and shaped ideological constructs such as national character, appropriate gender behaviour and class structures.[9] By analysing the multiple representations of Newton, I aim to recreate how he was perceived during the eighteenth century and to discuss how, collectively, they contributed to constructing the new category of a scientific genius.

Newton has now achieved a quasi-mythological status as England's greatest scientist, but neither he nor science enjoyed their current prestigious position. Genius and science both carried different meanings from now. Genius was traditionally attributed only to writers and artists, and was often regarded as a superior capacity differing in degree rather than kind from ordinary ability. Thus many of Newton's biographers maintained that he had achieved his great insights not from flashes of inspired creativity but through hard, patient thought. Aesthetic philosophers gradually came to emphasise creativity as the hallmark of genius, and this increasing focus on originality was reinforced by the legal establishment of proprietary authorship as the new copyright laws recognised ownership over literary works. A new Romantic vision emerged of an original genius driven from within by a forceful imaginative urge, a man distinguished by quite special intellectual and emotional characteristics.[10]

By the early nineteenth century, Newton's name had – according to the *Historic Gallery of Portraits* – 'become synonymous with genius'. That this accolade could be paid to a scientific innovator rather than to a literary author reflects the changing status of science. Previously, natural philosophers had often been satirised but they became increasingly successful at demonstrating the validity and usefulness of their research. Scientific knowledge became an essential component of polite culture, and men of science gradually established themselves as experts in new academic disciplines. As Britain started to become industrialised, and technological innovations gained importance, Newton became celebrated as the paradigmatic scientific genius, a new role model which his example had helped to construct.

Armed with a twentieth-century appreciation of Newton's singular genius, it is easy to forget that Newton was competing with other Enlightenment role models. In particular, Alexander Pope, associated as translator and editor with England's two iconic geniuses, Homer and Shakespeare, was the favoured classical model shaping Georgian masculinity.[11] The Enlightenment debates about genius were imbued with chauvinistic interests. One analyst of genius boasted: '*Bacon, Newton, Shakespeare, Milton,* have showed us, that all the winds cannot blow the *British* flag farther, than an original spirit can convey the *British* fame'.[12] Newton became incorporated within a pantheon of historical and contemporary Englishmen like Pope, Locke and Milton who were marketed to an ever-widening public. Examining the production and distribution of visual material makes it clear that Newton only gradually became differentiated from a diffuse group of eminent men collectively celebrated as 'British Worthies'. It was as part of broad transformations in attitudes towards genius, science and creativity that Newton became a national hero and also the prime example of a new category, the scientific genius.

This essay will illustrate how commercialising Newton's image contributed to these processes, concentrating on promotional strategies after his death. It will first describe representations generated through private patronage to exemplify how diverse visual projects consolidated Newton's reputation; will then turn to more explicitly commercialised projects; and will conclude by indicating how iconographic changes at the end of the century corresponded to Newton's emerging role as a scientific genius.

Although he was allegedly uninterested in art, the evidence suggests that Newton actively intervened in fashioning his public image. He sat for over twenty busts and portraits, paying large sums of money for several of them himself. While vanity may have influenced the deceptive youthfulness of his portraits, the extent of this self-representation was not unusual in England at this period. As Richard Steele commented, 'No Nation in the

World delights so much in having their own, or Friends, or Relations Pictures ... Face-Painting is no where so well performed as in England.'[13] Newton moulded how he was perceived amongst elite circles by displaying his image prominently in his own house and sending engravings to reward or influence colleagues. But for popular perceptions, the two portraits that were by far the most significant were the one by Kneller of 1702 (figure 3), subject of at least twenty different engravings, and the 1725 painting by John Vanderbank (figure 4). This was influential because George Vertue's engraving formed the frontispiece of the third edition of Newton's famous book on gravity, *Philosophiæ Naturalis Principia Mathematica* (Mathematical Principles of Natural Philosophy), a choice presumably approved by Newton. Numerous derivations of this engraving meant that from around 1780 it became familiar not only to the small international circle of people who read the *Principia*, but also to the wider audiences reading less specialised illustrated biographical and scientific publications.

Foreign writers often remarked on the English innovation of commemorating great men with public statues, a distinction reserved abroad for royalty. But this practice of honouring men of talent was initiated not by the state, but by private sponsors pursuing their own programmes of improvement. There were three major locations where Newton's image was displayed: Westminster Abbey, country estates and Cambridge University. Projects which promoted Newton were launched with diverse objectives, and as knowledge of them spread, they collectively contributed to making Newton a British hero.

One example of such a project was initiated by John Conduitt, who married Newton's niece, succeeded him at the Mint and inherited many of his possessions. He organised a posthumous publicity campaign which inevitably cast glory on himself by strengthening his associations with his famous uncle-in-law. In 1732, five years after Newton's death, he commissioned William Hogarth to paint *A Scene from 'The Indian Emperor'*, a conversation piece which is ostensibly a children's theatrical performance in Conduitt's town house, but was also designed as a tribute to Newton. Hogarth made visible the force of Newtonian gravity: a mother in the audience commands her daughter to pick up her fallen fan, and the juvenile actors on the stage seem bonded by this attractive power, a common visual metaphor for a moral harmonious society. From the mantelpiece, Michael Rysbrack's marble bust of Newton dominates the eminent spectators. Conduitt specified the iconography of the bas-relief below the bust, based on the sketch he had made for Newton's monument in Westminster Abbey, completed the previous year.[14]

Conduitt spent over £700 on Newton's monument (on the left in figure 5), one of a pair constructed at around the same time that separate

ISAACUS NEWTON· EQ.AUR.ÆT.83.

I.Vanderbank pinxit 1725   Geo.Vertue Sculpsit 1726.

Figure 4 'Isaacus Newton', line engraving by George Vertue (1726) of John Vanderbank's 1725 portrait. Reproduced by kind permission of the Wellcome Institute Library, London

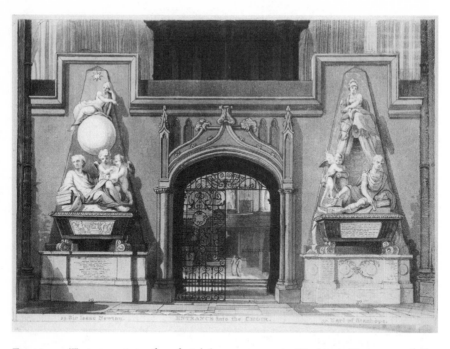

Figure 5 'Entrance into the choir' (monuments to Sir Isaac Newton and the
Earl of Stanhope), coloured aquatint by Anthony Pugin and Thomas
Rowlandson. Reproduced by kind permission of the Wellcome Institute Library,
London

the eastern part of the Abbey from the western nave. During the eighteenth
century, the Abbey became increasingly important as a tourist attraction,
and the nave became a public space for celebrating Enlightenment achievements. Unlike the gothic commemorations of royalty in the older religious
centre behind the altar, these were classical marble monuments commemorating contemporary heroes. Newton seems to be declaiming, yet his
horizontal posture suggests that he is dead, an ambiguity which enabled
this secular memorial to conform with Roman representations of life after
death as well as contemporary religious insistence that the virtuous dead
pass into the afterlife with their works. Like other funeral monuments, it
ensured the continuity and consolidation of Newton's social persona despite
the disintegration of his physical body; the exceptionally large pyramid
symbolised eternity.[15]

The iconography illustrates how our assessments of Newton have
changed. We celebrate him primarily for his work on gravity and light, but
his elbow rests on four tomes rather than two, because he was then also
famous for his studies in theology and ancient chronology. Unexpectedly

for us, the constellations on Astronomy's globe show not only the path of
the 1680 comet, but also how Newton dated the voyage of the Argonauts.
The scroll in his right hand shows the solar system, but also a converging
series, not something now appropriate for public commemoration. The
cherubs on the bas-relief depict Newton's innovations in chemistry and
coinage as well as his astronomical achievements.[16]

Pope's original sketch for the memorial includes an early version of his
famous couplet,

> Nature and Nature's Laws lay hid in Night:
> God said, *Let Newton be!* – and All was *Light*.

This was often reprinted in books and journals, occasionally accompanied
by a satirical version:

> *But* Pope *has his faults, so excuse a young spark,*
> *Bright* Newton's *deceas'd, and we're all in the dark.*[17]

Pope wrote epitaphs for several of the famous men who were later celebrated in the Abbey nave, and Newton was incorporated within a collective
declaration of English achievement which carried overtones of political
opposition. While his monument celebrated contemplative virtue, its partner
on the other side of the aisle was dedicated to active virtue: Lord Stanhope
was a military hero openly critical of Robert Walpole's corrupt authoritarian
regime.

Newton's monument was seen by a wider public than the tourists who
flocked to the Abbey itself because it was reproduced in engravings,
Newtonian medals and other pictures. Accounts in journals explained its
symbolism, and there were fierce debates about its artistic worth. Popular
journals reproduced this tribute: 'This grand and magnificent monument,
erected to real merit, is a greater honour to the nation, than to the great
genius for whom it was raised; and in this light it is viewed by all Europe.'[18]
As this privately funded monument erected by Newton's family became a
public expression of British intellectual supremacy, it reinforced Newton's
status as a national hero.

Personal initiative was also responsible for promoting Newtonian
ideology in country estates. Caroline, wife of George II, patronised an intellectual circle, including Newton, and she hung a Kneller portrait (a version
of figure 2) in her rooms. But in contrast to Conduitt's obsessive promotion of Newton, the Hanoverian queen was concerned to demonstrate
her allegiance to England. While the nave at Westminster Abbey came to
house a varied collection of monuments paid for by individual patrons, she
influenced projects specifically designed to provide a collective commemoration of national genius.

She engaged Kent to design a gothic Hermitage – completed in 1733 – for the royal gardens at Richmond. Its rustic exterior concealed a formal octagonal interior with spaces for five busts publicly referred to as 'Monuments of Genius'. Surprisingly for us, the central niche, lined with golden rays, was designed to display not Newton, but Robert Boyle (the other three geniuses were William Wollaston, John Locke, and Samuel Clarke). Although access to the grotto itself was limited, engravings of the Hermitage and the busts were marketed to wider audiences as sets and reproduced in books, often with eulogistic accompanying verses. Newton's role as a national intellectual exemplar was further enhanced by a poetry competition about the Hermitage in the Gentleman's Magazine and journal articles that debated Caroline's patronage of the arts. The acrimonious debates between the supporters of Leibniz and Newton were entrenched in political differences, and some commentators praised the Hanoverian Caroline's decision to choose British heroes like Newton rather than Leibniz, her compatriot.[19]

Kent also designed the Temple of British Worthies for Lord Cobham's garden at Stowe, England's most famous landscaped garden. This Temple symbolically faced the Temple of Ancient Virtue across a stream labelled the Styx that flowed through the Elysian Fields. Designed to be read allegorically, the gardens celebrated Whig ideals, and the sixteen Worthies commemorating British achievement included political and intellectual figures who embraced Whig virtues Cobham found lacking in Walpole's administration. A central bust of Mercury (leader of the souls of classical heroes) separated the active heroes from the men of thought (including Newton, Pope and Locke). As a natural philosopher, Newton represented the disinterested search for objective truth, but there were also close ties between Whig aspirations and Newtonian projects of improvement.[20]

The Elysian fields explicitly commented on modern corruption. Thus the classical heroes in the Temple on top of a hill were full-length statues on pedestals, while the British worthies below were only busts at eye-level. Subsequent visitors became increasingly oblivious of Cobham's political intentions, but the Temple of British Worthies continued to inspire sentiments of national achievement. 'Does not your Pulse beat high,' asked William Gilpin, 'while you thus stand before such an awful Assembly? Is not your Breast warmed by a Variety of grand Ideas, which this Sight must give Birth to?'[21]

As with the Abbey, Newton's representation reached wider audiences through publications: in the eighteenth century alone, there were over twenty editions of guides to Stowe. Verses like this were often reproduced:

But what is he, in whom the heav'nly Mind
Shines forth distinguish'd and above Mankind?

This, this is *Newton; He*, who first survey'd
The Plan, by which the Universe was made:

In this long country estate poem, only Milton and Shakespeare were celebrated as geniuses, suggesting both that scientific insight was not yet valued
as highly as literary originality, and that Newton's works had not had time
to satisfy the endurance criterion of genius.[22]

At Cambridge, individual initiative was also vital. In the middle of the
century, Robert Smith, Master of Trinity College, helped to make Newton
one of Cambridge's tourist attractions. Smith's promotion of Newton formed
part of his larger project to consolidate the College's international reputation and to establish the centrality of natural philosophy in the curriculum
of a progressive Whig University. To help achieve these ends, he donated
and solicited commemorative statues and portraits of Trinity's great men
to create a gallery displaying College achievement.[23]

Thomas Hollis, for example, donated his portrait of Newton by Enoch
Seeman. The mezzotint included a text by Voltaire extolling English natural
philosophy and a small cap of liberty advertising Hollis's republican ideals.
This engraving became so popular that subsequent collectors cut it out of
Hollis's *Memoirs*, but at the time, Newton had still not been constructed
as a singular genius. In 1755, William Sharpe wrote that Cambridge was
an ideal environment for fostering genius, drawing no distinction between
his three examples, Nicholas Saunderson and William Whiston – now largely
forgotten – and Newton.[24]

Smith commissioned Louis-François Roubiliac for the marble statue in
the Chapel (figure 6), an unusually early example of a public, secular
commemorative statue. Roubiliac sculpted Newton neither as a reclusive
scholar nor as a classical philosopher, but as a young and forceful public
figure personifying male beauty and Enlightenment rationality. Dressed in
elegant clothes, their fineness emphasised by the creasing shown in the
marble, Newton appears to be lecturing, tapping his prism – held like an
emblematic baton of power – in a traditional gesture of disputation. His
upturned eyes and slightly open mouth closely match Charles Le Brun's
illustration of ecstasy: Roubiliac has captured a genius enraptured by divine
inspiration.[25]

Smith also redesigned the Wren Library, persuading former students
to donate busts of eminent men associated with Trinity, including busts of
Newton and Francis Bacon, major ideological figurehead for the Royal
Society. Decorating libraries with sculptured rather than painted portraits
was a growing practice, but Smith's introduction of natural philosophers
was an innovative strategy which contributed to the accreditation of public
science. Writing in Smith's support, Elizabeth Montagu articulated the
growing split between what we now call the two cultures: 'so fine a Temple

Figure 6 'Statue of Sir Isaac Newton', stipple engraving by J. Whessel (1812), of Louis-François Roubiliac's statue, installed in Trinity College Chapel in 1755. Reproduced by kind permission of the Wellcome Institute Library, London

of the Muses should be adorned with all the arts of the ingenious as well as the studious nine especially in an age that honors the polite arts more than severe science.'[26] This quotation illustrates how visual representations not only contributed to promoting Newton's fame, but also enhanced the status of scientific activities.

Through his will, Smith financed Giovanni Cipriani's stained glass window which, completed in 1774, still dominates the Wren Library. To modern eyes, it gives a church-like aura to an academic retreat, but the scene was hugely controversial, at one stage concealed from tourists by a curtain. Clad in vibrant yellow, the muse of the College presents Francis Bacon and Newton to George III, enthroned before a Britannia-like Minerva. The window proclaims the national importance of this College's expertise and emphasises how, through Newton's innovations, natural philosophy will bring the British nation the utilitarian benefits promised by Bacon.

These diverse elite projects, formulated with differing objectives, placed representations of Newton in the public realm. By mid-century, Newton was embodied within various collective tributes to national achievement, while engravings and journals ensured that his individual image reached wider audiences. Newton's conversion into a British scientific hero was inextricably bound up with the establishment of science as a valuable public enterprise and with the growth of nationalist feelings in an increasingly commercialised society.

Particularly during the second half of the century, more explicitly entrepreneurial ventures enhanced Newton's fame by converting him into a commercial product. For instance, an ornate allegorical engraving titled *Truth Sought by Philosophers* shows 'PHILOSOPHY reprysented by a stately Woman' conducting a long line of men towards female Truth. The extended caption emphasises that Newton occupies the leading place. However, an eighteenth-century English plagiarist had simply copied and translated an older French engraving, substituting Newton's name for Descartes'.[27]

The most spectacular example of Newtonian commercialisation was the commemorative painting by Italian artists organised by an Irish entrepreneur, Owen McSwiny (figure 7). Recalling religious imagery, a divine ray of light shines over Newton's funeral urn to be refracted by a prism. Against the subdued browns of the classical background architecture, the spectral colours are repeated in the bright robes of the scientific muses near the picture's foot and of the ancient and modern philosophers studying diagrams and instruments. This was one of a set comprising twenty-four elaborate allegorical images of famous British men including Locke, Boyle and Archbishop Tillotson. While the originals were sold privately, MacSwiny marketed the engravings to a broader public. This international venture

Figure 7 'An allegorical monument to Sir Isaac Newton', line engraving by
L. Desplaces (1727–30) after D. M. Fratta after Giovanni Battista Pittoni, with
Domenico and Giuseppe Valeriani. Reproduced by kind permission of the
Wellcome Institute Library, London

provided a secular, patriotic equivalent of older religious iconography that portrayed new saints of the Enlightenment. McSwiny advertised them as 'British Worthies ... who contributed largely to carrying the Reputation and Credit of the British Nation to a much higher Degree than it was ever at before', proclaiming that his 'Collection of Pictures [was] fit for the Gallery of a Man of Taste ... that it might come into the hand of Many'.[28] He thus articulated how constructing Newton and his contemporaries as Enlightenment heroes lay at the conjunction of processes of nationalisation and commercialisation in a polite society.

Art historians are fascinated by McSwiny's paintings and engravings, but have ignored less ostentatious commercial ventures which seem iconographically less interesting. These were, however, enormously significant because they collectively affected public perceptions of a heroic Newton. For instance, an allegorical engraving by George Bickham was probably seen by far more people (figure 8): it hung in a church near the Mint and was published twice, five years after Newton's death, and again fifty years later with a eulogistic verse reprinted from a Stowe country estate poem.[29] It celebrates Newton as the Prince of Philosophers, who, following Renaissance tradition, has been posthumously elevated into an eternal star (although the cherub at the top appears to be gazing at the Goddess of Mathematics through the wrong end of his telescope).

As the markets for decorative 'furniture' expanded, entrepreneurs retailed increasingly cheap versions of elite representations to ever-widening markets. One important source was Kneller's 1702 portrait. Although this image was only available to selected audiences during Newton's lifetime, Conduitt subsequently allowed his original to be engraved for Thomas Birch's prestigious set of over a hundred 'Illustrious Persons of Great Britain' (figure 3). These included earlier heroes as well as famous contemporary figures, including Pope. The engraver, Jakob Houbraken, incorporated appropriate Newtonian attributes such as a traditional lamp of truth, a mathematical muse, and leaves of aloe, the plant which – like Newton's genius – only flowers once in a hundred years. The pyramid in the background represents eternity and recalls the Westminster Abbey monument. This high-quality folio engraving was sold separately and in books, and was often glazed for display in the houses of wealthy gentlemen.

Less privileged purchasers could see a pirated and much-simplified version in the *Universal Magazine*, reversed in direction because the engraver had traced it. The accompanying hagiographical article explained how Newton's fame had spread abroad, relating the anecdote which Conduitt helped to publicise of the French mathematician who inquired whether Newton ate, drank or slept like other men, allegedly declaring '*I cannot believe otherwise than that he is a* genius, *or a* celestial intelligence *entirely*

Figure 8   'Isaac Newton', line engraving by George Bickham (1787). Reproduced by kind permission of the Wellcome Institute Library, London

disengaged from matter.'[30] Like other myths of genius, this celebrated tale exemplifies the new canonisation of secular intellectual geniuses, as Newton inherited the superhuman capacities of survival previously attributed to saints. As the popularity of cheap prints grew, engravers marketed versions derived from Houbraken's faithful derivation which became decreasingly like the original Kneller (compare figures 3 and 9). Second-rate imitations achieved a sort of Newtonian brand identification in the journals, encyclopaedias and collective biographies of the late eighteenth- and early nineteenth-centuries, both in Britain and abroad.

As well as engravings, material objects also provided an important route for disseminating Newton's image. By mid-century, statues and busts had become a standard feature for decorating halls, libraries and staircases of private and public institutions. A French tourist noted how English aristocratic palaces, public meeting places and gentlemanly homes were all 'adorned with figures painted and engraved, and with busts of all sizes, made of all sorts of materials, of Bacon, Shakespeare, Milton, Locke, Addison, Newton'.[31]

For wealthy customers, Roubiliac and Rysbrack produced versions of Newton's bust similar to those they had created for public spaces like the Wren Library and the Hermitage. For instance, James West, the President of the Royal Society, commissioned Rysbrack to sculpt marble busts of Shakespeare and Newton for his new country mansion. Newton's socle is inscribed:

> NEWTONUS ANGLUS
> Promissum ille sibi voluit prœnoscere cœlum
>   Nec novus ignotas hospes adire domos

Loosely translated, this Ovidean elegaic couplet reads: 'He wanted to have a sneak preview of the heaven that he had been promised, and not go as a fresh guest to a strange house.' This classical quotation describing an English hero apparently refers to Newton's elucidation of the divine celestial blueprint, but was also chosen as an appropriate classical description for a bust of Pope.[32] The identity of these quotations underlines how Newton was bracketed with other Enlightenment figureheads as a marketable commodity, rather than being singled out as a unique genius. Although Pope is less famous now, he conformed more closely to Enlightenment classical ideals and was far more often represented than Newton. William Hayley's comic verse, written for Anna Seward when he discovered that his London stone cutter had sent him a bust of Newton instead of Pope, articulates the century's preference:

> Oh Jove! he exclaim'd if I wielded thy Thunder
> I'd frighten the Sculptor who ruins my hope;

Figure 9 'Isaac Newton', stipple engraving by R. Page (1818) after Godfrey Kneller's 1702 portrait. Reproduced by kind permission of the Wellcome Institute Library, London

Sure never did Artist commit such a Blunder
He has sent me a Newton instead of a Pope.[33]

But purchasers like West who held a previous interest in natural philosophy did deliberately choose busts of Newton. Roubiliac carved one for the Royal Society, and in Arthur Devis's conversation piece of John Bacon's London house, Newton's bust appears as one of four grisaille medallion portraits on the wall, complementing Bacon's fashionable display of expensive instruments of natural philosophy.[34]

Rysbrack and Roubiliac charged around £40 for their marble busts of Newton, and when in financial need, they sold models in painted terra cotta for about half that price, and plaster ones for a few pounds. Capitalising on Newton's growing fame, other sculptors (including Joseph Nollekens) marketed their copies of Roubiliac's bust at Trinity College, while imitators started to produce even cheaper versions of Newton. John Cheere, younger brother of the sculptor Henry Cheere, marketed statuettes around twenty inches high of men like Pope, Milton, and Newton, for around £1 12s. Similarly to Cheere's other Enlightenment role models, his Newton holds a classical pose, supplemented by the Muse of Astronomy copied from the Westminster Abbey monument. Like Wedgwood, who sold a blackened copy of Roubiliac's bust for around two guineas and a basalt replica of a Le Marchand plaque for a few shillings, Cheere developed special techniques to make his cheap and fragile plaster imitations resemble the robust expensive originals. Wedgwood correctly predicted to his business partner that 'Middling people will buy quantities at the much reduced price', but evidently regarded Newton as of only secondary marketable quality. Starting with the king and classical figures, the Etruria factory mass-produced over ninety reproduction heroes, buying many of the plasters in bulk from Cheere. It was only after his success at retailing Joseph Banks that Wedgwood suggested his series of 'Illustrious Moderns', in which Newton was just one of over 200 eminent Enlightenment men sold as jasper medallions to hang on the wall.[35]

Eighteenth-century gentlemanly collectors bought and exchanged gems; classic profiles of modern heroes were very popular, particularly Pope. Eminent men interested in natural philosophy and medicine, including Nevil Maskelyne and Richard Mead, acquired rock crystal seals engraved with Newton on one face, and intricate initials on another. Towards the end of the century, cheap glass imitations of such seals became fashionable. By 1795, Wedgwood's Scottish rival, James Tassie, was advertising thirteen cameos of Newton, around an inch high and selling at one or two pounds. At the University of Glasgow, from 1778 the annual prize for natural philosophy was a purse of gold and a Tassie medallion of Newton. An engraved gem of Newton by Nathaniel Marchant inspired one recipient to write a

patriotic poem about British international influence.[36] But the ultimate
in commercialisation for Newton, ex-Master of the Mint, were the mass-
produced halfpennies and farthings minted as local tokens of exchange.
These flimsy coins, often provided by forgers plugging gaps in series for
collectors, drew perfunctory visual discrimination between Newton and other
Englishmen converted into classical heroes.[37]

In around 1840, reminiscing on his undergraduate experiences at
Cambridge, William Wordsworth added the final two lines to his evocation
of

> The Antechapel where the Statue stood
> Of Newton with his prism, & silent face,
> The marble index of a Mind for ever
> Voyaging thro' strange seas of Thought, alone.

In this famous Romantic celebration of a disembodied scientific genius,
Wordsworth reworked older poetic tributes to Newton and reinterpreted
Roubiliac's vision.[38] Whereas Roubiliac had sculpted an Enlightenment
gentleman engaged in public discourse and inspired by God, Wordsworth
expressed Romantic perceptions of a solitary genius detached from normal
life. Wordsworth's contemporaries produced new representations of Newton
which similarly reflected changed attitudes towards science as well as
towards Newton and genius.

William Blake's famous image shows a naked, muscular Newton apparently seated on an underwater rock, arched with his measuring dividers
over a drawing of a semi-circle inscribed in a triangle. The complexities of
this print reflect the ambiguities of Blake's attitudes towards Newton and
towards science, and his dread that imagination and religion will be driven
out of the world by abstract attempts to circumscribe it mathematically.
Although Newton's features are here not unlike Blake's own, in contrast
with earlier portraits this is not a direct representation of Newton's own
body but a personification of abstract attempts to order the world. The
striking tensions between straight and curved lines, symmetrical and asym-
metrical shapes, definite and indefinite forms, encapsulate the confrontation
between the powers of reason and imagination.[39] Like Wordsworth's disembodied genius, Blake's Newton is no ordinary mortal, but a superhuman
creature with almost terrifying abilities.

In complete contrast, George Romney's purportedly realistic reconstruction of Newton's prism experiment (figure 10) was the first of a new
genre showing Newton as an active experimenter rather than a contemplative scholar. It parallels how, as part of their bid to validate the new
scientific disciplines, scientific polemicists were starting to create histories
celebrating heroic ancestors and their momentous discoveries. Romney
copied the prism from a diagram in Newton's *Opticks*, and here Newton

Figure 10 'Newton and the prism', stipple engraving by Meadows (1809) of George Romney's 1796 picture. Reproduced by kind permission of the Wellcome Institute Library, London

holds it like a magic wand capturing the divine light of inspiration. As their social standing became more secure, men of science could be portrayed engaging in manual activities which contradicted older ideologies of the privileged scholar gaining knowledge from books rather than experiments. Romney intended this picture to accompany one of Milton dictating to his daughters. Contemporaries admired the domesticity of the setting, which anachronistically and improbably shows the elderly Newton at home with his niece and a maid. But for some modern viewers, Romney's *Milton* and *Newton* reinforce visions of detached male intellects displaying the truths of nature to appreciative, servile women.[40] This change in critical appreciation illustrates how pictures can be constantly reinterpreted, a flexible ambiguity which makes the analysis of visual material so valuable for understanding how cultural heroes are formed.

As with Shakespeare, Newton's status as one of England's greatest geniuses was fashioned retrospectively and constantly reworked. Newton's Enlightenment commercialisation had ensured that he was displayed as a classicised English hero in mansions, public institutions and private homes. His conversion into a household name formed one aspect of the processes

through which science became legitimated as a nationalist enterprise bene-
fiting Britain's commercial and imperial expansion. Although criticised by
Romantic literati, men of science had gained an influential status in English
society by the early nineteenth century. Genius was no longer restricted to
superior capacities of reasoning but also characterised singular individuals
driven by an inner creative force. Wordsworth himself had articulated this
shift, 'Genius is the introduction of a new element into the intellectual
universe'.[41] As scientific and technological innovation became increasingly
important, Newton became represented as the exemplary type of a new
masculine category, the scientific genius. This remodelled Faustus figure
still moulds popular perceptions of scientific originality. Many diverse images
of Newton were created and they played a vital role in establishing his
reputation. Because so many of them survive, they now provide a rich
resource for analysing his construction as a national hero and scientific
genius.

Acknowledgements

I wish to thank the Royal Society and the Leverhulme Trust for research
grants contributing to this project. Amongst numerous colleagues who have
offered helpful suggestions, I am particularly grateful to Malcolm Baker,
Matthew Craske, Rob Iliffe, Ludmilla Jordanova, Milo Keynes, and Simon
Schaffer.

Notes

The substance of the present chapter overlaps with one of the chapters in the author's
Under Newton's Apple Tree (London, forthcoming).

1   Reproduced in B. Rackham, *Catalogue of the Glaisher Collection of Pottery and
    Porcelain in the Fitzwilliam Museum Cambridge* (Cambridge, 1987), 1, p. 117.
2   R. Iliffe, '"Is he like other men?" The meaning of the *Principia Mathematica*, and
    the author as idol', in G. Maclean (ed.), *Culture and Society in the Stuart Restoration*
    (Cambridge, 1995), pp. 159–76 and 'Isaac Newton: Lucatello Professor of mathe-
    matics', in C. Lawrence and S. Shapin (eds), *Science Incarnate: Historical
    Embodiments of Natural Knowledge* (Chicago and London, 1998), pp. 121–55, and
    S. Shapin, 'The philosopher and the chicken: the bodily presentation of disembodied
    knowledge', *ibid.*, pp. 21–50.
3   S. Crompton, 'On the portraits of Sir Isaac Newton; and particularly on one of him
    by Kneller, painted about the time of publication of the *Principia*, and representing
    him as he was in the prime of life', *Proceedings of the Literary and Philosophical
    Society of Manchester*, 6 (1866) 1–7, and '[untitled]', *Proceedings of the Literary and
    Philosophical Society of Manchester*, 7 (1867) 3–6. Kneller painted two versions of
    this portrait; see J. D. Stewart, *Godfrey Kneller* (London, 1971), p. 64; O. Millar,
    *The Tudor, Stuart and Early Georgian Pictures in the Collection of Her Majesty the
    Queen* (London, 1963), 1, pp. 27–28.

4   G. Becker, *The Mad Genius Controversy: A Study in the Sociology of Deviance* (Beverley Hills and London, 1978); R. Yeo, 'Genius, method and morality: images of Newton in Britain, 1760–1860', *Science in Context*, 2 (1988), 257–84; P. Theerman, 'Unaccustomed role: the scientist as historical biographer – two nineteenth-century portrayals of Newton', *Biography*, 8 (1985), 145–62.

5   Crompton, 'Portraits of Isaac Newton', 3 (referring to the frontispiece of D. Brewster, *Memoirs of the Life, Writings, and Discoveries of Sir Isaac Newton* (Edinburgh, 1855)); P. Barlow, 'Facing the past and present: the National Portrait Gallery and the search for "authentic" portraiture', in J. Woodall (ed.), *Portraiture: Facing the Subject* (Manchester and New York, 1997), pp. 219–38.

6   Stewart, Kneller, p. 64 and Millar, Tudor Pictures, I, p. 27–28.

7   T. Maude, *Viator, a Poem: or, A Journey from London to Scarborough, By the Way of York* (London, 1782), p. ii.

8   Many of these are reproduced in R. Westfall, *Never at Rest: A Biography of Isaac Newton* (Cambridge and New York, 1980), my major source for biographical information. There are no complete catalogues of Newton's portraits and their engravings. The best sources are D.E. Smith, 'Portraits of Sir Isaac Newton', in W. J. Greenstreet, *Isaac Newton 1642–1727* (London,1927), pp. 171–81; R. B. Webber, *A Descriptive Catalog of the Grace K Babson Collection of the Works of Sir Isaac Newton* (New York, 1950), pp. 203–21; D. Gjertsen, *The Newton Handbook* (London and New York, 1986), pp. 440–48; the archives of London's National Portrait Gallery.

9   M. Pointon, *Hanging the Head: Portraiture and Social Formation in Eighteenth-Century England* (New Haven and London, 1993).

10 The vast relevant literature includes M. H. Abrams, *The Mirror and the Lamp: Romantic Theory and the Critical Tradition* (Oxford, 1953); P. Murray (ed.), *Genius: The History of an Idea* (Oxford, 1989); M. Rose, *Authors and Owners: The Invention of Copyright* (Cambridge, Mass., and London, 1993).

11 W. K. Wimsatt, *The Portraits of Alexander Pope* (New Haven and London, 1965); J. Reily and W. K. Wimsatt, 'A supplement to *The Portraits of Alexander Pope*', in R. Wellek and A. Ribeiro (eds), *Evidence in Literary Scholarship: Essays in Memory of James Marshall Osborn* (Oxford, 1979), pp. 123–64. There were 66 basic portrait types of Pope, each including multiple variations. Since Pope died almost twenty years after Newton, the quantitative difference may be partly due to the increasing popularity of portraiture; C. D. Williams, *Pope, Homer, and Manliness: Some Aspects of Eighteenth-Century Classical Learning* (London and New York, 1993).

12 E. Young, *Conjectures on Original Composition* (London, 1759), p. 76.

13 From a 1712 letter to the Spectator, quoted in J. D. Stewart, *Sir Godfrey Kneller and the English Baroque Portrait* (Oxford, 1983), p. 58.

14 R. Paulson, *Hogarth: High Art and Low* (Cambridge, 1991), pp. 1–4; M. I. Webb, 'Busts of Sir Isaac Newton', *Country Life*, III (1952), 216–18.

15 D. Bindman and M. Baker, *Roubiliac and the Eighteenth-Century Monument: Sculpture as Theatre* (New Haven and London, 1995), pp. 9–23, 187–89; R. Llewellyn, *The Art of Death: Visual Culture in the English Death Ritual c.1500 – c.1800* (London, 1991).

16 Maude, *Viator*, pp. viii-xii; *Gentleman's Magazine*, I (1731), 159.

17 M. I. Webb, *Michael Rysbrack: Sculptor* (London, 1954), pp. 76–91; F. Haskell, 'The apotheosis of Newton in art', in Haskill (ed.), *Past and Present in Art and Taste: Selected Essays* (New Haven and London, 1987), pp. 1–15; *Universal Magazine*, 3 (1748), 249 and 34 (1764), 241; *Gentleman's Magazine*, I (1731), 159–60 and 11 (1741), 548.

18 J. Ralph, *A Critical Review of the Publick Buildings, Statues and Ornaments in, and about London and Westminster* (London, 1734), pp. 69–73; J. Physick, *Designs for English Sculpture 1680–1860* (London, 1969), p. 81; *Royal Magazine*, 9 (1763), 116–17, repeated in *Universal Magazine*, 34 (1764), 241–42.

19 J. Colton, 'Kent's Hermitage for Queen Caroline at Richmond', *Architectura*, (1974), 181–91; Webb, *Rysbrack*, pp. 146–54 and 'Busts of Newton'.

20 Webb, *Rysbrack*, pp. 135–37; Wilson, *Kent*, pp. 208–11; P. Willis, *Charles Bridgeman and the English Landscape Garden* (London, 1977), pp. 106–27, plates 111–58; J. D. Hunt, 'Emblem and expressionism in the eighteenth-century landscape garden', *Eighteenth-Century Studies*, 4 (1971), 294–317; R. A. Etlin, *The Architecture of Death: The Transformation of the Cemetery in Eighteenth-Century Paris* (Cambridge, MA and London, 1984), pp. 184–97; R. Paulson, *Emblem and Expression: Meaning in English Art of the Eighteenth Century* (London, 1975), pp. 19–34.

21 W. Gilpin, *A Dialogue upon the Gardens of the Right Honourable the Lord Viscount Cobham, at Stow in Buckinghamshire* (London, 1748), pp. 28–29.

22 G. West, *Stowe*, reproduced in J. D. Hunt and P. Willis (eds), *The Genius of the Place: The English Landscape Garden 1620–1820* (London, 1975), pp. 215–27 (quotation p. 219).

23 M. Baker, 'The portrait sculpture', in D. McKitterick (ed.), *The Making of the Wren Library* (Cambridge, 1995), pp. 110–37.

24 T. Hollis, *Memoirs of Thomas Hollis* (London, 1780), 1, p. 122; 2, p. 801; *Nature* (26 Mar. 1927), 466; W. Sharpe, *A Dissertation upon Genius (1755)* (New York, Scholar's Facsimiles and Reprints, 1973), p. 93.

25 W. K. Thomas and W. U. Ober, *A Mind for ever Voyaging: Wordsworth at Work Portraying Newton and Science* (Edmonton, 1989), pp. 161–72.

26 Baker, 'The portrait sculpture'; Montagu quoted in Bindman and Baker, *Roubiliac*, p. 120.

27 F. Haskell, 'The apotheosis of Newton in art', reproduced p. 10; J. Duportal, *Bernard Picart 1673 à 1733* (Paris and Brussels, 1928), p. 369.

28 Quotation from O. McSwiny, *To the Ladies and Gentlemen of Taste in Great-Britain and Ireland*. See Eugene Mac-Swiny, *Tombeaux des Princes Grands Capitaines et Autres Hommes illustres, Qui ont Fleuri dans la Grande-Bretagne vers la Fin du XVII. & le Commencement du XVIII. Siècle* (London, 1741); Haskell, 'Apotheosis of Newton in art', pp. 4–13; *The European Fame of Isaac Newton*, catalogue of 1974 exhibition at the Fitzwilliam Museum, Cambridge.

29 S. Kinns, 'Six Hundred Years'; Or, *Historical Sketches of Eminent Men and Women who have more or less come into Contact with the Abbey and Church of Holy Trinity, Minories, from 1293 to 1893* (London, 1898), pp. 399–43.

30 T. Birch, *The Heads of Illustrious Persons of Great Britain, On One Hundred and Eight Copper Plates* (London, 1756); *Universal Magazine*, 3 (1748), 289–301, quotation p. 295.

31 Pierre Grosely, quoted in Bindman and Baker, *Roubiliac*, p. 114.

32 Webb, *Rysbrack*, pp. 117, 221–22. I am grateful to David Money for the translation. Reilly and Wimsatt, 'Supplement to *Portraits of Pope*', plate 11, pp. 145–46. The lines are adapted from Ovid's *Fasti* and relate to Pope's *Essay on Man*.

33 Quoted in H. L. Thrale, *Thraliana: The Diary of Mrs Hester Lynch Thrale, 1776–1809* (Oxford, 1942), 2, p. 795.

34 E.G. D'Oench, *The Conversation Piece: Arthur Devis & His Contemporaries* (New Haven, 1980), pp. 45–46; Reilly and Wimsatt, 'Supplement to *Portraits of Pope*', pp. 150–51.

35 Webb, *Rysbrack*, pp. 197–99; J. V. G. Mallet, 'Some portrait medallions by Roubiliac', *Burlington Magazine*, 104 (1962), 153–58; G. B. Hughes, 'Portrait busts in black basaltes', *Country Life*, 132 (1962), 360–61; *The Man at Hyde Park Corner: Sculpture by John Cheere 1709–1787* (Leeds, 1974); A. Dawson, *Masterpieces of Wedgwood in the British Museum* (London, 1984), pp. 64–86; R. Reilly, *Wedgwood Portrait Medallions: An Introduction* (London, 1973); S. Taylor, 'Artists and philosophes as

mirrored by Sèvres and Wedgwood', in F. Haskell, A. Levi and R. Shackleton (eds), *The Artist and the Writer in France: Essays in Honour of Jean Seznec* (Oxford, 1974), pp. 21–39.

36   M. Henig, D. Scarisbrick and M. Whiting, *Classical Gems, Ancient and Modern Intaglios and Cameos* (Cambridge, 1994), pp. 281–83; J. M. Gray, *James and William Tassie: A Biographical and Critical Sketch with a Catalogue of their Portrait Medallions of Modern Personages* (Edinburgh, 1894), pp. 32–45; R. E. Raspe, *A Descriptive Catalogue of a General Collection of Ancient and Modern Engraved Gems, Cameos as well as Intaglios, Taken from the Most Celebrated Cabinets in Europe; and Cast in Coloured Pastes, White Enamel, and Sulphur, by James Tassie, Modeller* (London, 1791), pp. lxxv, 746, 799; *The Times*, 16 Sept. 1796, 3d.

37   C. Pye, *Provincial Copper Coins or Tokens, Issued between the Years 1787 and 1796* (London, 1796).

38   *The Prelude*, Book III, lines 60–63; Thomas and Ober, *Mind for ever Voyaging*.

39   D. D. Ault, *Visionary Physics: Blake's Response to Newton* (Chicago and London, 1974), pp. 1–4; P. Ackroyd, *Blake* (London, 1995), pp. 186–94; J. Gage, 'Blake's Newton', *Journal of the Warburg and Courtauld Institutes*, 34 (1971), 372–77.

40   S. Schaffer, 'Scientific discoveries and the end of natural philosophy', *Social Studies of Science*, 16 (1986), 387–420; W. Hayley, *The Life of George Romney, Esq.* (Chichester, 1809), pp. 314–15; J. Romney, *Memoirs of the Life and Works of George Romney, including Various Letters, and Testimonies to his Genius, &c.* (London, 1830), pp. 228–29, 235–37; H. Ward and W. Roberts, *Romney: A Biographical and Critical Essay with a Catalogue Raisonné of his Works* (London, 1904), 2, pp. 197, 201; Gage, 'Blake's Newton', 375.

41   M. Woodmansee, *The Author, Art, and the Market: Rereading the History of Aesthetics* (New York, 1994), quoted p. 39.

PART II

HEROES OF EMPIRE

The iconography of the exemplary life:
the case of David Livingstone

The exemplary life is invariably the envisioned life. Its power is conveyed not only by texts, but also through icons. Such an iconography develops its influence through repetition, and significant ideas can be projected through multiple and parallel imaging. Pictures thus underscore one of the prime characteristics of the exemplary life: a capacity to encapsulate sets of ideas which are projected through to new generations even when the particular paradigm which they represent has been overtaken by a wholly new one. The life, death and myth of David Livingstone well illustrate both these phenomena. Despite a trough in the 1860s, Livingstone's reputation remained that of an exemplary figure, heroically resolute and self-denying in his Protestant saintliness, from the 1850s until at least the 1950s. Despite the fact that his imperial economic and technical programme was recognised by many to be an impractical failure, he remained a central interpreter of and apologist for empire until the mid-twentieth century. He even became something of an icon of a particular brand of African nationalism, as is evidenced by the number of stamps which were issued by independent African states on the centennial of his death in 1973.[1]

The Livingstone myth was clearly a highly malleable one. Yet the life is riddled with paradoxes. As Tim Jeal demonstrated in his somewhat unsatisfactory biography of the missionary explorer, it is all too easy to debunk the man and his Victorian reputation: to trot out the old canard about the single convert, Sechele, who later recanted; to portray Livingstone as a sadly defective husband and father, as a poor leader of men, particularly white men, as an indifferent doctor, whose migrations and gyrations were as likely to produce error as success.[2] He sent missionaries to their deaths and his programme for settlement and cotton growing, based on the alleged navigability of the Zambezi and the Shiré proved to be the major chimera of nineteenth-century Central African history. Moreover, he went on searching for the sources of the Nile long after the problem had effectively been solved, and long after it was prudent for him to do so, not least in

terms of his personal health and the safety of the many parties sent out
to search for him.

Yet, during the partition of Africa and throughout missionary endeavour
in that continent, it was the example of Livingstone which was never far
from the lips of those seeking to justify European activities. Sir John Scott
Keltie of the Royal Geographical Society wrote that Livingstone turned
exploration in Africa into something of a holy crusade.[3] The Royal Scottish
Geographical Society was founded partly in his honour in 1884–85.[4]
Explorers, missionaries and administrators repeatedly appealed to the
example of Livingstone. Africans educated at mission stations were brought
up on stories of selfless sacrifice for Africa, as were children in the Sunday
schools of home, particularly in Scotland. Major celebrations surrounded
the Livingstone centenaries in 1913 (of his birth) and 1973 (of his death).
The Scottish composer, Hamish MacCunn, wrote a cantata in his memory.
His statue (one of only two) was set into the external wall of the Royal
Geographical Society and his bust appeared on the facade of the Foreign
Office. Memorials, statues and tablets were erected in places as diverse as
the Hebridean island of Ulva (the home of his paternal grandparents), the
principal Scottish cities, and at key points in Tanzania, Zambia, Zimbabwe
and Malawi. And in the inter-war years a major national memorial was
established in his name at Blantyre, Lanarkshire. It was opened in 1929
by the Duchess of York, now Queen Elizabeth the Queen Mother, and
secured remarkable visitor figures in the 1930s, 1940s and 1950s. Livingstone
was the subject of major documentaries and feature films in the 1920s
and 1930s.[5]

Some have seen all this activity as resulting solely from the manipulation of the Livingstone myth after his death. Jeal proposed that it was
H.M. Stanley who manufactured the legend through his remarkable
encounter with the explorer at Ujiji on the shores of Lake Tanganyika,
often seen as the greatest journalistic coup of the nineteenth century.[6]
Others have seen the editing of his final journals as the key, transforming
Livingstone's prime purpose from a fruitless search for the Nile into an
assault upon the so-called Arab slave trade.[7] In this respect, Dr Horace
Waller, editor and missionary, was a central figure, together with a variety
of personalities associated with the Universities Mission to Central Africa
and the Scottish missions (of both the Free and Established churches)
founded in Livingstone's name in Nyasaland (Malawi). Not the least of the
illustrations of the durability of the legend is that the African places associated with him, Livingstone in Zambia, Blantyre and Livingstonia in Malawi,
have retained their names.

This is partly because of the image of Livingstone's heroic death in
and for Africa, a death which seemingly brought out the best in his African

followers, James Chuma, Abdullah Susi and Jacob Wainwright, among others. For the Victorians, his death and the iconic death scene were the key. As scholars of English literature and funerary architecture, poetry and ceremony have amply demonstrated, Victorians elevated death into a major cultural as well as religious and spiritual phenomenon. The Livingstone death produced the major icon of resigned, noble sacrifice in the heart of Africa, a martyrdom almost Christ-like (and contemporaries did make that connection) in its potentially redemptive power. The icon was beautifully worked up by one of the principal engineers of the Livingstone myth, Horace Waller, who carefully interviewed Livingstone's followers in England. Livingstone was supposedly found on his knees, praying in the moment of death (figure 11). What followed was a sort of secular resurrection, the celebrated transportation of the sun-dried body to the coast by heroic and faithful followers, inspired by Livingstone's example to brave all sorts of dangers to return the body to his countrymen (figure 12). Inevitably, the death scene and what followed are prominently described and illustrated in all the many popular biographies of Livingstone that were written in the later nineteenth and twentieth centuries (there were at least a hundred of these). It comes as no surprise to find that other deaths were fitted into

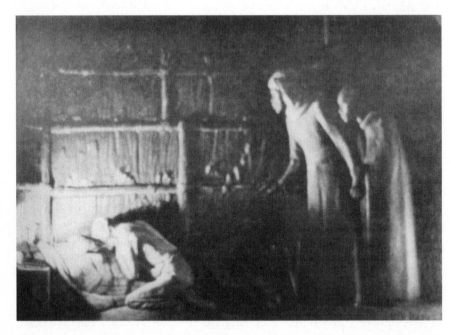

Figure 11   David Livingstone, the death scene, sculpture by C. d'O. Pilkington Jackson, The David Livingstone Centre, Blantyre. Reproduced by kind permission of the Centre and the National Trust for Scotland

the mould. W. P. Livingstone (no relation) described the death of Mary Slessor in West Africa as presenting 'a scene which suggested the final act in Dr Livingstone's life'.[8] Martyrdom was a fundamental requirement for a truly heroic myth and other self-sacrificing missionary deaths were thus

Figure 12   Carrying the body to the coast, LMS magic lantern slide, c. 1900. Reproduced by kind permission of the National Portrait Gallery, London

fitted into the major Livingstone precedent. Hence exemplary deaths, the ultimate self-sacrifice, became a crucial aspect of the self-confident projection and reception of the imperial project.

But the legendary exemplary life of Livingstone goes even deeper than this. It would have been unlikely to be so durable simply on the basis of a notable icon or the clever manipulation of his life after his death. Moreover, the ideas with which he was associated are much more extensive than simply Christianity and commerce or the extinction of the slave trade, even if that was the one which was noted most prominently on his celebrated tomb in Westminster Abbey.[9] The extraordinary epic of the return of his body to Britain from Central Africa on an Admiralty vessel, its reception, identification and lying in state at the Royal Geographical Society, the semi-state funeral attended by the Prince of Wales and the leading politicians of the day, were all based on something much deeper and wider than a heroic death and a holy crusade.

Historians and biographers have frequently passed over or missed the manner in which Livingstone was hailed as a sort of scientific messiah on his return to Britain in 1857. Having left Britain as a poor and unknown medical missionary in 1840, Livingstone returned as a major hero, who published a best-seller which swiftly made him the astonishing sum of £10,000 in royalties, who mixed with the grandest people in the land, stayed in great country houses, and was honoured by cities and universities throughout Britain and Ireland. His book, *Missionary Travels and Researches in South Africa*, signalled that he had satisfactorily reconciled science and religion in his travels.[10] The researches of the title were undoubtedly meant to be scientific and the inclusion of an illustration of a tsetse fly on the title page indicated Livingstone's entomological and zoological interests, among many others.

Indeed, Livingstone's scientific interests are strikingly projected through *Missionary Travels*. He had trained himself upon the natural history and geology of the Clyde Valley of his youth and had reconciled science and religion through his reading of the work of Dr Thomas Dick. He set about elevating his own scientific work in Africa by repeated references to notable scientists of the day: Sir Thomas Maclear, Astronomer Royal at the Cape, Sir Joseph Hooker, Director of Kew, and above all his dedicatee and later sponsor, Sir Roderick Murchison, geologist and president of the Royal Geographical Society. Yet Livingstone's work is also shot through with respect for African scientific knowledge. He noted Africans' understanding of river systems and recommended that other explorers should take careful note of African information. He was impressed by their knowledge of soils, insects, animals and plants which he considered superior to that of the peasantry at home. He proposed that the African pharmacopeia should be much more closely studied than he had found possible, although typically he then appended a very impressive and lengthy footnote.

Moreover, despite all the flaws in his observations of altitude, latitude and longitude, the precision of Livingstone's natural descriptions, his fascination with geology (for example, his remarkable passage on the geology of the Victoria Falls), with botany (appropriately commemorated in the mesambryanthemum or Livingstone daisy), with tree growth, with ants, with zoology (such as his intriguing calculations of the speed of the ostrich), with birds (he rightly spotted the migration of swifts from Europe to southern Africa), with types of soil – to name but a few of his manifold interests – had an indelible effect upon his readers, both contemporary and through the succeeding century.

The popularity of Livingstone's *Missionary Travels* is not far to seek. The fact is that Livingstone was a major painter in words who touched on many of the passions of the Victorians, in botany, in the creation of gardens in all senses, in geology, in natural history and its relationship to hunting, in hydrology and meteorology, not to mention ethnography and philology. The book is filled with 'sights', from the grand conception of the physical geography and geology of the continent to the minute attention to detail involved in spotting the worms in the eye of a rhinoceros. Both his telescopic and his microscopic gaze, without the benefit of those instruments, are everywhere in his work. He also projected a striking humanity and a sympathetic fellowship with Africans, combined with surprising shafts of humour. His prose is simple, supple and fluent (contrasting strikingly with that of his contemporaries, Carlyle or Ruskin), carrying the reader along most of the 684 pages of *Missionary Travels* as speedily as canoes running downstream on the faster-flowing stretches of the Zambezi. It was all of these characteristics which led to Livingstone's astonishing reception at Cambridge in 1857, and which also lent his travels so effectively to the wood block maker, the photographer, the sculptor, and the painter (although in the last case he fell out with the greatest, Thomas Baines, on the second, Zambezi expedition, and rather vindictively refused even to mention his name).[11] And it is in Livingstone's lionisation in 1857, and in an iconography thoroughly rooted in his character, personality and descriptive powers that we should see the roots of his continuing significance as an imperial interpreter and as a projector of popular science.

But the Reverend William Monk, who invited Livingstone to Cambridge in December 1857, took these attributes on to a much higher plane. Monk published Livingstone's lectures and provided a striking introduction for them. Above all, he was concerned to provide a visualisation of what he saw as remarkable events: 'The Senate House scene was worthy of the most graphic painting which pen or pencil could portray. There was a solemn majesty about it which all present must have felt.' Monk continued in painterly terms: Livingstone was a 'sun-burnt, care and travel-worn, yet happy man', who inspired his audience of students and dons, inducing thrilling moments of silence, breathless wonder, laughter, spontaneous bursts of applause and volley after volley of cheers. His sentiments had the capacity 'to melt the heart, subdue the being, and enchain the soul'. The achievement that he was seen to represent at this point in his life was indeed a messianic one, nothing less than (in Monk's words) 'the union of mankind into one common brotherhood of feeling, interest, sentiment and love, despite all differences of race, colour, clime, speech, condition and nationality'. And this was not some forlorn hope. Monk suggested that in Livingstone's words this 'union of mankind . . . seems actually to be brought about'.[12] Livingstone was thus depicted as fulfilling an early nineteenth-century dream, a dream that was to be shattered by social Darwinism, pseudo-scientific racism and all the social, political and intellectual para-phernalia of a more strongly racist imperialism later in the century.

Livingstone was also received as a major scientist. His host and chair for the Cambridge occasions was William Whewell, Master of Trinity. Another central participant was the venerable Adam Sedgwick, Professor of Geology in the University for many years. Sedgwick suggested that of all the occasions he had witnessed in the Senate House over the past fifty years, including visits of the sovereign, this was by far 'the greatest of all'. In a farewell speech in the combination room of Trinity, Sedgwick under-lined this by declaring that Livingstone had received the most enthusiastic reception which he had ever witnessed there during the past half century. Sedgwick's powerful endorsement went further. In Monk's book, he contributed a lengthy postscript to the published version of the lectures in which he assessed the scientific value of Livingstone's work under a number of headings: the vegetable kingdom, meteorology and climate, the animal kingdom, hydrography, physical geography, and geology, with a footnote on linguistics.[13]

Whewell and Sedgwick had their own agenda in promoting Livingstone as a major event at Cambridge. They were indeed using him as an exem-plary life, a grindstone upon which they could sharpen their particular natural philosophical axes. Both Whewell, a philosopher of natural philos-ophy who has been described as 'a meta-scientific critic', and Sedgwick had polymathic interests. They found in Livingstone not only an extraordinary personification of the successful fusion of religion and natural science, but also the very natural theology they were straining for. Livingstone was presented to his audience as achieving the goal of religious and scientific unity. He was a saintly empiricist who saw modern science and tech-nology as part of God's contemporary mission and message. Livingstone's

researches were shot through with a striking optimism which, despite
fever, exhaustion and the loss of journals and notes, permeates his work.
He wrote of insects 'being brimful of enjoyment', a phrase of which
the celebrated natural theologian William Paley would have approved.
Livingstone continued:

> Indeed the universality of organic life may be called a mantle of happy
> existence encircling the world and imparts the idea of its being caused
> by the consciousness of our benignant Father's smile on all the works of
> His hands.[14]

Later he wrote that the missionary enterprise should have the 'most extended
signification, including all the means by which God was bringing all His
dealings with man to a glorious consummation'. Among these were 'Men
of science, searching after hidden truths, which when discovered will, like
the electric telegraph, bind men more closely together . . .'[15] Passages
like this not only excited Cambridge scientists; they were to continue to
convey optimistic resonances through the century.

It is ironic that Livingstone was hailed as a major scientist and natural
theologian in the very year that the great revolt or Mutiny had broken out
in India, 1857. This is often rightly seen as a key moment, together with
the Morant Bay rebellion and the Governor Eyre controversy of 1865, in
the formulation of the harder racism of the later nineteenth century, a
racism which was underpinned by the social Darwinism which emerged out
of the epochal publication of Darwin's *Origin of Species* in 1859 and *The
Descent of Man* in 1871. Not surprisingly, Livingstone became an anti-
Darwinian and wrote to Sir Richard Owen to say so, indicating (rather
surprisingly) that he had never seen any evidence of struggle in Africa.[16]
His death in 1873 insulated him from the worst excesses of pseudo-scientific racism, but his influence continued.

It is in the perpetuation of some at least of his ideas that we can see
the intellectual significance of the exemplary life. There is a tendency to
suppose that Darwinian ideas, particularly in their perverted social muta-
tions, delivered a knock-out blow to the kind of natural theology and
pre-racist attitudes of Livingstone. In fact, a careful reading of the full
range of missionary memoirs and biographies of the later nineteenth and
early twentieth centuries indicates that Livingstone's approach survived
and was cherished. The exemplary hero can be interpreted as providing a
scientific popularisation that can be found sailing serenely on through the
tempests of scientific controversy generated by professional scientists.[17]

Livingstone's synoptic scientific and spiritual vision had two effects.
It elevated him above the constraints of denomination. He was a Congre-
gationalist, but his hosts at Cambridge were Anglicans. His cry to the

Cambridge audience to follow him to Africa, carried in inspirational capitals in Monk's book, resulted in the formation of an Anglican mission.[18] Missions of both the established and free churches in Scotland were founded in his name. Methodists and Plymouth Brethren acknowledged him, as did the Catholic founder of the White Fathers, Cardinal Lavigerie. Second, he was accepted as a practical visionary by one of the most influential figures of the day. Samuel Smiles, author of the remarkable best-seller, *Self-Help*, started out as a radical and auto-didact, but somewhere in his development he became convinced of the efficacy of empire as the ideal setting for the promotion of self-help.[19] The first edition of *Self-Help*, with its sub-title *With Illustrations of Conduct and Perseverance* was published in 1859. Both Livingstone's great success in 1857 and the Indian Mutiny were fresh in Smiles's mind. He saw India as a 'great field for the display of British energy' and was excited by such Mutiny heroes as Sir Henry Havelock and Sir Colin Campbell, Lord Clyde. But he described Livingstone's career as 'one of the most interesting of all'. Given his fascination with the lives of the engineers, it is not surprising that he particularly valued those heroic figures who seemed to him to combine self-advancement with practical virtues and spiritual values. Smiles admired Livingstone as a manual labourer who 'dug canals, built houses, cultivated fields, reared cattle and taught the natives how to work as well as to worship', while he regarded *Missionary Travels* as 'one of the most fascinating books of its kind that has ever been given to the public'.[20] After Livingstone's death, an engraving of the famous Annan portrait appeared as the frontispiece of all subsequent editions of *Self-Help*.

It is hard to underestimate the influence of *Self-Help*. By 1908, the book had passed through no fewer than fifty-six reprints. In the centennial edition, Asa Briggs suggested that it had sold 250,000 copies before the end of the century, outranking most other books of the period.[21] Readership must of course have been considerably greater than this, for it was the favourite reading matter of Mechanics' Institutes, Athenaeums and public libraries, not just in Britain but throughout the empire. Thus Smiles placed Livingstone at the centre of an empire of celebrated personalities achieving notable acts of self-improvement against exotic backdrops.

The influence of Smiles and the continuing popularity of *Missionary Travels* certainly helped Livingstone's reputation to survive its lowest point during the Zambezi Expedition of 1858–64. This expedition, generously funded by the British Government, destroyed the confidence of politicians in his ability to open up Africa. His geographical ambition, the navigability of the Zambezi into the interior of Africa, with all its related social and economic objectives – white emigration and endless fields of cotton, indigo and sugar – were miserable failures. His hope of developing all this through the liberating power of steam technology foundered on the rocks, shallows and cataracts of the River Zambezi by which he had set such store. His wife, much persecuted by his earlier travels and driven to drink, died when she came to join him in 1862. He fell out with almost all of his associates. Reports were never written and photographs (which could have created a whole new Central African iconography) never taken.[22] The first mission of the Universities' Mission to Central Africa, inspired by his visits to Oxford and Cambridge, failed and its first bishop, Mackenzie, died. A London Missionary Society Mission to the Zambezi resulted in the almost complete annihilation of two missionary families. The most powerful visual moment of the period was perhaps when the Rev. James Stewart, a fervent follower of Livingstone who described him, rather unexpectedly, as a 'great swell', threw his copy of *Missionary Travels* into the Zambezi.[23]

But Stewart was to be powerfully reconverted, like many others. The third act of the Livingstone life, the lonely and in many ways misguided search for the sources of the Nile, triumphantly reaffirmed Livingstone's status as one of the most resonant exemplary lives of Victorian times. Seven years of wanderings, the mystery of his disappearance within Africa, the arrival of news of his alleged murder, and the many search expeditions sent out for him, kept his name constantly in the press and before the public. Thus for years he was a mysterious figure, transported into another realm like so many of the mythic heroes of world traditions. His search was merely a metaphor for his personification of the sufferings of Africa, for his anguished crusade against the slave trade, and for his own images of openings and pathways to economic and spiritual regeneration. Ultimately, he returned, though as a corpse, bearing with it boons and revelations about the perceived needs of Africa. As in 1857, this reappearance galvanised many to action.

Smiles, Monk, Whewell, Sedgwick and Waller were now joined by almost a host of biographers, travellers, hunters, missionaries and traders, who continued to celebrate the exemplary life of Livingstone. Establishment figures were also not behindhand in celebrating his achievements. In 1913, the President of the Royal Geographical Society and ex-Viceroy, Lord Curzon, described Livingstone as 'the sincere and zealous servant of God ... the indefatigable servant of science ... [and] the fiery servant of humanity'.[24] By then, Livingstone's propaganda against the slave trade had attracted the epithet 'Liberator'. (This is now a contested word for the Zimbabwean authorities, to be removed from the grand statue overlooking the Victoria Falls.) Imperialists of course liked to think of themselves as liberators and Livingstone's convenient polemic continued to act as a valuable justifier of empire in East and Central Africa down to the magisterial works of Sir Reginald Coupland.[25]

But it must have been Livingstone's wider scientific and spiritual significance which attracted that somewhat mystical polymath, Jan Christian
Smuts, to him. In November 1929, Smuts addressed the Royal Scottish
Geographical Society in both Edinburgh and Glasgow. He complimented
his audience on the greatest service that Scotland had rendered to southern
Africa, 'the gift to us of David Livingstone', who was not only our greatest
explorer, but 'our greatest propagandist'.

> He taught the world that our sub-continent existed, and his plain unvar-
> nished report seemed such wild romance that Africa almost immediately
> became the Mecca of the adventurous spirits from every part of the world.
> Livingstone placed us in the limelight and we have been there ever since.
> We are no longer the Dark Continent.

To his theatrical reference to limelight, Smuts added the notably modern
notion that Livingstone offered a 'superb advertisement' for Africa. He 'lifted
the veil' from southern Africa and 'added more to knowledge of her mysterious interior than perhaps any other man has done'. Yet again, these
are strongly visual images. Smuts was even disposed to explain away
Livingstone's well-known dislike for the Boers. The South African prime
minister returned to an equally enthusiastic encomium upon Livingstone
in his rectorial address at the University of St. Andrews in 1934.[26] A somewhat different vision must have motivated the South African liberal writer
Alan Paton, author of *Cry the Beloved Country*, to write a play about
Livingstone entitled *Last Journey*. It reflects the spiritual potential inherent
in the co-operation between white and black symbolised by Livingstone's
last journey in search of the Nile headwaters and also the last journey of
his body to the coast.[27]

Thus, a set of powerful images of Livingstone, restlessly enquiring into
every conceivable human and natural phenomenon he encountered in Africa,
energising Cambridge (and later Oxford) with his natural theology and his
vision of an African future revolutionised by science and religion, and dying
on his last quest to 'lift the veil' can be found running through the visions
of explorers, hunters, missionaries, politicians and administrators of an
imperial Africa right down to the twentieth century. Livingstone somehow
elevated the programmes of all of these. But within these larger images of
an iconic Livingstone are to be found many more detailed portrayals which
had a greater quality of immediacy. Yet each of these illuminates part of
the vaster conception of the hero, scientist and saint in one. Through these
images Livingstone was projected to generation after generation as both
spiritual and secular hero.

One of the most potent is the illustration of Livingstone and the lion
which turns up in every book written about him. Livingstone's encounter

with the lion occurs early in *Missionary Travels* (figure 13). As a result of this incident, his right arm was seriously damaged. This affected his capacity to shoot and led to the unqualified identification of the body carried through Africa by James Chuma and Abdullah Susi. Livingstone himself loathed the engraving which was included in Murray's publication, dubbing the lion 'a dray horse' and nothing like the real thing. 'Everyone who knows what a lion is will die with laughing at it ... It really must hurt the book to make a lion look larger than a hippopotamus. I am really quite distressed about it.[28] However, all subsequent authors took it up and it was also included in a set of London Missionary Society slides produced at the turn of the century (figure 14). The image can be analysed in a number of ways. At its most basic, the missionary has briefly lost control of his environment. However, the lion is also the symbol both of Africa and of power. African chiefs liked to associate themselves with the lion, just as Indian rulers sought to identify with the tiger. There was also a myth, duly recorded by Livingstone, that some chiefs had a capacity to turn themselves into lions, participate in the hunt, and then return to human form. Livingstone's human frailty is symbolised in this encounter, but he survives. He is saved by one of his African followers, whom he had previously saved from a buffalo charge. The encounter therefore perfectly illustrates not only the

Figure 13   The attack by the lion, illustration from David Livingstone, *Missionary Travels and Researches in South Africa* (London, 1857)

capacity for co-operation between European and African, but the absolute
necessity of such co-operation if Africa is to be redeemed. The obvious
courage and heroism are incidental to this central message. It is true that
lions were fairly common in Central Africa, but it is noticeable that subsequent missionaries had a habit of replicating lion encounters. The lion

Figure 14 The attack by the lion, LMS magic lantern slide. Reproduced by
kind permission of the National Portrait Gallery, London

becomes the symbol of the host of continental demons that stand in the way both of modernisation (as with the building of the Uganda railway) and of spiritual renewal.

Many of the other icons of Livingstone involve the alphabet and reading (figure 15). The Book becomes the instrument of liberation, both in the sense of the Bible and of the more diverse books of knowledge. One of the many criticisms Livingstone levelled against the Portuguese was that neither in Angola nor in Mozambique were there any bookshops, the source of liberating education. Although Livingstone was clearly an able linguist, he did little to forward the process of translation and printing in Africa. Among the missionaries who followed him, however, the creation of westernised orthographies and the printing of testaments and other religious works became a major instrument of conversion and education. Printing shops at many missions became both a key support service and a major source of training. Livingstone's power lay in print.

Figure 15 Livingstone teaches Africans the alphabet, illustration from H. G. Adams, *The Life and Adventures of Dr Livingstone in the Interior of South Africa* (London, n.d.)

The image of Livingstone baring his chest, to understandably astonished Africans, is another image which turns up in many of the biographies
(figure 16). Often it is there without explanation, appearing to be merely
an act of quixotic courage, daring his assailants to kill him. In fact, as
Livingstone recounts the incident, he is revealing the whiteness of his
bosom, as he put it, contrasting with the brownness of his face, to indicate that he is indeed English and not like the Portuguese or half-caste
merchants, a slave trader. Instead, he insisted that he came from the tribe
which loved the African. There can be little doubt that Livingstone's
profound criticisms of both Boers and Portuguese (although he complimented the latter for their outstanding generosity and hospitality towards
him) helped to legitimate the demonising of those two peoples which was
such a characteristic of British attitudes towards southern and Central
Africa later in the century. For contemporaries and successors, the exemplary life could be exemplary in its negative as well as its positive lessons.

It is significant that when the Scottish National Memorial to David
Livingstone came to be established at Blantyre, Lanarkshire, in the 1920s,
a great deal of attention was paid to iconography. This constituted the

Figure 16   Livingstone bares his chest to Africans, illustration from H. G. Adams,
The Life and Adventures of Dr Livingstone in the Interior of South Africa
(London, n.d.)

creation of a shrine to a Protestant saint, complete with the gathering of
the relics. The extraordinary sculptures of C. d'O. Pilkington Jackson lay
at the centre of this iconography. These reveal the rites of passage of the
saint, each with a symbolic title: Faith, Vision, Truth, Courage, Mercy,
Renunciation, Endurance and Sacrifice. They were described as having

> figures ... about two and a half feet high, though they give the impres-
> sion of being life size. They are of reinforced cement, modelled on one
> side only, and each has a conical shaped background that gives, in a remark-
> able way, a sense of atmosphere and perspective ... The gallery is in
> darkness, illumination coming from hidden lamps placed above.[29]

Concentrating on 'Courage', here Livingstone calms the ardour of Africans
who appear to be Nguni warriors, full of echoes for the British viewer of
the fame and power of the Zulu (figure 17). Livingstone's relatively short
height is emphasised in comparison with the warriors on the left. He appears
to have disembarked from a canoe into a realm of some strikingly exotic,
but almost certainly unidentifiable plants. But the viewer should observe
what Livingstone is carrying. He has in his hand a sextant. His power lies
not in a gun, but in the scientific instrument of solar and lunar sights.

Figure 17   'Courage', Livingstone encounters Nguni warriors, C. d'O. Pilkington
Jackson sculpture, The David Livingstone Centre, Blantyre. Reproduced by kind
permission of the Centre and the National Trust for Scotland

Through the power of Western science, unlike his potential assailants, he knows where he is, or at least thinks he does. He is not so much the liberator as the navigator and it is through his confidence in this power that he is able to raise his hand in both blessing and peace. The geometry of the sextant has the power to conquer distance, to open up, to calm, and therefore to redeem. Similar analyses could be produced of the associated icons of 'Faith', 'Mercy', 'Truth', 'Renunciation', 'Endurance' and 'Sacrifice', although it is not possible to illustrate them all here. In these, the life of Livingstone in Africa, from family man to lonely searcher, is truncated into a few images, which glow in an appropriately iconic way. In 'Faith', the European family kneels in compassion for the African. In 'Truth', Africans again consider the power of the book, while in 'Mercy', the short stature of Livingstone is emphasised once more in a confrontation with an 'Arab' or Swahili slave trader, bearing his whip and other accoutrements of alleged cruelty (figure 18). In 'Renunciation' and 'Endurance' Livingstone turns from the easy way out, the route home with Stanley (figure 19), to his continuing search, in which the Nile sources have become merely a metaphor for Smuts's 'lifting of the veil'.

The continuity in the power of the Livingstone myth seems to offer substantial evidence for the contention that the projection and interpretation

Figure 18   'Mercy', Livingstone meets a slave trader, C. d'O. Pilkington Jackson sculpture, The David Livingstone Centre, Blantyre. Reproduced by kind permission of the Centre and the National Trust for Scotland

of empire in popular and other aspects of culture continue unabated until at least the Second World War. Livingstone was repeatedly invoked for both his spiritual and his secular, particularly scientific, importance, despite the fact that his science was in one sense overwhelmed by the dominant Darwinism of the later nineteenth century. His continuing role as interpreter was neatly symbolised by the creation of the National Memorial at Blantyre (itself one aspect of a Scottish cultural renaissance) and the erection of various statues at the Royal Geographical Society and at the Victoria Falls. The latter statue, to a certain extent, represented his appropriation by the white southern African community, although the Caledonian Society which funded it was also seeking to express a Scottish identity in an exotic location. Livingstone's scientific work and in particular his capacity to inspire medical missions continued to be celebrated in Lord Hailey's monumental *African Surveys* of 1938 and 1956.[30] Interestingly, the National Memorial was particularly eager to encourage visits from Africans from the 1930s onwards. African students in Britain were invited to see it as illustrating a set of key moments in the history of their continent. Moreover, much was made by Smuts and others of the creation of a Livingstone Institute at the eponymous town in Northern Rhodesia (Zambia).

Figure 19 'Renunciation', Livingstone says farewell to Stanley, C. d'O. Pilkington Jackson sculpture, The David Livingstone Centre, Blantyre. Reproduced by kind permission of the Centre and the National Trust for Scotland

The paradox of Livingstone is indeed that his own interpretations of future empire so often turned out to be inaccurate, but his life and death, despite the vicissitudes of the Zambezi expedition and its aftermath, offered almost endless opportunities for those interpreters who came after him. Livingstone was himself endlessly interpreted. And it is striking that Livingstone's role as the prime subject for an elevated interpretation of empire was always presented in such powerfully visual forms. The great word painter lent himself to any number of iconic images. He continues to influence modern tourist advertising, with at least two companies using his image in association with the Victoria Falls, quoting his famous remark about the scene so beautiful it must have been observed by angels in their flight (figure 20). Each of the Livingstone images offered a powerful echo of some aspect of the essence of empire's self-justification and must have acted as a significant influence on the many generations who were introduced to Africa through Livingstone as hero and exemplar. The flexibility of the Livingstone legend meant that it could be appropriated by all who

Figure 20   Travel advertisement, 1997

sought to interpret science, self-help, empire, missions and personal religious conviction. Moreover, as any number of missionary memoirs and biographies indicate, Livingstone's exemplary views on race and natural theology were given a longer life-span than Darwinists would have us believe. The Livingstone legend could itself be visualised and hence liberated and navigated in an astonishingly wide variety of ways.

Notes

1   P. J. Westwood, *David Livingstone: His Life and Work as Told Through the Media of Postage Stamps and Allied Material* (Edinburgh, 1986).
2   Tim Jeal, *Livingstone* (London, 1985, first published 1973).
3   J. Scott Keltie, *The Partition of Africa* (London 1893), p. 114.
4   John M. MacKenzie, 'The provincial geographical societies in Britain, 1884–1914', in Morag Bell, Robin Butlin and Michael Heffernan (eds), *Geography and Imperialism 1820–1940*, (Manchester 1995), p. 101.
5   John M. MacKenzie, 'David Livingstone: the construction of the myth', in G. Walker and T. Gallagher (eds), *Sermons and Battle Hymns: Protestant Popular Culture in Modern Scotland* (Edinburgh, 1990), pp. 24–42. M. A. Wetherall produced a lengthy documentary feature on Livingstone in 1925 and Hollywood followed with *Stanley and Livingstone* (starring Stanley Spencer and Cedric Hardwick, both hopelessly miscast) in 1939, as a paean of praise to Anglo-American co-operation.
6   Jeal, *Livingstone*, pp. 337–38, 342, 346–47.
7   Dorothy O. Helly, *Livingstone's Legacy: Horace Waller and Victorian Mythmaking* (Columbus, Ohio, 1987). H. Waller, *The Last Journals of David Livingstone, in Central Africa, from 1865 to his Death Continued by a Narrative of his Last Moments and Sufferings, Obtained from his Faithful Servants Chuma and Susi* (London, 1875).
8   W.P. Livingstone, *Mary Slessor of Calabar, Pioneer Missionary* (London, 1916), p. 331: 'it was a scene which suggested the final act in Dr Livingstone's life'. Like Livingstone, Slessor had read her book on the loom while working in a mill in Dundee and when news of Livingstone's death reached Britain, she was 'thrilled into action' to offer herself to the Foreign Mission Board; pp. 4 and 17.
9   'For thirty years his life was spent in an unwearied effort to evangelize the native races, to explore the undiscovered secrets, to abolish the desolating slave trade of Central Africa, where with his last words he wrote, "All I can add in my solitude is may Heaven's rich blessing come down on everyone, American, English or Turk, who will help to heal this open sore of the world."'
10 D. Livingstone, *Missionary Travels and Researches in South Africa* (London, 1857).
11 David and Charles Livingstone, *Narrative of an Expedition to the Zambezi and its Tributaries and of the discovery of Lakes Shirwa and Nyassa, 1858–1864* (London, 1865).
12 *Dr Livingstone's Cambridge Lectures together with a prefatory letter by the Reverend Professor Sedgwick*, edited with an introduction, life of Dr Livingstone, notes and appendix by the Reverend William Monk (London and Cambridge 1858), pp. ii–iii.
13 *Dr Livingstone's Cambridge Lectures*, pp. lxxxvii–xciii.
14 Livingstone, *Missionary Travels*, p. 609.
15 *Ibid.*, pp. 673–74.
16 J. M. MacKenzie (ed.), *David Livingstone and the Victorian Encounter with Africa* (London, 1996) (the catalogue of an exhibition at the National Portrait Gallery), p. 98.

17   I am grateful to my colleague, Professor John H. Brooke, for valuable discussion of theories of natural theology and the impact of Darwin.

18   'I beg to direct your attention to Africa. I know that in a few years I shall be cut off in that country, which is now open: do not let it be shut again! I go back to Africa to try to make an open path for commerce and Christianity: do you carry out the work which I have begun. I LEAVE IT WITH YOU.'

19   A. Calder, 'Samuel Smiles: the Unexpurgated Version' in *Revolving Culture: Notes from the Scottish Republic* (London, 1994), pp. 126–36. See also A. Calder, 'Livingstone, Self-Help and Scotland', in MacKenzie (ed.), *David Livingstone and the Victorian Encounter*, pp. 79–105. I am grateful to Angus Calder for discussion about Samuel Smiles and the Empire.

20   Samuel Smiles, *Self-Help*, centennial edition (London, 1959), pp. 244–46. *Self-Help* had reached its 71st impression in 1953.

21   Asa Briggs, introduction to the centennial edition, p. 7.

22   Charles Livingstone, David's brother, was appointed as the official photographer to the expedition, but his efforts were not a success. Successful photographs were, however, taken by John Kirk, doctor and botanist on the expedition, and these are now in the collections of the Scottish National Portrait Gallery in Edinburgh.

23   James Wells, *The Life of James Stewart* (London, 1909), p. 60. 'In his white trousers, frock-coat, and naval cap, he looked uncommonly smart and had a commanding air ... I could not help remarking to Mrs. Livingstone that the Doctor seemed to be a great swell.' Needless to say, Wells did not mention Stewart's attempt to throw Livingstone's influence into the Zambezi. This incident is to be found in J. P. R. Wallis, *The Zambesi Journal of James Stewart, 1862–1863* (London, 1952), p. 190. Stewart wrote that the book was 'nothing short of an eyesore, the very sight of its brown covers'. But once the heroic Livingstone was firmly established, Stewart attempted to score out the title of the book in heavy ink.

24   Quoted in MacKenzie, 'David Livingstone: the construction of the myth', pp. 36–7 and printed in full in J. I. MacNair, *David Livingstone: the Story in Brief* (Blantyre, 1929).

25   R. Coupland, *East Africa and its Invaders* (Oxford, 1938), pp. 155, 187, 305–07; R. Coupland, *The Exploitation of East Africa, 1856–90* (London, 1939), pp. 133, 137, 139–40, 141.

26   'Livingstone and After', an address given before the Royal Scottish Geographical Society in Edinburgh and Glasgow on 21 and 22 November 1929 in General J. C. Smuts, *Africa and Some World Problems* (Oxford, 1930), pp. 3–34. The specific quotations are on pp. 4–6. The rectorial address, entitled 'The Challenge to Freedom', was published in *Greater South Africa: Plans for a Better World: the speeches of J. C. Smuts* (Johannesburg, 1940), pp. 57–68. The Livingstone reference is on p. 59. I am grateful to Dr Donal Lowry for these references and the one that follows.

27   Peter F. Alexander, *Alan Paton: a Biography* (Oxford, 1995), p. 304.

28   MacKenzie, ed., *Livingstone and the Victorian Encounter*, p. 179.

29   J. I. MacNair, *The Story of the Scottish National Memorial to David Livingstone* (Blantyre, 1929), p. 24.

30   Lord Hailey, *An African Survey* (Oxford, 1938), pp. 1035, 1116, 1235, 1310. Interestingly, the references were reduced to one on medical missions in the revised edition of *An African Survey* (Oxford, 1957).

'Our King upon his knees'[1]: the public commemoration of Captain Scott's last Antarctic expedition

On Friday 14 February 1913 the National Anthem was sung in its entirety at St Paul's Cathedral for the first time in many years.[2] Four days earlier, news had reached London that a party from the British Antarctic Expedition had died on their way back from the South Pole. One of the largest congregations seen at St Paul's gathered to mourn the deaths of Captain Robert Falcon Scott, R.N., Petty Officer Edgar Evans, R.N., Captain Lawrence Oates of the 6th Inniskilling Dragoons, Lieutenant Henry Bowers of the Royal Indian Marine and Dr Edward Wilson.[3] Dean Inge observed that 'the rush for tickets was unparalleled.'[4] When King George V left the Cathedral after the service, the *Daily Mirror* reported that the National Anthem was taken up by the crowds gathered outside, 'the unrehearsed expression of a people's sorrow', and predicted that 'out of that sorrow and out of that anguish will be born a new patriotism, and from it will spring even a new desire for service to the nation and its head'.[5]

Over the last two decades a number of historians have highlighted the genesis of an aggressive imperial nationalism in Britain between the Indian Rebellion and the outbreak of the First World War.[6] John MacKenzie and Robert MacDonald have identified the commemoration of national heroes such as Dr Livingstone and General Gordon as a central feature of this new imperial nationalism.[7] Emphasis has been placed on the careful composition of heroic narratives, disseminated through an array of forms to nourish the popular culture of imperialism. Heroic myths have been interpreted as instruments of empire, which legitimated imperial expansion by subsuming ambiguities and doubts about imperial purpose within idealised narratives of individual heroism.

The following essay argues that this emphasis both on empire and on deliberate fabrication requires qualification. The first section briefly outlines the British response to the death of Captain Scott.[8] The second looks more closely at four examples of the commemoration of the disaster. The final section examines the range of meanings inscribed in the narratives inspired by Scott's last expedition. The pattern of the commemoration of the Antarctic disaster suggests that the heroes of the past should be interpreted less as instruments of social control, than as sites through which a range of imagined communities were capable of expression.

On 17 January 1912 five men from the British Antarctic Expedition arrived at the spot they calculated to be the South Pole. They had been preceded by a Norwegian expedition led by Roald Amundsen, which had reached the Pole a month before. The British explorers faced an 800 mile journey back to their base camp. Scott, Bowers, Evans, Oates and Wilson died on the return march. On 12 November 1912 a search party found the tent containing the bodies of Scott, Bowers and Wilson along with the letters and diaries which told the story of their last march. News of the disaster reached London by cable from New Zealand on Monday 10 February 1913.

The British press were the first to tell the story of Scott of the Antarctic.[9] Scott had sold the newspaper rights of the expedition to the Central News Agency for £2,000, and as a result the press coverage from the evening of Monday 10 February to Wednesday 12 February was based solely on a 2,500 word cable distributed by Central News. Composed by a committee of six of the expedition's officers,[10] the cable described the expedition's activities over the previous year and the assault on the Pole.[11] Two passages from Scott's sledging journal were quoted verbatim: Scott's account of the death of Captain Oates and a 'Message to the Public', written at the end of his journal. Scott wrote of Oates:

> He was a brave soul. He slept through the night hoping not to wake, but he awoke in the morning. It was blowing a blizzard. Oates said "I am just going outside and I may be some time." He went out into the blizzard and we have not seen him since. . . . We knew that Oates was walking to his death, but though we tried to dissuade him, we knew it was the act of a brave man and an English gentleman.

In his final 'Message to the Public', Scott blamed the disaster on excessive misfortune, rather than faulty organisation, and concluded,

> We are weak, writing is difficult, but, for my own sake, I do not regret this journey, which has shown that Englishmen can endure hardship, help one another and meet death with as great a fortitude as ever in the past. . . . Had we lived I should have had a tale to tell of the hardihood, endurance, and courage of my companions which would have stirred the heart of every Englishman. These rough notes and our dead bodies must tell the tale, but surely, surely, a great rich country like ours will see that those who are dependent on us are properly provided for.

The cable added that 'the southern party nobly stood by their sick companions to the end' and 'had retained every record and 35lb of geological specimens . . . [which] emphasises the nature of their journey'.

This first cable from New Zealand became the founding text of the story of Scott of the Antarctic, and contained the three key elements on which later narratives were based: Scott's 'Message to the Public', the account of Oates' death, and an emphasis on the scientific aims of the expedition.

The news of the death of Scott and his companions caused a sensation in Britain. The *Manchester Guardian* proclaimed: 'Nothing in our own time, scarcely even the foundering of the *Titanic*, has touched the whole nation so instantly and so deeply as the loss of these men'.[12] The *Newport Advertiser* declared that Scott's message 'told a story of heroism in the face of which the classic deeds of the Gods of the ancients paled into insignificance'.[13] An advertisement for the *Strand Magazine*'s serialisation of Scott's journals even described the 'Message' as 'the most impressive document ever read by man'.[14]

Such journalistic excess appears to have found a receptive audience. The *Daily Mirror*'s second 'Captain Scott Number' of 21 May 1913, which published for the first time the photographs taken by the explorers at the Pole, sold 1,342,000 copies.[15] This was by far the largest selling edition of the *Daily Mirror* in 1912 or 1913, and an overnight sales increase of 550,000 copies was unprecedented.

Crowded memorial services from St Giles' Cathedral, Edinburgh, to St John's Church, Cardiff, along with those in dissenting chapels and synagogues, were held throughout Britain. A national memorial service was swiftly arranged at St Paul's Cathedral for Friday 14 February, which the Dean (Dean Inge) observed 'excited extraordinary enthusiasm.'[16] For some the emotion of the occasion proved too much. The Reverend E. T. Griffiths, preaching in Gloucestershire on the Sunday following the news, referred to the death of Captain Scott and his party at the post of duty, at which his own voice failed and he fell down the steps of his pulpit and died.[17]

Four national memorial funds were opened, by the British Antarctic Expedition Committee, by the Mansion House, by the *Daily Chronicle* and by the *Daily Telegraph*, which collected funds to pay the expedition's debts, provide for the bereaved and erect a national memorial. Numerous local appeals were organised by publications such as the *Scotsman* and the *Yorkshire Post*, and by churches and local councils all over Britain. A disappointing initial response led to the amalgamation of the four national appeals into a single Mansion House Fund, which prompted a surge in donations, led by the King with £200.[18] The fund was closed in June after £75,000 had been raised.[19] This was a substantial sum. In the same year only £45,000 was raised for the 800 dependants of the 440 victims of the Sengenhydd mining disaster.[20] Admiral Beaumont, a member of the committee which administered the fund, even complained to Captain Scott's widow Kathleen that 'there is now more money than can be properly allocated. I always feared there would be'.[21]

Contributions came from all classes of society and from all regions of Britain. Schools, churches, businesses, service units and a wide variety of voluntary associations from Cheam Girls' Club to Alnwick Town Band collected money.[22] The *Scotsman* raised nearly £5,000, with one donation of £7 made up from the pennies donated by 1,700 pupils at a school in Galashiels.[23]

The bereaved were provided for through a combination of public and private finance. State pensions were awarded to the relatives of the deceased based on careful calculations of past income, so as to guarantee the Prime Minister Herbert Asquith's pledge that the bereaved would be placed 'in as good a pecuniary position as they would have been had the disaster not taken place'.[24] The bereaved also received £34,000 from the Mansion House Fund.[25] The social and professional status of the dead determined the amount each received. Trust funds worth £12,000 were awarded to Kathleen Scott and her son Peter. Petty Officer Edgar Evans' widow Lois and her three children, Norman, Muriel and Ralph, on the other hand, received a trust fund worth only £1,250.

Newspaper coverage, memorial services and fund-raising campaigns show the high level of interest in the deaths of Scott and his companions, while provision for the relatives of the dead presents a stark picture of social hierarchy in Britain before 1914.

Four key examples of the commemoration of Scott's last expedition will now be examined: the publication of Scott's sledging journals; the national memorial service at St Paul's; the reading of the story of the expedition to school-children; and the erection of public monuments to the dead explorers.

Several authors have followed Roland Huntford in highlighting the censorship of Scott's sledging journals as the central act in the construction of the legend of Scott of the Antarctic as national martyr, an act designed to salvage British pride following Norwegian victory in the race for the Pole.[26] This emphasis on censorship is misleading for three reasons. First, Scott's journals were not available in detail until the publication of the two volume *Scott's Last Expedition* by Smith Elder on 6 November 1913, by which time all major commemorative projects had been initiated.[27] Second, priced at 42 shillings, *Scott's Last Expedition* could only have reached a fraction of the readership which learned about the disaster through the press.[28] Third, a comparison of the published text with Scott's original exposes relatively few alterations, reflecting the conventions of popular biography, not an establishment conspiracy.[29] Only seventeen significant changes were made to Scott's account of the march back from the Pole, notably through the omission of critical comments about Petty Officer Evans. This 'editing' undoubtedly enhanced Scott's reputation by concealing unattractive aspects of his personality. However, the alteration or excision of only sixty-eight words in a sixty page account of the last march cannot explain the appeal of Scott's story. The two most significant passages, the account of Oates's death and 'Message to the Public', were published exactly as Scott had written them. Scott was not transformed into a heroic figure by the skilful excisions and embellishments of an editor's pen.

St Paul's was the natural venue for a national memorial service to honour the dead. The cathedral had staged memorial services following the deaths of General Gordon and Cecil Rhodes, as well as for the victims of the Boer War and the sinking of the *Titanic*.[30] The *Titanic* memorial service of April 1912 provided a model on this occasion, with a combination of hymns and biblical readings. Unlike the commemoration for General Gordon, no sermon was read.[31] Even so, the staging of the ceremony turned the Scott memorial service into a majestic display of the unity of the nation-state. Central to this display was the personal attendance of King George V, who, in the absence of the bodies of the explorers, provided the focal point of the ceremony. It was unprecedented for a British monarch to attend a service for someone who was not a member of a Royal Family and the King's presence was widely commented on.[32] A poem by T. B. Hennell inspired by the ceremony concluded 'Can you see the dome of the Golden Cross/And our King upon his knees?'[33]

The service reached a climax with Dean Inge's oration from I Corinthians xv. 20, which included the proclamation 'Death has been swallowed up in victory. Where, O Death, is your victory? Where, O Death, is your sting?' As the Dean's words faded, a drum-roll played by a member of the Coldstream Guards rose steadily in volume, heralding the *Dead March* in *Saul*. The names of the five dead men were intoned in the Prayer of Committal and the service concluded with the singing of the National Anthem.

Reports of the service closed a week of press coverage of the disaster, with the ceremony represented as a demonstration of national unity. The report in the *Star* was typical: 'The Memorial Service in St Paul's was a true national tribute to the heroic dead ... that noble assembly of the British people in the national cathedral – King, Prime Minister, Navy, Army, and the democracy. There never was a more spontaneous Requiem than this.'[34] The ceremony secured the position of the King at the head of the body politic. The energy generated by the service, by the crowds gathered outside, by the voices raised in communal song, by the rich Biblical language of sacrifice and solemn intonation of the names of the dead, was harnessed beneath the dome of St Paul's and channelled into the mute body of the King. In such moments the mystique of the monarchy was renewed.

As the bells of St Paul's struck twelve and the service began, one and a half million children in elementary schools in London and at least fifty other centres, including Birmingham, Brighton, Cardiff, Liverpool and Norwich were gathered together to hear 'The Immortal Story of Capt. Scott's Expedition – How Five Brave Englishmen Died' by Arthur Machen.[35] The story began:

> Children: You are going to hear the true story of five of the bravest and best men who have ever lived on the earth since the world began. You are English boys and girls, and you must often have heard England spoken of as the greatest country in the world, or perhaps you have been told that the British Empire . . . is the greatest Empire that the world has ever seen . . . when we say that England is great we are not thinking of the size of the country or of the number of people who live in it. We are thinking of much more important things, and if you listen to the story that is to be read to you, you will find out what greatness really does mean.

After a brief narrative of the progress of the expedition, Scott's account of Oates's death and the final section of the 'Message to the Public' were quoted in full. The story concluded:

> So these brave men died; and now you know what we mean when we say that they were great. They feared no danger, they never complained, they did their best, each one was willing to give up his life for the others, and when they knew that there was no hope for them they laid down their lives bravely and calmly like true Christian gentlemen.

The reading of this story was organised by the London *Evening News*, which, on Wednesday 12 February, had published a proposal beneath a large Union Jack with the headline 'Let us tell the children how Englishmen can die'.[36] The newspaper announced it had commissioned Arthur Machen to write a thousand word account of the disaster.[37] The Education Committee of the London County Council unanimously supported the plan for the story to be read to 750,000 children in L.C.C. elementary schools, to coincide with the St Paul's service.[38]

The state played its most significant role in the commemoration of the Antarctic disaster at mid-day on Friday 14 February 1913 through its control of public ceremony and national schooling. The service at St Paul's and readings to school-children appear at first to be an orchestrated expression of state power. Central government, however, played a peripheral role in

the organisation of both events. The national memorial service was organised by the Dean and Chapter of St Paul's, not the cabinet. Asquith's
cabinet letters to the King make no mention of the Antarctic disaster.[39]
The King's attendance at the service was almost certainly a personal choice.
Lloyd George's private secretary even wrote to the Royal Geographical
Society (R.G.S.) requesting tickets for the service and had to be informed
that applications should be directed to St Paul's.[40] The reading of Scott's
story to school-children was organised by a London evening newspaper,
motivated less by the desire to legitimate state authority, than by the wish
to increase sales. Decisions to request Machen's pamphlet were taken by
headmasters and local education officers, without direction from the Board
of Education.

This absence of central control can be seen most clearly in the erection of monuments to honour the dead. The Mansion House Fund
committee allocated £18,000 of the £75,000 raised to finance three memorials: a tablet in St Paul's, a polar research fund, and a statue in London,
which was to be the physical focus of the nation's commemoration.[41] A
competition for the statue was held and figure 21 shows the successful
design submitted by Albert Hodge, titled 'Pro Patria', which was chosen by
a committee headed by Sir Thomas Brock, designer of the Victoria Memorial
outside Buckingham Palace.[42]

Hodge proposed a granite pylon surmounted by a bronze statuary group.
'For King', 'For Country', 'For Brotherly Love' and 'For Knowledge', were
inscribed on each of the four sides, with bas-reliefs depicting scenes from
the expedition, and an extract from Scott's 'Message to the Public'.[43] Hodge
wrote that he wanted 'to teach the great lesson of heroism of the expedition, not by merely representing any incident but by telling the story for
future generations'.[44] The defiant posture and military costume, in combination with a triumphant Britannia, would represent the Antarctic disaster
as an emblem of national virility, standing forty feet high in the nation's
capital. Scott was to be represented as a warrior, dying 'Pro Patria'.

Yet this statue was never built. Kathleen Scott among others objected
to Hodge's design.[45] The President of the R.G.S., Douglas Freshfield, wrote
an official letter of complaint to Brock that the statue's

> general character is out of keeping with the occasion to be commemo-
> rated. We consider that a record of quiet protracted and heroic endurance
> calls for a design more reserved and less allegorical in conception. In
> particular the strained and somewhat theatrical attitude given to the
> figure grasping a military banner and apparently trampling underfoot nude
> bodies strikes Captain Scott's friends as singularly out of all connection
> both with polar exploration and the man it is designed to honour and to
> represent.[46]

Figure 21   Albert Hodge's design for a national memorial to Captain Scott

The protest was successful and the design substantially altered. In figure 22 we can see the more contemplative Scott that stands on top of the memorial today, represented as an explorer, not as a soldier.

The location of the statue was also contested. After the announcement of the disaster, Lord Curzon attempted to harness Scott's memory to the R.G.S., of which he had been President from 1911 to 1913. Curzon urged that the statue be erected in Hyde Park opposite Lowther Lodge, the lavish new premises to which the R.G.S. had moved in April 1913, largely as a result of Curzon's efforts.[47]

After this suggestion was made to the First Commissioner of Works, Lord Beauchamp responded that, while his department 'did not lag behind anybody in admiration of Captain Scott and his comrades . . . they found themselves barred by the jealous dislike which had been shown on more than one occasion by the public to any additions being made to the memorials in the Park'.[48] Curzon quickly lost interest after this rebuff, resigning from the committee responsible for choosing a design for the memorial.[49]

In fact, the Mansion House committee failed to secure a single site in London for the statue. The outbreak of the First World War and the death of Hodge in 1917 delayed matters further, and the project was almost abandoned in the early 1920s.[50] Eventually, a site was secured in Devonport, near the Admiralty House on Mount Wise, and the statue was finally unveiled in August 1925 (figure 22).[51]

While action on a national scale was paralysed by internal disputes and a lack of political will, the response of local communities was more decisive. By the time the statue on Mount Wise had been unveiled, at least thirty-three other memorials had been erected in Britain alone.[52]

Churches, schools and local councils in communities associated with the expedition proved particularly active in these commemorations. Parish subscriptions financed the erection of memorial tablets in Meanwood Church, Leeds, where Oates had worshipped, and St Peter's Church, Binton, where Scott's brother-in-law was the rector.[53] Stubbington House School, Fareham,[54] and Eton and Cheltenham Colleges each commemorated their old pupils, Scott, Oates and Wilson.[55] Public subscriptions in Cheltenham paid for the erection of a statue of its former resident, Dr Wilson, on the Promenade.[56] In Cardiff, the city which had donated most to the expedition's funds, four separate memorials were erected within four years of the announcement of the disaster: the figurehead of the *Terra Nova* and a clock tower in Roath Park; a bed in the City Hospital, and a bronze tablet in the City Hall.[57]

Officers and men in the armed forces also opened subscription lists to finance memorials, including a tablet in St Ninian's Church on the Isle of Bute, near Bowers's family home.[58] Most prominent was a statue of Captain

Figure 22   Completed national memorial statue, Mount Wise, Devonport

Scott, sculpted by his widow Kathleen, and paid for by naval officers. Unveiled in a semi-private ceremony at Waterloo Place, London, in November 1915, the only statue of Scott in the capital was far less didactic than Hodge's design, being inscribed only with the names of the dead and a short passage from Scott's 'Message to the Public'.[59]

The Church, representatives of national government, local authorities, the press and the people came together in an expression of national grief after the announcement of the Antarctic disaster. Yet no 'priest' constructed a 'myth' of Scott of the Antarctic to impose on British society. The commemorations were essentially generated by local communities, without central government direction. Studies of the Napoleonic, Boer and First World Wars have traced a similar pattern, whereby local government and civil society were the primary agents of public commemoration in Britain.[60] The popular appeal of Captain Scott and his companions was founded on the ability of their tragic story to be invested with a variety of meanings. Narratives of the disaster were less instruments of social control, than sites for the negotiation of collective identities, in which familial, professional, local, regional and national attachments were capable of expression.

Meaning was ascribed to the Antarctic disaster through the language of sacrifice. The deaths of the explorers were redeemed by their contribution to a higher cause. The identification of this higher cause, however, was contested. While Winston Churchill declared that the disaster demonstrated that officers of the armed forces would not fail the empire in the hour of need,[61] the Chief Rabbi, at the annual meeting of the Peace Society in 1913, hailed Scott as a hero for pacifists, prepared to sacrifice his life for science.[62] The final section of this essay examines three heroic representations of Captain Scott, as martyr of science, national icon and exemplar of manly character.

When setting out his expedition plans to the R.G.S. in 1910, Scott had announced that, while the attainment of the Pole for the honour of the nation was his primary aim, it was 'the plain duty of the explorer to bring back . . . every possible observation of the conditions under which his journey has been made'.[63] As a result the expedition sailed with one of the largest scientific staffs sent to the Antarctic. The assault on the Pole was to be the crowning achievement of an extensive programme of research in botany, geology, glaciology, marine biology, meteorology and zoology. The first cable from New Zealand reported that the explorers had dragged 35lbs of geological specimens until their deaths, thereby enabling the disaster to be represented as a sacrifice in the name of scientific research. *Nature*, for example, paid tribute to the explorers, who had 'laid down their lives in the pursuit of geographical knowledge'.[64] In particular, both the R.G.S. and

the network of international geographical societies with which it was associated, commemorated the explorers as 'martyrs of science'.[65] The scientific
aims of the expedition guaranteed the selflessness of the explorers' sacrifice.

Outside the scientific community, Scott was more frequently raised as
a national rather than scientific martyr. Fears of national decline, mass
physical deterioration and elite decadence were prominent features of
Edwardian political discourse.[66] Before sailing south, Scott had declared
that the 'quest [for the Pole] becomes an outward visible sign that we are
still a nation able and willing to undertake difficult enterprises, still capable
of standing in the van of the army of progress'.[67] When news of the disaster
reached Britain three years later, the Mental Deficiency Bill was passing
through Westminster, Lord Roberts was lecturing in support of the National
Service League, and R. H. Benson had published a scathing attack on standards at Eton. Scott's last 'Message', in which he had written that 'I do
not regret this journey, which has shown that Englishmen can endure hardship, help one another, and meet death with as great a fortitude as ever
in the past', was amplified against this background. The explorers' sacrifice
was redeemed by the inspirational legacy bequeathed to the nation. The
Daily Mirror's hints for dinner-table topics, for example, included 'Is England
decadent? The old tiresome question. May it not now be answered "No!"
as we read of such men as Scott and his companions'.[68]

Scott's example was raised as an antidote to national decline. Baden-
Powell hailed the explorers as fellow scouts, arguing that 'there is plenty
of pluck and spirit left in the British race after all. Captain Scott and
Captain Oates have shown us that'.[69] St Catherine's Press published Scott's
'Message to the Public' with a dedication 'To those who have high hope
for Young England'.[70] An introduction entitled the 'British Way' declared
that the explorers had shown 'how Englishmen still can die quietly and
faithfully in the English way'.

The easy slippage between English and British indicates a more general
ambiguity in representations of the nation. The commemoration of the
disaster articulated a vocabulary of race based on a common cultural inheritance rather than biology. Comparisons with past heroes were frequent,
with Scott compared to Sir John Franklin in particular, but also with Nelson,
Gordon, Drake, Raleigh, Livingstone, Wolfe and Cook. Within this pantheon
of national heroes, explorers were praised for their deeds in the epic struggle
between man and nature. Yet the nation itself remained undefined. Accounts
of the disaster were rarely explicitly imperialist. Out of a group of forty-
one leaders published in thirteen newspapers between 10 and 15 February
1913, which I have examined, only six articles even mentioned the empire.[71]

The nebulous character of this nationalist language was the basis
of its appeal. But the place of the monarchy was crucial. The King's

unprecedented attendance at St Paul's and his presentation of awards to the surviving members of the expedition, secured the disaster as a sacrifice for the nation. Flags, anthems and Royal ceremonial marked the elevation of the dead explorers to the heroic status of national martyrs.

Yet, apart from brief messages of condolence, the King was silent. The commemoration of the disaster was not harnessed to any explicit imperialist or racist ideology. Scotsmen, Welshmen, Englishmen, the residents of Galashiels, Cardiff and Devonport, all imagined their own nation under the crown.[72] The *Terra Nova* sailed into Cardiff in June 1913 with the city's arms at her foremast, the Welsh Dragon at her mainmast, the Royal Yacht Squadron burgee at her mizzenmast and the White Ensign at her peak, a fitting symbol of the range of identities capable of expression through the story of Scott of the Antarctic.[73]

What united those across the social and political spectrum who celebrated Scott's sacrifice was not the belief that imperial expansion was sanctioned by divine right, but the subscription to a common vision that character was forged through struggle.[74] The martyr of science, national icon, imperial scout and hero of pacifists, were underwritten by the representation of Captain Scott as an exemplar of manly character.

Scott's plea for those dependent on the explorers to be properly provided for placed the bereaved at the centre of representations of the disaster. Photographs of Kathleen and Peter Scott filled the newspapers.[75] The frontpage of the *Daily Sketch* after the national memorial service, for example, showed Scott flanked by his wife and son.[76] Narratives of the disaster reasserted traditional gender roles in a period when suffragette campaigns had placed relations between the sexes at the forefront of the political agenda. Antarctic exploration was an exclusively male activity. No woman set foot on Antarctica until Caroline Mikkelsen in 1935. The Bishop of London declared that Scott's 'Message' had 'raised human manhood throughout the world',[77] while a leader in the *Manchester Guardian* was entitled simply 'These were men'.[78] Scott even reached the pinnacle of modern images of masculinity, the cigarette brand, advertised under the slogan 'Cool like the iceberg'.[79] Captain Scott, the Edwardian 'Marlboro Man'.

An examination of over 110 newspapers and periodicals has revealed that, although the superiority of Amundsen's methods was acknowledged,[80] the disaster was almost universally acclaimed as a heroic sacrifice. Socialists and suffragettes alike celebrated the tragedy. The radical press, including the *Daily Herald, Daily Citizen, Clarion, Truth, New Witness* and *New Age*, hailed the explorers as heroes. Alex Thompson in the *Clarion* declared that the men who 'start Labour and socialist papers undertake the work in the spirit which led . . . Scott to the South Pole'.[81] The *Daily Herald* praised the disaster as an inspiration which transcended nationality:

They have done service and brought honour not simply to Britain – we are tired of these pretentious and unreal race distinctions – but to humanity and its seeking and soaring spirit . . . The achievement has touched responsive chords in the hearts of millions of men and women engaged in grim or deadly though less showy tasks . . . consciously or unconsciously they have had a new place in the commonwealth of heroism.[82]

Criticism was not directed at the explorers, but both at the sentimentality of the press, and at the authorities who failed to recognise the 'everyday heroes', the striking taxi-drivers or miners, who acted in the spirit of Captain Scott.[83]

The Women's Freedom League postponed a protest which would have clashed with the St Paul's memorial service, while the *Vote* recorded that 'women suffragists did not fail to pay their tribute to the brave adventurers'.[84] In an article on the suffering endured by suffragettes, Christabel Pankhurst declared:

There is, indeed, nothing to match the spirit of the militants, unless it be the spirit shown by Captain Scott and his brave companions. There is universal mourning for these dead heroes, but it is only the militant women who really understand and share the spirit that moved them in their work and in their death.[85]

Pankhurst singled out Captain Oates for praise. Four months later the death of Emily Davison at the Derby mobilised the same language of sacrifice, with John chapter 15 verse 13, 'Greater love hath no man than this, that a man lay down his life for his friend', invoked for Davison as it had been for Captain Oates.[86]

This is not to suggest that admiration for Scott's achievement was universal. The death of Princess Diana has demonstrated how press reports offer an imperfect reflection of public attitudes. Both *Justice* and the *British Socialist*, for example, offered little comment on the disaster, suggesting indifference if not contempt. Many still believed that polar exploration was a waste of resources. In 1914 the popular *Pimple* series of comic films turned to polar exploration with the release of *Lt. Pimple's Dash to the Pole*, indicating a popular irreverence obscured in the aftermath of the disaster.[87] Yet the celebration of the heroism of the explorers by socialists and suffragettes reveals a shared subscription to the belief that character was forged through struggle. The language of sacrifice transcended political divisions.

A week after the announcement of the Antarctic disaster a number of newspapers reported that Percy Lambert had set a new land speed record at the Brooklands Track, covering over 103 miles in one hour in his Talbot car.[88] A day earlier, King George V had postponed his visit to the Olympia Aeroplane Exhibition to attend the St Paul's memorial service.[89]

Scott sailed south at a moment when transportation and communications were being rapidly transformed.[90] Cables had rendered transcontinental communication almost instantaneous, moving images of the Antarctic were projected into picture theatres from Hastings to Hull, cars travelled at over 100mph and flight confirmed the technological mastery of the forces of nature. Yet an assault on the Pole relied on animals and men. Scott's last expedition was one of the final expressions of a language of exploration, in which scientific research was combined with heroic adventure. In the future, technological developments would reduce the need for exposure to risk during the observation of the natural world. Explorers would be transformed from scientific travellers to seekers of sensation, from Captain Scott to Richard Branson.[91]

A chorus of voices commemorated the Antarctic disaster, as a variety of communities invested Scott's story with different meanings. This chorus was not orchestrated by a conductor. Central government made little attempt to raise Scott and his companions as imperial heroes. Meaning was ascribed to the disaster through the language of sacrifice. The identification of the cause for which the explorers died, however, was contested, as different accounts proclaimed the sacrifice, in the words of Albert Hodge's national memorial statue, 'For Knowledge', 'For King', 'For Country', 'For Brotherly Love'. Each memorial has its own story to tell.

The commemorative projects outlined in this essay were generated by the conjunction of an active local state and vibrant civil society, which characterised Edwardian Britain. Scott's story was not harnessed to a hegemonic discourse of empire or Englishness. The pattern of the commemoration of the Antarctic disaster suggests that historians should move beyond the model of the heroic myth, instrument of ideology, and look more closely at the ways in which the celebration of 'exemplary lives' served as a site for the negotiation of individual and collective identities. The appeal of the imagined community of the nation in Britain on the eve of the Great War did not reflect the strength of the British state in imposing an imperialist ideology, but the absence of a state-sponsored nationalist agenda. The monarchy lay at the malleable heart of representations of the nation, allowing the local, Scottish and Welsh identities embedded in civil society expression alongside a loosely defined rhetoric of national and imperial service. Articulated through the rituals of monarchy rather than an explicit ideology, the elusive character of the imagined nation in Britain has been the foundation of its enduring appeal.

Notes

1   T. B. Hennell, 'St Paul's, February 14', *Daily Mirror*, 14 Feb. 1913, p. 3. I would like to thank Becky Conekin, Jennifer Davis, George Jones, Adam Tooze, Jay Winter and the editors for their comments.
2   *Guardian*, 21 Feb. 1913, p. 259.
3   *British Weekly*, 20 Feb. 1913, p. 603.
4   Magdalene College, Cambridge, W. R. Inge diary, vol. 24, 14 Feb. 1913.
5   *Daily Mirror*, 15 Feb. 1913, p. 4.
6   See, for example, E. Hobsbawm and T. Ranger (eds), *The Invention of Tradition* (Cambridge, 1983); John M. MacKenzie, *Propaganda and Empire: the Manipulation of British Public Opinion, 1880–1960* (Manchester, 1984); R. Colls and P. Dodd (eds), *Englishness: Culture and Politics 1880–1920* (London, 1986); G. Dawson, *Soldier Heroes: British Adventure, Empire and the Imagining of Masculinities* (London, 1994); R. H. MacDonald, *The Language of Empire: Myths and Metaphors of Popular Imperialism, 1880–1918* (Manchester, 1994); K. Castle, *Britannia's Children: Reading Colonialism through Children's Books and Magazines* (Manchester, 1996).
7   John M. MacKenzie, 'David Livingstone: the construction of the myth', in G. Walker and T. Gallagher (eds), *Sermons and Battle Hymns: Protestant Popular Culture in Modern Scotland* (Edinburgh, 1990), pp. 24–42; John M. MacKenzie, 'T. E. Lawrence: the myth and the message', in R. Giddings (ed.), *Literature and Imperialism* (Manchester, 1991), pp. 150–81; John M. MacKenzie, 'Heroic myths of empire', in John M. MacKenzie (ed.), *Popular Imperialism and the Military: 1850–1950* (Manchester, 1992), pp. 109–37; MacDonald, *Language of Empire*, esp. chapter 3.
8   The Irish response to the Antarctic disaster is beyond the scope of this chapter, which will focus on England, Scotland and Wales.
9   Scott Polar Research Institute, Cambridge (hereafter SPRI), MS 1453/61, Draft of agreement between R. F. Scott and Central News, no date (1910).
10 SPRI, MS 559/11, A. Cherry-Garrard diary, 28 Jan. 1913. The committee comprised Lt. E. R. G. R. Evans; Surgeon E. L. Atkinson; Lt. H. L. L. Pennell; Lt. V. L. A. Campbell; Lt. W. M. Bruce; and Francis Drake, Assistant Paymaster.
11 *The Times*, 11 Feb. 1913, p. 8.
12 *Manchester Guardian*, 15 Feb. 1913, p. 10.
13 SPRI, MS 1453/40, *Newport Advertiser*, no date.
14 *Wide-World Magazine*, Aug. 1913, p. 8.
15 'Circulation of the *Daily Mirror*', *Circulation Manager*, Feb. 1914, p. 17.
16 Magdalene College, Cambridge, W. R. Inge diary, vol. 24, 14 Feb. 1913.
17 *British Weekly*, 20 Feb. 1913, p. 610.
18 *The Times*, 20 Feb. 1913, p. 6.
19 SPRI, MS 1464/5, 'Captain Scott Fund – Report of the Committee', July 1913.
20 W. Soulsby, 'Mansion House Funds', *The Times* 'City of London' number, part 1, 8 Nov. 1927, pp. xii–xiii.
21 SPRI, MS 2, L. Beaumont letter to K. Scott, 6 May 1913.
22 SPRI, MS 1453/40, 5th List of donations, 27 Feb. 1913.
23 *The Times*, 19 Mar. 1913, p. 12.
24 *The Times*, 22 Feb. 1913, p. 5; Public Record Office, London (hereafter PRO), T164/404, 'British Antarctic Expedition', no date (Feb.–April 1913).
25 SPRI, MS 1464/5, 'Scott Fund Report'.
26 R. Huntford, *Scott and Amundsen* (London, 1993), p. 563–64; R. Huntford, *Shackleton* (London, 1996), pp. 360–62; L. Bloom, *Gender on Ice: American Ideologies of Polar Expeditions* (Minneapolis, 1993), pp. 13–14, 113–14, 117, 128; C. Alexander, *The Endurance: Shackleton's Legendary Antarctic Expedition* (London, 1998), p. 9.
27 L. Huxley (arr.), *Scott's Last Expedition*, 2 vols. (London, 1913).

28 A cheap edition was not published until the 1920s.

29 I have compared the published version with *The Diaries of Captain Robert Falcon Scott: a Record of the Second Antarctic Expedition 1910–12 – vol. vi Sledging Diaries November 1911–March 1912, British Museum Add. Mss. 51033, 51034, 51035* (Tyler's Green, Bucks., 1968). The journals were arranged for publication by Leonard Huxley of Smith Elder and Apsley Cherry-Garrard, a member of the expedition, with some additional assistance from Scott's friend, J. M. Barrie.

30 W. Sinclair, *Memorials of St Paul's Cathedral* (London, 1909), chapters xxxi–xxxii. See also S. Daniels, *Fields of Vision: Landscape Imagery and National Identity in England and the United States* (Cambridge, 1993), ch. 1.

31 St Paul's Cathedral, London, W. R. Inge scrapbook 'St Paul's, 1911–24', orders of service.

32 For example *Pall Mall Gazette*, 14 Feb. 1913, p. 1.

33 Hennell, 'St Paul's, February 14'. The poem was set to music by Lady Barrett Lennard and published by Novello under the title 'Gallant gentlemen all!'.

34 SPRI, MS 1453/40, *Star*, no date.

35 SPRI, uncatalogued folder of ephemera concerning *Discovery* and *Terra Nova* expeditions, A. L. Machen, 'The immortal story of Captain Scott's expedition'.

36 SPRI, MS 1453/40, *Evening News*, 12 Feb. 1913.

37 A. L. Machen, author, folklorist and actor, joined the *Evening News* in 1910. He invented the story of the 'Angel of Mons' at the beginning of the First World War.

38 Greater London Record Office, London County Council Education Committee minutes, 12 Feb. 1913, p. 222.

39 Department of Western Manuscripts, Bodleian Library, Oxford, MS Asquith 7, Cabinet letters 1913–14.

40 Royal Geographical Society, London (hereafter RGS), 'R. F. Scott correspondence block, 1911–20: file j', J. S. Keltie letter to G. N. Curzon, 13 Feb. 1913.

41 SPRI, MS 1464/5, 'Scott Fund Report'. A bronze memorial tablet by S. Nicholson Babb was unveiled in St Paul's on 5 May 1916. The polar research fund financed the establishment of the Scott Polar Research Institute in Cambridge in the 1920s.

42 PRO, WORKS 10/121, L. Earle letter to W. Soulsby, 9 July 1914.

43 The most detailed description of the statue, written by Soulsby, appeared in *The Times*, 11 July 1914, p. 6.

44 SPRI, MS 559/76/1, A. Hodge letter to A. Cherry-Garrard, 15 July 1914.

45 SPRI, MS 2, L. Beaumont letter to K. Scott, 14 Sept. 1914.

46 RGS, 'R. F. Scott corr. file g', D. Freshfield letter to T. Brock, 21 Aug. 1914.

47 SPRI, MS 1464/5, 'Scott Fund Report'.

48 *Parliamentary Debates* (H. L.), 5th series, vol. xiv, 6 Aug. 1913, cols. 1628–9.

49 India Office, London, Mss Eur F 112/53, W. Soulsby letter to G. N. Curzon, 3 Nov. 1913.

50 PRO, WORKS 20/121, L. Earle letter to W. Soulsby, 19 Dec. 1922 and reply, 20 Dec. 1922.

51 PRO, WORKS 20/121, Secretary to HM War Office letter to L. Earle, 30 Apr. 1923.

52 For a full list of memorials see M. H. Jones, 'The R.G.S. and the Commemoration of Captain Scott's last Antarctic Expedition', Ph.D. dissertation, University of Cambridge, 2000.

53 *Church Times*, 7 Nov. 1913, p. 649; *Stratford Herald*, 1 Oct. 1915.

54 SPRI, MS 1464/23, G. D. Robin letter to Hannah Scott, 5 Apr. 1913.

55 *Eton Chronicle*, 28 May 1914, pp. 569–70; G. Seaver, *Edward Wilson of the Antarctic: Naturalist and Friend* (London, 1933), pp. 11–12.

56 'Memorials to the Antarctic heroes', *Geographical Journal*, 44 (1914), 214–16.

57 A. M. Johnson, *Scott of The Antarctic and Cardiff* (Cardiff, 1995), pp. 46–63.

58 SPRI, MS 1464/23, E. Bowers letter to Lady Macartney, 12 Feb. 1914.

59   RGS, 'R. F. Scott corr. file b', Invitation to ceremony, 27 Oct. 1915.
60   A. W. Yarrington, *The Commemoration of the Hero: Monuments to the British Victors of the Napoleonic Wars* (London, 1988); A. Warren's chapter in this volume; A. King, *Memorials of the Great War in Britain* (Oxford, 1998).
61   *The Times*, 5 June 1913, p. 5. Churchill chaired Commander Evans's first public lecture on the expedition.
62   The Chief Rabbi, Dr Hertz, spoke of his hope that 'military virtues would no longer be glorified, that the non-military virtues – those displayed by Captain Scott for example – the non-military virtues will be glorified and force will no longer be resorted to', *Herald of Peace and International Arbitration: the Organ of the Peace Society*, 2 June 1913, p. 43.
63   R. F. Scott, 'Plan of the British Antarctic Expedition, 1910', *Geographical Journal*, 36 (1910), 12.
64   'The British Antarctic Expedition', *Nature*, 13 Feb. 1913, p. 650.
65   See, for example, C. R. Markham, 'Robert Falcon Scott', *Geographical Journal*, 41 (1913), 220.
66   See, among many, J. Harris, *Private Lives, Public Spirit: a Social History of Britain, 1870–1914* (Oxford, 1993).
67   R. F. Scott, 'Plan of the British Antarctic Expedition, 1910', pp. 11–12.
68   *Daily Mirror*, 13 Feb. 1913, p. 7.
69   R. Baden-Powell, *The Scout*, 31 Jan. 1914, p. 515.
70   *Captain Scott's Message to England* (London, 1913).
71   I examined the *Daily Chronicle, Daily Express, Daily Graphic, Daily Mail, Daily Mirror, Daily News and Leader, Daily Sketch, Daily Telegraph, Evening News, Manchester Guardian, Pall Mall Gazette, Scotsman* and *The Times*.
72   J. S. Ellis, 'Reconciling the Celt: British national identity, empire, and the 1911 investiture of the Prince of Wales', *Journal of British Studies*, 37 (1998), 391–418, has recently emphasised the inclusive character of the investiture ceremony of 1911.
73   SPRI, MS 1453/40, unnamed newspaper cutting, no date; Johnson, *Scott of The Antarctic and Cardiff*, p. 50.
74   For the language of character see S. Collini, *Public Moralists: Political Thought and Intellectual Life in Modern Britain, 1850–1930* (Oxford, 1991).
75   *Daily Graphic*, 13 Feb. 1913, p. 1; *Daily Mail*, 11 Feb. 1913, p. 6; *Daily Mirror*, 15 Feb. 1913, p. 3.
76   *Daily Sketch*, 15 Feb. 1913, p. 1.
77   SPRI, MS 1464/23, A. Winnington-Ingram letter to Lady Ellison Macartney, 18 Feb. 1913.
78   'These were men', *Manchester Guardian*, 12 Feb. 1913, p. 6.
79   *John Bull*, 10 May 1913, p. 685.
80   'A fight against fatality', *Daily Mail*, 12 Feb. 1913, p. 4; *Westminster Gazette*, 13 Feb. 1913, p. 2; 'The hero as explorer', *Nation*, 8 Nov. 1913, p. 260.
81   *Clarion*, 4 Apr. 1913, p. 4.
82   'Other Poles to be reached', *Daily Herald*, 17 Feb. 1913, p. 10.
83   H. Russell Smart, 'Scott's last message', *Daily Herald*, 15 Feb. 1913, p. 6.
84   *Vote*, 14 Feb. 1913, p. 2.
85   C. Pankhurst, 'Above the law', *Suffragette*, 14 Feb. 1913, p. 274.
86   *Suffragette*, 20 June 1913, p. 602.
87   *Bioscope*, 26 Feb. 1914, p. 942.
88   *Daily Express*, 17 Feb. 1913, p. 2.
89   *Daily Telegraph*, 15 Feb. 1913, p. 11.
90   See S. Kern, *The Culture of Time and Space, 1880–1918* (London, 1983).
91   The entrepreneur Richard Branson made four attempts to circumnavigate the world by balloon in the 1990s.

Baden-Powell : two lives of a hero, or two heroic lives?[1]

In December 1995, Channel Four's *Secret Lives* series took as its subject Robert Baden-Powell, Boer War hero of the defence of Mafeking, and later founder of the Boy Scouts and Girl Guides. In making the film, Dai Richards used material from the authoritative biography by Tim Jeal, which had subjected Baden-Powell's extraordinary life and career to psycho-historical analysis. With the help of a consultant psychiatrist, the programme suggested that the driving force of its subject's personality lay in a craving for maternal affection and in a Peter Pan-like desire never to grow up, elements which were combined with a repressed homosexuality and traces of sado-masochism. The programme was made by an experienced documentary maker, and the film company was well-established and reputable. Baden-Powell was not the only 'famous' figure to be subjected to critical scrutiny in the series; earlier life-stories by other film makers had also dismantled the reputations of Marie Stopes, the Duke of Windsor, and Princess Margaret. Finally, the film included engaging comment on Baden-Powell's life by his daughter, and from some of those who had also known him personally, as well as an appreciative and positive summary by Tim Jeal himself.[2]

Despite these counter-balancing features, the documentary was almost universally disliked by the critics. The television critic of the *Sunday Times* was simply one of the more extreme examples:

> This programme was a desperately po-faced, politically correct outing of the founder of the scout movement, one of those under-the-skin, behind-the-psyche, in-the-knicker-drawer bits of invasion that have sold so many written biographies in the last 10 years and are now becoming the staple of television. Last week, we saw the Duke of Windsor and Marie Stopes have their pants pulled down and their privates inspected. Baden-Powell is an awfully big soft target. There was a pretty comprehensively nasty biography of him a couple of years ago and, really, what is Armani man to make of an old geezer in shorts and a lot of little boys today? Say no

more. A woggle's as good as a winkle to a blind Baloo. We were depress-
ingly assured that the siege of Mafeking had nothing to do with what any
of the people involved in it imagined, it was actually all about racism and
abusing black people, and that scouting was really all repressed homosexuality, class war and incipient fascism. These matt-black, Groucho club
insights are so tediously, yawningly, fashionably obvious that one wonders
why they bother. The palpable fact that Baden-Powell used his fame to
bring enormous joy to millions with the best intentions in the world was
uncomfortably alluded to and then left so that we could get back to the
really important stuff like sex and class and social engineering.[3]

All of this is pretty extraordinary. Baden-Powell had died in 1941, and
his most famous military exploit, the defence of Mafeking was nearing its
centenary. The Scout and Guide movements had long outgrown the early
vision of their founder as expressed in his handbook, *Scouting for Boys*
(1908), and had become integral parts of their local and national communities, not just in Britain and its former Empire, but throughout the
developed and developing world. At the moment of the film's making, both
movements were re-establishing themselves rapidly in the former Soviet
Union and eastern Europe, after decades of prohibition.

This chapter takes as its starting point the title of William Hillcourt's
official biography (written with the help of Baden-Powell's widow, Olave
(1889–1977), *Baden-Powell: The Two Lives of a Hero* (1964), with its assumption that its subject had some unique mix of personal qualities that enabled
him to lead two such extraordinary lives. It asks whether it is not better
to see Baden-Powell more as a man with an almost dual personality, each
half of which was made heroic more by circumstance and timing than by
any inherent mix of personal qualities or talents, and through which he
became the vehicle of society's values and concerns. In attempting to understand his public status, it re-examines the nature of that popular reputation
following the relief of Mafeking in May 1900, and how it was used by
Baden-Powell and others, enabling him to launch a highly idiosyncratic
training movement for boys eight years later. It then shows how the numer-
ical success of the Boy Scouts, and later the Girl Guides, had the effect
of transforming Baden-Powell's public reputation from that of imperial
adventurer to that of world citizen for peace and reconciliation, a position
acknowledge in 1920 by his nomination as Chief Scout of the World.
Finally, it looks at how those two heroic reputations have continued to be
issues of contemporary influence and interest and why the *Secret Lives*
programme could still agitate critics well-used to the public's taste for journalistic exposure.

Two contemporary press cuttings point up the contrast in Baden-
Powell's public reputation:

He is appalling in his versatility ... He is a bachelor and an all round good fellow.

(*Birmingham Daily Post*, 19 May 1900)

If any of us were asked to name the man, or the woman, who in our lifetime has rendered the greatest service to the rising generation, we should find it difficult to find an alternative to Lord Baden-Powell. The creation of the Boy Scouts – with their counterpart the Girl Guides – was his work and his alone ... that is surely an achievement to which it is hard to suggest a parallel.

(*The Times*, 9 January 1941)

The story of Baden-Powell's early life and military career is now familiar through Jeal's comprehensive biography. Similarly, the siege of Mafeking from September 1899 until May 1900, its daily rhythms, its military insignificance, and Baden-Powell's personal role have all received detailed analysis, both positive and hostile. It is interesting that among Victorian military heroes – Havelock, Gordon, Roberts – it should be Baden-Powell who continues to attract such detailed scholarly attention. Jeal's balanced assessment of the seige, of Baden-Powell's contribution and style as a commander, and of his treatment of those beseiged, both black and white, is unlikely to be superseded. After 219 days of isolation, the unofficial news of the town's relief by Colonel Mahon provoked unparalleled scenes of patriotic rejoicing in Britain, the Empire, and in other parts of the English-speaking world. These celebrations (which Churchill noted as more exuberant than those which followed the signing of the Armistice in 1918), were as widespread and surprising as the spontaneous reactions to the death of Diana, Princess of Wales ninety-seven years later. They have been little studied, either as public events or as expressions of popular feelings or values. Mafeking night (or nights and days would be more accurate) is usually quoted as the standard example of the growth of late nineteenth-century imperial and military enthusiasm. If particular celebrations are cited, it is to repeat the newspaper reports relating to the City of London and the West End. Only Richard Price has used Mafeking crowds to support his argument that jingoist enthusiasm was particularly reflected among the lower middle class.[4]

Mafeking celebrations deserve more extended treatment than is appropriate for the purposes of this chapter, but their range and variety, and the remarks upon them, help to define the public status being invested in the besieged town's insouciant commander. The general comment of the *Yorkshire Evening Press* for Saturday 19 May 1900 was typical; it noted that public enthusiasm was all the greater because of Mafeking's small size and military unimportance, and because the sufferings had been mainly endured by civilians and natives, 'a little band of heroes of both sexes, who with unswerving faith in their commander, and buoyed up, possibly more than they themselves knew, by his infectious spirit of cheerfulness and uncomplaining patience, have undergone for the honour of the Empire at the most isolated of all British posts'. The Bristol paper, the *Western Daily Press* noted on the same day: 'It was his personality, his audacity, his perennial cheerfulness, his gay humour, his reserve, his military skill that drew all eyes to Mafeking.'

Moving beyond these general explanations, the range, the variety and the spontaneity of the celebrations are their most striking features. Geographically, almost every village, town and city participated in the general rejoicing. These public celebrations were not officially orchestrated; indeed it was widely commented that no flags flew in Whitehall, because news of the relief had not been formally confirmed. In large cities, in particular, the popular rejoicing was quickly adopted and managed by the civic and religious authorities, once people began pouring out into the streets and made their way towards the city's centre. Processional routes were arranged, civic orations delivered, special religious services hurriedly put together and sermons preached. Half-day holidays for children were announced for the Monday, while workers took time off work for themselves. But these were reactions, not planned events, and those slow on the uptake found themselves under pressure, particularly if they suggested that adults should not take any holiday. Outside the large urban centres, celebrations were necessarily more improvised, and, in the smallest villages, church bells were rung, bunting paraded (doubtless left over from the Diamond Jubilee two years before), and processions held, following almost any available local band.[5]

The crowds, though sometime boisterous, were almost universally law-abiding, perhaps partly as a result of the participation of significant numbers of women, a point noted in the press. There were examples, not very many, of pro-Boer shopkeepers being attacked or having their shop windows broken and looted, but in the main the law-breaking was confined to drunkeness, which the magistrates treated with indulgence. In Bristol, interestingly, the crowd was described as more exuberant and less deferential than that which had greeted Queen Victoria on her visit to the city the previous November.

There also appears to have been little religious or denominational difference among those celebrating. At Halesowen in the West Midlands, the town's procession was led by the Primitive Methodist Band, while in the rather contrasting communities of Harrogate and Kirkbymoorside in Yorkshire, it was the local temperance bands that led the way. In Bristol, the Wesleyan Methodist preacher drew the attention of his congregation to the fact that like Baden-Powell, John Wesley had been an old Carthusian. Equally, when they could be mustered, local Volunteers and other patriotic bodies took a prominent role, but not to the exclusion of religious or other voluntary groups. In a number of towns, boys or young men's organisations took a prominent part, usually prompting favourable comment. Thus in Manchester, Owen's College students briefly took possession of the Royal Exchange, setting off crackers, before joining the main procession. In York, students from St John's College paraded through the city carrying lighted torches, while in Bristol, it was the Boys' Brigade that took a leading role in the march from the centre of the city to the Downs. Nor were the celebrants only from middle- or lower middle-class suburbs. Raucous sounding of klaxons by young men on bicycles characterised the celebration in the London districts of Poplar and Stepney, while in Bristol many of the crowds came from the poorer suburbs to the east of the city. In the west Yorkshire towns of Brighouse and Elland, the mills closed and boys dressed up in khaki and collected for local relief funds. Politically, too, the celebrations were seen as of a non-party nature. In Leeds, news of the relief was received at the Liberal Club with 'the utmost enthusiasm', while an attempt to give the rejoicing a party-political character in Huddersfield prompted hostile comment. The veteran radical M.P. Henry Broadhurst in a speech in Manchester distinguished carefully between his views about the war and his personal praise for Baden-Powell himself, while even *Reynolds News*, with its daily by-line, 'the Boer War – the Capitalists' War', commented that the defence of Mafeking had been 'as fine a thing as has been done in military history'.

In short, the Mafeking celebrations were popular, patriotic and imperial, politically, socially and denominationally wide-ranging, and reflected the civic and cultural variety of the communities from which they sprang. While not typical, the experience of the grimy town of Dudley in the West Midlands was representative, with its civic procession made up of named organisations as well as individual citizens: the Ambulance Corps, the Castletown Minster Troupe, St Thomas' Church Army Band, the Athletic Club, Christ Church Band, and the uniformed ranks of the local postmen. National newspapers caught the mood in trying to explain this totally unexpected outburst of national exuberance. Perhaps surprisingly, *The Times*, in its leader of 21 May, did not sound off with a sonorous paean of imperial jubilation, but commented:

> Apart from other considerations, there is a general feeling that Mafeking is an affair of the people rather than the army . . . Throughout the Empire it is instinctively felt that at Mafeking we have the common man of the Empire, the fundamental stuff of which the breed is built . . . the essential thing is the recognition, unconscious, perhaps . . . that we have here a demonstration of the fundamental grit of the breed, the unassailable qualities that have made the Empire, in spite of foolish generals and the secular ineptitude of officials.

Perhaps even more surprisingly, the *Manchester Guardian* of 19 May commented:

> And, indeed, in a sense the whole world is with us in our rejoicings over the relief of Mafeking. Heroes after their death are said to have no nationality, but to become citizens of the world. In this sense, Colonel Baden-Powell and his garrison . . . are men of whom the world may feel proud . . . And the story is all the more moving because the defence is the achievement not so much of professional soldiers as, to a great extent of men and women before the war we should not have been able to distinguish from the average Englishman in the colonies.

If the Mafeking celebrations are seen as a popular patriotic event, and as the medium by which idealised qualities of the 'breed' were endorsed, then the man at the centre of these rejoicings was seen as encapsulating all that was idealised; a sporting pluck and determination, a maverick and imaginative individualism, and a capacity to win out against the odds through wit, insouciance and skill. In a war dominated for the first time by popular journalism, all these qualities were attributed to Baden-Powell. For the rest of his life he remained, at least in part, a sporting, patriotic and popular British imperial hero, whose actions at Mafeking had prompted a more popular response than those of many 'greater' military or naval commanders.

In all the contemporary eulogies and the popular biographies that followed, it is important to identify the qualities that were *not* attributed to Baden-Powell, as well as the ones that were. Despite the idealised reminiscences provided by his former headmaster, Dr W.Haig Brown, Baden-Powell was not usually represented as exemplifying all that was best in a games playing public school elite. He was sporting, certainly, but more a characterful individualist than a team player; quick-witted, but not academic, more inclined to go out in search of adventure in the neighbouring woods than to listen to pie-jawing about leadership. Nor was he portrayed as an ideal officer and gentleman. In fact, as we have already seen in the extract quoted from *The Times*, his military qualities were counterposed to those of the brasshats, who had brought Britain's reputation to such a low ebb in Black Week the previous December. Once again, it was Baden-Powell's individual soldierly qualities that were highlighted: his scouting talents and ability to improvise and second-guess the enemy, his loyalty and dedication, his capacity to bring out the best in civilians as well as soldiers, and his lack of stuffiness or of concern for protocol, as shown in his eccentricities of dress and impulsive theatricality. Manly, again certainly, if that meant a concern for health and fitness, but not if it implied a rigid adherence to hierarchies, deference or elaborate codes of honour. If Baden-Powell was to join a pantheon of British military heroes, it would be in the company of Drake, Raleigh, Nelson, Lawrence, Wingate, Bader and, possibly, Montgomery, rather than Wellington, Roberts, Kitchener, Allenby or Mountbatten.[6]

Though Baden-Powell himself can have had no immediate knowledge of the scale or nature of the celebrations at home and around the world, his reputation was quickly exploited commercially. Memorabilia were on sale almost immediately; songs, marches, even a so-called 'descriptive Fantasia', were composed and published in his honour. Individual souvenirs of all kinds were produced; plates, mugs, rolling pins, paper weights, egg cups, mustard jars, and portraits on silk or linen. Items in metal were also manufactured; statuettes, horse brasses, pub tables, and, most bizarrely, a clothes mangle with an inset portrait of Baden-Powell in cast iron on the stand. Popular biographies were quickly published, using Baden-Powell's own earlier military and journalistic writing, recording his campaigns against the Ashanti and the Matabele, and supplemented by highly embellished accounts of his childhood and schooling, submitted by his mother and Dr Haig Brown. The general tone is reflected in the words of R. J. Bremner Smith: 'Writer, soldier, actor, athlete, sportsman and painter – he has something of each and all of these occupations. He is the beau ideal of the soldier, with the additional advantage of something of the romantic in his character. Here's luck to him.'[7]

Although home on sick leave between June 1901 and January 1902, Baden-Powell had little chance to take the measure of his new public status until his permanent return to England as Inspector-General of Cavalry in March 1903. Though its potential did not immediately become clear to him, his new posting gave him the opportunity to travel around the country and to appreciate the range of organisations, military as well as civilian and patriotic, that were anxious to secure his imprimatur. Tim Jeal and others have carefully traced the evolution of Baden-Powell's new training scheme, and how his ideas oscillated between the militaristic and the civic before settling in the form outlined in *Scouting for Boys*, published in fortnightly parts in early 1908. For the purposes of the present chapter, what is important is the process whereby Baden-Powell was able to ues the public's perception of him as a popular, patriotic hero so that within six years he could become the inspiration and the leader of a new youth training organisation with broad socio-cultural appeal to both boys and girls. By 1910 there were an estimated 100,000 Boy Scouts, challenging all the existing provision for boys and young men.

The Scouting phenomenon is easier to explain once the extent of Baden-Powell's public reputation as the hero of Mafeking is recognised. On his return from Africa, civic leaders around the country welcomed him to their cities, leaders of the religious denominations and organisations for moral reform sought his advice and endorsement. Interestingly, these requests often came more from the evangelical or nonconforming tradition rather than from the Anglican establishment; they came also from the Boys' Brigade, the Church of England Men's Society, the Young Men's Christian Association and the temperance and anti-smoking movements. Of course, his support was also sought by those with a more explicitly militaristic agenda – by public schools' Officer Training Corps, by those interested in the promotion of rifle-shooting, and most obviously by Lord Roberts and his National Service League, with its aim of securing the introduction of compulsory cadet training. Among those concerned with the moral and religious development of the young, it was Baden-Powell's emphasis on the training of the individual soldier through scouting and reconnaissance that proved attractive and adaptable to work in the local club, brigade, church or inter-denominational group.[8]

As a result of these various overtures, Baden-Powell gradually came to realise that he was more than a famous soldier. He had acquired a status that could open door among civic, ecclesiastical, landed and industrial patrons across the country, including the royal household; nor was he in the pocket of any particular interest group. Baden-Powell enjoyed this newly acquired public status, which vindicated his own self-image in contrast to the long years of professional frustration and family disappointment in the decade and a half before the Boer War. He was also well-suited to the new age of popular journalism for boys and adults alike. He brimmed over with ideas (not all of them consistent one with another), which he could present in a snappy form, he had skills as a popular artist and cartoonist, and he had established contacts with the press as a campaigning soldier. He liked the public occasion, its formality, theatricality and atmosphere of performance, which could draw on his abilities for mimicry and characterisation, giving him the chance to occupy centre-stage with all its potential for individuality and surprise. Until Mafeking these qualities had been confined to barracks. From Mafeking onwards they were vital supporting elements in the process by which Baden-Powell became the visionary youth leader, and, eventually, an evangelist for international harmony.

But, of themselves, these qualities were not enough. Baden-Powell may have had a public status, but he needed something else if he was to become more than a leading member of the military establishment, who could receive a popular hearing on matters of duty, discipline, and the future of the Empire. He needed a patron, and he had to find a way in which to present his ideas on boy training coherently and attractively. The first he found in Sir Arthur Pearson, publishing magnate, imperialist and enthusiast for child health and improvement. Baden-Powell was not a man experienced in civilian organisations, or in the ways of business, and Tim Jeal has shown the importance of Pearson's contribution in encouraging him to write *Scouting for Boys*, in supporting the experimental camp at Brownsea Island, and in launching the boys' paper, *The Scout*. He also bank-rolled the early Scout office organisation, and clearly was using his public hero for business as well as philanthropic purposes.

In style and presentation, both *Scouting for Boys* and *The Scout* showed their pedigrees in the popular adult and boys' literature of the time: short stories, snippets of advice, cartoons, puzzles and useful practical tips, all set in an imperial or frontier environment of world-wide adventure. *Scouting for Boys*, in particular, with its Camp Fire Yarns, nature stories, hints on camp and field craft, along with its advice on health and self-improvement at home and on the frontier, is a scrapbook of material from boys' comics, spy and detective fiction, and the writings of social and imperial pundits on the future of the race and the needs of youth. This combination was to be an outstanding publishing success. *Scouting for Boys* went through numerous editions and translations and was still selling 40,000 copies a year forty years later, making it according to Tim Jeal the most popular twentieth-century publication after The Bible. Almost at a stroke, it transformed Baden-Powell's reputation from that of popular patriotic hero into pundit and social visionary for youth.

Scouting for Boys has been dismissed by many commentators as the handbook of a defensive and anxiety-ridden military and social establishment. To see it merely as a product of a man concerned about imperial degeneration, fitness and social Darwinism, is, however, to ignore the book's imaginative individuality, which enabled it to transcend the immediate circumstances of its composition. It is original in two important respects, both of which derived from its author's own character and experience, and both of which help to explain how Baden-Powell was able to redefine his public status between 1908 and 1910. First, *Scouting for Boys* was scarcely a conventional training manual. It was idiosyncratic, and highly individualistic and unhierarchical, rejecting mass drill in favour of the development of the personal character of the soldier or scout through field craft and reconnaissance. In the non-military sphere, it connected youthful training and useful citizenship for the first time, and introduced the idea of play as a key element in engaging the attention of the boy himself. Nor was this play simply team games or sportsmanship, but a whole range of activities set in a recreative environment of camp or the outdoors. With its emphasis on character formation it was inherently flexible and, suitably adapted, appropriate for boys or young men, as well as for girls and young women. As an integrated training scheme, it brought together uniquely for its time the idea of individual personal self-development, civic preparedness and training, and outdoor education and play.

Secondly, Baden-Powell created an imaginative world within which this recreative training would take place, which drew heavily on his own personal feelings and experiences, and which also found a powerful resonance in the minds of those influenced by him, child and adult alike. His vision of camp life also tapped feelings of anti-urbanism, of a desire for a simpler, more 'natural' life, and of an unspoken pantheism – feelings constrained by the ecclesiological niceties and denominational differences of the existing training and moral improvement organisations for children. It also allowed a freedom from Edwardian social constraints (for both men and women), at times expressed through peculiarities of dress and ceremonial, which derived directly from Baden-Powell's own eccentric theatricality and fascination with display, and of which the Scout hat, the short trousers and Scout staff were only the most obvious and photogenic examples. *Scouting for Boys* allowed the boy to become an imperial frontiersman, the hero of a *Boys Own Paper* adventure, and Sherlock Holmes, all in a single week in camp. Later, younger boys as Wolf Cubs became the young Mowgli in the community of the jungle, playing safely under the watchful eyes of Akela, Bagheera, and Baloo. As his movements grew Baden-Powell also invented new forms of ritual for adults, which drew substantially on the woodcraft idioms he had learned from Ernest Thompson Seton and later John Hargrave, and which also used a remodelled chivalric motif of Arthurian dedication and service.

Scouting for Boys is therefore more than a tract of its times, although it is certainly that as well. It is a direct product of Baden-Powell's own personal experience and character. Just as his style and conduct at Mafeking had created a popular soldier-hero, who transcended military categories, so *Scouting for Boys* was a unique creation, which drew deeply on existing, if often divergent and contradictory social and cultural concerns, and which was able to secure a popular response beyond the existing workers with boys. Its publication gave Baden-Powell a new and powerful status above that of Lord Roberts, Ernest Thompson Seton, and William Smith.[9]

Scouting for Boys certainly made a difference. Within two years, there were an estimated 100,000 Boy Scouts in Britain, and girls and women were pressing Baden-Powell to set up a parallel training scheme for girls. Thereafter, Baden-Powell's life was almost exclusively devoted to the work of Scouting and, later, Guiding. Proclaimed Chief Scout of the World at Olympia in 1920, his two movements had an estimated five million members world-wide by 1939, and from 1918 until his death in 1941 he had the status of world citizen and prophet of international harmony through youthful brotherhood and reconciliation, a vision symbolically celebrated in the great four-yearly international camps, or jamborees, that have been held ever since. Honoured by almost every country in the world, nominated for the

Nobel Peace Prize, his reputation was unchallenged except by a few left-wing critics at home and by fascist and communist regimes abroad.[10]

How had this come about? Clearly, Baden-Powell had not anticipated such a response in writing his original training manual; it had been geared to a domestic market with its imperial themes prompting a response around the white Dominions. No one had anticipated its success in the United States, Europe, and, increasingly, in Africa and Asia. One explanation might be simply that Baden-Powell was a man for all seasons and that, just as *Scouting for Boys* had reflected the social preoccupations of 1908, so the popular growth of Scouting and Guiding on the ground just carried Baden-Powell in its wake. Such was his egoism, the argument might continue, and his lack of systematic thought that he could easily re-invent himself so as to remain at centre-stage of the two movements that had made him.

Baden-Powell was certainly adaptable, the magpie cast of his mind picked up each novel enthusiasm of the moment, prompting a quick sketch or idea. He was also sensitive to changing currents of educational thinking, to the enthusiasm for woodcraft, to the rise of post-war internationalism, and to the fad for fitness in the 1930s. All were grist to the mill of Scouting and Guiding, movements which reflected the diversity and contradictions within his own character, and apart from which Baden-Powell, and later his wife, had little separate personal identity; they were Chief Scout and Guide, first, second and last. By the same token the weaknesses of the Scout and Guide ideologies were theirs also; a failure fully to understand the significance of differences of race, class and gender in contrasting societies around the world, a naive belief in the power of pulling together to make a better world, and an almost complete disregard for the necessity of the political process in resolving disputes and making progress. As a result their movements faltered in the 1930s. Apparently reaching the limits of their expansion at home, they were challenged abroad by the complex cultural and racial politics of India and South Africa. Failing to understand fully the threat posed by Fascism and National Socialism, they were often too ready to warn of the dangers of Soviet Communism.[11]

Having said this, and recognising that Baden-Powell's second heroic life was the unexpected result of the success of the Scouts and Guides, it is still true that both movements directly reflected the characteristic inputs of their Founder. If Baden-Powell's role in the defence of Mafeking created one sort of British hero, his contribution to the dynamic development of the two largest youth organisations in the free world created another giving him an international status. While it is almost impossible to separate Baden-Powell from the movements he founded after 1910, the flexibility of his training scheme and his personal identification with it helps to explain how he and his wife could be accepted easily as Chief Scout of the World and World Chief Guide in the internationalist environment after 1920.

As a training scheme it contained a number of paradoxical elements. It was inherently flexible with a disciplined individualism that could appeal to traditionalist and reformer alike, while the emphasis on good character was also a concept simultaneously flexible and hard-edged, capable of being used in single-sex and co-educational environments. The scheme could similarly transcend differences of religious denomination or faith, and could take root in very different racial cultures, simultaneously being regarded as both in the vanguard of reform and as supporting the existing system. There was, also, the focus on civic service and a social ethics of an explicit, but non-mandatory kind. Scout and Guide organisations around the world were often close to the state, but could not be subsumed within it, and as such they could be seen as supporting the varieties of democracy, even if those democracies were not fully free. Similarly the outdoor emphasis, and the social ideology of the camp as a distinctive training environment, was a feature which seems to have had a global appeal for most of the century. Scouts and Guides do not meet and express their solidarity in meetings, or congresses, or through the passing of resolutions; they gather together in great multi-national world camps, in visual statements of their common humanity, and as advertisements for their collective ideologies. Baden-Powell did not invent the camp, but he certainly invented the idea of an international jamboree of Scouts and Guides. Finally, Baden-Powell brought many of these training ideas together in the notion that youth could make a difference. While much of his thinking was socially and politically conformist, its fundamental individualism implied, not only that the solitary or Lone Scout could fashion a better life for himself, but also that the massed ranks of Scouts and Guides could create a better world, despite politicians, brass-hats and grey-beards. In doing so it contributed significantly to the strands of thinking, which later led to the World College movement, Voluntary Service Overseas, Community Service Volunteers and the Peace Corps.[12]

These latter elements touched profound feelings in the decade after 1918, and can be seen in the press comment on the Scout international gatherings held in 1920, 1924 and 1929. At the first, where Baden-Powell was proclaimed as Chief Scout of the World, *The Times* pre-featured the boys 'League of Nations' about to gather at Olympia, and endorsed the youthful exuberance seen in the displays as a welcome contrast to the conformity of manners before 1914:

> The natural instincts of boys and girls have the same purposive basis, but the Gradgrinds of the Victorian Age tried to repress them and replace them by a monotonous acquirement of knowledge. The Boy Scout movement,

as conceived by Sir Robert Baden-Powell, is a return to a natural education. It aims at drawing out from boys the best that is in them ... Self
help and service to others become complementary. Individualism is trained,
but finds its greatest advantage as a contribution to the common good.

Four years later, *The Times* commented in its leader on the Scout movement: 'It is in the widest sense international. It is essentially an organisation
for the promotion of peace. Only the most sour of its critics can detect
the cloven hoof of militarism.' Again five years later, at the 'Coming of Age
Jamboree' at Arrowe Park, outside Birkenhead, which was attended by five
thousand Scouts from around the world, *The Times* featured the event on
five successive days with headlines of 'World Youth Shows the Way : a
World Without Barriers', 'Youth's Inspiring Pageant', 'Prince's Clarion Call
to Youth', and 'Here is a Power for Peace'. Its feature on the first day had
set the tone, 'There is something about this gathering of the youth of the
world which makes the pulse beat faster, and makes one envisage a world
with its peoples of all nations living together in harmony and in one accord.'
It is probably still true, seventy years later, that the four-yearly World Scout
Jamborees are the largest single gatherings of young people that regularly
take place.[13]
     By the time of his death, and as earlier obituary notices indicated,
Baden-Powell's exemplary status had been transformed. While the defender
of the town of Mafeking might still be seen as demonstrating the best in
British qualities, he was now regarded as one of the very few world citizens, who through his own very individual creations of the Scout and Guide
movements had set down models of international, youthful humanity acting
as examples of what could be achieved, and as a contrast to the sordid
concerns of the existing adult world. If the model seemed simplistic or
naive to such a world, so much more powerful was its implied message.[14]
     In the more than fifty years since his death, Baden-Powell's reputation
has inevitably faded, although as the responses to the *Secret Lives*
programme showed, it still has a greater charge than that of almost any
other late Victorian hero. For the most part, the problem (if it is so defined)
of Baden-Powell's legacy is one confined to the Scout and Guide Associations
themselves, and how they treat their Founder. At the most basic level, this
was made uncomplicated since he died in Kenya and was buried there,
making it difficult to create shrines or centres of pilgrimage. As a lesser
alternative, Gilwell Park, the Scout international training and woodcraft
centre in Epping Forest, from which Baden-Powell took his title, became
for some a place where 'the spirit of Scouting' continued to burn most
fiercely.
     The question of maintaining the Founder's ideals was more problem-
atic. Baden-Powell had wanted his family to exemplify Scouting values, and

his widow, Olave, thirty-five years his junior, certainly saw it as her role to maintain and perpetuate her late husband's image. She kept up until shortly before her death in 1977 a continuous progress around the world as the World Chief Guide, enthusing volunteer adults and young alike, and serving as constant reminder of her husband's achievement. As for their children, not all could live up to their parental expectations of them as the ideal members of Scouting's first family, and Peter, their only son, found his father's reputation a particularly burdensome inheritance.[15]

As the memories of Balden-Powell faded, the use and invocation of his founding authority became problematic for the movement's post-war leadership. Lady Baden-Powell clearly thought towards the end of her life that the United Kingdom Scout Association insufficiently revered the achievements and vision of her husband, and found alterations in the language of the Scout Law and Promise especially distressing. On the other hand, both the UK Scout and Guide Associations, have given representatives of the Baden-Powell family a privileged status. Patience, the present Lady Baden-Powell, was Commonwealth Chief Commissioner for Guides between 1980 and 1985, while her husband, the present Lord Baden-Powell, was being seriously canvassed in 1981 as a candidate to succeed Sir William Gladstone as Chief Scout. Part of those discussions focussed on the issue of whether the Scout Association should continue to seek its national leadership from among the Founder's family.[16]

More significant than questions of familial apostolic succession within both Associations are those of constitutionality. The unique position of the Chief Scout within the UK Scout Association continues to reflect the custom and practice of Baden-Powell's own lifetime, in which the Chief Scout has little formal power under the Association's Royal Charter (subsequently amended), but was, by custom, expected to provide inspiration and leadership to the movement. On the other hand, the formal responsibility for the affairs of the Association lies in the hands of an elected executive committee of its Council members, creating a confusing relationship with the potential for discord. For the most part, while the Scout and Guide Associations reflect in their deeper constitutional assumptions and practices the ideology and practice of their Founder, this is little appreciated by contemporary volunteers, who simply assume that is the way the movements do things.[17]

Nevertheless, both Associations, do use the heroic status of the 'Founder' and his life for didactic and political purposes. During his life, frequent reprintings of *Scouting for Boys*, published selections from his voluminous other writings, and new or re-used short journalistic pieces in which Baden-Powell deployed illustrations from his own experience, all had the effect of drawing attention back to his own life. Since his death, *Scouting for*

Boys and his other writings remain core texts, not so much as the movement's definitive training manuals, but as a quarry for authoritative extracts
to support contemporary arguments.The Scout Law and Promise, as originally drafted by Baden-Powell, remains the fundamental basis of the
Scouting and Guiding 'philosophy'; its paralleling of the Old and New
Testament, with its ten Laws (originally nine) and shorter Promise, reinforces its defining status. Not surprisingly, attempts to amend or modernise
its content and language provoke considerable introspective heart-searching
in both movements. Finally, the distinctive uniforms, with their badges,
beads, cords and thongs, plumes, tabs, staves, hats and shorts (much modified in the UK since the late 1960s), along with the distinctive ceremonies
of Investiture, Scouts' Owns (non-denominational forms of worship), Camp
Fires and chivalric Vigils, act as reminders of Baden-Powell's idiosyncratic
and theatrical personality. Modification and updating occur, but the debates
around these changes in public identity remind the present-day leadership
of the Founder's contribution. Finally, the language of authority is a continuing reminder of the movement's pedigree. From early in the movement's
development, Baden-Powell was known as 'The Chief', and from the 1920s,
he and his wife were referred to as 'The Two Chiefs' within the two movements. After his death, the title continued among his peers as 'The Old
Chief'. Within the United Kingdom national association, the title Chief
Scout is still used, and only recently the Guide Association has substituted
the title of Chief Guide for Chief Commissioner. Outside the United
Kingdom, different rules and conventions apply. Baden-Powell's successors
(Lords Somers, Rowallan, and Sir Charles (later Lord) Maclean) continued
to be Chief Scouts of the Commonwealth until 1975 but not of the World.
Nevertheless, different national associations continued to give iconic status
to Baden-Powell himself, and it was a perception of the greater reverence
shown by the Boy Scouts of America to the memory of her husband that
led Olave, Lady Baden-Powell, to donate a large part of her husband's artefacts and archives to them in the 1970s.[18]

Outside those involved in the work of the Associations, Baden-Powell's
status remained largely unquestioned for nearly thirty years after his death.
The Scouts and their Founder had, of course, been objects of the cartoonist's
art and of the musical hall gag from the outset. But it was not until the
late 1960s that social commentators and academic historians began to
re-examine the life and attitudes of the hero of Mafeking. A whole succession of studies appeared to dismantle his exemplary status. His military
capacities and administrative conduct at Mafeking were questioned, while
the intentions lying behind the writing of *Scouting for Boys* were increasingly placed within an academic context, which saw Edwardian England as
a beleaguered society in social and political terms. Tim Jeal's authoritative

and exhaustive biography, published in 1989, appeared to bring the process of re-assessment to a conclusion, in which he fairly and in great detail examined the Mafeking seige and the writing of *Scouting for Boys*, placing both within a convincing and sympathetic portrayal of an individual life. All of which makes the reaction to the *Secret Lives* documentary, with which this chapter began, the more surprising. It was not so much that there was no material on which to base a revisionist portrait. Baden-Powell's attitudes to race, for instance, especially during his military career, continue to attract scholarly attention, and it is clear that he probably retained Anglo-Saxonist assumptions throughout his life.[19] What clearly irritated the critics was not so much the revisionism itself (there were nothing like the same protests about other figures featured in the series) but rather its psychological method. It was not that Baden-Powell remained a too-heroic figure to be touched by revisionism (Churchill, after all, had been through many a revisionist mill), but that a public reputation was taken as being diminished or compromised by a Freudian reading of his upbringing and character. In this particular case, the critics seemed to be saying that public and private scrutiny should not be intertwined in the way that the programme intended. Public achievements and private feeling should be regarded as separate spheres, especially when those achievements were visible in every local community.

Notes

1   The author would like to thank The Scout Association and The Guide Association for permission to consult material in their keeping, and in particular Mr. Paul Moynihan and Mrs Margaret Courteney and their staff in their respective archives departments. He would also like to thank his co-editor for his constructive comments on earlier drafts.

2   For background on Baden-Powell's life and career, T. Jeal, *Baden-Powell* (London, 1989); J. Springhall, *Youth, Empire and Society: British Youth Movements, 1883–1940* (London, 1977); M. Rosenthal, *The Character Factory: Baden-Powell and the Origins of the Boy Scout Movement* (London 1986); R. H. MacDonald, *Sons of the Empire: the Frontier and the Boy Scout Movement, 1890–1918* (Toronto, 1993); T. Pakenham, *The Boer War* (London, 1979); A. Warren, 'Sir Robert Baden-Powell, the Scout Movement and citizen training in Great Britain, 1900–1920', *English Historical Review*, CI (1986), pp. 376–99, A. Warren, 'Citizens of the Empire: Baden-Powell, Scouts, Guides and an Imperial Ideal', in John M. MacKenzie (ed.), *Imperialism and Popular Culture* (Manchester, 1986), pp. 232–57; A. Warren, 'Popular manliness: Baden-Powell, Scouting and the development of manly character', in J. A. Mangan and J. Walvin (eds), *Manliness and Morality: Middle Class Masculinity in Britain and America, 1880–1940* (Manchester, 1987), pp. 199–220; A. Warren, '" Mothers for the Empire ?": The Girl Guides Association in Britain, 1909–1939', in J. A. Mangan (ed.), *Making Imperial Mentalities: Socialisation and British Imperialism* (Manchester, 1990), pp. 96–110; B. Willan, 'The Siege of Mafeking', in P. Warwick (ed.), *The South African War: the Anglo-Boer War, 1899–1902* (London, 1980), pp. 139–60.

3   *Sunday Times*, 10 Dec. 1995.

4   W. S. Churchill, *Great Contemporaries* (London, pbk. 1959), p. 298; R. Price, 'Society,
    status and jingoism: the social roots of lower middle class patriotism, 1870–1900',
    in G. Crossick (ed.), *The Lower Middle Class in Britain, 1870–1914* (London, 1977),
    pp. 89–112. Since writing, the author has had the benefit of reading Kit Good,
    '"Perfect Saturnalia" – Mafeking Night in Huddersfield and Lancaster', University
    of Lancaster M.A. thesis, 1998, which among other themes highlighted draws atten-
    tion to a distinctively civic element in the celebrations.

5   Examples are taken from the provincial press in the days following the news of
    the relief: *Birmingham Daily Post*, 19, 21, 22 May 1900; *Bristol Times and Mirror*,
    19, 21 May 1900; *Leeds Mercury*, 19, 21 May 1900; *Manchester Guardian*, 19, 21 May
    1900.

6   W. F. Aitken, *Baden-Powell* (London, 1900); H. Begbie, *The Story of Baden-Powell:
    the Wolf that Never Sleeps* (London, 1900); J. S. Fletcher, *Baden-Powell of Mafeking*
    (London, 1900); R. J. Bremner Smith, *Col. R.S.S. Baden-Powell* (Soldiers of the
    Queen Library, London, 1900); anon, *The Hero of Mafeking* (London, 1900).

7   P. Oosthuizen, *Boer War Memorabilia: the Collector's Guide* (London, 1987); quota-
    tion from Bremner Smith, *Col. R.S.S. Baden-Powell*, p. 16.

8   For background to the Scouting movement see footnote 2 above.

9   For secondary background see footnote 2 above. Also Lieut.-General R. S. S. Baden-
    Powell, *Scouting for Boys: a Handbook for Instruction in Good Citizenship* (London,
    1908); his *Yarns for Boy Scouts* (London, 1909), *Scouting Games* (London, 1910), and
    with A. Baden-Powell, *Handbook for Girl Guides* (London, 1912).

10 Figures of membership are derived from the annual reports of the Girl Guides
    Association (now the Guide Association) and from L. Nagy, *250 Million Scouts*,
    (Chicago and London, 1985). Baden-Powell's international status was marked by his
    treatment during his world travels. In April 1926, after he had been received at the
    White House, Baden-Powell and President Coolidge jointly attended the National
    Council of the Boy Scouts of America. Within the British Empire, the Baden-
    Powells would usually stay at Government House, and on the Scout and Guide
    cruises in the 1930s, for instance on the *S.S. Calgaric* in 1933, they were received
    either by a member of the Royal Family or by the Head of State in each of the
    Baltic countries visited. In countries within the Empire, such as India and South
    Africa, ethnic or religious differences within Scouting and Guiding were a matter
    of concern for the civil authorities and visits by the Baden-Powells were used to
    try to effect a reconciliation, in the case of India in early 1921 at the request of
    the Viceroy, Lord Chelmsford. See W. Hillcourt with Olave, Lady Baden-Powell,
    Baden-Powell: Two Lives of a Hero (London, 1964), pp. 368–69, 376–77, 390–91;
    E. Wade, *Olave Baden-Powell, the Authorised Biography of the World Chief Guide*
    (London, 1971), pp. 88–89.

11 Jeal, *Baden-Powell*, pp. 488–566; Warren, 'Citizens of the Empire', 'Popular
    Manliness', 'Mothers for the Empire'.

12 See Baden-Powell's Last Message, found among his papers after his death, reprinted
    in *Scouting for Boys*, 35th edition (London, 1991), p. 274.

13 Extracts from *The Times*, 9 Aug. 1920 p. 11d; 1 Aug. 1924, p. 13c; 31 July to 5 Aug.
    1929 (quotation from 31 July, p. 5a).

14 See the account of Baden-Powell's presence at the World Jamboree in the
    Netherlands in July 1937 in Hillcourt, *Baden-Powell: Two Lives of a Hero*, pp. 402–05.

15 Jeal, *Baden-Powell*, pp. 518–53; Olave, Lady Baden-Powell, *Window on My Heart:
    the Autobiography of Olave, Lady Baden-Powell, G.B.E.*, as told to M. Drewery
    (London, 1973); Wade, *Olave Baden-Powell*.

16 Personal knowledge.

17 The Boy Scouts Association Royal Charter 1912, and subsequently amended, Scout
    Association Archives.

18   For the major writings of Baden-Powell after the publication of *Scouting for Boys*,
      see Jeal, *Baden-Powell*, p. 591. For the many editions of *Scouting for Boys* and the
      mass of Baden-Powell's other writings in *The Scout, The Headquarters' Gazette* (later
      The Scouter), and his responses to journalistic invitations, see the Scout Association
      Archives.

19   For evidence of Baden-Powell's racial assumptions see his early military writings,
      his actions in summarily executing Chief Uwini in 1896, the continuing debate about
      racism and the conduct of the siege of Mafeking, and Baden-Powell's artistic repre-
      sentations of Africans and Jews, mentioned in footnote 2 above.

PART III

ANCIENT HEROES AND HISTORIC EXEMPLARS

Roman heroism and the problems
of nineteenth-century empire: Aeneas
and Caractacus

Military prowess, with or without the additional advantages of domestic
virtue or religious distinction, or the potential to be a father to the nation,
attracted enormous popular interest throughout the nineteenth century as
kingdoms and empires rose and fell by more or less violent means. As if
the Duke of Wellington and General Gordon were not enough for the
British public, the interest extended back into the remote past to include
Aeneas and Caractacus. The hero of Virgil's Roman epic and the unavailing
defender of British freedoms against Roman invasion are on the face of it
an unlikely pair: the successful and the defeated hero, the smooth proto-
Roman and the shaggy ancient Briton, heroic magnificence versus heroic
moustaches. But both heroes enjoyed a nineteenth-century afterlife in
Britain, on the page and on the stage, in music and the visual arts,
in middle to lowbrow as well as in highbrow culture. This now-forgotten
fame affords unexpected insights into the preoccupations and tensions of
nineteenth-century society.

In the case of Aeneas, exemplar and father of Roman greatness, posthumous celebrity was hardly surprising. He was part of what every schoolboy
and some schoolgirls knew, particularly if they had been taught Latin or
persuaded to sing in the school production of Purcell's opera *Dido and
Aeneas*, immensely popular after its rediscovery and publication in 1840.[1]
Whether they had actually studied Virgil's *Aeneid* or not, most people had
at least vaguely heard of the Trojan hero who escaped from burning Troy
and told his story to a fatally fascinated Dido before travelling on to conquest
and victory in Italy, where his descendants established the world-conquering
might of Rome.

Caractacus (more correctly, if less familiarly, Caratacus or Caradoc), a
father-figure of British nationality, almost a saint and a martyr within
the spectrum of possible heroes, though he seems to have died in his
bed, is perhaps a bit more unexpected. A military leader who desper-
ately tried to stop the Roman advance through England, an honour he

shared with the better-known Boadicea or Boudicca, he was eventually, inevitably, defeated, betrayed and carried off to Rome in chains in AD 51. Impressive and forthright even in defeat, a more than Roman exemplar of military heroism and love of country, he and his family were pardoned and generously treated by the Emperor Claudius and ended their days in Rome.[2]

But where Aeneas, son of the goddess Venus, was a literary legend, Caractacus, son of King Cunobelinus or Cymbeline, was more or less real. Coins stamped with the head of the father had been found in Colchester. The son was mentioned by the reputable ancient historians Tacitus and Dio Cassius as well as the much later Byzantine annalist Zonaras[3] who recorded the stirring detail that, seeing the splendours of Rome, Caractacus enquired what the Romans wanted with the hovels of the British. British historians took note.[4] All this made father and son real enough to get into the *Dictionary of National Biography*. Aeneas the mythical man of destiny could serve as a prototype of British men of destiny, particularly if one thought of Britain's Empire with approval as a natural extension of the nation, as Greater Britain. But the historical Caractacus was already a national hero, particularly if, like Linda Colley,[5] one thought of the nation in terms of difference, as that which defines itself against the ethos and the expansionism of other peoples and nations, especially empire-building Romans and Frenchmen. Legend and myth played their part in his story, of course, for in the Welsh Triads he is grouped with his father Cunobelinus and King Arthur as a legendary champion of ancient Britain.[6]

These contrasting heroes, legendary or historical, illustrate fundamental ambiguities in Britain's national self-image throughout the long nineteenth century, between the French Revolution and the First World War. Was imperial Rome, founded by the descendants of Aeneas, a brutal conqueror or a source of universal peace and order? Was Britain, once a Roman colony despite the resistance of Caractacus, a vulnerable if self-contained community or was her fate to be the new Rome, destined to repeat, perhaps as farce, perhaps triumphantly, some or all of that long tragic history of world dominion, decline and fall?

Who could say? Past and present could be read in so many different ways. The rich, unstable, sometimes unnerving ambiguity of the cherished Roman model serves to challenge the homogeneity and self-confidence often attributed to the nineteenth-century discourse of empire. In 1874 the poet Arthur O'Shaughnessy, easily diverted from problems of reptile conservation in the British Museum, invoked as it might be Virgil's imperial legend of Aeneas and the fragile dreams of his own generation when he sang in 'The Music-Makers' of how

... out of a fabulous story
We fashion an empire's glory:
One man with a dream, at pleasure,
Shall go forth and conquer a crown ...

But O'Shaughnessy acknowledges that, while the dreamer may escape from
the present into the dreams which mingle past and future, there is no
escaping the loss and sacrifice of past glories since the future is built upon
them. The poet goes on to say:

We, in the ages lying
In the buried past of the earth,
Built Nineveh with our sighing,
And Babel itself in our mirth;
And o'erthrew them with prophesying
To the old of the new world's worth:
For each age is a dream that is dying;
Or one that is coming to birth.[7]

The emotional and ideological ambiguities of this kind of dreaming,
mingling empire-building and the decay of empire, were already established
in the nineteenth-century imagination in Turner's massive atmospheric
paintings of 1815 and 1817 depicting the building and the decline of
Carthage's mercantile empire, associated respectively with sunrise and with
sunset. Rome had defeated Carthage, which is why Virgil and Roman
Destiny could not permit Aeneas to stay with Carthaginian Dido. But
mercantile Carthage was often seen as a type of mercantile Britain. The
counterpoint of imperial aspiration and anticipated eclipse was reflected in
the contrasting bravura and melancholy of Elgar's brilliantly self-reflexive
musical setting of O'Shaughnessy's 'Music Makers'. The music was
composed for the Birmingham Festival of 1912, a time when national and
imperial self-questioning had become much more acute. Colonial expansionism in South Africa had led to military humiliations and near defeat
in the earlier part of the Boer War. And 1912 was also the year of the Ulster
gun-running: serious trouble was brewing yet again in divided Ireland,
Britain's first colony and the first to start challenging metropolitan authority.

Despite, or because of, such misgiving, Aeneas had a loyal following
in late-Victorian and Edwardian Britain. The Earl of Cromer, retired from
being Britain's proconsul in Egypt, addressed the Classical Association on
Ancient and Modern Imperialism in 1909. It was clear to him that the Greeks
were far too undisciplined to run an empire properly, but the austere and
practical Romans, imbibing the atmosphere of empire distilled in the *Aeneid*,
had no difficulties of this kind. Virgil was described as 'an enthusiastic
Imperialist, ... probably a true representative of the Roman public opinion

of his day'.[8] Clearly Virgil-reading Britons were meant to inherit the imperial mission of Virgil-reading Romans.

But Virgil's Aeneas, tearful, priggish and brutal by turns, unscrupulous
in his private life at least from the point of view of deserted Dido, was an
awkward role-model, and the parallel with slave-owning imperial Rome
was always tricky and uncomfortable. This was particularly apparent in
nineteenth-century realist and anti-imperialist assessments of the politics
of empire which have often been underplayed or overlooked by modern
historians. With rather disconcerting frankness the Cambridge Professor of
Modern History, J.R. Seeley, conceded in 1883 that any route to empire
involved a measure of brutality and repression, but claimed that in British
colonial history as in Virgil's Aeneid there were gleams amid darkness, righteous pioneers who 'remind us of Abraham and Aeneas'.[9]

The artful association of Abraham and Aeneas, the biblical and the
political hero, nudges Virgil and imperial enterprise away from their literary
antecedents in Greek epic, the almost cheerful military brutalities of Homer's
Iliad and the more or less irresponsible adventures of Homer's Odysseus,
one of the models for Aeneas. It gestures instead at Old Testament notions
of divine and national destiny and a chosen people.

But this was special pleading. Aeneas, the Aeneid and the Roman imperial model had always been rather problematic in Britain, open to moral
and political objections. Mr Gladstone was particularly effective at articulating such objections. His first major parliamentary intervention in
foreign affairs had been to oppose Palmerston in the Don Pacifico debate
in 1850 when the promise of security associated with the Roman affirma-
tion civis Romanus sum ('I am a Roman citizen') had been daringly applied
to British nationals overseas, including the rather dubious Don Pacifico,
mistreated by a mob in Athens. Mr Gladstone did not care for Lord
Palmerston's tone:

> What then, Sir, was a Roman citizen? He was a member of a privileged
> caste; he belonged to a conquering race ... Is such, then, the view of the
> noble Lord, as to the relation that is to subsist between England and other
> countries?[10]

This anti-imperial deconstruction of the mystique of imperial Rome antic-
ipates Walter Benjamin's uncomfortable insight that there is no monument
of civilization that is not also a monument to barbarism. Views of the
proto-imperial Aeneas, the Aeneid and Roman civilization could never be
completely divorced from blood-stained power-politics, ancient and modern.

Gladstone read Virgil constantly throughout his adult life, from 1829
to 1880, according to his now-published Diaries. He particularly admired
the second book of the Aeneid, which included the famous account of the

Trojan Horse. Even in his eightieth year he whiled away a train journey by re-reading it. He was never happier than when bandying Virgilian quotations in the House of Commons with other Oxford classicists such as Robert Lowe. But despite this he much preferred Homer. In 1857, perhaps unconsciously safeguarding his own position as a righteous and religious liberal reformer, he claimed that for all its splendours the *Aeneid* had insincerely perverted Homeric tradition in the interests of a corrupt court (the imperial court of Virgil's patron Augustus) and that it had condoned the moral deficiencies of an unsatisfactory hero, the man who loved Dido and left her. From his different perspective the Baptist Evangelical writer John Foster similarly saw Virgil as secondary to Homer, granted him 'elegance and tenderness' but complained that 'none of the personages intended for heroes take hold enough of the reader's feelings to assimilate them in moral temper'.[11]

The cultural fortunes of Aeneas in Italy and France had something to do with this moral hostility. The grudging Gladstone complained that where 'Homer has the full force and play of the drama, Virgil is essentially operatic'.[12] The perspective was comfortably British, almost Philistine – a term Matthew Arnold had not yet popularised in cultural debate – because opera was still regarded as an extravagantly artificial art-form, characteristically composed and performed by foreigners, especially Italians. Gladstone's remarks were published during the period when the French romantic composer Hector Berlioz was at work on his ambitiously Virgilian opera *Les Troyens*, the second half of which was eventually performed in Paris as *Les Troyens à Carthage* in 1863. There seems to be no evidence that Gladstone ever heard, or even heard of, this work: if he did, its brilliantly stylised emotional excess would presumably only have confirmed his judgement of Virgil. But Gladstone may well have known or heard something of Italian operatic treatments of the Virgilian Aeneas. He knew the country and read and wrote about Italian literature, and Italian operas such as Pietro Metastasio's celebrated *Dido abandonnata* were regularly performed in London.

French and Italian inflections of the Aeneas legend had political as well as aesthetic significance. When the great French critic Sainte-Beuve tried to lecture on Virgil at the Collège de France in 1855 he was shouted down and the lectures had to be abandoned, not because they were inadequate but because he owed his appointment to the new French Emperor Napoleon III and the lectures by the court professor of Napoleon on the court poet of Augustus offended liberal and radical sentiment. Victor Hugo had admired Virgil in youth but he came to detest the *Aeneid* in the 1850s at much the same time as he came to detest Napoleon III and for much the same anti-imperial reasons.[13]

Eighteenth-century Italy with its courts and aristocratic patrons of the arts had continued to sponsor Virgil, as Augustus had once done. Giambattista Tiepolo had painted Virgil's Aeneas in heroic mode as a series of frescos on the walls of the Villa Valmarana in 1757. As the art-historian Michael Levey has argued,[14] the formal rhetorical grandeurs of such classical paintings had their counterpart in opera devoted to classical themes. One of the most influential of these was Metastasio's *Dido abandonnata* (1728), a libretto which attracted a surprising range of musical settings over the next hundred years. The conventions of the Italian *opera seria* favoured a happy ending, which posed particular problems for Virgilian operas. The *Aeneid*, probably unfinished, ends grimly and abruptly with Aeneas' slaying of Turnus whose soul flees unconsenting to the shades below. In Virgil's narrative the episode of Dido and Aeneas ends either with the death of Dido or with her uncomfortable post-mortem encounter with Aeneas in the underworld. Metastasio's solution to this formal problem, in a version of his opera performed at the Spanish court in 1754, was to stage Dido's funeral pyre but then follow it with a *Licenza* or 'Envoy' in which Neptune looks far into the future. Like Virgil in the *Aeneid*, Metastasio moves beyond the immediate situation to open up a grand historical vista, setting this particular episode in the larger and rather more positive political context of international tranquillity and ultimate peace on earth, the famous *pax Romana* to be achieved by Aeneas' descendants. It has been noted that this was designed to flatter the peace-loving policies of Ferdinand IV of Spain after the Treaty of Aix-La-Chapelle (1748) which ended the War of the Austrian Succession.[15]

The works of Metastasio, poet in residence at the imperial court of Vienna, were available in English translation from 1800, and even before that his *Dido abandonnata* had been performed in London. In 1792 an adaptation by Prince Hoare was staged at the Haymarket, with some new music by Mr Storace (and a great deal of older music by nine other composers which had survived from previous versions). The libretto was modified for English purposes. Aeneas begins the opera with an accompanied recitative:

From downy rest, and calm delights of peace,
Once more her heroes glory wakes to arms.[16]

This can be seen against the general background of imperial glory and the success of British arms in India in 1792: the first performance was on 23 May, and on 25 February of the same year Lord Cornwallis had defeated Tippoo Sultan of Mysore and compelled him to concede half his territories.[17] The concluding Masque of Neptune, originally quite Virgilian, was also updated for English purposes. Neptune is made to say to Ascanius, son of Aeneas:

> Immortal kings, a godlike race,
> From thee their bright descent shall trace;
> Third from thy Sire shall Brutus rise,
> Who, far beneath yon western skies,
> Ordain'd to empire yet unknown,
> On Albion's coast shall fix his throne,
> And, crown'd with laurels, spoils, and fame,
> Shall change to Britain Albion's name.

The opera ended with a chorus of Sea Gods and Nymphs singing

> Renown, thy trumpet loudly sound!
> From pole to pole proclaim around
> Great Albion's name,
> The theme of Fame.[18]

 But despite all this operatic flag-waving the production was a flop: the form was too elaborate and artificial for English audiences, with too much singing of recitative between the big choruses. It may also have been that the proto-imperialist hero was more popular at the courts of foreign emperors than among the subjects of a constitutional monarchy. The most successful nineteenth-century versions of the story flatly refused to take Aeneas seriously. I have found no record of 'straight' theatrical or operatic treatments in England during this period, apart from revivals of older works such as *Dido abandonnata* and Purcell's *Dido and Aeneas*. Even at the high point of late-Victorian imperialism, in 1893, Aeneas was a figure of fun in the burlesque *Dido and Aeneas* at the Strand Theatre. H.S. Granville put on *Aeneas, or Dido Done* at the Cork Opera House in 1868. F.C. Burnand, later editor of *Punch*, got his own back on school classics with a burlesque, variously entitled *Dido. A Tragical, Classical and Original Burlesque* or *Dido, the Celebrated Widow* which ran for eighty nights in 1860 and was successfully revived in 1865, reaching a far more popular audience than the productions of the Italian Opera. Aeneas was played by a woman, which was not uncommon in Virgilian operas, but the widow Dido was played by a man: epic or operatic dignity was subverted by the pantomine roles of principal boy and the Widow Twankey. There were some truly dreadful puns, and some good moments. Aeneas engages in earnest dialogue with a talking fish. Trojan maritime adventure acquires a robustly British dimension when the Virgilian Cave of the Winds is introduced to the tune of 'A Life on the Ocean Wave':

> A life in Aeolian Cave
> A home 'mid the rocks so steep,
> How quiet we all behave,
> While the Winds their cradles keep.

Best of all, the heroic business of nation-building and the founding of Carthage is immortalised in song, to the tune of 'Campdown Races':

(Dido)	The Carthaginians sing a song
(Chor.)	Dido, Dido!
(Dido)	The walls of Carthage nine miles long.
(Chor.)	Dido, Dido, da!
(Dido)	Ye build 'em all the night;
	Ye build 'em all the day;
	For a tanner, for a tizzy, for a joey, for a bob,
	Not a penny more or less your pay.[19]

Nineteenth-century Englishmen were often tepid, if not ribald, about Aeneas and Virgil as the court poet of the Emperor Augustus because, unlike Metastasio's original audiences, they had no cause to recall imperial courts from Madrid to Vienna with any particular affection or loyalty. Nor did they have much sympathy with the vainglorious swaggerings of the Emperor Napoleon III of France: no-one liked the renewed threat of French invasion they seemed to represent. The notion of Empire, given literary currency by Virgil and recent political currency by both Napoleons, seemed to involve European Empire and so threatened British sovereignty, a recurring British nightmare. It was not until later in the nineteenth century, after the collapse of the French Second Empire, that the word 'imperialism' in English began to have positive connotations. Despite repeated parliamentary warnings about over-extension, often illustrated from Roman history, the idea and the mystique of a *British* Empire which might be compared with the old Roman Empire made some headway again and Virgil-reading imperial ideologues such as Lord Cromer and J.R. Seeley began to get a hearing.

But even then many, if not most, people were a little unhappy about Aeneas, politically and aesthetically. Given the choice between a rather literary and piously public hero ruthlessly sacrificing everything to a blood-stained vision of Roman destiny on the one hand, and the more romantically personal modes of heroism on the other, they preferred Dido to Aeneas. Both Berlioz and Purcell had found it easier to write tender haunting arias for suffering Dido than for ambitious Aeneas. It was Dido, not Roman triumphalism, that induced the tender-hearted young Berlioz to overcome his initial dislike of Virgil. If, on the other hand, one's taste was for blood and uncomplicated heroism, as Mr Gladstone's probably was, then the heroes of Homer were more promising material than Virgil's hero, a little pallidly derived from them.

This enthusiasm for Homer rather than Virgil, which can be traced back to the later eighteenth century, arose out of and helped to reinforce the Pre-Romantic and Romantic enthusiasm for the primitive and the

craggily original, sometimes expressed in terms of landscape. In the eighteenth century Thomas Warton had complained that while Homer was
original like Mount Atlas with its vast rough rocks, gloomy pines and cedars
and awe-inspiring torrents, Virgil was articifical and derivative like the
Capitoline Hill in Rome, covered with the temple of Jupiter which was
'adorned with the spoils of conquered Greece'.[20]

Homer in this respect was the literary equivalent of the Romantic
tourist's version of Scotland or Wales, attractively rugged, craggy, shaggy
and wild. The romantic aesthetic which reinvented Homer in these terms
also reinvented Caractacus as the hero of remote British fastnesses,
including wild Wales where he retreated to continue the sturggle against
the Romans. The poet Thomas Gray had in a sense prepared the way for
nineteenth-century constructions of Caractacus and for Romantic Celticism
in conjunction with the politics of defiance in his poem 'The Bard' (1755–7).
This celebrates poetic defiance of the invading English of Edward I in the
picturesque remoteness of the Welsh mountains. It is not difficult to substitute the Romans for the English and the Emperor Claudius for Edward I.
The continuing significance of Gray's 'Bard' in the nineteenth century is
illustrated in the Northumbrian artist John Martin's spectacular painting
The Bard (1817), now in the Laing Art Gallery in Newcastle, which follows
Gray quite closely, depicting the wild bard with his harp against a spectacular mountain landscape, overlooking a column of advancing hostile
soldiers far beneath across a foaming river. On closer inspection the landscape is not Welsh but partly Alpine (to be fashionably picturesque) and
partly local, for Martin has relocated the bard among the dramatic crags
of Allendale Gorge in Northumbria, close to home.

This was convenient. Craggily heroic resistance, preferably accompanied by musical, poetic or prophetic incantation, could be relocated in
different parts of the country to articulate the mystique of imperilled but
also imperishable nationhood. This turned the difficulty of reconstructing
the precise topography of Caractacus' campaigns in England and Wales or
the Welsh borders into an advantage because Caractacus could be wherever picturesque national sentiment wanted him to be – in Colchester, in
Wales, or, for Edward Elgar, in the Malvern Hills at his back door.

Gray's close friend William Mason put Caractacus on the stage again,
in 1759, with inset Pindaric odes and a chorus of bards which clearly indicate Gray's influence. There had been earlier appearances: under the name
Caratach he had been unhistorically related to Boadicea (sometimes known
as Boudicca or Bonduca) in John Fletcher's play *Bonduca* (1613–14) and
some later productions adapted the piece to give him greater prominence.
He had long featured in standard histories such as Thomas Carte's *General
History of England* (1747) and Oliver Goldsmith's popular *History of England*

(1764), not to mention Goldsmith's equally popular and much reprinted *Roman History* (1769). Under the stimulus or perceived threat of foreign foes, usually the French, Caractacus was retrospectively constructed as a patriotic hero, a national or proto-national champion comparable to the German Hermann or Arminius or the French Vercingetorix, and like them attractive to nationally minded sculptors and artists.[21] The secret of his posthumous success was that he could be celebrated in the dominant and influential cultural idiom of those who had defeated him. Just as Tacitus had used the rhetorical conventions of Roman history, including constructed set-piece speeches, to commend a foreign hero, with wife and family, from whom decadent Romans might learn something, so the sculptor Thomas Banks used his time in Rome and his acquired familiarity with the conventions of Graeco-Roman sculpture to produce his heroically classical and yet also heroically British *Caractacus and his Family before Claudius* (1774), a marble *alto-relievo* exhibited at the Royal Academy in 1780, now at Stowe School. The best-known Victorian sculpture of Caractacus was that by J.H. Foley (1860), commissioned for the Mansion House in London, with smaller copies in bronze available for private purchasers. There is one at Cragside, the Armstrong family home in Northumberland. Athletic and dignified, left arm outstretched in heroic defiance, grounded battleaxe in his right hand, a Celtic or Germanic *übermensch* with Nietzschian moustaches bristling ferociously, this Caractacus still startles visitors on their way up the stairs to the picture-gallery. The competition for fresco designs to redecorate the Palace of Westminster in the 1840s called for subjects illustrating English history or English literature. Seventeen of the 140 cartoons submitted related to Romano-British history and of these no fewer than five represented Caractacus, including the entry by G.F. Watts which won first prize in 1843.[22]

The appeal of Caractacus in middle-class Protestant England was domestic and religious as well as public: it was not just that he was British and a patriot admired even by the conquering Romans but that he was an exemplary married man with a family and that with some ingenuity he could also be linked with the early days of Christianity. Virgil's Aeneas was distinctly pagan, and Virgil himself could be only partly reclaimed for Christianity by his appearance in Dante's *Divine Comedy* since the Christian poet kept him out of Paradise. Aeneas was also strongly patriarchal, concerned about his father and his son but ruthlessly subordinating relationships with women to political necessity. But the Caractacus of Tacitus is an enlightened Christian gentleman in the making: he respects both his own wife and the lady Agrippina, wife of the emperor, thanking her in the same terms as he had thanked Claudius for sparing his life, treating her as equal in dignity to her husband in the British manner as Tacitus represents it. The poet Martial had mentioned a British lady called Claudia and her husband Pudens, and St Paul had mentioned a Claudia and a Pudens among the Christians at Rome (2 Timothy 4:21). Classically educated British churchmen could not resist the coincidence of names, even though the dates were difficult. Since the sixteenth century protestant divines had used these alleged Britons in the Bible to argue for a personal link between St Paul and ancient Britain: if early British Christianity was so early that it was not directly dependent on centralising Roman influences then the triumphalist claims of Counter-Reformation Roman Catholicism were ill-founded.[23]

With a little further ingenuity, relying on the thoroughly unreliable tradition of the Welsh Triads, Claudia could be represented as the daughter of Caractacus, brought up in Rome with her parents under the patronage of Claudius (hence the name Claudia) but still identified with and drawn back to her native country to spread the Gospel. The scholarly F.W. Farrar, writing as an historian, dismissed this conjecture as 'an elaborate rope of sand',[24] but in his fictional recreation of Nero's Rome, *Darkness and Dawn* (1891), Farrar the novelist was happy enough to go beyond the evidence and invent a Roman Pudens and a Claudia who was both British and Christian and a daughter of Caractacus. Other historical novelists and fantasists could not help trying out the same idea because it simultaneously baptised patriotic antiquarianism and gave British Christianity comparable antiquity and dignity with the early church of the Roman catacombs. The traveller and poet C.M. Doughty's forgotten epic *The Dawn in Britain* (1906–7), much admired in its day by the poet Edward Thomas, mingles different traditions and legends as it fancifully brings together Joseph of Arimathea, Caractacus, a British Claudia and her husband the Roman Pudens.

Reclaiming Caractacus and his relatives not just for the Church and the British nation but for the British decencies of home and family was greatly assisted by the composer of 'Home Sweet Home'. Henry Bishop, in his own private life a reckless home-breaker and adulterer, always knew what the public wanted. His first major work was the music for a ballet of *Caractacus* (1808) which emphasised Welshness and Caractacus before he got to Rome. This may have been mainly an excuse for harp-music as the harp was a popular instrument for amateur music-making in well-to-do middle-class homes, not yet eclipsed by the piano, and the rather costly engraved musical score could be purchased either in parts or as a whole. Atmosphere was established by an oboe melody with harp continuo based on a Welsh Air. The wordless poetry of motion was varied with a simple glee, *Larghetto cantabile*, of the kind that could be sung in the drawing-room: 'Breathe my Harp, ye groves resound.' Needless to say, there was a harp accompaniment.

The most famous and ambitious musical treatment was Elgar's cantata for the Leeds Festival of 1898. But this comes out of a tradition. Most of the other treatments were shamelessly patriotic and also subliminally pious. Both Caractacus and Christ himself had been brought before the Roman authorities. The chorally mediated story of the paraded prisoner, perhaps jeered and derided, which could nevertheless end with glory and thanksgiving, was musically and dramatically akin to the Passion narrative as interpreted by Bach or Handel, frequently performed in the nineteenth century, particularly at Easter time, to large audiences and congregations. The Welsh musician Joseph Parry, remembered chiefly for hymn-tunes such as 'Aberystwyth', composed an elaborate choral ballad of *Caractacus (in Rome)*,[25] with Welsh and English words. It was scored for tenors and basses in four-part harmony, designed to appeal to the growing number of Welsh male-voice choirs trained on works such as Handel's *Messiah*. The *Messiah* concludes with the triumphant singing of 'Blessing and honour, glory and power' and Parry's score concludes with 'All glory to Claudius! Carádoc is free!'

The application to modern Britain could be simply that Britons never, never will be slaves, so that there was an historical inevitablility about freeing 'Caractacus of Britain,/The island of the free', to quote the conclusion of one particularly stirring treatment.[26] But Elgar's librettist, his friend Harry Acworth, had perhaps unconsciously imitated the prophetic technique of Prince Hoare's Virgilian opera and indeed of Virgil's *Aeneid* by ending with a prospect of the future, a vision of once-conquered Britain as the new and greater Rome. The flag-waving is quite specific and literal. The concluding chorus, frequently marked triple forte (*fff*), equates Britain's empire with the guarantee of freedom and equality under the law, in contrast to Roman slavery:

> And where the flag of Britain
> Its triple crosses rears,
> No slave shall be for subject,
> No trophy wet with tears;
> But folk shall bless the banner,
> And bless the crosses twin'd,
> That bear the gift of freedom
> On every blowing wind.[27]

This brassy imperial self-confidence determinedly extracted from the Caractacus story, which is after all a narrative of defeat by an imperial power, commended itself to brass bands and their audiences. The military bandmaster Lieutenant Charles Godfrey arranged a suite from Elgar's *Caractacus* as a test-piece for the Belle Vue national brass band competition in 1903 and it was extremely popular.[28]

One might expect Caractacus to be as popular on the page as he was on the band-stand or the concert-platform at this period. To some extent he was. The enormous expansion of the reading public and the new availability of cheap reading material for mass audiences coincided with the popular enthusiasm for empire. In an earlier epoch *Caractacus. A Metrical Sketch in Twelve Parts* (1832) had had little impact. But *Caractacus, Champion of the Arena* (c.1885), an illustrated boys' adventure-story selling at a shilling, was much more exciting, designed to reach the same popular audience as the Jack Harkaway and Robin Hood stories issued by the same publisher. The historical Caractacus had never fought as a gladiator in the arena, though he might have done if Claudius had not pardoned him. But the artistic licence served to bring Caractacus into the arena of popular culture and entertainment, sharing the ring with prize-fighters and other sporting heroes. At a more sophisticated level G.J. Whyte-Melville's novel *The Gladiators* (1863) reworked the Caractacus theme without mentioning him by name by taking a young British warrior in chains to Rome and then insinuating him into the imperial court. G.A. Henty, author of such imperial fictions as *With Clive in India* or *With Kitchener in Khartoum* made similar use of the Caractacus story in *Beric the Briton. A Story of the Roman Invasion* (1893). Caractacus himself is mentioned only in passing, but Beric is partly modelled on him. He is presented as a British freedom-fighter who is forced to serve as a gladiator in Rome but by great good fortune is also able to make good use of Roman libraries. It is not difficult to imagine him as a model for and a back-formation from nineteenth-century 'native' princes from India or Africa being educated at Oxford. He ends up as a Romano-British provincial governor, acquiring from the conqueror the much-needed lessons in discipline and civility which after many centuries will allow Britons to attain political maturity and perhaps to be conquerors and imperial rulers in their turn.

Both these novels explore for a wide audience the paradox and the accommodation made apparent in Banks's classically heroic sculpture of defeated British heroism or Elgar's neo-Virgilian transformation of British humiliation into imperial destiny. They negotiate and come to terms with the historical necessity of Roman conquest and Roman culture in the invention, articulation and development of eventually imperial British heroism and nationality.

Caractacus, with covert help from the less satisfactory Aeneas and from Roman imperial ideology, provided late-Victorian Britain with a means of bridging the political and imaginative gulf between coloniser and colonized, conquest and freedom. He helped the British public to accommodate latter-day British colonialism. Although he already existed, it was necessary to reinvent him. He assuaged colonial guilt, since Britain could be magnanimous as Claudius had been and could think of itself as committed to establishing peace as the Roman descendants of Aeneas were supposed to be. Caractacus' success in Rome soothed the misgivings about colonial adventure arising from the collective unconscious of a former colony which had known humiliation and defeated hope. It helped to reconcile national sentiment to the possibly valuable discipline of Roman administration and to the imposed civility stemming from military conquest and occupation. Perhaps it was now Britain's destiny to transmit this acquired discipline and civility to other nations and other peoples.

Notes

1   W. H. Cummings, *Purcell* (London, 1881), p. 33; J. A. Westrup, *Purcell* (revd. edn., London, 1975), pp. 116, 123–24.

2   Tacitus, *Annals* 12.33–7; Dio Cassius 60.20.1–2

3   Zonaras, *Annals* 11.10

4   T. Carte, *A General History of England* (London, 1747–55), I, pp. 110–11; O. Goldsmith, *An History of England* (London, 1764), I, pp. 25–26.

5   L. Colley, *Britons: Forging the Nation* (London, 1994), p. 5.

6   S. Smiles, *The Image of Antiquity: Ancient Britain and the Romantic Imagination* (New Haven, 1994), p. 42.

7   J. H. Buckley and G. B. Woods (eds), *Poetry of the Victorian Period* (3rd edn., Glenview, Illinois, 1965), pp. 760–61.

8   Earl of Cromer, *Ancient and Modern Imperialism* (London, 1910), p. 14.

9   J. R. Seeley, *The Expansion of England* (London, 1883), p. 135.

10 W. E. Gladstone, Speech in the House of Commons, *Hansard*, 3rd series, CXII, cols. 586–7: 17 June 1850.

11 [W. E. Gladstone], 'Homer and his successors in epic poetry', *Quarterly Review*, 101, pp. 80–122; J. Foster, *Essays in a Series of Letters* (26th edn., London, 1854), pp. 268–69; J. Morley, *Life of Gladstone*, 2 vols. (London, 1905–6), II, p. 721; F. M. Turner, *Contesting Cultural Authority: Essays in Victorian Intellectual Life* (Cambridge, 1993), pp. 284–321.

12 W. E. Gladstone, 'Homer and his successors', p. 89.

13 R. E. Mulhauser, *Sainte-Beuve and Greco-Roman Antiquity* (Ohio and London, 1969), pp. 60–61; G. M. Harper, *Charles-Augustin Sainte-Beuve* (Philadelphia and London, 1909), pp. 312–13; G. Highet, *The Classical Tradition* (Oxford, 1949), p. 406.

14 M. Levey, 'Tiepolo's treatment of classical story at Villa Valmarana', *Journal of the Warburg and Courtauld Institutes*, 20 (1957), 298–317.

15 P. Metastasio, *Dido abandonnata*, in his *Opere*, ed. Mario Fubini (Milan and Naples, 1968), p. 87.

16 [Prince Hoare], *Dido, Queen of Carthage* (London, 1792), p. 1.

17 J. C. Marshman, *The History of India* (4th edn., Serampore, 1868), I, pp. 448–63.

18 [Prince Hoare], *Dido, Queen of Carthage*, p. 41.

19 F. C. Burnand, *Dido* (London, [1860]), pp. 5, 11, 15.

20 R. D. Williams, 'Changing attitudes to Virgil', in D. R. Dudley (ed.), *Virgil* (London, 1969), pp. 127–29.

21 Smiles, *The Image of Antiquity*, p. 42.

22 F. Knight Hunt (ed.), *The Book of Art: Cartoons, Frescoes, Sculpture, and Decorative Art, as Applied to the New Houses of Parliament* (London, 1846); T. S. R. Boase,

'The decorations of the New Palace of Westminster', *Journal of the Warburg and Courtauld Institutes*, 17 (1954), 319–58.

23   J. B. Lightfoot, *The Apostolic Fathers: St Clement of Rome*, 2 vols. (London, 1890), I, pp. 76–79.

24   F. W. Farrar, *Life and Work of St Paul* (London, 1879), p. 681n.

25   J. Parry, *Caractacus (in Rome): a Choral Ballad* [Welsh and English words by Rev. D. Adams], (London, [c.1900]).

26   F. Aylward, *Caractacus of Britain* [song with words by R. H. U. Bloor], (London, 1901).

27   E. Elgar, *Caractacus* [Op. 35], (London, 1905), pp. 297–99.

28   J. Crump, 'The identity of English music: the reception of Elgar 1898–1935', in R. Colls and P. Dodd (eds), *Englishness: Politics and Culture, 1880–1920* (London, 1986), p. 169.

The Red Queen and the White Queen: exemplification of medieval queens in nineteenth-century Britain

Queens you must always be; queens to your lovers; queens to your husbands and your sons; queens of higher mystery to the world beyond, which bows itself, and will for ever bow, before this myrtle crown, and the stainless sceptre, of womanhood . . .[1]

'Well, this *is* grand!' said Alice. 'I never expected that I would be a queen so soon – and I'll tell you what it is, your Majesty . . . it'll never do for you to be lolling about on the grass like that! Queens have to be digni-fied, you know!'

So she got up and walked about – rather stiffly just at first, as she was afraid that the crown might come off: but she comforted herself with the thought that there was nobody to see her, 'and if I really am a Queen' she said . . . 'I shall be able to manage it quite well in time'.[2]

The year 1865 saw the publication of two very different works: John Ruskin's *Sesame and Lilies* (from which the first of these quotations comes) and Lewis Carroll's *Alice's Adventures in Wonderland*. In Carroll's classic fantasy tale and its sequel *Through the Looking-Glass* (from which the second quotation is taken), the young heroine encounters worlds which reflect – but in a comi-cally distorted form – the figures and ideas she would have met in the text-books and improving literature which were integral to the education of Victorian girls and young women. Among these works was *Sesame and Lilies*, and in its second section – 'Of Queens' Gardens' – Ruskin addressed the issues of female education and reading matter. Both Carroll and Ruskin invite the reader to consider the nature of queenship and the possibility of its imi-tation by Victorian middle-class girls and women. Such a link was almost inevitably made in an age presided over by Victoria, a queen who embodied bourgeois domestic virtues and tastes for the nineteenth-century public.

But while Ruskin embarks upon the mythological and metaphorical eulogy of the good woman figured as queen, Carroll wickedly plays with the exemplars of good and bad queens common in nineteenth-century

historical biographies of women. Among the characters Alice encounters in
the course of her adventures are no less than three queens, the Queen of
Hearts, the Red Queen, and the White Queen. As exemplars – both good
and bad – for Alice, who joins their ranks in Chapter 9 of *Through the
Looking Glass* (1872), they prove to be all equally unappealing: abandoning
the burdens of queenship, Alice swiftly reverts to her natural self.

However, not all female writers and readers of Victorian educational
literature were able to sweep aside the Ruskinian injunction to 'be no more
housewives, but queens' with the dispatch of an Alice. This chapter will
examine the nineteenth-century historiography surrounding two medieval
queens of England, Eleanor of Aquitaine (wife of Henry II) and Philippa
of Hainault (wife of Edward III). It will focus mainly on the treatment of
these two women in works of history, textbooks and collective female biography, analysing the use of their lives to popularise and inculcate domestic
virtues in a juvenile and female audience. In the early nineteenth century,
in fact, Eleanor and Philippa appear as straight-faced versions of the Red
Queen and the White Queen, classic exemplars of the way in which bad
and good women behave.

But exemplification is an inherently unstable enterprise: characters can
burst out of the interpretative straitjackets tightened around them, refusing
to be confined in an exemplary mould. Such was the case with Eleanor of
Aquitaine, whose vital character and varied life eventually resisted definitions of her as a Bad Woman. From the middle of the century, she became
the subject of more sympathetic investigation, while Philippa of Hainault
– whose life much more easily elided with that of the Victorian ideal woman
– was eventually neglected. But Eleanor's 'escape' from the ideology which
attempted to identify her as simply a Bad Queen is not merely a matter of
scholarly reinterpretation in the face of historical evidence. Undoubtedly,
it represents the triumph of academic history over a neo-classical and philosophical approach to history-writing which favoured the construction of
exemplary stereotypes. But it also reflects interactions between a popular
ideology concerning gender roles and the society which at once produces
it and is also influenced by it, reproduces it and yet redefines it. Like
Eleanor's, Victorian middle-class women's lives rarely did fit into the mould
of the ideal woman, and – as a natural result – there were always contradictions and fissures in the heart of the ideology itself. As Lewis Carroll's
playful presentation of the Queen of Hearts, the Red Queen, and the White
Queen shows, all didactic exemplifications are potentially flexible, and open
to re-inventions.

Scholars working in the field of nineteenth-century women's history and
gender studies have traditionally emphasised the importance of a domestic

ideology dominated by the theory of the separate spheres, which has been adopted as an organising concept for historians of the period.[3] This interpretative schema, allocating the domestic and moral sphere to women and the political and public sphere to men, has been used to explain the lives of women of all ranks and classes. While research into the lives of working-class and aristocratic women has weakened the overall thesis, the lives of middle-class women have seemed to be closer to this paradigm. However, this conception of the complementary roles of the sexes has been challenged, both as historical fact and as a useful interpretative framework for the lives of middle-class women.[4] A far more complex picture of the reality of Victorian women's lives is emerging, but it is wise not to discard the theory of the separate spheres too peremptorily. Whatever its weakness in respect of individual case-studies, it is difficult to over-estimate the impact of the separate spheres *as a contemporary ideology* by which nineteenth-century women defined themselves and were defined by men. Some women may well have ignored or defied it. Others – both men and women – engaged with it, working out strategies for life within it, and endlessly restating, reaffirming, and reinterpreting it. Amanda Vickery may be right to suggest that it was 'simply a defensive and impotent reaction to public freedoms already won'.[5] Nevertheless, it was a staple subject of contemporary debate and an undeniable cultural phenomenon.

Not surprisingly, domestic ideology played a role in the wide range of historical literature which proliferated in nineteenth-century Britain. Under the aegis of a Romantic, picturesque, and expansive historiography, writers of history – who included historians, antiquaries, novelists, textbook writers and literary hacks of every description – began to include in their writings social groups who had been largely excluded from the historical record. Women were such a marginalised category, and the discovery and celebration of 'women worthies' was one of the most vigorous sub-genres of the period. Many of the writers of female biographies were women[6]: in the early and mid-nineteenth century, history-writing was a pastime open to amateurs.[7] Following the tropes of eighteenth-century neo-classical history, their presentations of prominent women frequently exploited them as exemplars of virtue and vice for their (largely female) readership. The creation of a pantheon of women worthies was an enterprise entirely in keeping with the spirit of the Victorian period, a female response to Carlyle's definition of history as the 'biographies of great men'. It was also an essential stage in the development of women's history.[8]

But eminent women were not all like the little girl with the curl in the middle of her forehead: they were not always either very, very good, or horrid. The characters of women such as Eleanor of Aquitaine contained contradictory and paradoxical – in other words, human – qualities which

did not make them susceptible to straightforward representation as either
Good or Bad Women. But the tension between real and ideal lay deeper,
affecting even the exemplary status of uncomplicated Good Women such
as Philippa of Hainault. Contradictions in the construction of remarkable
women as exemplars of the Victorian ideal woman appeared in the heart
of the ideology itself. While the Victorian ideal woman was confined to the
private sphere, women whose lives appeared in the historical record had
clearly ventured into the public arena. While the choice of a woman to
serve as an exemplar demanded historical documentation, those who were
most worthy were – by definition – least known and least knowable. The
celebration of women worthies was thus – in itself – an equivocal project:
the truly Good Woman would surely efface herself too fully to leave evidence
of her life sufficient to justify a biography.

    To a large extent, the choice of a queen for biographical study eased
these problems. Unlike all but a few outstanding female figures, queens
and other royal women had traditionally received the attention of historians and chroniclers: something of their lives was known. They had achieved
their public profiles effortlessly and innocently through birth and blameless unions: their appearance in the historical record was a function of
their rank and not a reflection on their character. Through no fault of their
own, their lives crossed the divide between the public and the private
spheres: their actions, their virtues and vices, were at once personal and
political. In their lives, the legitimate exercise of woman's social, cultural,
moral, and religious influence within the home was writ large for all to
see. This was particularly the case with queens from the medieval period,
when the court was at once the king's home and household and the centre
and focus of political power. Naturally, it was all the easier to highlight
the importance of domestic virtues for one's readership, if the exercise –
or the absence – of these attributes in the subject of a biography could be
shown to have affected the lives not only of other family members, but
of nations.

    Accordingly, biographies of queens and other royal women prolifer-
ated in nineteenth-century Britain, climaxing in the multi-volumed works of
Agnes and Elizabeth Strickland – *The Lives of the Queens of England*
(1840–48) and *The Lives of the Queens of Scotland* (1850–58) – and Mary Anne
Everett Green – *The Lives of the Princesses of England* (1849–55). These
women historians did not begin the fashion for female royal biographies,
nor did their publications put an end to it: in the 1820s, Elizabeth Ogilvy
Benger published biographies of Anne Boleyn (1821) and Elizabeth of
Bohemia (1825) and in the early twentieth century Ida Ashworth Taylor was
still producing popular lives of Lady Jane Grey (1908) and Christina of
Sweden (1909). Biographical sketches of the lives of queens also appeared in

collections of biographies of women – such as Mary Hays's *Female Biography or Memoirs of Illustrious and Celebrated Women* (1803) and Ellen Clayton's *Women of the Reformation* (1861), not to mention biographical anthologies of both men and women.[9] In addition, of course, their characters and actions received attention in history textbooks – particularly early nineteenth-century ones, which were written mainly by women, such as Elizabeth Penrose's *History of England* (1823) – and in multi-volumed histories.

Biographical treatments of the reigning monarch, Victoria, aptly demonstrated both the usefulness and the problems of using queens as exemplars for middle-class Victorian women. Unlike other eminent women – saints, writers, philanthropists, and so forth – Victoria was not remarkable for undertaking extraordinary actions which took her out of the private sphere. As one recent scholar puts it, among eminent women 'Victoria's only ticket for admission is her royalty : the Queen's main achievement is that *in spite of sovereignty* she is just like an ordinary good woman'.[10] As has been frequently pointed out, commissioned portraits of the queen and family reinforce the idea of Victoria as part of an ideal bourgeois family: Edwin Landseer's *Windsor Castle in Modern Times* (1841–45), for instance, presents Albert as hunter-gatherer, energetic denizen of the public sphere, who rests on his return home after a shoot, attended by his daughter and doting wife, whose femininity is symbolised by the posy which she carries.[11] The gap between this domestic queen, as presented in text and image, and her middle-class female counterparts was narrowed by this apotheosis of Victoria as the bourgeois queen.

Nevertheless, there remained an unsettling element in this image of Victoria: however domestically she was presented, she was still a queen – a reigning monarch no less – and thus a powerful political figure. As Nicola J. Watson has shown, profound unease was evident when Victoria was compared to the most illustrious queen regnant in British history, Elizabeth I: although associated with a Golden Age in English history, the Virgin Queen was undeniably lacking in feminine and domestic virtues. Victorian vacillations between images of Gloriana as a barren old maid, betrayed by her own vanity, and as a child princess, not yet embarked on her problematic reign and romances, witness to the difficulties of presenting Elizabeth as an exemplary predecessor of Victoria.[12] The alarming potency of Victoria's political role was diffused by stressing the constitutional limitations on the nineteenth-century monarch. In accounts of her life, Victoria appears a figurehead rather than a monarch: the mere advisor of her governments, the presiding presence in an empire created and administered by energetic men, the mother of Europe.[13]

This presentation of Victoria as a constitutional monarch echoes the nineteenth-century treatment of earlier queens, who were similarly disarmed of direct political power by their Victorian biographers. As most were consorts, it was all the easier to present them as wielders of influence rather than power: intercessors, advisors, helpmeets, rather than the genuinely powerful political players they often were. This was true for that other dangerous sixteenth-century queen regnant, Mary Queen of Scots, whose government is often described in sympathetic accounts as 'maternal'.[14] Power in the political sphere was presented as domestic qualities exercised in the public domain. But this process of disarmament was simultaneously a means of empowerment: by presenting the political actions of queens as 'maternal' or 'womanly', the private sphere was enlarged, making the domestic virtues of the ideal Victorian woman into a springboard for ventures into the public arena.

This apparently contradictory reading of historical and biographical representation of queens can be justified by reference to an unimpeachably conservative source – John Ruskin's *Sesame and Lilies*. Ruskin's interpretation of the role of women in society is by no means a narrow one: calling women to exercise 'a true queenly power, not only in their households merely, but over all their sphere', he explicitly states that they have 'a public work or duty, which is . . . the expansion of [their personal role in the home]'.[15] As S. A. Weltman has argued, Ruskin advanced a theory of queenship which offered Victorian women 'a powerful political and mythological model for the broadening of their scope of action, thereby redefining the traditionally domestic arena to include a broad range of philanthropy and social activism'.[16] Admittedly Ruskin was merely adopting an argument which women had already developed (and, moreover, in an attempt to divert their attention from the vexed issue of political rights). The rhetoric of the domestic ideology – of woman's legitimate domestic influence – was already being used by 1865 to justify the role of Victorian women in a variety of public arenas: local politics, culture, philanthropy, the church ministry, nursing.[17] But Ruskin's endorsement of a potentially active and influential role for women in 'Of Queens' Gardens' is a striking demonstration of the elastic capacity of the queenly exemplar.

Nineteenth-century treatments of Eleanor of Aquitaine and Philippa of Hainault serve to illustrate the successes and failures of exemplification. While Philippa was uniformly praised as a good queen and lent herself to representation as a Victorian ideal woman, Eleanor's image was much more unstable. Initially perceived as a jealous harpy and then as the female epitome of domestic vice, she was gradually reconsidered as a woman and, for the first time, a ruler.

Inevitably, nineteenth-century interpretations of both queens relied heavily on their previous historical reputations. At the beginning of the nineteenth century, Eleanor of Aquitaine was known primarily – and almost

only – from her appearance as the vengeful wife of Henry II, in the traditional account of the death of Fair Rosamund. This account, according to
D. D. R. Owen, has its origins in the work of several fourteenth-century
chroniclers. The tale of Eleanor's discovery of her husband's mistress, whom
she forces to commit suicide, had accumulated *en route* to the nineteenth
century all the paraphernalia of the maze at Woodstock, the skein of embroi-
dery silk (by which Eleanor finds her way to Rosamund), and the choice
between the dagger and the bowl of poison offered by the jealous queen
to her rival. Ballads, such as the sixteenth-century pamphleteer Thomas
Deloney's *Fair Rosamund*, popularised the tale among a wide audience. This
ballad, with the related *Queen Eleanor's Confession*, appeared in Bishop
Thomas Percy's *Reliques of Ancient Poetry* (1765), a collection of early
English verse. An early printed version of the *Confession* carried an appalling
illustration which established the visual iconography of the tale: the queen,
in crudely drawn ermine robes, with the crown attached to her head like
a glorified bun, admonishes Fair Rosamund, a blob in widow's weeds who
clutches an outsized goblet.[18]

While Eleanor of Aquitaine's image at the beginning of the nineteenth
century was decidedly negative, Philippa of Hainault had long enjoyed a
very favourable press. The main source for her life was Jean Froissart's
Chronicles, a source which – in the 1805 translation of Thomas Johnes of
Hafod – had enormous prestige in the early nineteenth century: its preoccupation with chivalry, battles, and court pageantry chimed in well with
the interests of early nineteenth-century medievalism of the genre popularised by Walter Scott and Kenelm Digby. Froissart had been, of course,
a countryman of Philippa's and one of her household clerks, and not
surprisingly his portrait of Edward III's queen was highly complimentary.
Even before 1800, like Eleanor of Aquitaine, Philippa was established in
the iconography of English medieval history through a traditional historical anecdote: the tale of the burghers of Calais, as related by Froissart.[19]
In this well-loved historical episode, she rescued the hostages demanded
by Edward III – after the surrender of the French port to his siege – by
pleading successfully with her husband for their lives. Philippa twice
featured prominently in Benjamin West's canvases for the King's Audience
Chamber at Windsor, commissioned by George III and painted between
1787 and 1789. While the subject-matter of the painting of *Queen Philippa
at the Battle of Neville's Cross* (1789) is unusual, that of *Philippa interceding
with Edward III for the burghers of Calais* (1789 also) is but one of many
late-eighteenth century depictions of this scene.[20]

Early nineteenth-century portrayals of Eleanor and Philippa in history
textbooks by women writers shed light on the processes of exemplification in the case of the two queens. The movement away from anecdotal

narrative towards an emphasis on didactic stereotyping was a slow transition: textbooks are inherently the guardians of tradition. Although the tale
of Fair Rosamund was already meeting with considerable scepticism, many
authors were nevertheless unable to resist an appealing story. In her
Historical Prints of 1821, Emily Taylor comments equivocally that 'There
are a great many romantic tales recorded respecting Henry the Second
and Rosamund Clifford'. However, after asserting firmly that Rosamund
definitely existed and made Eleanor 'very angry', she repeats the tale.[21] The
illustration on the facing page shows Eleanor, supported by a party of armed
men, presenting the dagger and bowl to a kneeling Rosamund; in the background, Rosamund's maids clutch each other in alarm. The tale of Rosamund
was to continue to haunt the pages of nineteenth-century history textbooks
for a considerable time. Charles Dickens, in his deliberately old-fashioned
A Child's History of England (1852), still included it, although he finished
with a disclaimer:

> But I am afraid – I say afraid, because I like the story so much – that
> there was no bower, no labyrinth, no silken clue, no dagger, no poison. I
> am afraid that Fair Rosamund retired to a nunnery near Oxford and died
> there, peaceably.[22]

Dickens's conclusion was somewhat undermined by Frank Topham's frontispiece to the first edition of *A Child's History*, which illustrated four
well-loved anecdotes from English history, of which 'Eleanor and Fair
Rosamund' was one.[23]

However, the days of historical anecdotes based only on such traditional sources as popular ballads were clearly numbered, despite the
rearguard action of a Charles Dickens. In an 1842 satirical work by his
contemporary and rival, W. M. Thackeray, *Miss Tickletoby's Lectures on
English History*, the tale of Fair Rosamund had been held up to ridicule,
accompanied by a parody of the illustrations which frequently accompanied the story. In this image, Rosamund appears as a plump young lady
comfortably knitting, while the queen who confronts her is a scrawny and
hatchet-faced old woman (figure 23).[24] Other early nineteenth-century textbooks had shown a change in the presentation of Eleanor. The majority of
the most prominent of these textbooks were written by women, such as
Elizabeth Penrose[25] and Maria, Lady Callcott,[26] and employed a domesticised and didactic perspective on English history which – though not the
preserve of female writers of history – had a particular appeal for them.
This approach aimed to teach children – both boys and girls – domestic
and private virtues, such as familial duty, personal integrity, and social
benevolence, through examples of good and bad conduct drawn from history.
In this project, heroism and its reverse were viewed as rooted in everyday

She preferred, it is said, the prussic acid, and died, I have no doubt?

Figure 23 W. M. Thackeray, 'Queen Eleanor and the Fair Rosamund', from *The Oxford Thackeray* (London, 1908), ed. G. Saintsbury, VII, p. 288

domestic behaviour and thus accessible to girls as well as boys (other models of heroism which stressed political, civic, or chivalric virtues exercised in the public arena were obviously less inclusive of the female reader). Nevertheless, the exemplary conduct held up for imitation was susceptible to gender stereotyping: the characteristics of a good father, son, husband, and brother were not the same as those of a good mother, daughter, wife, and sister.

The lives of medieval kings and queens lent themselves easily to this domestic mode of exemplarity, as here private and family life affected the course of history in a highly visible fashion. While this trend towards domesticised history in some cases ensured the continuing vitality of the anecdotal tradition, in the case of the tale of Fair Rosamund, it undermined it. This anecdote – an embarrassing narrative of adultery, jealousy, and revenge – did not lend itself to moralising commentary of any sort. This – with increasing scepticism concerning its accuracy – seems to have led to its exclusion. Accordingly, the writers of many early nineteenth-century textbooks, such as Penrose and Callcott, concentrated on Eleanor's conduct as a wife and mother: while this, too, revealed her in an unflattering light, it allowed the textbook writer to portray her didactically as a straightforward exemplar of the Bad Queen.

In the 1846 edition of her extremely popular *History of England* (1823), Elizabeth Penrose – better known as Mrs Markham – presents Eleanor as an argumentative divorcée of 'an unamiable and jealous temper', who marries a man 'many years older than herself'. She not only 'gave him much vexation by her own conduct, but also encouraged her children to behave undutifully to him'.[27] In case we have missed the point, Mrs Markham glosses her account of the rebellion of Henry II's sons against him with the comment:

> My opinion is, that they [the sons] acquired habits of disobedience to their father by seeing how little harmony subsisted between him and their mother. When children see their parents disagree, they seldom learn to treat them with duty or respect.[28]

Maria, Lady Callcott, adopted much the same line in *Little Arthur's History of England* (1835), in which she represents Henry II as marrying Eleanor for her riches, although she was 'very ill-tempered, and in all ways a bad woman'.[29] Henry receives his just deserts for such a mercenary marriage in his miserable home life, according to Lady Callcott. Once again, Eleanor features as the bad mother and the destroyer of family harmony: Lady Callcott comments that 'She brought up [her] children very badly, and instead of teaching them to love their father, she encouraged them to disobey him in everything.'[30] In these portrayals of Eleanor as a bad wife and mother, there is clearly no room for the story of Fair Rosamund, in which Eleanor appeared as a wronged – if vengeful – wife. Nor is there space for the consideration of her considerable political abilities in accounts which focus on Eleanor's domestic conduct as the cause of wider political conflict.

While Eleanor lent herself to portrayal as bad wife and bad mother in early nineteenth-century textbooks, Philippa of Hainault was equally useful as the model of the virtuous wife and mother. In Emily Taylor's *Historical Prints* (1821), the tale of the burghers of Calais is the subject of an illustration in which the queen's 'warm intercession',[31] accompanied by tears, softens her stern husband's resolve. Mrs Markham comments that 'Queen Philippa is mentioned by all historians in terms of the highest praise. She and Edward lived together in uninterrupted harmony forty years.'[32] Lady Callcott, claiming that Philippa was 'one of the best, and cleverest, and most beautiful women in the world', praises her as a mother who brought up her children 'wisely and well'.[33] For these early nineteenth-century textbook writers, Philippa's virtues as a wife and mother were reflected in her beneficial influence on English politics. This was exemplified for both Mrs Markham and Lady Callcott by her intercession with Edward III on behalf of the burghers of Calais, but also by other actions, such as her energetic rallying of an army to repel the Scottish invasion at Neville's Cross: such political interventions are viewed as the actions of a devoted wife.[34] In addition, Lady Callcott attributes to her a wide range of benefits – including assisting the foundation of churches and a new college at Oxford, inviting Froissart to England and encouraging him to write his *Chronicles*, and acting as patron to Chaucer and to scholars translating the Bible into English – as well as serving as regent of England in the absence of Edward.[35]

From the 1840s, historical accounts of many prominent women, written for women by women, began appearing in considerable numbers. Often using archival material, the best of these publications brought to light much new information, but even these well-researched works frequently showed no real critical analysis of their sources. One such publication was Agnes and Elizabeth Strickland's *Lives of the Queens of England* (1840–48): although only Agnes Strickland's name appeared on the title page, both sisters contributed to the research and the writing of the *Lives*, each taking final responsibility for a group of subjects. The sisters' biographies of British queens have been described as 'womanist' in their approach: while promoting their subjects and often sympathising with the female situation in their historical works, the Stricklands were uninterested in actively advocating women's rights or campaigning for reforms to better the social, economic, or political condition of women. In the mid-1850s, for instance, Agnes

Strickland refused to sign the petition to parliament for reform of married women's property rights.[36]

Despite their apparent endorsement of the domestic ideology of the separate spheres, the Stricklands' works show unexpected fissures in their attempt to present their subjects as ideal Victorian women. In their efforts to establish a canon of royal 'women worthies', the sisters sometimes found themselves confronted with a dilemma: how to celebrate a bewildering variety of characters while making them conform (at least partially) to the demands of domestic ideology. For Elizabeth Strickland – the sister credited with the authorship of the accounts of Philippa and Eleanor – this endeavour was reasonably straightforward when a subject lent herself to presentation as the ideal Victorian woman, but in the case of a less malleable subject, a new approach was called for. This could involve a judicious stretching of the bounds of domestic ideology to include an open acknowledgement – or even a celebration – of women's involvement in the public sphere: such an involvement could be vindicated as a natural extension of women's rightful domestic, social, cultural, and moral influences. By comparing Elizabeth Strickland's lives of Philippa and Eleanor with the popularisations of these biographies in Mary Howitt's *Biographical Sketches of the Queens of England* (1851), it can be shown that these developments are not unique to the Stricklands' works but were current in a wide range of historical biographies of women by women published in the early and mid-Victorian period. In these works, an approach to female biography which has been described as 'womanist' shades into one which is clearly feminist.

Elizabeth Strickland's biography of Philippa in the *Lives* – where the queen appears in the full glory of her 'beautiful and near perfect character'[37] – reads like an expanded version of the comments of Mrs Markham and Lady Callcott. She is the ideal wife, who moderates her husband's ruthlessness, secures his virtue, and even pawns her jewels to finance his French wars. At her death, 'the happiness, the good fortune, and even the respectability' of Edward III and his family dissolves.[38] In her lifetime, as well as intervening on behalf of the burghers of Calais, she also persuades Edward to forgo the punishment of some carpenters who have erected an unstable scaffold from which she herself has fallen. As a mother, she again sets an example: contrary to custom, she breastfeeds the Black Prince and later attempts to save him from a marriage with the flighty Joan of Kent. In addition, she promotes the economic and social welfare of her adopted country, encouraging coal-mining in Tyneside and founding the cloth industry at Norwich. 'Like a beneficent queen of the hive', Strickland enthuses, 'she cherished and protected the working bees.'[39] Her interventions in politics are conducted in a suitably womanly way: at the battle of

Neville's Cross, when she leads the English forces in the absence of Edward, she does not exhibit the 'vulgar personal bravado of the fighting woman', retiring to pray when her troops engage battle.[40] In fact, most of her political activities are confined to peace-making, as in her promotion of the Treaty of Bretigny.

The value of Philippa of Hainault as an exemplar *par excellence* of the Good Queen and the Good Woman was confirmed – even as the Stricklands were writing – by Queen Victoria herself. In the 1840s and 1850s, the Queen and Prince Consort held a series of fancy dress balls with themes from English history. At one of these events, the Plantagenet Ball of 1842, Victoria and Albert appeared as Philippa of Hainault and Edward III, associating themselves with a successful, fruitful, and long-lived marriage which was seen as a model of bourgeois domesticity.[41] Edwin Landseer's depiction of Victoria and Albert in their costumes (1842–46) once again shows his sensitivity to complex questions of power and gender posed by Victoria's role as sovereign. The appearance of Albert as Edward III – a sovereign – and Victoria as Philippa – his consort – subtly reinstated the conventional gender roles of man and wife. In the picture, Albert is in the act of stepping down from the dais on which two equal thrones stand, gallantly offering his hand to Victoria, who is firmly placed on the highest step. His deference to her as monarch (it is he, not she, who is bound to obey) is presented as a knight's chivalric devotion to his lady. This identification of Victoria and Albert with Philippa and Edward linked the Victorian court to the industrial classes by a timely reminder of Philippa's role in protecting the French burghers and fostering the cloth industry in East Anglia. During a year of economic distress and Chartist protest, it was an attempt to defuse criticism of the elite and their lifestyles and to reaffirm the authority of the monarch as head of state.[42]

However, the image of Philippa was not quite as uncomplicated as this wholesale royal adoption of her may suggest. Across Strickland's laudatory account, for instance, hangs a shadow of historical criticism: when recounting the tale of the burghers of Calais, Strickland is forced to consider the doubts cast on 'this beautiful incident' by French historians, and in particular, their unflattering comments on Philippa's subsequent seizure of the property of one of the rescued burghers. 'Biography', as Strickland comments regretfully, 'seldom permits us to portray a character approaching perfection.'[43]

This newly sceptical approach to Froissart – which Strickland wishes to ignore – is given more rein in Mary Howitt's *Biographical Sketches of the Queens of England*. Largely a plagiarism of the Strickland sisters' *Lives*, this work initially appears as even more uncritical than their narrative. This impression is confirmed by the illustrations, provided by the publisher,

Henry G. Bohn, which are absurdly idealized (figure 24): these, and the subtitle of the work, *The Royal Book of Beauty*, link the *Biographical Sketches* into the keepsake, books of beauty, and annual tradition of the 1820s and 1830s. But – although Howitt quotes copiously from Strickland's *Life* in her account of Philippa – we are pulled up short by her reflections on Strickland's account of Philippa's passive role at the Battle of Neville's Cross, which she compares with Patrick Abercromby's *Martial Achievements of the Scots Nation* (1711), a source offering a less idealized account of the queen's conduct. 'We fear', writes Howitt, 'the foregoing extract must convict the fair biographer of Philippa in a *suppressio veri*, arising in an amiable desire to exhibit the subject of her memoir to the utmost advantage.'[44] Strickland's main source, Froissart, is treated equally dismissively. After quoting the tale of the burghers from the *Chronicles*, Howitt comments that it is 'highly probable' that it is 'almost entirely fictitious'.[45] Howitt's quiet attempt to destabilise Philippa's exemplary role may reflect her feminist sympathies: a friend of Bessie Rayner Parkes and Barbara Bodichon, she was involved (unlike Agnes Strickland) in efforts leading to the passage of the Married Women's Property Act of 1857. In an interesting royal parallel, she and her husband William were often compared by their friends to the joint monarchs, William III and Mary II: Mary Howitt was evidently not a submissive consort but a partner in power.[46]

The life of Eleanor of Aquitaine proved far more problematic for Elizabeth Strickland than that of Philippa and necessitated a more revisionary interpretation. Like Lady Callcott and Mrs Markham, Strickland dwells on Eleanor's lack of domestic virtues. As the wife of Louis of France, her first husband, she is portrayed as 'not a little licentious' and prone to 'disgusting levity' in her flirtations and affairs with a variety of men, including Raymond of Poitou (her own uncle), a Turkish emir, Geoffrey Plantagenet and his son, Henry Plantagenet (her future second husband).[47] Her early political interventions prove to be disastrous: she hinders military manoeuvres by accompanying her husband on Crusade in the frivolous guise of an Amazon,[48] and leads Louis into 'the only act of wilful injustice which stains the annals of his reign', when she persuades him to support her sister's illegal marriage with military action.[49]

But Strickland, writing from a womanist perspective, points out that Eleanor's troubles are not all of her own making. Whatever her failings, her second husband Henry II is also no paragon of domestic virtue. The Fair Rosamund incident is discussed at considerable length, as Strickland attempts to separate truth from legend, and Eleanor's encouragement of her sons' rebellion against her husband is attributed to her anger over Henry's liaison with his putative daughter-in-law, Alice of France.[50] She also emphasises the importance of Eleanor's cultural role in the

Figure 24 E. Corbould (artist) and W. H. Engleton (engraver) from *Biographical Sketches of the Queens of Great Britain* (London, 1851), ed. M. Howitt, between pages 124 and 125

Anglo-Norman empire, a subject touched upon only lightly by earlier writers, claiming that the queen brought 'the arts, the idealities [sic], and refinements of life' to the rugged people of the north.[51] Moreover, Strickland argues that Eleanor's subsequent long years of captivity at the hands of Henry II teach her wisdom – 'Adversity evidently improved the character of Eleanor of Aquitaine' – a suggestion of complex character development which undermines her exemplary status as Bad Queen.[52] Strickland also complicates the interpretation of Eleanor as a Bad Woman by countering an admission that the queen is a bad wife with a presentation of her as a devoted (if not always wise) mother. On the platform of this domestic virtue, she justifies Eleanor's political activism, using her private function as a mother to vindicate her public role. She describes Eleanor as feverishly active in negotiating Richard's liberation from the Duke of Austria and in raising his ransom, and then acting as peace-maker between Richard and his rebellious brother John. Significantly, she acknowledges Eleanor's sustained and independent role as a powerful political figure, both in England and in her own domains (unlike Philippa, she was a sovereign in her own right in her native duchy and thus periodically exercised independent authority). Not for Eleanor the occasional womanly interventions of Philippa. Rather the emphasis is laid on the queen's role as the virtual co-ruler of England during Richard I's reign, where her government is characterised by 'acts of mercy and wisdom'.[53]

Nor is it just Eleanor's maternal role which is exploited to justify her activities in the public arena; her cultural role is also used as a springboard for wide-ranging interventions. Linking her cultural and governmental roles, Strickland remarks that the 'political sovereignty of her native dominions was not the only authority' that Eleanor exercised, for she was also 'chief reviewer and critic of the poets of Provence' and 'herself a popular troubadour poet'.[54] This ambitious claim made her not only the patron of cultural progress, but also an artist in her own right, extending her role as handmaiden of the arts beyond 'womanly' bounds. Strickland closes with an assessment which combines her more sympathetic consideration of Eleanor's character with a rudimentary awareness and admiration of her role as a political figure: 'Eleanora of Aquitaine is among the very few women who have atoned for an ill-spent youth, by a wise and benevolent old age. As a sovereign, she ranks among the greatest of female rulers.'[55]

Interestingly, when the more feminist Mary Howitt plagiarises this queen's life for her *Biographical Sketches*, she exhibits none of the scepticism with which she treated Strickland's account of Philippa. Her narrative of Eleanor's later life is even more laudatory than that of Strickland, while her conclusion directly echoes Strickland's: commenting that Eleanor 'stands pre-eminent among the great women of her age', she opines that the follies and crimes of her early life were atoned for by the sorrows and wisdom of her later years. She deserves 'admiration rather than blame from us'.[56]

What did subsequent scholars make of these mid-century models of queenship? Both queens' lives were revised as writing of medieval history in popular forms moved away from an anecdotal tradition based on Shakespeare's history plays, the contents of chapbooks, and credulous readings of the works of those few chroniclers earlier in print. But while Eleanor ultimately benefited from the development of history as an academic discipline, Philippa ceased to command much attention and became marginalised in the twentieth century. Although this may result partly from the fact that Eleanor is simply the more significant and fascinating, the twentieth-century historiographical reputations of the two queens cannot be explained fully without reference to their nineteenth-century status as exemplary figures.

With the publication of *The Dictionary of National Biography* in the 1880s and 1890s appear the first lengthy considerations of both queens by male historians, with some scholarly pretensions, and with the fruits of the development of medieval studies upon which to draw. These provide points of comparison with the accounts of Elizabeth Strickland and Mary Howitt; they also show how Strickland's and Howitt's partial redemption of Eleanor from the category of Bad Queen prepared the ground for serious scholarly consideration of her political role, a consideration which Good Queen Philippa would not receive.

Both writers – Thomas Andrew Archer, who wrote the article on Eleanor and William Hunt, who wrote that on Philippa – were regular contributors to the *D.N.B.* who between them spanned the period from the sixth century to the eighteenth. Both seem to be partially dependent on Strickland's biographies for basic narratives of the lives of the queens, but both attacked these biographies, thus asserting their freedom from these quintessentially picturesque accounts of their subjects. Archer condemned Strickland's account of Eleanor's Amazonian activities in the Crusades,[57] while Hunt bluntly described her story of Philippa's contribution to the ransom of Bertrand du Guesclin as 'worthless'.[58] Both copiously reference their other authorities, mainly a wide range of chroniclers, and provide far more critical comment on them than Strickland had ever attempted. In his entry on Philippa, for instance, Hunt discounted Froissart's and Jehan the Bel's accounts of her role in the battle of Neville's Cross with the comment that 'As it is not confirmed by any known English or Scottish authority, it must be regarded as extremely doubtful, especially as both the Flemish chroniclers were evidently mistaken as to the situation of the battle.'[59] However, his narrative of the tale of the burghers of Calais concludes with the comment that 'there is not the slightest reason for doubting the truth of this story'.[60] Archer's entry on Eleanor, which is remarkably free

of moralising comment on her lifestyle, concentrates on the possible political motivations of the parties involved when considering the traditional
accounts of (for instance) her intrigue with Raymond of Poitou and her
divorce from Louis. It clearly benefited greatly from the publication of many
important sources for Eleanor's life in William Stubbs's Rolls series.

This combination of a critical attitude to sources with the attempt
to construct a morally neutral political narrative is characteristic of
late nineteenth-century historiography. It foreshadows developments in late
twentieth-century research on English medieval queens, now a thriving
industry: early scholars in this field approached their subjects as biographers, but the recent studies have 'instead sought to dissect the ways in
which queens pursued and exploited means to power', analysing their political offices rather than their lives.[61] Interestingly, Hunt is unable to sustain
such an objective and politically focussed narrative as he closes his entry
on Philippa of Hainault: here her image as the exemplary Good Queen
proved too powerful. He slips briefly into the language of Strickland: 'She
was prudent, kindly, humble and devout; very liberal and pitiful, graceful
in manner, adorned, Froissart says, "with every noble virtue, and beloved
of God and all men".'[62]

Interpretations of Philippa never seem to have broken out of their
mid-nineteenth-century 'worthy woman' mould, largely because it was an
appropriate one, one which chimed in perfectly with the image which the
queen herself had promoted six centuries earlier. But one full-length biography of this queen has been published in the twentieth century. Written
by a female popular historian, Blanche C. Hardy, the author of biographies
of Arabella Stuart (1913) and the Princesse de Lamballe (1908), it is clearly
a latecomer in the Strickland tradition. This impression is confirmed by
the frontispiece illustration, which is the image of Philippa that had appeared
earlier in Mary Howitt's *Biographical Sketches* (figure 24).

Meanwhile, Eleanor of Aquitaine has attracted almost continuous
attention in the twentieth century. Biographies, in both French and English,
both popular and scholarly, have appeared in every decade but one from the
1930s onwards,[63] while fictional presentations have included both the play
and film versions of James Goldman's *A Lion in Winter*. Late twentieth-
century scholarship has produced a collection of symposium essays, edited
by W. W. Kibler, *Eleanor of Aquitaine: Patron and Politician* (1976), and
D.D.R. Owen's full-length study *Eleanor of Aquitaine: Queen and Legend*
(1993), as well as a variety of articles on specific aspects of her life and career.
While the image of Philippa of Hainault remained frozen in its
nineteenth-century manifestation, Eleanor – a powerful, energetic, and com-
pelling figure – has become something of an icon for the twentieth century.

Notes

1 *The Works of John Ruskin*, ed. T. Cook and A. Wedderburn (London, 1904–12), XVIII, p. 139.

2 L. Carroll [C. Dodgson], *Alice's Adventures in Wonderland and Through the Looking Glass*, ed. H. Haughton (London, 1998), p. 220.

3 M. Vicinus, ed., *Suffer and Be Still: Women in the Victorian Age* (London, 1972), and L. Delamont and L. Duffin, eds, *The Nineteenth-Century Woman: Her Cultural and Physical World* (London, 1978).

4 M. J. Peterson, *Family, Love, and Work in the Lives of Victorian Gentlewomen* (London, 1987); A. Vickery, 'Golden Age to separate spheres?: a review of the categories and chronology of English women's history', *Historical Journal*, 36:2 (1993), 383–414.

5 Vickery, 'Golden Age to Separate Spheres?', 414.

6 R. Maitzen, '"This Feminine Preserve": historical biographies by Victorian women', *Victorian Studies*, 38 (1995), 371–93.

7 R. A. Mitchell, '"The busy daughters of Clio': women writers of history from 1820 to 1880', *Women's History Review*, 7:1 (1998), 107–34.

8 B. G. Smith, 'The contribution of women to modern historiography in Great Britain, France, and the United States, 1750–1914', *American Historical Review*, 89 (1984), 709–32.

9 S. Oldfield, *Collective Biography of Women in Britain, 1550–1900: A Selected Annotated Bibliography* (London, 1999) for a fuller listing of biographical anthologies featuring women subjects.

10 A. Booth, 'Illustrious Company: Victoria among other women in Anglo-American role model anthologies', in M. Homans and A. Munich (eds), *Remaking Queen Victoria* (Cambridge, 1997), p. 72.

11 S. Schama, 'The domestication of majesty: royal family portraiture, 1500–1850', *Journal of Interdisciplinary History* 17:1 (1986), 156–57; A. Munich, *Queen Victoria's Secrets* (London, 1996), pp. 134–36.

12 N. J. Watson, 'Gloriana Victoriana: Victoria and the cultural memory of Elizabeth', in Homans and Munich (eds), *Remaking Queen Victoria*, pp. 79–104.

13 E. Langland, 'Nation and nationality: Queen Victoria in the developing narrative of Englishness', in Homans and Munich (eds), *Remaking Queen Victoria*, pp. 13–32.

14 For instance, Agnes Strickland's account of her life in A. and E. Strickland, *The Lives of the Queens of Scotland and Princesses Connected to the Royal Succession* (Edinburgh, 1850–58), III–VII. This is also discussed in J. E. Lewis, *Mary Queen of Scots: Romance and Nation* (London, 1998), pp. 181–86.

15 *The Works of John Ruskin*, XVIII, pp. 120, 136.

16 S. A. Weltman, 'Be not Housewifes, but Queens': Queen Victoria and Ruskin's domestic mythology', in Homans and Munich (eds), *Remaking Queen Victoria*, p. 105.

17 P. Hollis, *Ladies Elect: Women in English Local Government 1865–1914* (Oxford, 1987), pp. 472–73; F. Prochaska, *Women and Philanthropy in Nineteenth-Century England* (Oxford, 1980), pp. 7–8.

18 D. D. R. Owen, *Eleanor of Aquitaine: Queen and Legend* (London, 1993), pp. 114–48. The image is reproduced on page 157.

19 J. Froissart, *Chronicles*, trans., ed., and selected by G. Brereton (1968, this edn. 1978), pp. 9–29, is a useful introduction to Froissart and the history of the *Chronicles*.

20 R. Strong, *And When Did You Last See Your Father? The Victorian Painter and the British Past* (London, 1978), pp. 25, 78.

21 E. Taylor, *Historical Prints, Representing Some of the Most Memorable Events in English History* (London, 1821), p. 24.

22 C. Dickens, *The New Oxford Illustrated Dickens* (Oxford, 1958), p. 220.

23 *Ibid.*, facing p. 120.

24 W. M. Thackeray, *The Oxford Thackeray*, ed. G. Saintsbury (1908), VII, p. 288.

25 For her life and career, see R. A. Mitchell, 'Elizabeth Penrose', *The New Dictionary of National Biography*, eds H.C.G. Matthew and B. Harrison (forthcoming, Oxford, 2004).

26 R. B. Gotch, *Maria Callcott, the creator of 'Little Arthur'* (London, 1937) is the only biography of Lady Callcott.

27 E. Penrose ['Mrs Markham'], *A History of England from the First Invasions of the Romans to the End of the Reign of George IV* (London, 1823; this edn., 1846), pp. 78–79.

28 *Ibid.*, p. 86.

29 M. Callcott, *Little Arthur's History of England* (London, 1835; this edn., 1856), p. 60.

30 *Ibid.*

31 Taylor, *Historical Prints*, p. 40.

32 Penrose, *History of England*, p. 149.

33 Callcott, *Little Arthur's History*, p. 88.

34 Penrose, *History of England*, p. 244.

35 Callcott, *Little Arthur's History*, p. 88.

36 C. C. Orr, 'Agnes Strickland, historian of women, and the Langham Place Group', in a paper delivered at the Age of Equipoise Conference, Trinity and All Saints College, Leeds, 15–16 July 1996, coined the term 'womanist' for the stance of Agnes and Elizabeth Strickland. See also U. Pope-Hennessy, *Agnes Strickland: Biographer of the Queens of England, 1796–1874* (London, 1940), especially p. 243.

37 A. and E. Strickland, *The Lives of the Queens of England* (London, 1840–48; this edn., 1845–48), II, p. 310.

38 *Ibid.*, II, p. 360.

39 *Ibid.*, II, p. 311.

40 *Ibid.*, II, p. 331.

41 Schama, 'The domestication of majesty', pp. 155–85.

42 *Ibid.*, p. 161; Munich, *Queen Victoria's Secrets*, pp. 27–31.

43 Strickland, *Lives of the Queens*, II, pp. 336–37.

44 M. Howitt (ed.), *Biographical Sketches of the Queens of England: The Royal Book of Beauty* (London, 1851), p. 129. Although presented as the editor of the letter-press, Howitt was almost certainly the author.

45 Howitt, *Biographical Sketches*, p. 135.

46 A. Lee, *Laurels and Rosemary* (London, 1955); J. Dunicliff, *Mary Howitt: Another Lost Victorian Writer* (London, 1992).

47 Strickland, *Lives of the Queens*, I, pp. 292, 298–301.

48 *Ibid.*, I, pp. 296–97.

49 *Ibid.*, I, pp. 293–94.

50 *Ibid.*, I, pp. 315–19, 332–36.

51 *Ibid.*, I, p. 288. The extent of Eleanor's influence on the arts and the development of the conventions of courtly love is the subject of debate in several essays in W.W. Kibler (ed.), *Eleanor of Aquitaine: Patron and Politician* (London, 1976).

52 Strickland, *Lives of the Queens*, II, p. 49.

53 *Ibid.*, I, p. 350.

54 *Ibid.*, I, p. 293.

55 *Ibid.*, I, p. 358.

56 Howitt, *Biographical Sketches*, p. 63.

57 L. Stephen and S. Lee (eds), *The Dictionary of National Biography* (London, 1885–1901; repr. 1993), VI, p. 594.

58 *Ibid.*, XV, p. 1052.
59 *Ibid.*, XV, p. 1051.
60 *Ibid.*
61 J. C. Parsons, 'Family, sex and power: the rhythms of medieval queenship', in J. C. Parsons (ed.), *Medieval Queenship* (Stroud, 1994; second edn., 1998), pp. 1–2.
62 *Dictionary of National Biography*, XV, p. 1053.
63 These include A. Kelly, *Eleanor of Aquitaine and the Four Kings* (London, 1950) and M. Meade, *Eleanor of Aquitaine, A Biography* (London, 1977).

Ruskin and Carlyle: changing forms
of biography in *Fors Clavigera*

Victorian perceptions of history were closely bound up with images of the
heroic. The lives of exemplary individuals were seen to form the narratives
of the past, and to gesture towards patterns for the future.[1] Not only did
critics and historians identify heroes and heroines within history, they
created a cultural climate that favoured the appearance of contemporary
heroes, to be revered and emulated in their own lifetime. Carlyle and Ruskin
made significant contributions to this development, for they had much to
say about the role of the heroic in history. As their reputations grew, each
came to be seen by many as heroic in their own right – fearless prophets
crying out against the shallowness and corruption of the age. Ruskin, born
in 1819, was twenty-four years younger than Carlyle, and often presented
himself as his disciple. It is partly for this reason that twentieth-century
readers have been inclined to see his thinking on heroism as an extension
of Carlyle's earlier work. But the personal and intellectual relation between
the two men was dynamic, and at times combative. It cannot be understood in terms of a simple model of discipleship. The purpose of this
chapter is to re-examine Ruskin's treatment of the exemplary force of biography in the light of Carlyle's work, and to suggest that the nature of
Ruskin's debt to Carlyle is more mixed, and more critical, than has often
been recognised.

   Ruskin's early understanding of the interaction between biography, autobiography, history, and fiction was formed by his eclectic reading. Novelists
(Samuel Richardson, Walter Scott, Maria Edgeworth) suggested the potential moral force of fictional biography, while poets (Byron, Wordsworth)
could amplify the autobiographical impulse into spiritual insight. But the
writer who confirmed the link between history and biography in Ruskin's
mind was Thomas Carlyle. Ruskin did not meet Carlyle until around 1850,
and was not among the early converts to his writing. His first encounter
with Carlyle's views on the heroic in history left him unimpressed. He wrote
to his family friend and first editor, William Henry Harrison, shortly after

the appearance of Carlyle's *Heroes and Hero-Worship,* in the spring of 1841, 'What are these Carlyle lectures? People are making a fuss about them, and from what I see in the reviews, they seem absolute bombast – taking bombast, I suppose, making everyone think himself a hero, and deserving of "your wash-up", at least, from the reverential Mr. Carlyle.'[2] First-hand acquaintance with *Heroes and Hero-Worship* did not improve Ruskin's opinion, 'Read some of Carlyle's lectures. Bombast, I think; altogether approves of Mahomet, and talks like a girl of his "black eyes".'[3] Ruskin's Protestantism was at its most fervent in the early 1840s, and Carlyle's studies of 'paganism' and 'Islam' in 'The Hero as Divinity' and 'The Hero as Prophet' may well have seemed to him sacrilegious.

It was not until Ruskin encountered the more soberly written *Past and Present* (1843), with its measured eulogy of the medieval Abbot Samson, that he began to take a serious interest in the man he was eventually to acknowledge as the 'master' to whom he 'owed more than to any other living writer'.[4] The debt is particularly evident in Ruskin's developing views on biography. Like Carlyle, Ruskin was sharply critical of the contemporary phenomenon of 'lionism', which seemed to him no more than commercial publicity-mongering. Again like Carlyle, he insisted that the symbolic significance of the hero could only be properly interpreted in conjunction with an understanding of the solidly factual realities of the heroic life. For both men, history and hero-worship were inseparable, making moral sense of the narrative of the past, 'Universal History, the history of what man has accomplished in this world, is at bottom the History of the Great Men who have worked here', as Carlyle had famously asserted in *On Heroes, Hero-Worship, and the Heroic in History.*[5] In this series of six impassioned lectures, first delivered in May 1840, he acclaims the heroes of the past. But the significance of the hero is not confined to history. Carlyle's argument is that the languid perplexities of a confused age could only be resolved by the direct and semi-divine command of the 'great man', who would kindle the impotence of doubt into the vitality of belief. Carlyle's rather fevered celebration of the heroes of history, whether mythological, literary, military, or spiritual, is as political as it is literary. His eclectic examples of greatness in action – Odin, Mahomet, Dante, Shakespeare, Luther, John Knox, Johnson, Rousseau, Burns, Cromwell, and Napoleon – serve to indicate his own cultural interests, and also to demonstrate his contempt for what seemed to him the limitations of democracy, and the emptiness of utilitarianism. The liberal programmes of a reforming Parliament, no matter how well-intentioned, would never resolve the nation's miseries. The decisive intervention of a heroic man could sweep them away.

Though Carlyle's influence echoes through many of Ruskin's texts, it is particularly strong in *Fors Clavigera,* Ruskin's serial publication of the

1870s. *Fors Clavigera*'s view of history reflects many of the assertions of *Heroes and Hero-Worship*. But the oddly disparate heroes in Carlyle's collection of lectures are very differently characterised from the equally diverse list whose biographies figure in the versions of history told in *Fors Clavigera*. Carlyle is primarily interested in those whose active heroism, by whatever means, moves and shakes the world. Ruskin's approach to biography takes a more inward, self-reflective, and often very much more sceptical turn. His exemplary lives often have as much to do with failure as with success. They represent a necessary corrective to any tendency to over-simplify Victorian approaches to what was involved in the greatness of a life, and in its limitations.

Ruskin's relations with Carlyle's literary example were always complicated, and sometimes tense, and this was so partly because of the ambivalence with which Carlyle himself functioned as hero in Ruskin's mind. Carlyle was indeed a hero. But he was also a friend, occasionally an unpredictable friend, and in some ways also a rival.[6] He could not be translated into a safe literary image insulated by distance and time. The two men were particularly close in the mid-1870s, when Ruskin was actively engaged with the serial publication of *Fors Clavigera*, and with the associated activities of the utopian Guild of St George, on whose newly acquired land Ruskin hoped to provide his readers with practical models for the revival of pre-industrial communities. In the spring of 1874 Ruskin promised that he would write to Carlyle as regularly as he had once written to his own father, John James Ruskin, 'who had his letter every day, whether there was anything in it or not'.[7] In later years Ruskin habitually addressed his letters to Carlyle to 'Dearest Papa'. But, like other father-images in Ruskin's life, Carlyle eventually appeared to him as deeply flawed. In 1886, five years after Carlyle's death, Ruskin wrote to his American friend Charles Eliot Norton: 'How many wiser folk than I go mad for good and all . . . like poor Turner at the last, Blake always, Scott in his pride, Irving in his faith, and Carlyle because of the poultry next door.'[8] Ruskin himself had suffered his first bout of serious mental illness in 1878, and subsequent breakdowns meant that in 1886 he had a long and painful history of mental instability to look back on. The memory of Carlyle, like that of Turner or Scott or John James Ruskin, was absorbed into the outline of a complex self-image, representing imperfect and finally frustrated greatness, greatness run mad. There is in Ruskin's composite writing of the 1870s and early 1880s a shift from the resonance of the Carlylean public statement to a more privately textured analysis, as Ruskin attempts to comprehend and come to terms with the process of recording his own darkened life.

Fors Clavigera was begun in 1871, and published more or less monthly, with some long gaps, until 1884. With its difficult and allusive title, its episodic publication, and its rebarbative style, it has become one of the least read texts among Ruskin's expansive late writings. Its form is a mixed one. It is publicly addressed, to the 'workmen and labourers of Great Britain'. But it is also a collection of letters, a literary form implying private and personal communication. The densely referential methods of *Fors* seem initially to suggest that its appeal can never have been anything other than esoteric, and that its influence must always have been confined to a few very highly educated readers. In fact, however, its contemporary readership was surprisingly diverse, though never large. It included followers from working populations alongside the leisured middle classes, together with some influential and wealthy opinion-formers.[9] Women were among Ruskin's most devoted followers in his later years, and they formed a substantial proportion of the readership of *Fors*. The assorted nature of this audience suggests that one of the features that makes *Fors Clavigera* an innovatory and fruitful text is its steady refusal to be contained within conventional categories of writing. It is simultaneously public and private, aesthetic and political, historical and contemporary. Its material is obscure and learned, but its style is often oddly direct.

The re-modelling of biography is one of the most significant ways in which these strange letters break down barriers between different forms of writing and different patterns of reading. The letters of *Fors Clavigera* persistently tell stories of exemplary lives – soldiers and artists, kings, peasants, and writers. Some of these tales are told in extensive detail, some exist in brief references. Some are narratives of heroism, some of folly, while others describe lives that are both heroic and foolish. All are didactic, for Ruskin shared Carlyle's settled conviction that the purpose of biography is to teach us how to do the world's work. Central to this educative process is the telling of *Fors Clavigera*'s most resonant life-story, of the narrative that shapes all of Ruskin's later writing – the story of his own life. It becomes progressively clearer to the readers of *Fors* that it is this story, emerging from the constructs of memory rather than the formal disciplines of history, that lies behind the others. Biography and autobiography are not wholly distinct within Ruskin's teaching strategies. What is to be gathered from recalling the lives of other people is not easily separated from what we can learn from remembering our own lives.

In the earlier letters of *Fors,* Ruskin's focus is sometimes on lives that seem to him to be of national resonance. Written at a time when accelerating social and political change, together with the cataclysm of the Franco-Prussian war, had led to a widely shared sense of uncertainty, these initiating letters are deeply interested in where Englishness comes from, and what its destiny might be. Ruskin chooses to describe 'English ghosts',[10] lives that exemplify the virtues and the corruptions of national character, that have combined in the formation of the unhappy condition of the national life he sees around him in 1871. Some of these lives are located in the medieval period, for Ruskin's renewed interest in medieval history and literature in the 1870s is one of the shaping forces behind *Fors*. An early example comes in his letter of March 1871, later entitled 'Richard of England', and featuring King Richard I, a long-standing English hero through his association with the Robin Hood legends. In Ruskin's account, however, Richard's brand of heroism emerges as uncomfortably problematic:

> Men called him 'Lionheart', not untruly; and the English as a people, have prided themselves somewhat ever since on having, every one of them, the heart of a lion; without enquiring particularly either what sort of heart a lion has, or whether to have the heart of a lamb might not sometimes be more to the purpose.[11]

Richard's peculiarly English vigour, as Ruskin defines it, is practical and down-to-earth, not without worldly use or worldly honour, but finally deficient because it fails to recognise the higher spiritual laws, which should govern national behaviour. It may seem odd, not to say perverse, for Ruskin to single out this peculiarly un-English king to typify English character, since few kings have had less immediate contact with their kingdoms than Richard, who spent only six months of a ten-year reign there. But this is rather the point, and Ruskin has no hesitation in describing Richard as a true 'representative of one great species of the British squire'.[12] Good-humoured, selfish, and thoughtlessly courageous, Richard emerges from Ruskin's account as an irrepressibly child-like figure, never where he should be, refusing to fulfil the duties proper to his role. Through his barbed description of Richard's dashing but inadequate life, Ruskin reproaches the irresponsibility of the English aristocracy of his own time: 'And it remains true of the English squire to this day, that, for the most part, he thinks that his kingdom is given him that he may be bright and brave; and not at all that the sunshine and valour in him is meant to be of use to his kingdom.'[13]

The lion-hearted Richard emerges from this sceptical analysis as a much diminished figure. He is very far from the shining literary image of Arthur the 'blameless king', still under construction in Tennyson's great medievalist text, *Idylls of the King* (1859–85), another composite work which attempted to build a restored sense of national identity out of modern corruption. Ruskin had, indeed, objected to the Arthurian medievalism of the *Idylls* on the Carlylean grounds that Tennyson's poetry was woven out of the ideal rather than the real, out of fiction rather than fact. He had written to Tennyson in 1859:

Great power ought not to be spent on visions of things past, but on the living present . . . I cannot but think that the intense, masterful and unerring transcript of an actuality, and the relation of a story of any real human life as a poet would watch and analyze it, would make all men feel more or less what poetry was, as they felt what Life and Fate were in their instant workings.[14]

Ruskin's Richard embodies this conviction; his is a real human life, exemplary in its deficiencies rather than its triumphs. The meaning of such a life is by no means confined to the past. Ruskin uses Richard to under-write his own immediate political purposes, and as confirming the need for a newly regenerated aristocracy, one of the central premises of *Fors Clavigera*'s reforming agenda.

The edged and reductive irreverence with which the kingly Richard is treated is a reminder of the curious blend of traditional Christian values and robust anti-authoritarianism that made *Fors* so attractive to disaffected idealists, and to the ambitious workmen and self-educated young women who were often its most committed readers. But Richard is very unlike Ruskin, and in general Ruskin is more deeply interested in lives which touch at least in part his own personality and his own remembered experience. The novelist Walter Scott qualified on both grounds. Scott, whom Ruskin had first read as a child, figured among that small charmed circle of writers who had been a feature of his youth, and who were also identified with the Edinburgh of his father, John James Ruskin. Like Carlyle, Scott contributed to Ruskin's shadowy sense of Scotland as the place of origin, the place where his own life and thought was fathered. In writing of Scott in a series of *Fors* letters in 1873, Ruskin's tone is darker, gentler, and more elegiac than it is in his descrip-tion of the quintessentially English King Richard as the brisk and cheerful squire. Scott is given something closer to fully heroic status in Ruskin's inter-pretation, though here too the heroism is finally qualified and problematic.

Scott was a writer, and in belonging to the literary and cultural world of Ruskin's childhood he serves as a more intimate model for Ruskin's sense of his own work. The financial ruin that followed Scott's ambitions to live like a laird on the proceeds of insecure investment darkened his later years. In his stubborn and honourable labour to pay off his overwhelming debts, Scott reminded Ruskin of his own father, whose early manhood was devoted to the repayment of debts incurred by the economic failure. Courageous in the face of adversity and disappointment, proud, and tirelessly produc-tive, Scott as a historical novelist seemed to Ruskin to demonstrate an allegiance to the defeated values of the past that confirmed his own crit-ical project. But Scott's life also appeared to prefigure the decline that Ruskin feared for himself, for the fiction of his final years provided sombre evidence of his decaying powers.

Interestingly, though Ruskin draws heavily on Lockhart's biography[15] to give a detailed account of the circumstances of Scott's early life, he explicitly and vehemently denies any intention of giving his readers anything approaching a 'life' of Scott. Scott's example is to challenge and instruct, not to reassure or to entertain. Ruskin's readers

> must please to remember that I am only examining the conditions of the life of this wise man, that they may learn how to rule their own lives, or their children's, or their servants'; and, for the present, with this partic- ular object, that they may be able to determine, for themselves, whether ancient sentiment, or modern common-sense, is to be the rule of life, and of service . . . You are always willing enough to *read* lives, but never willing to *lead* them.[16]

What Ruskin emphasises unrelentingly in his selection of characteristic details from the life of Scott is their use as a moral model of old-fashioned virtue, as it might be contrasted with the utilitarian dreariness of modern common-sense.

Memory, rather than scholarship, draws the outlines of Scott's lost world, as Ruskin repeatedly interweaves his stories of Scott with the recol- lected details of his own family life. At one point he turns from the image of Scott's sternly upright mother, who is reported never to have allowed her back to touch the chair, to that of his own equally erect Scottish mother, Margaret Ruskin: 'I have seen my own mother travel from sunrise to sunset, in a summer's day, without once leaning back in the carriage.'[17] These admirably vertical ladies, 'obedient . . . to the severest laws of morality and life',[18] are favourably compared with the limp and drooping girls that Ruskin observes in his own time, slumped into a 'languid Paradise of sofas and rocking-chairs'.[19] The contrast between the uncompromising, prickly women lovingly remembered in Scott's life and in Ruskin's own childhood, and the self-indulgently malleable modern girls is curiously like that between the stiffly angled pinnacles and crockets of the medieval Gothic that Ruskin admired and the sophisticated curves of the Renaissance architecture that he so loathed. Similarly, it is another version of the contrast between the disciplined faith of the past and the venal modernity that has succeeded it, a difference for Ruskin which is never to the advantage of the present. Such juxtapositions constitute the basis of Ruskin's biographical method in *Fors Clavigera*. The terms of the comparison matter far more to his inter- pretation of the lessons of biography than does historical accuracy, about which he is always disarmingly casual, noting that he is 'not solicitous at all to avoid mistakes; for being entirely sure of my main ground, and entirely honest in purpose, I know that I cannot make any mistake which will inval- idate my work'.[20] The reality of fact is for Ruskin a moral phenomenon, rather than a simple matter of empirical verification.

Ruskin's approach to the story of his own life was formed by the same beliefs that motivate his work as a biographer. It was in *Fors Clavigera* that Ruskin first tried to set down an account of his early life, in a scattered narrative which he began in October 1871, and continued in brief and inter-mittent episodes in letters up to May 1876. These fragments were later expanded and published separately between 1886 and 1889 as his celebrated autobiography, *Praeterita* (meaning 'things past'). It is in the latter form that the autobiography is now most often studied. Yet to read *Praeterita* is often an oddly disorienting experience, for without its intended context in *Fors Clavigera* many dimensions of Ruskin's multiple narrative are lost. Twentieth-century scholarship has shown just how far Ruskin fashioned fact into narrative in describing his own life. More than one motive directed this remodelling process. Nostalgic, often comic, and self-deprecating, Ruskin's autobiographical account was in part an attempt to win the sympathy and affection of his beloved young Irish friend, Rose La Touche, with whom he was forbidden direct correspondence throughout much of the early 1870s. This partly accounts for the rather misleading emphasis on the damaging severity of his upbringing, since one of his purposes was to persuade Rose, whose parents objected to Ruskin's courtship, that parents do not always know best in denying their children's wishes.[21] Alongside this intensely private design, however, is Ruskin's intention to use the outline of his own imperfect life to illuminate our understanding of how all should live. He explains to his readers, 'Have patience with me in this egotism; it is necessary for many reasons that you should know what influences have brought me into the temper in which I write to you.'[22] In one of the later autobiographical passages of *Fors Clavigera*, Ruskin returns to his main purpose in including autobiography as an integral part of his polemic, asking how far the 'salutary' modes of his early education might be made 'attainable for young people in general'.[23] His answer is a sober one. His development had been made possible by vanishing traditions of mutual service. The new world of 'the modern school board'[24] will, he suggests, produce no more children like the fortunate and eager young Ruskin lovingly and critically remembered in *Fors*.

Like his biographies, Ruskin's autobiography is primarily didactic. Restored to its original setting in *Fors Clavigera*, it often seems more political, and less personal, than the gentler pages of *Praeterita*. Ruskin remembers, for instance, how as a child he had accompanied his wine-merchant father on his annual sales tours,

> and in reverentest manner I thus saw all the noblemen's houses in England; not indeed myself at that age caring for the pictures, but much for castles and ruins, feeling more and more, as I grew older, the healthy delight of uncovetous admiration, and perceiving, as soon as I could perceive any

political truth at all, that it was probably much happier to live in a small house, and have Warwick Castle to be astonished at, than to live in Warwick Castle, and have nothing to be astonished at; but that, at all events, it would not make Brunswick Square in the least more pleasantly habitable, to pull Warwick Castle down. And, at this day, though I have kind invitations enough to visit America, I could not, even for a couple of months, live in a country so miserable as to possess no castles.[25]

The half-bantering tone disguises a serious purpose. Again, the basis of Ruskin's method is comparative, setting old-fashioned sentiment against modern common sense. What he describes as his 'old Tory'[26] notions of kinghood and greatness are juxtaposed with the implied littleness of contemporary republicanism, and reminiscence becomes the means of political comment. Yet the noblemen who ought to have been living in the castles were failing in their duty, having reprehensibly decamped to the fashionable squares and crescents of London. They are seen as persistently deficient, irresponsible in the same way as Richard the Lionheart. Ruskin remembers his childhood custom of wearing a gilded oak-apple on 29 May in honour of the Restoration of Charles II, but asserts that this emblem of an inadequate king soon failed to satisfy him: 'As I grew older, the desire for red pippins instead of brown ones, and Living Kings instead of dead ones, appeared to me rational as well as romantic; and gradually it has become the main purpose of my life to grow pippins, and its chief hope, to see Kings.'[27] Here as elsewhere in *Fors Clavigera* nostalgic sentiment slips into the declaration of utopian reforming aspiration. The example of defective dead kings is outweighed by the prospect of better living ones.

In his later years, Ruskin grew ever more vehement in his mistrust of the growing contemporary enthusiasm for the writing and reading of biographies of the great and the dead. It had at one time looked likely that he would himself contribute to the movement by producing the life of Turner which he seemed better qualified than anyone to write. In 1860, he had noted in the final volume of his *Modern Painters* (1843–60):

> And the lesson we have finally to learn from Turner's life is broadly this, that all the power of it came of its mercy and sincerity; all the failure of it, from its want of faith. It has been asked of me, by several of his friends, that I should endeavour to do some justice to his character, mistaken wholly by the world. If my life is spared, I will.[28]

But as the years went by, Ruskin came to feel that Turner's best biography was to be found in his works. He recorded his decision not to write a life of Turner in *The Queen of the Air* (1869): 'Of Turner's life, and of its good and evil, both great, but the good immeasurably greater, his work is in all things a perfect and transparent evidence. His biography is simply, "He did this, nor will ever another do its like again".'[29]

Ruskin's growing suspicion of contemporary biographies was deepened by his reluctant participation in the corrosive controversy generated by the publication of James Anthony Froude's biographical studies of Carlyle in the early 1880s.[30] It was a conflict in which Ruskin found himself awkwardly placed. He had known Froude for years, and respected him. It was, indeed, through Froude's editorship of *Fraser's Magazine* that Carlyle had found in 1862 an outlet for Ruskin's own writings on political economy, later published as *Munera Pulveris*. Carlyle and Froude had long been associated in Ruskin's mind as among the few active champions of his work. In 1873 he claimed in a letter to Carlyle that his writing gave him no pleasure, 'except because you and Froude and one or two other friends still care for it'.[31] In 1874, he wrote an admiring letter to Froude: 'I am not the institutor, still less the guide . . . but I am the Exponent of the Reaction for Veracity in Art which corresponds partly to Carlyle's and your work in History, and partly to Linnaeus's in natural science. You put the real men before us instead of ideal ones.'[32] In general, Ruskin approved of Froude's vigorous and occasionally unflattering portrait of Carlyle. But he was also a close friend of Charles Eliot Norton, the American scholar who, together with Carlyle's niece Mary Aitken, vehemently objected to Froude's uncompromisingly 'real' approach to Carlyle's life. At first, Ruskin attempted to make peace between his two friends, writing to Norton in 1882, 'I am very fond of Froude, and am with him in all that he has done and said, about C, if it *had* to be said or done, at all and I never saw anyone more deeply earnest & affectionate in trying to do right.'[33] Later Ruskin was increasingly angered by Norton's high-handed and proprietorial attitude to Carlyle's memory. One of his final letters to Norton, written in 1889, returns to the subject: 'What ever put it into your head that *you* could understand Carlyle better than Froude or I could?'[34] The increasingly acrimonious quarrel became a source of considerable personal distress in the troubled years of Ruskin's later life. He even contemplated setting the record straight by writing a biographical study of his own, writing to Norton in 1886 that he was 'not so anxious about your having your ideal Carlyle, as getting my own extremely positive view of him – and his Miss Welsh – put into such photography as I can, through my spectacles – readjusted on nose'.[35] But Ruskin was at this point in his life too ill for the sustained effort such a work would have required.

Froude's biographical work seemed to Ruskin to be of the kind that Carlyle himself had sanctioned, in that it made a serious attempt to tell the truth about a life as it has really been lived. Yet the outcome had been destructive, resulting only in misunderstanding, bitterness, and damage to Carlyle's reputation and influence. Readers of Froude's edition of Carlyle's *Reminiscences* had been no better able to respond to its teaching than readers of *Fors Clavigera*. Ruskin wrote to George Richmond in 1881 that those who had disapproved of the *Reminiscences* had been able to perceive nothing, 'but the bits of brick that hurt their own puffy personages, and see and feel nothing of its mighty interests – its measureless pathos'.[36] If Froude's serious and honest work had done little good, other more popular celebratory biographies seemed to him to offer nothing more than false reassurance or empty entertainment:

> Lives in which the public are interested are scarcely ever worth writing. For the most part compulsorily artificial, often affectedly so, – on the whole, fortunate beyond ordinary rule, – and, so far as the men are really greater than others, unintelligible to the common reader, – the lives of statesmen, soldiers, authors, artists, or any one habitually set in the sight of many, tell us at last little more than what sort of people they dealt with, and of pens they wrote with; the personal life is inscrutably broken up, – often contemptibly, and the external aspect of it merely a husk, at the best. The lives we need to have written for us are of the people whom the world has not yet thought of, – far less heard of, – who are yet doing the most of its work, and of whom we may learn how it can best be done.[37]

This was written in 1883, just before *Fors* came to the end of its run of publication, as part of a Preface to 'The Story of Ida', a biography of a Tuscan peasant girl who had died at the age of nineteen. It was written by Ruskin's artist friend Francesca Alexander, who had been a friend of Ida.[38] By this time Ruskin's labours for the Guild of St George and *Fors Clavigera* had come to seem largely futile gestures. The work of Francesca Alexander, which interested him deeply, represents a very different interpretation of the exemplary force of biography.

That Ruskin here presents the life of a girl, a life first told by a woman, is an indication of how far he had moved from the uncompromisingly masculine Carlylean model, always exclusively focussed on the idea of the 'Great Man'. It is worth noting how often Ruskin's positive cultural references towards the end of his life are centred on women. It is also notable, and a further indication of how Ruskin had come to question the precedents of Carlyle and his own earlier evangelically Protestant work, that Ida is not only a woman, but a woman whose moral strength is grounded in devout Catholicism. The strength of her faith now seemed to him to matter much more than the allegiance to any particular religious tradition. 'This is the story of a Catholic girl written by a Protestant one, yet the two of them so united in the Truth of the Christian Faith, and in the joy of its Love, that they are absolutely unconscious of any difference in the forms or letter of their religion.'[39] Though Ruskin seems never to have been seriously tempted to convert to Catholicism, and was sometimes exasperated by the more florid aspects of Catholic custom, he had become increasingly impatient with what he wrote of in 'Notes on the Priest's Office'[40] as the corrosive self-assertion of 'the typical modern English Protestant, ignorant alike of painting, sculpture and music, and complacent in the drab of his individual Papacy'.[41] Ida was an especially virtuous Catholic, at least as Alexander remembered her, and her story amounts to a secularised and semi-fictional hagiography of a pious and sentimental kind that has not been to the taste of the late twentieth century. Indeed, it was hardly to the taste of the late nineteenth century either, and *The Story of Ida* has never been widely admired. Despite its claims to veracity, it is clear that it was greatly influenced by literary traditions of the holy deathbed, from Richardson's Clarissa to Dickens's Little Nell. Here, once again, the shadow of Rose La Touche falls over the page. Through Alexander's lingering description of Ida's death, brought about by the fecklessness of an unworthy lover, Ruskin approaches the memory of Rose's deathbed. In her last meeting with Ruskin, Rose had recited the hymn 'Jesu, lover of my soul' to him.[42] But the point of Ida's life and death, as Ruskin presented it in one of the periods of respite from the bouts of mental illness that were gradually reducing his old age into inactivity, lay in the perceived reality of the story, not in its symbolic power or its autobiographical reference, though for him it evidently had both of these. Ida's life was one of service and self-renunciation. Ruskin admonishes his readers: 'Of invented effects of light and shade on imaginary scenes, it seems to me we have admired too many. Here is a real passage of human life, seen in the light Heaven sent for it.'[43] In this, returning to the parallels with which I began, Ruskin remains close to Carlyle. Biography, and autobiography, are drawn together in his writing by the shared moral energy of fact, and it is this that gives them their continuing power to teach and to reform.

However, if we look back to what Carlyle had claimed for heroism in *Heroes and Hero-Worship*, deep-seated differences emerge. Carlyle insists on the active influence of the great man:

> He is the living light-fountain, which is good and pleasant to be near. The light which enlightens, which has enlightened the darkness of the world; and this not as a kindled lamp only, but rather as a natural luminary shining by the gift of Heaven; a flowing light-fountain, as I say, of native original insight, of manhood and heroic nobleness: – in whose radiance all should feel that it is well with them.[44]

This is close to the Romantic concept of genius, the man who is singled out by Heaven to be a source of light, or a 'flowing light-fountain', in Carlyle's energetic metaphor. But the passive and saintly Ida receives the light of Heaven, reflects it, and is seen by it, but she does not, in Carlylean fashion, emit it. Our last glimpse of Ida is as sanctified body, lying on her bed illuminated by the sunset. More than forty years after Carlyle published

Heroes and Hero-Worship, Ruskin has come to distrust the self-determining autonomy of Romantic concepts of greatness, with their attendant dangers of pride, madness, misunderstanding and irresponsibility, dangers which had written themselves into the narrative of his own life. Increasingly, he returned to an older model of heroism, characterised by faithful service, obedience, and resignation. Editing the story of Ida, which was itself an act of service, was one of the last things Ruskin did before taking up the fragmented story of his own life again, the autobiography he had begun in *Fors Clavigera* and continued in *Praeterita*. It was a story that was never to be completed, and ends in the silence that overtook Ruskin's final years of illness in Brantwood. This most eloquent and articulate Victorian, who had himself become such an exemplary figure to his diverse and numerous followers, might seem a quintessentially representative example of the Carlylean image of the great man. Yet Ruskin's later life and work combine to suggest that his response to Carlyle's potent model of biography grew increasingly complex, and disillusioned, in his final years.

Notes

1   See A. D. Culler, *The Victorian Mirror of History* (New Haven and London, 1985), J. W. Burrow, *A Liberal Descent: Victorian Historians and the English Past* (Cambridge, 1981), and R. Chapman, *The Sense of the Past in Victorian Literature* (London, 1986) for fuller accounts of the uses of history in Victorian culture.

2   *The Works of John Ruskin*, eds E. T. Cook and A. Wedderburn, 39 vols. (London, 1903–12), XXXVI.25. Subsequent references to this edition will give volume and page numbers only.

3   *The Diaries of John Ruskin*, eds J. Evans and J. H. Whitehouse, 3 vols. (Oxford, 1956–9), I, p. 199.

4   XII.503.

5   *The Works of Thomas Carlyle*, ed. H. D. Traill, Centenary Edition, 30 vols. (London, 1896–99), V.1. Subsequent references to this edition will give volume and page numbers only. The lectures are usually known by the title they subsequently acquired, *Heroes and Hero-Worship*.

6   The two men had quarrelled sharply and rather publicly in 1867, though their friendship was quickly repaired. See *The Correspondence of Thomas Carlyle and John Ruskin*, ed. George Allen Cate (Stanford, 1982), pp. 27–30; 131–41.

7   *Correspondence of Carlyle and Ruskin*, 19 May 1874, p. 184.

8   *The Correspondence of John Ruskin and C. E. Norton*, eds J. L. Bradley and I. Ousby (Cambridge, 1987), 28 Aug. 1886, p. 494.

9   See B. Maidment, 'Interpreting Ruskin: 1870–1914', in J. Dixon Hunt and F. Holland (eds), *The Ruskin Polygon: Essays on the Imagination of John Ruskin* (Manchester, 1982), pp. 158–71; J. Stoddart, *Ruskin's Culture Wars: Fors Clavigera and the Crisis of Victorian Liberalism* (Charlottesville and London, 1998), pp. 1–22.

10   XXVII.51.

11   XXVII.53–4.

12   XXVII.54.

13   XXVII.57.

14   XXXVI.320–1.

15   J. G. Lockhart, *The Life of Sir Walter Scott*, 10 vols. (Edinburgh, 1839).
16   XXVII.606–7.
17   XXVII.609.
18   XXVII.611.
19   XXVII.609.
20   XXVII.602.
21   The publication of *The Ruskin Family Letters: The Correspondence of John James Ruskin, His Wife, and Their Son, John, 1801–1843*, ed. Van Akin Burd, 2 vols. (New York and London, 1973) first made it clear that Ruskin's childhood was much warmer and happier than the somewhat bleak account in *Praeterita* suggests. The point is confirmed in Hilton's *John Ruskin: The Early Years* (New Haven and London, 1985), pp. 8–32; and in Sheila Emerson's *Ruskin: The Genesis of Invention* (Cambridge, 1993), pp. 2–34.
22   XXVII.167.
23   XXVIII.391.
24   XXVIII.392.
25   XXVII.170.
26   XXVII.171.
27   XXVII.171.
28   VII.442.
29   XIX.397.
30   Froude's edition of Carlyle's *Reminiscences* appeared in 1881, only a month after Carlyle died. His four-volume biography soon followed: *Thomas Carlyle: A History of the First Forty Years of His Life, 1795–1835*, 2 vols. (London, 1882), and *Thomas Carlyle: A History of His Life in London, 1834–1881*, 2 vols. (London, 1884).
31   *Correspondence of Carlyle and Ruskin*, Oct. 1873, p. 173.
32   XXXVII.83.
33   *Correspondence of Ruskin and Norton*, 30 Aug. 1882, pp. 447–48.
34   *Ibid.*, 13 June 1889, p. 507.
35   *Ibid.*, 28 Apr. 1886, p. 490.
36   *Correspondence of Carlyle and Ruskin*, 20 May 1881, p. 45.
37   XXXII.5–6.
38   Francesca Alexander was an American, brought up in Florence, who enthusiastically collected and illustrated the old songs and street ballads of the country people of Tuscany. An account of her friendship with Ruskin in the 1880s is to be found in *John Ruskin's Letters to Francesca, and Memoirs of the Alexanders*, ed. L.Gray Swett (Boston, 1931); see also J. Marsh and P. Gerrish Nunn (eds), *Pre-Raphaelite Women Artists* (Manchester, 1997), pp. 138–39.
39   XXXII.7.
40   Included in Part III of Ruskin's edition of Francesca Alexander's *Roadside Songs of Tuscany* (Sept. 1884), XXX.116–26.
41   XXXII.121.
42   Ruskin described the meeting in a letter to Francesca Alexander, dated 16 Mar. 1886. See *The Winnington Letters: John Ruskin's Correspondence with Margaret Alexis Bell and the Children at Winnington Hall*, ed. Van Akin Burd (London, 1969), p. 83.
43   XXXII.6–7.
44   V.2.

PART IV

EXEMPLARY TYPES

'Martyrs to a nice sense of honor': exemplars of commercial morality in the mid-nineteenth-century United States

For two centuries it has been said that individuals who suffer financial failure in America can rebound to success much more readily than they could in Europe. Bankruptcy, instead of carrying a stigma, is virtually a test of fitness for doing business. The English visitor Henry Fearon wrote in 1818 that 'failure in trade, so far from being a cause of loss, or a subject of shame, is generally the means of securing a fortune; and . . . no kind of disadvantage or disgrace attaches to the individual' who has suffered it. In 1857 a German, Count Adam de Gurowski, remarked that 'an individual, unsuccessful in any branch or line, rises as quickly as he fell; dusts himself off, and rushes again into the same or another enterprise, without any great injury to his name or credit'.[1]

To many Europeans this facility to fail without dishonour indicated an alarming absence of moral restraint, which they attributed to the American economy's free-booting character, to mobility, the frontier, and to rugged individualism. Gurowski noted that Americans moved around and changed occupation 'with a rapidity and ease neither thought of nor possible' in Europe. With a whole continent open before them, it seemed, Americans might behave as they wished. The Scottish radical exile William Russell was shocked at the practices he encountered in Middletown, Connecticut, in the 1790s. 'Here a man may break his word with impunity . . . He may have been two or three times a bankrupt and be known to have defrauded his creditors', but as soon as he had regained wealth he would 'be received in the first company'. The suspicion was widespread that American economic expansion was achieved at the expense of all standards of honesty and decency.[2]

In fact, however, commercial morality was a constant theme in American public and private discourse. Except between the late 1840s and the mid-1860s, when slavery dominated national politics, questions about the conduct of economic life defined most differences between political parties. Debates about bankruptcy laws, imprisonment for debt, and the currency revolved around questions of equity and fair dealing. Commercial correspondence was constantly preoccupied with the rules of good behaviour and their violation. Anxieties about trade and its risks produced an endless stream of jokes and humorous anecdotes. Far from being indifferent to standards of economic morality, many Americans were deeply concerned about them.

Behind the public debates and private anxieties were some fundamental difficulties. On one hand, standards of honesty seemed to demand strict attention to property rights and the satisfaction of obligations. On the other, economic development seemed to require a flexible attitude to debt. The United States Constitution itself reflected this dilemma: it prohibited 'Law[s] impairing the obligation of Contracts', implying that debt-relief was unacceptable, but also gave Congress the power to 'establish uniform Laws on the subject of Bankruptcies throughout the United States', measures that could shelter debtors from the demands of their creditors.[3] The expansion and turbulence of the American economy prompted efforts to identify the acceptable behaviour that could assure individuals a reputation for good character. Various forms of writing, published and unpublished, held up exemplars of economic morality for emulation.

This chapter traces the development of these exemplary discourses in the uncertain business world of the mid-nineteenth century.[4] As the first part of the discussion suggests, there was no single American tradition for treating the issues of debt and bankruptcy. Nor did economic or political conditions indicate a clear path for resolving them. Business morality became largely a matter for individual self-regulation. Debates over exemplary behaviour were focussed by the consequences of the financial panic of 1837, which caused widespread failures, especially in the north-eastern states. One result was a short-lived attempt to operate a federal bankruptcy statute, but a more permanent outcome was the development of commercial credit-reporting to regulate the granting of credit. Accordingly, the second part of the chapter examines credit reports, and their construction of notions of exemplary behaviour. This was not a value-neutral process. The evangelical origins of credit-reporting and its roots in small-town business activity ensured that the concepts it employed drew heavily on pre-existing moral and religious precepts. Credit-reporting and its standards influenced the conduct of economic life, but did not prevent business failures. As individuals struggled to recover from financial disaster, they had to face not just material obstacles but the imputation of unworthiness that accompanied relief from debt. The final part of the discussion suggests how, in biographical and autobiographical narratives, those who recovered from financial failure constructed ideals of exemplary conduct designed to repel the suspicion of dishonesty. The notion that recovery from debt was a process of moral, as well as monetary, redemption helped to legitimise the return of former bankrupts to full participation in business activity.

This analysis of American discourses of commercial morality provides a case-study of the creation and adoption of notions of exemplariness. It traces a process by which economic conditions influenced groups in American society concerned with moral as well as material success, leading them to identify characteristics that they regarded as exemplary for the conduct of business transactions. Institutions and personal experience in turn combined to cause individuals to apply these characteristics to their evaluations and portrayals of their own and others' characters. Like any construction of exemplariness, these discourses were prescriptive, and need not have shaped actual conduct. However, in the hands of certain groups in the 1830s and 1840s, concepts of exemplary behaviour passed from prescriptive literature into credit reports, and gained the power to influence economic life. Their subsequent adoption in biographical and autobiographical narratives suggests that certain people internalised them, using them to help fashion their sense of worthiness and self-identity. They were congruent with other contemporary efforts to understand and control behaviour, particularly those connected with evangelical moral and social reform. Exemplariness became a means of moral justification and redemption. Because it was a construction of particular social groups, however, it also became an instrument of social distinction and exclusion.

Whether in plantation economies, where society was dominated by the patronage of powerful families, or in freehold farming regions, early American economic life was dominated by local exchange among neighbours, family, and kin. Incurring debt and extending credit were inherent in these exchanges; as a deposition in a 1790s Delaware court case put it, the plaintiff and defendant 'did neighbor with each other, by borrowing & lending, etc.'. In agricultural-based economies with long crop and trade cycles, indebtedness was normal and expected. J. Hector St. John de Crèvecoeur noted in the 1780s that 'it is vain to say: Why do they borrow? . . . It is impossible in America to till a farm without it.' Debts ran for long periods and were regarded as part of the give and take of life; indeed, as a Massachusetts epitaph of 1833 suggests, they were so normal as to be a metaphor for life itself:

> Lord he was thine and not our own,
> Thou hast not done us wrong,
> We thank thee for that precious loan
> Afforded us so long.[5]

'Neither a borrower nor a lender be' was not a precept that many early Americans could observe. Over long distances, where dealings were between strangers, credits shorter, and risks greater, elaborate efforts were made through correspondence and personal connections to establish a basis of trust. Merchants' letters embodied the construction of what one recent scholar has termed 'narratives of reliability', on which the minimisation of risk could be based.[6]

Still, attitudes to economic fluctuation and misfortune had varied with cultural context in the colonial period. The planters of colonial Virginia had built their tobacco-exporting economy on long debts to British merchants. It is not surprising that, when Mason Locke Weems compiled his life of George Washington as an exemplar for American youth, he should have spun a famous tale about the young Washington's honesty, but said little about the planter's economic conduct. In Puritan New England failure in hard times had been tolerated. Large numbers of people in a web of reciprocal obligations might support those who went under, by extending credit or forgiving debts. Usury statutes and price controls attempted to limit the degree to which individuals could profit from such accommodations. Quakers in Pennsylvania and elsewhere were bound to different obligations in their dealings with one another. Here, prices and interest rates were usually subject to agreement between individuals, rather than formal regulation, and there was an emphasis on the honest discharge of contracts. Bankruptcy – the failure to repay debts for any reason – was a disgrace that could bring exclusion from the group. Quaker economic morality in many ways anticipated the individual, promise-based 'will theory' of contract that would come to govern most American commercial law by the middle of the nineteenth century.[7]

The massive expansion of the American economy between the mid-eighteenth and mid-nineteenth centuries, and the creation of national markets in a wide range of commodities and services, led to a shift away from local exchange practices towards those of a contract-based system. Expectations about honesty focussed increasingly on the behaviour and responsibility of individuals. Concern with individuals' business reputations increased. Yet economic expansion could not sweep away older borrowing and lending practices, because demand for capital far outstripped personal savings or the sources of commercial capital available. Credit – generated in myriad personal, local, and commercial networks – made up the deficiency.

With growing demand for cash, but no uniform or regular currency before the 1860s, there was increasing willingness to treat as cash privately made paper promises that remained valid as long as they might be honoured. Personal promissory notes and bills of exchange circulated widely. Prominent citizens, merchants, and other individuals frequently endorsed their neighbours' or customers' notes, easing the flow of credit. Banks, the first of which were founded in the 1780s, and which multiplied in the early nineteenth century, issued their own notes. In many states these were by law redeemable in specie, but they often circulated without regard to the ease or even possibility of redemption. Banks regularly defaulted, through fraud or mismanagement. Printers issued regular 'banknote reporters' listing defaulted, withdrawn or counterfeit notes, but retailers would have needed large books, updated daily, to keep track of them. People accepted forged and uncurrent notes regularly. Estimates of their proportion in the total range from 10 per cent in the early decades of the century, to as high as 80 per cent between 1863, when a national paper currency was introduced for the first time, and 1865 when the government created the United States Secret Service to combat forgers. Easy credit and floods of banknotes of dubious value all contributed to an inflationary pressure that helped the economy expand despite its shortage of capital.

The dangers of being swindled, or caught out with worthless goods or notes, meant that trade was always risky. Serious interruptions to credit from any cause, domestic or international, could send the whole economy plunging. Serious crises in 1819, 1837, and 1857 were interspersed with more minor reversals, and usually followed by periods of depression. The 1837 panic was preceded by several years of sharp inflation, and followed by a depression that lasted until the mid-1840s. Some commentators explained these upswings and downswings in biblical terms of alternating plenty and famine, blaming them on human actions and frailties. *Hunt's Merchants' Magazine* connected the panic of 1837 to the rapid inflation and expansion of the middle of the decade: 'When the profits of trade happen to be greater than ordinary, overtrading becomes general; and if any sudden change occur in the state of the commerce or currency . . . a revulsion must inevitably ensue.'[8]

Panic and depression threw thousands out of work and many businesses, even successful ones, into financial ruin, and focussed public attention on debt and failure. Avoiding failure, remarked *Hunt's Merchants' Magazine* in 1848, was 'a subject of grave importance'. Like other journals, it issued doom-laden estimates of the proportion of business people who could expect to face ruin in the course of their lifetimes. A Massachusetts writer estimated that year that no fewer than 97 per cent of businesses would collapse over a period of twenty-five years, and similar claims were often repeated. A manual on retailing published in 1869 reckoned that 60 per cent of businessmen 'either entirely fail and go out of business, or make some compromise with their creditors', another 25 per cent managed to remain solvent until they died, and only 15 per cent could expect to earn sufficient to pass on their business and retire at the age of fifty.[9]

Whenever depression set in, traders noted the need to adjust their practices in light of it. 'Most of my sales now a days are for cash', wrote the merchant Asa Clapp of Portland, Maine, at the start of the 1837 panic, 'I have been very unfortunate in my credit operations the last year, and met with heavy losses.' Many extended this observation to blame the credit system itself for depressions. Having lost heavily himself by the practice, for years the publisher Matthew Carey attacked the habit of endorsing friends' and neighbours' notes. After 1837, commercial journals urged traders to purchase their goods for cash, and not on credit, whenever possible, citing the 'abuse of credit' as the cause of hard times. During the 1857 panic, the same refrain sounded. 'The great cause of all the present financial trouble', wrote a young manufacturer in a private letter, 'is, the long credit given in business, and if the result shall be short credits and prompt payments, much good will have come out of a great evil.'[10]

The 1837 panic also prompted fierce debate between Democratic supporters of the banking policies of the Jackson and Van Buren administrations, and their opponents in the newly formed Whig party. Both broadly agreed that the credit system was at fault; but while Democrats argued for tight money and a sharp reining-in of credit, Whigs advocated a federal bankruptcy law that could protect failed businesses worthy of resuscitation and permit their return to solvency.[11]

The extension of national markets had provoked a reversal of opinions regarding the control of currency and credit. Farming advocates who in the eighteenth century would have favoured the emission of paper money and relaxed attitudes to credit and debt repayment became advocates of hard money and restrictions on commercial credit for speculative gain. Many such people became supporters during the 1820s of Andrew Jackson, and swung behind the Jacksonian anti-'aristocratic' attacks of the 1830s on the Second Bank of the United States. They were joined by members of Workingmen's parties keen to secure both the abolition of imprisonment for debt – still a practice in various states – and measures to compel payment of wages owed to artisans and labourers. Meanwhile, prominent among supporters of the Whig party that coalesced in opposition to Jackson in the mid-1830s were representatives of north-eastern commercial groups who had once been advocates of hard money and creditors' rights. Now, after 1837, it was Whigs who advocated bankruptcy laws to extend protection to debtors, and electoral success in 1840 gave them their opportunity. 'A wisely regulated credit is a grand instrument, which freedom creates, and sustains, and with which it works', suggested the Whig *New York Tribune*. The instruments of this system would be a Federal Bankruptcy Act, permitted by the Constitution but not attempted since the beginning of the century, and private efforts at restraint and self-regulation, according to moral principles. Recalling portrayals of Andrew Jackson as an unbridled tyrant, the *Tribune* argued that 'Credit is the circulating medium of

England, and of all countries which are rich and transact a great and prosperous business. Specie is the circulating medium of Spain and Turkey and
all poor and miserable despotisms.'[12]

The Whig federal bankruptcy statute enabled debtors to obtain protection from their creditors, not only at the petition of creditors anxious to
secure their position, but also at the instance of debtors themselves. Many
Democrats and Workingmen opposed the federal bankruptcy law and similar
state measures, arguing that they gave unfair advantage, both to large debtors
who owed money to labourers and artisans, and to powerful creditors who
might use the law to obtain preferential treatment in any scheme for
partial repayment. Having regained control of Congress, Democrats repealed
the federal statute in 1843, though some state bankruptcy laws remained
on the books. Yet Whig politicians and judges found alternative ways of
providing some measure of protection for debtors. The most striking instance
was their support for New York's pioneering Married Women's Property
Act of 1848, as businessmen realised that it could enable them to put property in their wives' names to evade creditors.[13]

Commentators fiercely attacked as 'un-Christian' devices that enabled
debtors to hide property or pay off preferred creditors, and the association
of debt with dishonesty – never far from the surface of discussion – was
reinforced. Ralph Waldo Emerson would write in 1860 that 'Wall Street
thinks ... that in failing circumstances no man can be relied on to keep
his integrity', adding that this was his own reflection too. To the extent
that prosperity brought 'the habit of expense, the riot of the senses, the
absence of bonds, clanship, fellow-feeling of any kind', it was logical to feel
'that when a man or a woman is driven to the wall, the chances of integrity
are frightfully diminished'.[14] The importance of maintaining the evidence
of integrity increased.

Appropriating vivid metaphors for the discussion of economic crisis and
failure, both published and private writings reflected ambivalence about
where responsibility for it lay. Many wrote of the crisis of 1837 as 'turbulence', a 'storm', or a 'tornado', suggesting that it was a force of nature,
beyond human control. But others emphasised the individual reaction to
this potentially hostile 'nature'. To say that a business was 'proceeding swim-
mingly', 'staying afloat', 'drowning', or 'sinking' implied a struggle which
tested the mettle of a trader's character; 'failure' was the loss of control or
resolve. Success and failure also affected human relationships. In good
times, things went 'smilingly', but in bad times people were 'embarrassed'.
The notion of financial 'embarrassment' reflected the impact of loss and
debt on personal connections, and stressed the significance attached to
individuals' roles in shaping the nation's economic fortunes.[15]

If responsibility for the economy's condition lay with individuals' decisions and behaviour, crucial to its success would be the ability to inculcate correct standards, and to distinguish between those who would uphold them and those who could not. Exemplary behaviour, and its opposites, were defined in these contexts.

The commercial, manufacturing, and agricultural press already dripped with advice about how to behave properly in a credit system. 'The way to *get credit* is to *be punctual*', the *New England Farmer* proclaimed in 1829, 'The way to *preserve it*, is, *not to use it much*.' Similar sentiments appeared in private correspondence. When some family friends had '*failed* in business – after making a loss in the *short time of two or three years*, of more than $20,000 Dollars!!!', the Massachusetts lawyer Edward Dickinson reflected, '[S]o the world goes . . . They enjoyed it while they could . . . A little more economy might have saved them, still . . . A warning to all young men, to be prudent & industrious.' Credit should be awarded on the basis of reputation. 'Trust no stranger . . . Trust no man upon appearances . . .', the *New England Farmer* warned, 'Beware of a gaudy exterior. Rogues usually dress well. The rich are plain men.' Above all, use discrimination about a man's character, for 'what is character worth, if you make it cheap by crediting all alike?'[16] These guidelines were applicable to a face-to-face economy. How could they be applied more broadly in long-distance trade among an ever-increasing volume of traders and traffic?

Personal experience led individuals to attempt new ways to guard against a recurrence of the business failures of the late 1830s. Prominent in taking action was the evangelical merchant and abolitionist Lewis Tappan, who had been deeply affected in 1837 by the bankruptcy of his brother's firm, Arthur Tappan & Company, one of New York's leading mercantile houses. The Tappan brothers' wealth, their prominence in evangelical and reform circles, and their philanthropy, had made the firm a figurehead of Christian capitalism, an assurance that doing well and doing good could go together. Its collapse in the panic shocked the commercial and religious worlds. Lewis, after writing an article entitled 'Confessions of a bankrupt' for the New York *Evening Post* in 1838, set out to prevent a repetition.

Collecting commercial data on individuals, including evidence about their lives, might enable traders and investors to avoid the risk of failure through the default of others by choosing their debtors more systematically. Though his was not the first to be formed, and there would be unseemly competition with rivals, Tappan's new venture, the Mercantile Agency, established in 1841, became the first successful credit-reporting firm, a direct forerunner of the Dun & Bradstreet company that was to become pre-eminent in the field by the end of the century. Started in New York to provide data on inland customers to the city's merchants, the

Mercantile Agency established a national network of correspondents, though Tappan's abolitionist sympathies caused difficulties in the South. The Agency succeeded so well that after only eight years Tappan sold it, noting that 'God has prospered me in my pecuniary affairs so that I can now support my family without further accumulation.'[17]

In its first two decades the Agency collected abundant evidence about the causes of business failures. Firms or individuals were exposed as suffering from insufficient capital, excessive debt, imprudently endorsing notes, unpunctuality in payment, failing to pay even when means existed, holding too much capital in real property, and, not least, outright incompetence.[18] But the purpose of credit reports was not to chart the causes of misfortune; it was to try to avoid it in the first place by indicating where credit might safely be granted. The Agency relied on its local correspondents to report on individuals. Initially Tappan's principles and connections led him mainly to use lawyers and other propertied men with evangelical leanings, such as Edward Dickinson, whose letter was quoted earlier – a Mercantile Agency correspondent from Hampshire County, Massachusetts. As they sent in their reports to New York, these men between them established a set of exemplary personal characteristics on which sound credit might be based. They also identified, of course, the kinds of behaviour that creditors should want to shun.

Credit reports on artisans and small traders during the 1840s and 1850s illustrate the qualities that city merchants sought before extending credit. Men and women were described as 'safe, honest, and trustworthy', as 'upright, intelligent [and] enterprising', as 'careful, prudent . . . honest and reliable.' One firm of young partners were described as 'Honest, faithful men, careful and prudent, and good workmen', another as 'intelligent well educated religious men'. A well established firm was simply as 'good as gold'. One artisan 'attends to his business faithfully and constantly', another was a 'shrewd, economical manager' who 'makes money'. These character judgements were backed up, wherever it could be obtained, by information about property, the size and nature of each business, and other indications of wealth or success. Reporters used their own local or professional knowledge, asked questions, referred to public tax and property records (and to private bank records if they could), listened to rumours, and kept their eyes open.[19]

Often the process of enquiry suggested the need for caution in extending credit. Men were 'of not much account, slow in payment and hard to collect from', 'unreasonably and unwarrantably slack', were 'negligent and [had] not thrifty habits', or were just 'worthless', or 'good for nothing'. Again, specific information supported these judgements. A storekeeper's 'bundles . . . come marked C.O.D.', another was 'embarrassed for

ready money in consequence of building an expensive house', a third 'adver-
tizes largely' – a possible sign that business was poor.[20]

These local reports to the Mercantile Agency fed small-town information and values back to the commercial systems centred on large cities.
They revealed when an 'industrious and careful man' put his own credit at
risk by endorsing another person's notes or standing as surety for him, or
when 'an honest industrious' craftsman who 'means well' was 'rather slow
to pay'. One tradesman had 'a large family of daughters [and] cant do much
more than support his family'. A newly established druggist, 'a fine young
man . . . promising . . . assisted by his mother', made friends of whom the
Agency reporter did not approve – '[I] do not think the company is quite
select enough for a young man in business' – and within a year was rated
simply as 'bad'. 'He has no standing here as a mechanic or citizen . . . I
cannot recommend him' was a report on one jeweller in 1856, and it seems
unsurprising that a year later the man was being sued for unpaid debts.
'He don't pay', wrote the Agency correspondent, 'and the only way is to
give the Execution [i.e. court order] to an officer and let him take the
goods.'[21]

As it turned out, however, good reputation and 'good credit' proved no
guarantee of continued success. Circumstances often upset the reporters'
attempts at sound judgement. One shopkeeper started with a reputation as
'a respectable Merchant [who] appears industrious and honest', but hard
times undid this: first he was 'in the borrow', and then found to be 'slack,
wanting good business traits, not a very shrewd manager'. His payments
slowed, and a reporter commented that he 'should rather give credit to a
man more prompt'. Later, he failed, trying to settle his debts at 20 cents
on the dollar, and ended up as an employee, 'entirely unworthy of being
trusted' with credit. Frequently the descent to failure was sudden and unpre-
dicted. A 'thrifty and improving' manufacturing firm posted notice of
insolvency 'to the surprise of the people here'. A storekeeper regarded as
'a well-bred accurate merchant . . . entitled to credit' was rumoured to have
endorsed notes heavily and then did a flit, removing 'nearly every thing
from his store and not in day light'. Surprised by unexpected failures,
commercial correspondents hastened to insist that they had taken reason-
able steps to secure information. A Boston silk-dealer returning bad notes
to a Connecticut supplier in 1855 assured him that 'We have been very
much Disappointed in the failure of these Concerns[.] We made enquir[y]
through the Mercantile Agency and every other available source, and they
stood well.'[22]

Equally, though, there were individuals who made good after poor starts
or initial failures. A paper manufacturer who had 'formerly failed' was nevertheless worthy of credit 'as long as business is good', and in fact managed

to survive the crises of the 1850s to expand his firm significantly. One jeweller, first described as 'bad' and 'dissipated', managed to accumulate property from his work so that within a decade his business was 'sound' and his credit 'undoubted'.[23] Credit reports, as well as serving as agents of failure for those unable to meet the demands of the marketplace, could also help the process of restarting after failure that the American economy was said to permit.

Credit reporting was not just a response to economic depression. It was an instance of what the historian Neil Harris termed 'the operational aesthetic' – a disposition to enquire into how things worked. Harris's prime example was the public fascination with the tricks and performances of the museum-owner and impresario Phineas T. Barnum, who himself went bankrupt in 1856, and then rebounded.[24] But other examples abounded, from the detective fiction of Edgar Allen Poe, with its emphasis on the techniques of crime and detection, to articles in the journal *Scientific American*, founded in 1846, that described processes in the inventor's workshop, the laboratory, and the factory. The fascination with process was not limited to technical matters. It was strongly concerned with the moral characteristics of individuals, and with the use of narrative forms to explore these. Accordingly evangelical-inspired reform movements produced many instances of the 'operational aesthetic' at work. Temperance tracts catalogued the medical, psychological, and social effects of alcohol. Abolitionists and escaped slaves published the first detailed accounts of the realities of slavery. Phrenology, widely popular among reformers in the 1840s, represented one of the first attempts to map the physiological roots of individual human characteristics, and had powerful moral overtones.

Credit-reporting marked the application of the 'operational aesthetic' to the commercial world. Knowledge of any individual's means and business habits provided evidence of his or her creditworthiness that could be used to avoid bad risks. This information could be provided at a distance, to suit the needs of traders in an expanding national market, but it could also be obtained on one's neighbours and acquaintances, so potentially freeing trade from the influences and irrational preferences of kinship and friendship. Like other contemporary efforts to understand 'how things worked', credit-reporting sought to emphasise the moral, as well as purely operational, aspects of economic behaviour.

Credit reporting did not in fact make trade more predictable. Failures continued. But its feedback of behavioural judgements into commercial decisions helped to systematise the application of exemplary characteristics in business, and to invest business with moral respectability. After the long depression of the early 1840s, two Boston authors published biographical

sketches of the 'rich men of Massachusetts', specifically to illustrate the
rewards that might be gained by the right sort of behaviour. 'Our leading
object', they wrote, 'has been to furnish *encouragement to the young*, from
the contemplation of SUCCESS.' They distinguished wealth earned by hard
work and good character from that acquired by marriage, inheritance, or
speculation, and directed their readers' attention to 'success resulting from
a suitable combination of those sterling qualities, Perseverance, Energy,
Carefulness, Economy, Integrity, Honesty'. They turned the positive aspects
of the discourse of credit reporting into exemplary tales for youth.[25]

Narratives of economic respectability became a staple of biographical
and autobiographical writing. An account published in 1849 about a Boston
timber-wharf owner named Solomon Piper employed typical language and
tone:

> Whatever of worldly prosperity may have fallen to his lot is but the natural
> result, under Providence, of patient, persevering industry, guided by an
> ordinary sense of prudence ... No golden prospect of acquiring sudden
> wealth by speculation was ever able to tempt him from the "even tenor of
> his way", deeming a slow but less certain prospect of gain more conducive
> to rational and permanent happiness.

Only the fact that it appeared in a book entitled *Genealogy of the Family
of Solomon Piper*, compiled by Piper himself, with a note that '[T]he above
biographical sketch of Solomon Piper has been inserted at the particular
request of friends', gave this particular example a parodic quality. Piper
enjoyed financial success. At the time he wrote, his wealth was estimated
at $100,000, and a decade later he was declaring property in excess of
$255,000 to the Boston tax assessors.[26]

However, alongside such pious justifications of accumulated wealth
appeared stories of a parallel kind, of failures or bankrupts who had restored
themselves to credit. Narratives of this sort had their source, in addition
to prescriptive literature and the language of credit reporting, in the proceed-
ings of bankruptcy courts. Bankruptcy sheltered debtors from the claims
of their creditors; the fact that in the United States, unlike some parts of
Europe, individuals could declare themselves bankrupt voluntarily, fuelled
suspicions among sceptics and political opponents of bankruptcy statutes
that the system was a cover for dishonesty. However, debtors could obtain
discharge from bankrupt status by giving evidence that they had recouped
their losses. The strongest claims for discharge came from those who could
repay their debts in full. Court records bulged with bankrupts' testimony
about their struggles to regain financial solvency. By 1851 the New York
diarist George Templeton Strong could disparage the 'interesting martyrs
to a nice sense of honor' who recounted their tales of hardship to the court
so as to restore their business reputations.[27]

Told to the judge, such tales had an obvious material purpose. But their frequency in memoirs and autobiographical sketches suggests that they also shaped the self-identity and self-regard of individuals who had suffered misfortune. They formed part of an effort to portray business as an activity that took place within, not beyond, moral bounds. In an economy where failure was common, to have failed but subsequently 'repaid all his creditors, and in full' became one of the hallmarks of exemplary character. Arthur Tappan himself was reputed to have repaid debts of one million dollars by the late 1840s.[28] Many lesser figures charted a heroic struggle to repay the lesser amounts that they owed. This was more than just good business. Along with other contemporary discourses about religious belief, the use of alcohol, and various medical practices, it was imbued with moral significance. The rebound from failure to success became a trope of mid- and late nineteenth-century life-narratives. As two examples will illustrate, such rebounds resulted not from luck, or even skill, but from moral fitness. To claw oneself back from bankruptcy to full credit was to achieve a form of redemption.

Samuel L. Hill of Northampton, Massachusetts, having assumed the debts of the utopian community he had once led, set up as a silk manu- facturer in the late 1840s. But, as his son wrote in a memorial essay, he 'soon ... had his feet swept from under him by the failure of a brother manufacturer, whom he had assisted, and on whose notes he was an indorser'. Thus began a grim effort to overcome the threat of bankruptcy. It began with calm calculation. 'He carefully looked his affairs over, made his estimates and decided that under ordinary circumstances, by the strictest economy, he would be able, if allowed to continue, to pay all his indebt- edness in a very few years.' Then there were negotiations, in which Hill's character, reputation, and persuasiveness were crucial for success. 'He visited his creditors, obtained a five years extension of time in which to pay them, and commenced anew a hard, self-denying upward climb.' Initial success gained him help from a wealthy investor who, 'having confidence in him, furnished working capital', and became his partner in a firm that 'became favorably known in the business world'. With this backing, Hill could expand his factory and repay his creditors, one by one, within the five years given him. This triumph, secured 'by his indomitable energy, perseverance, and frugality', was marked by an emblem of esteem. 'The chest of tea presented to him by the last creditor, a New York ... importer ... became the symbol to him of the completion of a long contest in which he had proved a conqueror.'[29]

More than financial success in itself, the honest struggle back to solvency confirmed moral worth. Hill's was, above all, a 'self-denying' struggle, requiring the practice of 'frugality' and the rigorous exercise of 'perseverence'. Yet the memoir implies that Samuel Hill was already morally fit for the task. His misfortune derived not from his own failings, but from the 'failure of a brother manufacturer' whom he had assisted. Nowhere does it suggest that Hill's 'long contest in which he had proved a conqueror' was also one of self-conquest. A memoir of a Chicago lawyer, Emery A. Storrs, by contrast, emphasised that the path back from financial embarrassment might also be a curative purge of bad habits. It was a process of self-redemption that could – like religious conversion – mark the driving-out of old sins.

Established as an attorney and minor politician in Buffalo, New York, in the 1850s, Storrs succumbed to his own ambitions. '[H]e began to live beyond his means, and, as has been the history of many others in this world of deceit, too sudden success, though really merited, encourages a downfall. To gratify the demands of vanity and the caprice of fashion . . . he purchased an elegant residence.' To maintain this, he borrowed what he could, 'and when this resource failed him, he resorted to other shifts, . . . not altogether commendable.' Embroiled in real estate speculation from which 'his expectations . . . colored as they were by his fancy, were almost fabulous', he was caught out by the 1857 panic and suffered 'a most humiliating fall from his briefly maintained high estate'. After an unsuccessful attempt to restart himself in New York City, Storrs moved to Chicago. There, in America's fastest-growing city, it was probably tempting to forget the past and begin again with a clean slate. Storrs, however, embarked on a long, grinding, silent struggle to establish himself and to repay his Buffalo creditors. His biographer presented his achievement in doing this, 'dollar for dollar, with full interest', as the moral turning point in his career and the guarantee of his future respectability. In this telling, Storrs's financial achievement was his apotheosis, the symbol of his emergence as a reformed person.[30]

It was not coincidental that credit reporting was instituted by evangelicals. If its influence, through the feedback to urban commercial decisions, would work as intended, credit information could effect a moral 'change' on individuals comparable to that of a temperance pledge or the conversion experience itself. Like these, it offered an incentive to individuals to exercise their free will against the powerful, uncontrollable determination of the market.

Evangelical tropes of self-denial, self-control, and self-improvement also marked many of the biographical and autobiographical accounts of individuals' journeys from failure to restored success. But the biographical narratives that stressed repayment of debt uncoupled the estimation of moral worth from a simple reading of economic success. When 'determination' – the uncontrollable forces of the market – did bring about business failure, 'free will' could still let an individual shape a career and achieve redemption by the application of stern moral principles. The heroic stories of those who struggled to repay their debts in full served as a repellent to the imputation of European and other critics that America's rebounding bankrupts were beneficiaries of dishonesty. By making repayment of debt a moral achievement, they insulated debtors from the suspicion of gaining 'something for nothing'.

As elsewhere in the evangelical universe, however, individuals did not undergo their suffering or secure their achievements alone. The effort to maintain or rebuild good credit was, for example, deeply gendered. The best recourse for a 'sinking' trader, some moralists argued, was to recognise the inevitability of his fate and preserve his character by conceding defeat 'manfully'. Similarly, the path to redemption and repayment required 'manly' virtues. But just as in spiritual matters, so in financial affairs, women could play a significant role in their menfolks' fates, for good or ill.

On one hand, women with insufficient virtue could fatally undermine a man's credit. Credit reporters noted instances of unwise family expenditure, occasionally attributing this – using a familiar trope – to the influence of wives or daughters. Emery Storrs's memoir slyly implied that his downfall stemmed from his wife's desires for fashionable display, noting that he purchased his large Buffalo house 'against his own better judgment'. A Boston newspaper was more explicit in 1853, when it claimed that 'a man's wealth depends more on his *wife* than [on] his income. Some women will cause their husbands to become rich on five hundred a year. Others can scarcely keep out of jail on five thousand.' Women, by their own ability to uphold or subvert exemplary moral standards, could exercise critical control over their menfolk's economic and moral fortunes. 'If married men are poor', the paper concluded, 'in nine cases out of ten it is their wives' fault.'[31]

Bad women got men into trouble, but good women could keep them out of trouble, or redeem them if they stumbled. When one New Yorker ruined in the 1819 panic recounted his years of struggle to revive his fortunes in a memoir written – significantly – in the 1850s, he stressed his wife's assistance in the process. The compilers of *The Rich Men of Massachusetts* attributed the success of the evangelical manufacturer Samuel Williston to the fact that 'he was moral, industrious, and frugal, and took a wife possessing the same qualities'. Indeed Emily Graves Williston's 'shrewd propensity to calculate the cost of all articles of living', and her 'disposition to earn an honest living in some way, rather than thriving on the hard unrequiting toils of others', had led her – not Samuel – to make the invention that formed the basis of the Williston family fortune.[32]

Exemplary narratives of the kind we have examined help explain the social context for economic success and failure in the mid-nineteenth-century United States. They suggest how contemporaries rebutted the European suspicion that easy recovery from failure was a mark of dishonesty, while demonstrating that this suspicion was one that they widely held themselves. At the same time, such narratives help explain how rapid recovery from failure did become an aspect of American economic life, not by divorcing business from morality but by seeking to anchor business behaviour within concepts of a moral universe.

It is, however, in the nature of exemplary texts to present themselves as normative, and we should not make the mistake of assuming that the accounts examined here were 'typically American' in character. They were the products, not of 'Americans' in general, but of particular groups operating in certain circumstances. These were pre-eminently the narratives of an American-born, Protestant middle class, who were seeking to project their own behavioural values not just to bolster their own position or to demand conformity from others, but to mark themselves out from groups they wished to exclude.

Credit-reporting allowed businessmen to select those from among their own class whose character and behaviour appeared to merit the award of credit. The inclusion of financial, as well as behavioural information, however, was a means to ensure that people without means, however worthy their character, were kept out of the credit system. Those without property or business experience, or without the backing of those who had these, were excluded. Credit reporting, therefore, had a strong class dimension. Wage-earners were unlikely to benefit from it, because they could rarely demonstrate both the financial and moral prerequisites for commercial credit.

Furthermore, as the historian David A. Gerber has demonstrated, nineteenth-century credit reports contained much evidence of ethnic bias, most particularly against Jews, whose business practices were frequently prejudged to be dishonest. This imputation of dishonesty worked as an effective bulwark of anti-semitism precisely because it undercut the moral grounds for a favourable business decision. An individual might have sound property and business practices, but the prejudiced assumption that his 'group' acted 'dishonestly' justified excluding him from the circle of those entitled to credit.[33]

Ironically, of course, it was to inoculate themselves from the very same suspicion of dishonesty that American businessmen had constructed their own narratives of exemplary behaviour in the first place. Their tropes were building-blocks in the creation of a bourgeois culture, part of the bourgeois self-fashioning that accompanied the rapid social change and economic expansion of the nineteenth-century United States. Narratives of exemplary business character did not resolve the issues of debt and failure, or heal the political divisions that continued to surround economic questions. They did not prevent failure, and they did not stop dishonesty. They did not address the fundamental issues of access to resources, wealth, and equality in an emerging capitalist economy. Yet in bridging some of the disparities between a strong evangelical ideology and the practices of business life, and in charting means for success out of the vagaries of an unstable economic system they helped construct some of the enduring myths and patterns of American capitalism.

Notes

1   H. B. Fearon, *Sketches of America* (London, 1818), pp. 379–80; Count A. G. de Gurowski, *America and Europe* (New York, 1857), p. 371.
2   M. Durey, *Transatlantic Radicals and the Early American Republic* (Lawrence, Ks., 1997), p. 217.
3   U.S. Constitution, article I, section 10; article I, section 8.
4   On changes in American economy and society, see C. Sellers, *The Market Revolution: Jacksonian America, 1815–1846* (New York, 1991). Recent studies of failure in American business include E. J. Balleisen, 'Navigating Failure: Bankruptcy in Antebellum America', Ph.D. dissertation, Yale University, 1995.
5   Delaware case quoted in B.C. Smith, *After the Revolution* (Washington, DC, 1986), p. 76; J. H. St. J. de Crèvecoeur, 'Thoughts of an American farmer on various rural subjects', in *Letters from an American Farmer and Sketches of Eighteenth Century America* (Harmondsworth, 1981), p. 273; gravestone inscription for Capt. Azariah Lyman, Westhampton, Mass., in T. Bridgman, *Inscriptions on the Grave Stones of Northampton, and of other Towns in the Valley of the Connecticut* (Northampton, Mass., 1850), p. 162.
6   T. L. Ditz, 'Shipwrecked; or masculinity imperiled: mercantile representations of failure and the gendered self in eighteenth-century Philadelphia', *Journal of American History*, 81 (1994–95), 51–81.
7   On Virginia, see T. H. Breen, *Tobacco Culture: The Mentality of the Great Tidewater Planters on the Eve of Revolution* (Princeton, 1985), M. L. Weems, *The Life of George Washington; With Curious Anecdotes, Equally Honourable to Himself and Exemplary to his Young Countrymen* (Philadelphia, 1809), and H. E. Sloan, *Principle and Interest: Thomas Jefferson and the Problem of Debt* (New York, 1995); on New England, see C. Clark, *The Roots of Rural Capitalism: Western Massachusetts, 1780–1860* (Ithaca, NY, 1990), pp. 28–38; on Pennsylvania, M. M. Schweitzer, *Custom and Contract: Household, Government, and the Economy in Colonial Pennsylvania* (New York, 1987), p. 60.
8   *Hunt's Merchants' Magazine*, 1 (Nov. 1839), 436.
9   *Hunt's Merchants' Magazine*, 18 (March 1848); *Massachusetts State Year-Book and Handbook of General Information* (Boston, 1848), p. 217; S. H. Terry, *The Retailer's Manual* (Newark, NJ, 1869), p. 17.
10 Asa Clapp to Hall & Laughton, Portland, Me., 24 July 1837, Clapp Letterbook, Asa Clapp Papers, Library of Congress, Washington DC; *Hunt's Merchants' Magazine*, 1 (Nov. 1839), 517; Henry F. Hills to Adelaide Spencer, Boston, 28 Oct. 1857, Hills Family Papers, Amherst College Archives, Amherst, Mass.
11 Balleisen, 'Navigating Failure', passim. On political ideology, see D. W. Howe, *The Political Culture of the American Whigs* (Chicago, 1979), and J. Ashworth, *"Agrarians" and "Aristocrats": Political Ideology in Antebellum America* (Cambridge, 1983).
12 *New York Weekly Tribune*, 23 Oct. 1841.

13   N. Basch, *In the Eyes of the Law: Women, Marriage, and Property in Nineteenth-Century New York* (Ithaca, NY, 1982), pp. 136–61.

14   Ralph Waldo Emerson, 'Wealth', in D. McQuade (ed.), *Selected Writings of Emerson* (New York, 1981), p. 701.

15   The terminology of indebtedness and panic is discussed in Clark, *The Roots of Rural Capitalism*, pp. 199–203.

16   'How to be rich', *New England Farmer* (23 Oct. 1829), 112; Edward Dickinson to Emily Norcross, Amherst, Mass., 19 March 1828, in V.R. Pollak (ed.), *A Poet's Parents: the Courtship Letters of Emily Norcross and Edward Dickinson* (Chapel Hill, 1988), p. 196.

17   Note dated 1 June 1849, Lewis Tappan Papers, Container 14, Library of Congress (microfilm). On the origins of the Mercantile Agency, see J. D. Norris, *R. G. Dun and Co., 1841–1900: the Development of Credit-Reporting in the Nineteenth Century* (Westport, Conn., 1978), pp. 3–23, and B. Wyatt-Brown, *Lewis Tappan and the Evangelical War against Slavery* (Cleveland, 1969).

18   These examples are drawn respectively from the following entries in R.G. Dun and Co. Collection, Baker Library, Harvard University Graduate School of Business Administration: Maine, vol. 3, p. 61, p. 55, p. 37; Pennsylvania, vol. 79, p. 34; Maine, vol. 3, p. 43; New York, vol. 16, p. 77, p. 141.

19   Entries respectively in Massachusetts, vol. 46, pp. 9, 4, 17, 50, 10, 3, 8, 2, R. G. Dun and Co. Collection.

20   Massachusetts, vol. 46, pp. 7, 13, 9, 93, 81, 3, 2, R. G. Dun and Co. Collection.

21   Massachusetts, vol. 46, pp. 14, 11, 3 and 12, R. G. Dun and Co. Collection.

22   Massachusetts, vol. 46, pp. 6, 4; Maine, vol. 3, p. 37, R. G. Dun and Co. Collection; A. & J. C. Batchelor to O. S. Chaffee, Boston, 15 Feb. 1855, O. S. Chaffee Correspondence, ms. no. 69972, Connecticut Historical Society, Hartford.

23   Massachusetts, vol. 46, pp. 5, 104, R. G. Dun and Co. Collection.

24   N. Harris, *Humbug: The Art of P. T. Barnum* (Chicago, 1973).

25   A. Forbes and J. W. Greene, *The Rich Men of Massachusetts: Containing a Statement of the Reputed Wealth of about Fifteen Hundred Persons, with Brief Sketches of more than One Thousand Characters* (Boston, 1851), p. iii.

26   Piper genealogy and 1860 tax return quoted in P. R. Knights, *Yankee Destinies: the Lives of Ordinary Nineteenth-Century Bostonians* (Chapel Hill, 1993), p. 63; for Piper's wealth in 1850, see Forbes and Greene, *The Rich Men of Massachusetts*, p. 50.

27   Quoted in Balleisen, 'Navigating Failure', p. 263.

28   Wyatt-Brown, *Lewis Tappan*, p. 241.

29   C. A. Sheffeld (ed.), *The History of Florence, Massachusetts* (Florence, Mass., 1895), pp. 208–9.

30   I. E. Adams, *Life of Emery A. Storrs: His Wit and Eloquence, as Shown in a Notable Literary, Political and Forensic Career* (Chicago, 1886), pp. 80–2.

31   *Boston Evening Transcript*, 13 May 1853, quoted in Knights, *Yankee Destinies*, p. 37.

32   Forbes and Greene, *The Rich Men of Massachusetts*, pp. 143–4.

33   D. A. Gerber, 'Cutting out Shylock: elite anti-semitism and the quest for moral order in the mid-nineteenth century American market place', *Journal of American History*, 69 (1982–83), 615–37.

'With a lofty moral purpose': Caroline Martyn, Enid Stacy, Margaret McMillan, Katharine St John Conway and the cult of the good woman socialist

In August 1895, the well-to-do daughter of the Chief Constable of a cathedral town came to Liverpool to work. She was twenty-eight years old, a neat, intelligent young woman with a handful of positions as a governess and schoolteacher behind her.[1] However, although she was still working, broadly as an educator, Miss Caroline Martyn had not been summoned by the Liverpool School Board, nor at the behest of some wealthy merchant seeking a guiding influence for his daughters. Rather, she had come at the invitation of the local Fabian Society and Independent Labour Party, as one of the most popular socialist orators of the time to undertake a week's intensive campaigning in a district where socialism was beginning to take root. As an overture to this propaganda work, her arrival was marked by a profile and portrait on the front page of the *Liverpool Labour Chronicle*, joint monthly journal of the Fabians and ILP. Written by John Edwards, a well-known activist in both societies, and also the *Chronicle's* co-editor, it began, irresistibly, with a challenge, not to a contemporary audience, but to another age, perhaps even to ourselves:

> When the story of the progress of Socialism in England comes to be written, I wonder what the historian will say about the little band of women who have done so much to inspire the movement with a lofty moral purpose.[2]

Edwards cited Katharine St John Conway, Enid Stacy, Caroline Martyn and Margaret McMillan as the most prominent members of the little band. These good women socialists, he continued, were raising politics to an almost religious standing, both by their presence as women and through the high moral tone of their propaganda work, as writers for the socialist press and as itinerant speakers travelling the length and breadth of Britain. And, despite the much-repeated claim that women have been hidden from history, a diverse range of historians have agreed with him. From the earliest participatory accounts of British socialism through to current work, there is striking acknowledgement of the importance of a small group of female propagandists, especially this particular four. However, as one might expect, on closer examination a gap emerges between the primary sources and secondary comment. Later writers have tended to present the four (with sporadic additions including Isabella Ford, Ethel Annakin, Margaret MacDonald and Ada Nield) as a group, emphasising their similarities. Henry Pelling, for example, identifies amongst the 'little band of socialist lecturers' tramping the length and breadth of 1890s Britain 'several . . . well-educated women, still in their twenties'.[3] Stephen Yeo, largely basing his essay on the British socialist revival in the 1890s on an interrogation of the lives of forty-six individuals including eight women, commented on 'the over-whelming popularity and presence of four of these . . . [who] were consumed more avidly by meeting attenders and devoured more frequently than their numbers suggest'.[4] Both agree with John Edwards as to the identity of the key four women.[5] Such undifferentiated grouping, however, is unusual in contemporary accounts. Although commentators in the 1890s did group the women together, the listings were frequently punctuated by adjectives which hinted at differences between individuals, helping to define a particular personality for each.

It is on the construction and significance of these 'public' personali-ties that I wish to concentrate in this chapter. My main focus will be on the presentation, publicising and reception of their proselytising within the wider socialist movement.[6] Using this approach it will become clear that there were often gaps between what the four actually said (or in many cases wrote), and, typically, what they were perceived to have said by the wider socialist movement. The perceptions emerged through the reports of their meetings within the socialist press, and through the reaction to their propaganda writing. My aim is to show that what was of real interest to the wider (and predominantly male) socialist movement was not the indi-viduals themselves, but the particular facets of an acceptable feminine behaviour which they represented. In other words, what was being created and provided was a multi-faceted role model, that of a good woman socialist.

The need for such role models was great. The 1890s were a uniquely dynamic period in the developing culture of the labour movement and British socialism, in which the boundaries and definitions of the political sphere were constantly being tested and expanded. Art, music and litera-ture sat alongside religion and economics in the movement's search for an alternative, all-embracing socialist lifestyle.[7] Many of these activities were advertised and documented through a flourishing and varied socialist press. As well as the large national papers, such as the organisationally inclined *Labour Leader* and *Justice* and the independent *Clarion*, there were a host of smaller papers including the *Liverpool Labour Chronicle*, *Keighley Labour Journal* and the *Bradford Labour Echo*, all of which revealed the richness and diversity of this culture at branch level.[8] The period also coincided with increased interest in the so-called 'woman question', a broad and far-reaching debate regarding the nature of women's position in society. Definitions of public and private underlined this debate, underpinning the argument about the role of women in politics. By the time the Independent Labour Party was formed in 1893, both the Liberal and the Conservative Parties had already recognised that women could play an important role in maintaining party fortunes. Through their auxiliary organisations, the Women's Liberal Federation (WLF) and the Primrose League, hundreds of upper- and middle-class women had already discovered for themselves 'the stimulation and fascination of politics'.[9] Simultaneously, they had created a role model for aspiring workers, through a tendency to limit themselves to particular questions deemed of feminine interest, and inspired by a sense of 'mission'.[10] Feminist periodicals such as the *Englishwomen's Review* reported enthusiastically on their activities, creating an impression of women's politics as being associated only with the Conservative or Liberal Parties.[11]

The success of the Primrose League Dames and their WLF rivals did not go unnoticed within socialist circles. However, the image of women politicians as belonging 'almost exclusively to the upper and upper middle classes' was a difficult one to dislodge.[12] Paradoxically the claims of the ILP to be 'the most sympathetic of all political groups to the "woman question"' did not help matters.[13] Equality of membership meant that there was no obvious need for a separate women's organisation within the ILP, whereby socialist women could meet together for the purpose of self-definition. Attempts at creating such bodies met with little success, except at a very local level.[14] Indeed, socialist women were often amongst the fiercest critics of such initiatives, believing them to represent a backward step towards the 'reactionary sex distinction' practised by other political parties.[15] To define a suitable role model for potential women socialists, a different forum was required. Therefore, it was largely within the socialist press, rather than within the structure of an auxiliary organisation, that the ideal of the good woman socialist was created. Katharine St John Conway, Margaret McMillan, Caroline Martyn and Enid Stacy began to appear together in its columns, giving the false impression that they were the only women socialists available.[16] This group presentation did not lead to any blurring of their individual personalities. On the contrary, commentators tended to dwell on particular aspects of each individual woman, the effect being that the four together added up to all that an exemplary female socialist might be.

Some grouping of the four women is understandable. They actually had much in common, not least their gender, which, despite changes in social attitudes by the 1890s, still set them in a minority within the world of politics.[17] Furthermore, they had each taken up socialism through similar convictions, often at great personal cost, and had adopted a punishing lifestyle of itinerant speaking engagements, eking out a small livelihood from expenses and bits of journalism. They were roughly of an age. (In 1895, when John Edwards wrote about them, Enid was twenty-seven, Caroline and Katharine twenty-eight, and Margaret thirty-five.) They came from similar social backgrounds and were all well-educated. Katharine St John Conway and Enid Stacy had attended university. Enid held a degree from London University, whilst Katharine, who had attended Cambridge, took the tripos examinations before women were entitled to hold degrees, but nevertheless used the letters B.A. after her name. Caroline Martyn and Margaret McMillan were from slightly less enlightened backgrounds, but had both benefited from longer formal education than most Victorian girls, and had been prepared for the 'suitable' career of governess. Yet these common features in terms of education were never mentioned when they were discussed collectively in the press. Instead the main emphasis in reports of their activities was upon their essentially feminine characteristics. Katharine's physical appearance often attracted comment, as did her charismatic appeal as a speaker. She was the sweetheart of socialism, 'Bonnie Kate' whose 'silvery eloquence' drew the crowds and placed her on a par with Keir Hardie as an attraction.[18] The older Margaret McMillan was a mystic prophetess, 'eloquent and fervent', who could reduce an audience to tears with her soaring rhetoric.[19] Caroline Martyn was a deeply serious and religious personality who was almost canonised by her followers.[20] Enid Stacy, slightly the youngest of the four, was 'our Enid' the joker, always ready to stop a heckler with her quick wit, and famed for her athletic ability through, among other things, her ability to make socialist speeches from the roofs of moving tramcars.[21]

So this group of four women, whom Stephen Yeo has told us were 'consumed' more avidly than any other socialists, appear to have been quite deliberately marketed as embodying distinctive feminine characteristics.[22] Such a characterisation has not been uncommon in the twentieth century. From the 'Four Marys' stories of the 1950s through to the 'girl band' phenomenon encapsulated by the Spice Girls in the 1990s, the modern media have collectively marketed small groups of individually very different women in order to give them the broadest possible appeal. In 'the little band of women' socialists we find a similar situation: Katharine the sweetheart of the movement, Margaret the prophetess, Caroline the saint and Enid the comedienne. Their public characters appear to have been shaped to take into account certain aspects of their personalities but to ignore others, especially such features as they had in common.

One facet of their socialism which provides a good example of this selective marketing is in the use that each woman made of religious and ethical socialism. Contemporary observers were repeatedly struck by the strong links which existed between religion and socialism in late Victorian Britain, both in its Christian Socialist aspect and in the less deistical but highly idealised 'new life', which moved emotional focus 'away from the service of God to the service of man'.[23] Keir Hardie himself felt that within socialism 'more inspiration . . . has been drawn from the teachings of Jesus than from any other source'.[24] Similar sentiments informed the propaganda work of the four women, each of whom had particular personal reasons for drawing on religious rhetoric. Religion played an important role in their lives. Katharine Bruce Glasier, who had converted from Congregationalism to High Anglicanism, first encountered socialism whilst in church, a story which she frequently repeated on socialist platforms.[25] She was a contributor to the Labour Church journal *The Labour Prophet* and co-wrote the ILP's early pamphlet 'The Religion of Socialism,' one of the key texts of Christian Socialism. This topic became the subject of one of her most popular lectures, repeated throughout Britain. Margaret McMillan, a contributor to the *Christian Socialist,* often allowed a religious rhetoric to creep into her prose. 'Great forces are silently waking, a new Gospel trembling on the lips of the workers', she informed an audience at Keighley Co-Operative Hall which had gathered on Christmas Eve to hear her lecture on 'Peace.'[26] Enid Stacy was not as explicitly religious as this, but religion was of crucial importance in her life. She was a member of the Christian Social Union, and, following her marriage to the Reverend Percy Widderington around 1897, combined the role of a busy clergyman's wife with an active political profile.[27] Yet despite the claims of all four women to a devout religious side, Caroline Martyn was the only one to be clearly characterised in this way by contemporary commentators, consistently portrayed as the personification of feminine religion, and variously described as 'a good woman', 'possessed of a strong nature, of high moral aims', and 'holy enough for any cause'.[28]

Part of the explanation for this is clear. Caroline was a deeply involved Anglican, who wore her religion very much on her sleeve, which possibly explains why Henry Pelling later chose to call her 'austere'.[29] She served a term as sub-editor of the *Christian Weekly*, and her socialist propaganda shone with a vision of the future in which socialism brought humanity to a more Godlike state. 'Not in vain was the Saviour of the World . . . born of woman', she wrote in her first major article, 'The man to be, the perfect man . . . expression of the highest goal, must be born of the great and noble mother.'[30] At one of her earliest public meetings in Bolton, a member of the audience remarked that she was 'a splendid speaker [who] has evidently pleased ... the religious section of the Labour movement'.[31] However, without wishing to diminish her religiosity in any way, it is remarkable that it is this one aspect which is consistently emphasised when her work is discussed. The promotion of Caroline consistently as the *religious* woman socialist above all other, drew attention away from the religious aspects of Margaret, Katherine and Enid, making it easier for them to represent other characteristics.

There was often a common popular reaction to these proselytising women socialists, and their gender appears to have given them a greater freedom to use sentimental or rhetorical language than was available to their male counterparts. Commentators were initially unsure as to whether Katharine or Margaret deserved top billing as the most feminine or womanly socialist. Both were credited with the remarkable powers of persuasion particular to their sex. An early member of Katharine's audiences remarked in 1892 that it was 'possible that [she] was getting more applause than a woman less young and attractive might have got but that was all doing good to socialism. She had a peculiar magnetic influence over her audiences.'[32] Another report of a different meeting concluded, 'upon retiring, the audience did *not* sing God Save the Queen. Rather, judging from the enthusiasm, the unexpressed desire in most minds present was God Save Kate Conway.'[33] Katharine's marriage to John Bruce Glasier in 1893 meant that she was no longer free to be quite so much the 'darling' of the movement. However, although her biographer claims that she 'dwindled into a wife', her new status as one half of socialism's foremost couple did little immediately to distract commentators from their obsession with her physical charms, which now appeared almost as a bizarre socialist form of courtly love.[34] Thus amid references to the 'girlish ... slender ... delicate ... sweetness' of 'Bonnie Kate', or the 'Maid of Orleans', readers were also reminded that she is now Katherine St John Conway (Mrs Bruce Glasier).[35] With Katharine married, Margaret, described in *The Labour Annual* as a woman 'of the highest culture and with the inspiration of a prophetess' began to emerge as the leading *unmarried* woman socialist.[36] She so enraptured her audiences in Bradford that they responded with a lengthy verse poem in the local *Labour Echo*. The report of her speech begins:

> When Mystic Margaret in our Hall
> Her wondrous teaching gives
> Responsive to her Sovereign Call
> The dead past wakes and lives![37]

Enid and Caroline were equally popular and persuasive speakers, but their rhetoric, although often similar to that of Margaret and Katharine, was largely characterised in different ways.

Enid Stacy's image was that of a quick-witted and humorous speaker She appears to have played the comedienne much more readily than the saint, sweetheart or prophetess. Commentators described her repeatedly as 'Our only Enid', 'young' and 'winsome.' Enid's first biographical sketch in *The Labour Annual* described her as being 'rather proud than otherwise of being a New Woman', thereby identifying her directly with a range of advanced and feminist beliefs. As Lucy Bland has recently explained, the 'New Woman' may well have been a journalistic construction, but there was general agreement that a New Woman would, at the very least, be 'given to reading advanced literature, smoking . . . and travelling unchaperoned often on a bicycle'.[38] Publicly adopting the persona of a 'New Woman' actually allowed Enid to bring a more radical edge to her propaganda, an aspect largely denied to the other three women.[39] This is most apparent in the reports on her speeches on women and socialism, in which she is characterised as someone who is expected to go beyond the pale. Enid was able to use her position as court jester to embody more radical feminist ideas and so subvert some of the more overtly misogynist writings of certain leading socialists. One of her main targets was Nunquam (Robert Blatchford), the editor of *The Clarion*. Nunquam and his editorial board member Dangle (Alec Thompson) frequently published hostile opinions on leading women, socialist or otherwise, which they concealed beneath claims of chivalry. Enid attacked this practice in 'Man's Chivalry', a piece she wrote for *The Clarion* in 1894. Inspired by the *Clarion's* recent refusal to criticise Mrs Humphrey Ward's latest book on the grounds that any criticism levelled by men against a female author would be 'unchivalrous', it gave scope for Enid to be at her outrageous best:

> if [woman's] efforts must not be judged because of their great sensitiveness and delicacy, then they had better cease to make effort and do work which may not be judged. If they are strong enough to do the work, to write the books, to paint the pictures, then they are strong enough to bear the criticism . . . If they are not strong enough . . . Let them be shut out of every avenue of public work and retire to a purely private and domestic sphere.[40]

The lengthy article then attacks Nunquam and Dangle by name on particular points, and concludes with Enid admitting that, on a recent visit to a historical monument where the staircase had crumbled and been replaced with a ladder, she 'climbed that ladder'. This action, which refers to an earlier comment by Dangle regarding appropriate female activities, was later used throughout the socialist press as a metaphor for Enid's abilities, 'our Enid can climb ladders' being a typical remark.[41]

The two targets of 'Men's Chivalry' appear to have taken this in good part. 'She means well but she is young', chided Nunquam in the following edition. Nevertheless, he had published her piece, albeit contextualised within an atmosphere of amused male toleration. Enid was the one member of the group from whom such sentiments were to be expected, and so tolerated. She alone managed to penetrate the male 'clubbable' atmosphere of the *Clarion* and to banter with its editorial board. While Enid carried on this light-hearted feud with Nunquam and Dangle, Caroline Martyn used the paper to take a sideswipe at another editorial board member, The Bounder (Edward Fay), author of a ponderous weekly column describing his lengthy journey, or 'tour' as he preferred to call it, around Britain. This was never one of the *Clarion*'s more popular pieces. 'When is the Bounder going to finish that confounded tour of his?' was one reader's response. So Caroline began her account of her visit to Belgian socialists thus: 'There is a superstition abroad amongst Clarionettes whereby they believe that men only are capable of tours ... still when [a woman] does venture from home she does not confine herself within the small limits of an island'.[42] Her remarks passed without comment. On this occasion, the bait was not taken. Whilst the male editorial board would happily tease and be teased by Enid Stacy, they were unwilling to include Caroline Martyn in their word games. The inference would seem to be that one socialist comedienne was enough.

Although the New Woman became Enid's public persona, she was far from being a sexual radical. Both she and Katharine Conway were appalled in their early days as Fabian lecturers at the views of fellow Fabian, Walter de Mattos, a keen advocate of free love. Enid wrote to the Fabian Society Secretary, Edward Pease, that support for such an idea was 'doing the cause of socialism some apparent good and very much real harm ... as a woman I feel that I cannot ... with any regard for my self-respect ... have any connection officially, however slight, with a man whose views of life and manner of living are so degrading.'[43] Later historians, Caroline Steedman in her biography for example, have suggested that Margaret McMillan was probably the real sexual radical of the group, although she too stopped short of embracing free love.[44] But if so, this was a strand largely ignored at the time. It was Enid alone who was promoted as the woman socialist who was, in her own words, 'unconventionally conventional'.

Moving beyond the personifications of sweetheart, prophet, saint and joker, there are other striking elements within the propaganda of the four which, although evidenced in print at the time, rarely attracted comment, possibly because they did not offer an easily accessible role model for women socialists. All four women were well educated, and they were more than willing to place their knowledge at the disposal of the socialist movement. Yet despite showing a clear grasp of economic theory, they were never encouraged to stray onto what was seen as masculine territory. Instead, their considerable intellectual talents were seen as more fitting the arts in an early example of what has become a classic twentieth-century gender division within education. Margaret McMillan, 'probably better read in Marxist economics and socialist theory than the other members of the ILP leadership', was happy to spread her learning, and delivered a series of lectures on 'Modern economists' to the Leeds Labour Church.[45] Whilst these attracted little attention within the wider socialist movement, her work within art history received a rapturous reception. In 'Classics for Labour Men', she provided a series of articles for the *Bradford Labour Echo* to 'enable those who have not had the benefit of a university education to thoroughly understand and properly appreciate the large number of pictures which crowd the walls of our fine art gallery'.[46] Such publicity demonstrates that the socialist readership preferred to have Margaret as a representative of high culture rather than as a commentator on economic or political affairs. Similarly Enid, praised as 'one of the cleverest speakers in the labour movement, which is saying a great deal', was equally applauded for having 'none of the disagreeable qualities of the ordinary blue stocking about her'.[47] Instead, readers appreciated much more that men and women possessed significantly different qualities of mind. Men came to socialism, she believed, via their intellect, 'then their feelings and sympathies are touched'. With women, 'a different order prevails. Touch their quick and ready sympathies, then render the feeling ... stronger and lasting.'[48] It was this assumed and fundamental difference between men and women that women socialists were expected to both replicate and respond to.[49]

In reading about the characters and activities of these good woman socialists, it is striking how much more there is to their propaganda than either their contemporaries or later historians have recognised. In part, this has arisen because of the way in which contemporary socialist writing characterised each of them in a one-dimensional fashion. There was a desperate need to capitalise on any enthusiasm that women may have felt for socialism and to create a blueprint for their activity.

There is a final complication to our late twentieth-century perspective on the roles open to women within the socialist movement. The extent or even existence of something resembling a spirit of sisterhood within socialism, encouraging women to prioritise gender alliances over class-based ones, remains open to argument. Certainly socialist theory favoured class over gender, although there are numerous examples of this being subverted by individual women. But there is another more problematic side to this question which arises from the actions of socialist women. This could sometimes take a personal form, as ideologies about personal freedom spilled over into messy affairs and marital breakdowns.[50] At other times, female propagandists could not contain their obvious irritation at the quality of the 'raw material' with which they were working. Enid Stacy won a severe rebuke for a piece she published in the *Clarion* called 'Hats and Bonnets'. It was intended to describe how the constraints of working-class life denied thousands access to any form of beauty. Enid used as her main metaphor a window display she had seen in a milliner's shop in Oldham.

> The Colours! Merciful powers, what did I behold? Blue recklessly mingled with mauves and greens, purples enlivened with scarlets and crimsons, rose pinks and magenta in excruciating companionship with red and orange, flowers, laces and ribbons, feathers in gaudy profusion – the whole forming a combination enough to make the eye sore and strange . . .

This is not just about hats, she argues, but a clear demonstration that 'the majority of our girls are without the line of neatness or fitness, and what is even worse, perhaps, are entirely devoid of a knowledge of the simplest laws of colour, . . . unable to appreciate . . . delicacy and beauty'. This is wholly to be expected from their 'spending the first years of life in the monotonous ugliness of the schoolroom', progressing to 'the weaving shed, brought up in the midst of mill chimneys and the soot, dirt and smoky gloom'.[51]

Hard on the heels of this article came an outraged response from 'An Oldham mill girl,' who claimed that there was no better dressed class of working girls than herself and her colleagues. Vigorously contesting the slurs Enid had cast on the dress, homes and musical taste of the girls, she concluded that just like Enid, 'we also love the scent of the heather and to hear the bleat of the lambs'.[52] Enid was unrepentant. 'I fear' she responded, 'that girls who dress tastefully [in mill towns] are the exceptions . . . and that my words do truthfully apply.'[53] The appeals to the common interests of all women within socialism must have been somewhat muted by outbursts such as these, and by the individual jealousies awakened by the popularity of charismatic female propagandists.

If we are to accept that these women were more important (and less unique) within the history of socialist culture than has usually been assumed, some reason must be given for the shortness of their careers as socialist women. Marriage clearly placed no restrictions on their activities.[54] Nor did motherhood. Enid Stacy still undertook lengthy speaking tours after the birth of her son, including one to the USA in 1902.[55] Katharine St John Conway's four children did little to diminish a life of political activity until her death in the 1950s. On the other hand, Caroline Martyn, who had often complained of the way the movement was turning her into a 'speaking machine', died suddenly of pleurisy in Dundee in 1896 during a particularly strenuous campaign.[56] Similarly, Enid Stacy refused to give up work when complications occurred in her second pregnancy, and consequently died from an embolism.[57]

But more general developments within British socialism offer a more convincing explanation. The emergence of the Labour Party from the Labour Representation Committee led to a distinct and organised working-class presence in parliament, but also pulled the focus of the labour movement away from the social and cultural towards the parliamentary. Although women recruits remained important, female role models were less critical, especially as the parliamentary woman did not yet exist. Also relevant was the formation, in 1903, of the Women's Social and Political Union (WSPU), by a group of ILP women, many of whom had worked closely with Caroline, Katharine, Margaret and Enid for the previous decade. Much WSPU 'militancy' involved tactics of direct propaganda lifted from socialism, although more frequently practised by socialist men than by women. The enthusiasm with which the WSPU cast off 'conventional' female political behaviour provided a new role model for political women, which simultaneously made the older ones anachronistic and obsolete. The age of the good woman socialist would appear to have passed.

Notes

1   Further biographical information can be found in *Dictionary of Labour Biography* (London, 1987), vol. 8, pp. 158–60.
2   *Liverpool Labour Chronicle*, Aug. 1895.
3   H. Pelling, *Origins of the Labour Party* (Oxford, 1965), p. 155.
4   S. Yeo, 'A new life: the religion of socialism in Britain, 1833 – 1896', *History Workshop Journal*, 4 (1977), 5–56.
5   For examples of similar descriptions which include the same four women at their centre and demonstrate the range of additions, see H. Tracey (ed.), *The Book of the Labour Party, its History, Growth, Policy and Leaders* (London, 1925), p. 106, which names Enid Stacey [sic], Katharine St John Conway, Margaret McMillan, Caroline Martyn, Isabella Ford, Mary MacArthur and Margaret Bondfield; H. Tracey (ed.), *The British Labour Party, its History, Growth, Policy and Leaders* (London, 1948), p. 47 replaces Isabella Ford with Emmeline Pankhurst; and H. Snell, *Men, Movements and Myself* (London, 1939), p. 113 takes a broader definition of 'socialist' and names Annie Besant, Beatrice Webb, Enid Stacy, Caroline Martyn, Katharine Conway, Ethel Annakin and Eleanor Marx.
6   The main concentration will be on work done for the Independent Labour Party, with which all four women were associated. This did not preclude their working for smaller groups on occasions, however, so the general word 'socialist' will be used in the text.
7   See C. Waters, *British Socialists and the Politics of Popular Culture 1884–1914* (Manchester, 1990) for examples of its extent and success.
8   For an extensive list of local socialist publications see G.B. Woolven, *Publications of the Independent Labour Party* (Society for the Study of Labour History, 1977).
9   Jeannie Churchill, quoted in B. Campbell, *The Iron Ladies: Why do Women Vote Tory?* (London, 1987), p. 11.
10 C. Hirshfield, 'Fractured faith: Liberal Party women and the suffrage issue in Britain, 1892 – 1914', *Gender and History*, 2:2 (1990), 173–97. Hirshfield also demonstrates that this model of obedience did not extend into the twentieth century.

11 There are many reports in the *Englishwomen's Review*; for example, 'Political men on the political work of women', 15 Jan. 1896, pp. 24–6.

12 E. Stacy, 'Women's work and the ILP', *The Labour Annual* (1895), p. 117.

13 J. Hannam, 'Women and the I.L.P. 1890–1914', in D. James, T. Jowitt and K. Laybourn (eds), *The Centennial History of the I.L.P.* (Halifax, 1992), pp. 205–28, esp. p. 205.

14 Enid Stacy raised the idea of separate women's associations at the 1894 first annual conference of the ILP. Some local groups, notably the Women's Labour Party of Glasgow, resulted, but no co-ordinated national body.

15 Elsie Harker, letter to the *Labour Leader*, 11 Apr. 1896.

16 This presentation of them as 'unique' is discussed by June Hannam, '"In the comradeship of the sexes lies the hope of progress and social regeneration": women in the West Riding ILP c.1890 – 1914' in J. Rendall (ed.), *Equal or Different? Women's Politics 1800–1914* (Oxford, 1987), pp. 214–38.

17 For recent biographical interpretations of each individual see C. Steedman, *Childhood, Culture and Class in Britain: Margaret McMillan 1860–1931* (London, 1990); L. Thompson, *The Enthusiasts: a Biography of John and Katharine Bruce Glasier* (London, 1971); A. Tuckett, 'My Aunt Edith', *North West Labour History Bulletin*, 7:1 (1980–81), 41–48.

18 Liverpool local report, *Clarion,* 24 Feb. 1894; Liverpool University Library, Glasier Papers, John Bruce Glasier to Elizabeth Bruce Glasier, 2 July 1896.

19 *Bradford Labour Echo*, 18 Jan. 1896.

20 See *Liverpool Labour Chronicle,* Aug. 1895; *Fraternity*, July and Aug. 1896.

21 *Clarion*, 16 Feb. 1895.

22 Yeo, 'A new life', p. 25.

23 The words of Beatrice Webb, quoted by Pelling, *Origins of the Labour Party*, p. 155. An interesting if perplexed contemporary account of the persistence of religiosity in British socialism can be found in A. Hamon, *Le Socialisme et le Congrès de Londres: étude historique* (Paris, 1897), p. 28. For further discussion of the links between religion and socialism in late Victorian Britain, see L. Smith, 'Religion and the ILP', in James, Jowett and Laybourn (eds), *Centennial History*, pp. 259–76.

24 K. Hardie, 'The ILP' in A. Reid (ed.), *The New Party Described by Some of its Members* (London, 1895), p. 264.

25 *Bradford Labour Journal*, 30 Sept. 1892.

26 *Keighley Labour Journal*, Jan. 1894.

27 *Clarion*, 11 Sept. 1903.

28 *Liverpool Labour Chronicle,* Aug. 1895; *Keighley Labour Journal*, 1 Aug. 1896; *Bradford Labour Echo*, 26 June 1897.

29 Pelling, *Origins of the Labour Party*, p. 155.

30 C. Martyn, 'Woman in the world', *Labour Prophet*, July 1895.

31 *Clarion*, 12 May 1894.

32 Glasier Papers, W. de Mattos to E. Pease, 13 May 1892.

33 National Museum of Labour History, Wallasey ILP minute book, 13 Nov. 1894.

34 Thompson, *The Enthusiasts,* p. 86.

35 *The Liver*, 17 Feb. 1894 has her as 'girlish in appearance, very slender and delicate looking'. Other examples from reports of meetings in Scotland and Lancashire are cited by Thompson, *The Enthusiasts*, p. 77. For examples of the juxtaposition of her maiden and married names see Wallasey ILP minute book, 13 Nov. 1894; *Bradford Labour Echo*, 5 Oct. 1895.

36 *Labour Annual* (1895). Enid Stacy was engaged by this time, whilst Caroline Martyn's image was never that of a socialist 'sweetheart'.

37 *Bradford Labour Echo*, 18 Apr. 1896.

38 L. Bland, *Banishing the Beast: Early Feminism and Sexual Morality* (Harmondsworth, 1995), p. 144.

39 I discuss ways in which socialist women worked with the idea of the 'New Woman' in more detail in my '"Giving them something to do": how the early ILP appealed to women', in M. Walsh (ed.), *Gender and Labour* (Aldershot, 1999), pp. 119–34.

40 *The Clarion,* 28 June 1894.

41 *Bradford Labour Echo,* 14 Sept. 1895.

42 *Clarion,* 20 July 1895.

43 Glasier Papers, Enid Stacy to E. Pease, 13 May 1892.

44 Steedman, *Margaret McMillan,* pp. 123–25.

45 *Ibid.,* pp. 160–61, 78.

46 *Bradford Labour Echo,* 20 Sept. 1895.

47 *Ibid.,* 14, 24 Sept. 1895.

48 *Labour Prophet,* Aug. 1893.

49 At least one historian seems to have made the same assumption (without presumably reading their work) when he wrote that 'The lives of [Katherine, Margaret, Caroline and Enid] illustrate the moral fervour on the New Socialism ... their enthusiasm began with slight intellectual substance', although their academic record shows that this was not the case: S. Pierson, *Marxism and the Origins of British Socialism* (Ithaca, 1973), p. 168.

50 The relationship of Katharine Conway and Bristol socialist Dan Irving attracted particular attention. See Thompson, *The Enthusiasts,* p. 71. Sally Blatchford was one of the few socialist wives to admit to sexual jealousy. See L. Thompson, *Robert Blatchford: Portrait of an Englishman* (London, 1951), p. 141; Steedman, *Margaret McMillan,* p. 252.

51 *Clarion,* 28 Apr. 1894.

52 *Clarion,* 12 May 1894.

53 *Clarion,* 26 May 1894.

54 This claim is made in D. Howell, *British Workers and the Independent Labour Party 1888–1906* (Manchester, 1983), p. 334.

55 Her letters to her husband during this tour explicitly detail the pain she feels at separation from baby Gerald. See Working Class Movement Library, Salford, Lancs., Anglea Tuckett Papers, Enid Stacy to Percy Widderington, 29 Dec. 1902.

56 Letter from Isabel Fyvie Mayo to Keir Hardie, *Labour Leader,* 1 Aug. 1896. Mayo returns to this theme even more forcibly in her 1910 autobiography, *Recollections of What I Saw, What I Lived Through, and What I Learned, during more than Fifty Years of Social and Literary Experience* (London, 1910).

57 Obituary, *Clarion,* 11 Sept. 1903.

The batsman as gentleman: inter-war cricket and the English hero

'The simple intensity with which the tragedies and triumphs of games are experienced and shared between the generations', wrote Violet Bonham-Carter, 'keeps boyhood green in Englishmen all through their lives.'[1] One sport, she went on, stood out from the rest as a means of transmitting common values and enthusiasms: 'The almost sacramental approach to cricket shared by English fathers with their sons must be as unintelligible to a foreign mind as any mystic tribal rite.'[2] This contribution to Sir Ernest Barker's *The Character of England* was published in 1947. In the same year Denis Compton broke the record for the number both of runs and of centuries scored in a season. Cricket was at its apogee. The terrible winter with its freezes and fuel shortages had given way to a fine summer, banishing the memories of war and making economic privation easier to bear. England, it seemed, was restored to itself as cricket once again took its place at the heart of national life, played and followed throughout the country by men of all social classes. Men like Jack Hobbs and the young Len Hutton had been as important as any soldier or explorer as role models for inter-war English boys. Girls and women were given marginal roles as spectators and tea-makers. Changing media coverage of the game, national advertising campaigns and male conversation within the family had made a handful of great players into household names.[3]

Cricket was a peculiarly English and conservative institution. Nationalisation and the welfare state followed in the wake of the Second World War. Yet cricket remained unchanged, still structurally divided at the highest level between working-class professionals and public school amateurs. Only 'gentlemen' could captain their county and the 'players' were expected to call them 'Sir' or 'Mr.'. Lord Hawke's famous outburst 'Pray God, no professional shall ever captain England' was made in 1925.[4] No professional did until Len Hutton in 1952. Ironically, he was still debarred from being captain of his county team. Professionals changed separately from amateurs, were lodged in poorer accommodation, often entered the ground by separate gates and had their initials placed after their names on the scorecard. Social distinction was integral to cricket.[5] Part of its deeper appeal, especially to the middle and upper classes, no doubt arose from the idea of natural hierarchy. This went hand in hand with the gentry associations and pastoral landscapes evoked in so much cricket writing, including de Selincourt's *The Cricket Match* (1924), A. G. Macdonell's *England Their England* (1933) or Edmund Blunden's *Cricket Country* (1944), a poet's wartime tribute to rural England.[6]

'First-class' cricket – the term is revealing in itself – was formulated around the traditional loyalties of the county rather than the modern city. It was not run by an elected national association but by a self-perpetuating, private club of ex-public school cricketers, the Marylebone Cricket Club (MCC), the inner circles of which were dominated by the House of Lords. The lore and rituals of the game as distinct from its rules were largely unwritten, rather like the English constitution, and its moral vocabulary – 'straight bats', 'sticky wickets', 'not cricket' and so forth – was derived from the playing fields of the public schools. The code of amateurism, which dominated so much of English sport for a century, was a seamless fusion of birth and wealth, of aristocratic honour and bourgeois competition. Amateur sport combined the revived 'chivalric' ideal with the idea of a 'moral market place', where 'laissez-faire' co-existed with strict standards of personal conduct.[7] Common rules permitted the competitive principle to flourish whilst 'fair play' emphasised the wider moral purpose. 'Not playing the game' and 'not cricket' came to stand for anything that fell below gentlemanly standards of good behaviour.[8]

The game had grown at a phenomenal pace in the later nineteenth century. From a largely southern, rural base, cricket became the staple summer sport of northern industrial towns. Bolton had 111 cricket teams in 1914, Oldham 139, and even Sunderland in the far north-east without a county side had 108.[9] Spectator demand was met by a mixture of local league teams and county cricket. However, it was international 'test matches', especially the biennial series against Australia, which provided the arena for the emergence of the cricketer as a national hero.

The best bowlers, though famous in their day, were not turned into popular national symbols. The batsman had to face the might of the opposing team alone with only his legs protected, while the bowler had to toil for his laurels with less risk of injury and without the same obligation to be stylish. For this reason few of the gentlemen chose to bowl, which further reinforced the prestige of the batsman. W. G. Grace was a case in point. He was a very fine bowler, but it was for his batting that he was universally known as 'the Champion', 'The Old Man', 'the best loved Englishman' of later Victorian England. He had a mastery of the whole range of shots, going forward or back, which set the standard for those who followed him.[10]

The batting heroes of the late Victorian era were mainly public school boys, whose education and circumstances allowed them to play cricket every day. A few surpassed even the best professionals. Amateurs such as C. B. Fry outclassed professionals like Arthur Shrewsbury and Bobby Abel, 'The Little Guv'nor' from Rotherhithe. In the Edwardian era, however, a new breed of professional came to the fore, who looked for inspiration, not so much to the likes of Bobby Abel but to the public school amateur. It is with this very small, but highly visible, group of 'nature's gentlemen' that this chapter is concerned: Jack Hobbs and Herbert Sutcliffe, Frank Woolley and 'Patsy' Hendren, Wally Hammond, Len Hutton, Bill Edrich and Denis Compton, whose playing careers collectively spanned more than half a century, from Hobbs's first game under the watchful eye of the ageing W. G. Grace in 1905 to Compton's retirement in 1957.

Three inter-linked questions suggest themselves. First, there is the style and the nature of the performance itself. How was the aesthetic of cricket understood, transmitted and given wider meaning? Second, the complex issues of social class arise. How did the lives of the great players illustrate the distinctive structures and possibilities of inter-war English society? Third, there is the question of identity. In what ways did style and status combine with 'character' to fashion the batting hero into an exemplary Englishman?

Cricket was transformed in the later nineteenth century in stylistic terms. It was no longer enough for a batsman to be merely effective, to defend stubbornly or heave and swipe at a loose ball. The cricketer's body was now a site of aesthetic display. As the public school amateur took charge of the game and much of the writing about it, the great player was expected to execute a range of 'classic' shots with perfect technique and timing. An 'orthodoxy' was established, the mastery of which was the basis for the new aesthetic of batsmanship. This was the province of a dozen or so clean-shaven public school boys who succeeded the more rustic Dr Grace in what came to be known as 'The Golden Age' from 1890 to 1914.[11] Amongst the most famous were Archie MacLaren and the Hon. F. S. Jackson (from Harrow School), Gilbert Jessop, and C. B. Fry, the Oxford and England batsman, rugby and football international, world long jump record holder and editor of a boys' magazine that bore his name. Marjorie Pollard, England's leading women's hockey player and cricket pioneer, 'felt I must curtsey when the names of Fry, Jackson, Spooner, Warner, MacLaren, Ranji, Tom Emmett and many others were dwelled upon (they were never just mentioned in our house)'.[12]

Relatively few spectators could see such great players at any one time. Only Saturday afternoons were free for the bulk of the working population, and there was no first-class cricket on Sundays. This meant that the many followers of the sport might only see a great batsman once a year or even less. Only a small fraction of fans could see a test match at any one time. On the other hand, the top batsmen often played for twenty to thirty years, so a man like Jack Hobbs would have been watched by a very large number of people over his entire career as a county and England player. Local heroes could often be seen at the end of a day's play, when admission charges were reduced in the late afternoon, as schools and offices were closing. The news that Hammond was batting was well-known to clear offices in Bristol before 1939. Very few footballers or other sportsmen enjoyed the same prolonged exposure to the public. The cricket public could expect to have seen the great players a few times in the flesh but relied on the local and national press for regular reports on their progress.

The journalist was both interpreter and creator of the sporting hero. By the mid-1930s over three-quarters of the English population saw a morning paper, which now always included a sports section. The major provincial press gave extensive coverage to cricket. In the 1930s nearly three-quarters of households in Leeds took the *Yorkshire Evening Post*, which was famous for cricket journalists such as A. W. Pullin ('Old Ebor') and his successor J.M. Kilburn.[13] The suffusing of cricket with a peculiarly English aesthetic, however, came most famously from the *Manchester Guardian* and the pen of its cricket correspondent and music critic, Neville Cardus, who claimed 'he had received "the Grace of Art" through the vision of a single MacLaren off drive', and compared 'Tom Hayward's serene and classic batsmanship to the music of Bach'.[14]

Cardus became a cult figure for the more literary cricket lover.[15] Cricket books and biographies emerged as a thriving form of popular hagiography, recounting the hero's rise from obscurity by dint of natural talent and application and offering a sanitised, selective account of the life. The bulk of the English public, however, followed the doings of great players through a more mundane mixture of words and pictures, ranging from cigarette cards to the multi-page picture spreads, combining the action shots and relaxed portraiture made possible by the lightweight Leica camera. This was a special feature of the new weekly, *Picture Post*, which had over eight million readers by 1950. The batsman could now be caught in mid-stroke, instead of posed or at rest, sweeping, hooking or driving in classic fashion, alongside a detailed account of the game.[16] The new cinema newsreel began to feature sporting clips, and from 1927 live radio commentary brought the game and its greatest moments into the home. When Hutton broke Bradman's record for the highest test score at the Oval in 1938 almost eight million households had a radio licence and the first television cameras caught the event.[17]

The new media possibilities gave an unprecedented range and vividness to sports reporting. In cricket, a trio of batsmen, whose careers spanned the First World War, became celebrated national figures. Alongside Jack Hobbs of Surrey, there were Frank Woolley of Kent and 'Patsy' Hendren of Middlesex. This trio, who were the highest run-scorers in the history of the game, were eulogised by Cardus and company. Even a sober Yorkshireman such as J. M. Kilburn thought Woolley had 'the calm maturity of Kentish meadows'.[18] Hobbs and Woolley played together in nineteen Tests between1909 and the outbreak of the First World War. Both came into Test cricket at a time when only one professional could regularly hold a batting place in the England side, and both men subscribed to the myth of the Edwardian 'Golden Age'. When Woolley finally took his leave in 1938, aged 51, he 'doubted whether English cricket has really recovered from the effects of the war' and the decline of the amateur.[19] Hobbs broke all the batting records, but said cricket would be a better game if they were not kept. No amateur could have said more.

Alongside these survivors of the Golden Age came the new inter-war professional heroes. No-one could match the force and power of Wally Hammond in his prime. Watching Hammond's 240 at Lord's in 1938, J. M. Kilburn noted the crowd's reaction: 'the clapping applauded the effectiveness of the stroke, its product in runs; the spontaneous cries of wonderment were tribute to the magic of the stroke's creation'.[20] Edrich and Compton produced a similar reaction after the war, batting with aplomb and abandon for Middlesex and England, piling up the runs in cavalier fashion. Edrich was a fighter, afraid of nothing, living up to his wartime pilot's reputation, going back in to bat after having his cheekbone broken by the 'typhoon' bowling of Frank Tyson. If Edrich stood for courage, Compton was the 'Happy Warrior', a natural, picking up the game 'on the Hendon by-pass' but playing with the flair and dash of a Golden Age amateur. The Australian cricket journalist A. G. Moyes had the impression that Compton played 'for the fun of the thing', adding that 'earning his living is a secondary consideration – he lives for me not for the runs he made but for his manner of making them'.[21]

The other two leading batsmen of the inter-war era, Herbert Sutcliffe and his Yorkshire protégé Len Hutton, offered a distinct and important variation in style. Both were amply endowed with the fierce determination and stubbornness that was part of the county's culture. Cricket was an important expression of regional personality. Lacking the complete polished elegance of Hobbs, Sutcliffe was a supremely effective batsman who made 26 partnerships of 100 with 'the Master'. Hutton, too, had a remarkable ability to apply himself for long periods, and like Sutcliffe had an untutored mastery of orthodox batsmanship They brought a northern seriousness, which, combined with the more carefree southern style, sought to create a composite picture of the Englishman's character.

These men not only played like gentlemen, they looked like gentlemen. The dress code and etiquette of cricket allowed them to enjoy the more casual summer style associated with wealth, good birth and leisure, whilst not appearing to dress up. This killed two birds with one stone, not just advertising a man's physical vigour and attractiveness, but suggesting a certain social distinction. 'Whites' were all-important and had to be 'immaculate'. Playing in dirty or crumpled whites was unthinkable for the great players. Hobbs was always beautifully turned out and Hammond abhorred collecting green marks on his flannels. No one, however, carried the cult of the immaculate cricketer further than Sutcliffe. Hutton recalled how Herbert would 'arrive with a flat case in addition to the old fashioned cricket bag so that flannels and shirts were kept spotless and creases remained razor sharp'. He ordered consignments of silk from Thailand to make up into cricket shirts in his Leeds sports shop.[22]

The ideal of an upright bearing and good posture, combined with a calm, composed expression, reflected in part the influence of neo-hellenism on the late nineteenth century. 'Fry could, alike in form and function, have stepped out of a frieze of the Parthenon', as H. S. Altham, one of the game's leading historians and myth-makers, remarked.[23] The batsman cut a distinguished figure, striding from the pavilion gate or calmly taking up his stance at the wicket with a body language that suggested an easy authority. The players' bodies were unprotected except for pads and gloves and a cap, vulnerable yet self-confident. They had to face fast bowling without showing fear, without flinching or making an ugly shot. A 'glorious' cover drive with the batsman making a full follow-through as he watched the ball race to the boundary was considered one of the great sights in cricket. Hammond was the master of this shot, which was said to linger in the mind of those who saw it long after the result was forgotten.

Alongside this physical ideal of the new sporting gentleman, a new cinematic image of male beauty spread during the period between the wars. This began to influence cricket from the 1930s when Sutcliffe's 'glossy' black hair and 'twinkling' eyes made him 'the Clark Gable of cricket'.[24] Compton's good looks were openly discussed and his hair was the subject of a national advertising campaign after the Second World War. A photo of Len Hutton's wax model being prepared in Madame Tussaud's revealed an assistant, hard at work on parting the hair with the precision that male fashion required, whilst another adjusted the blazer. This was a neat, leisured, suburban kind of male beauty, a visual contrast to the besuited 'Sunday best' of the respectable working classes.

It was not only in their style of play and appearance that the 'players' increasingly resembled the 'gentlemen'. In their speech, their place of residence and choice of home, in the education of their children and in their subsequent business careers, England's batsman heroes became solidly middle class. In sharp contrast to professional football, where great players sometimes drifted back into manual labour, cricket's heroes were monuments to social mobility. Being a gentleman no longer required membership of the landed elite or the liberal professions. However, rising from the working class into the higher reaches of the middle class in one generation was still rare. Plenty of professional cricketers moved into the world of small business, but only the best rose beyond the lower middle class.

This made the social mobility of the top players all the more striking. Their playing success brought them new possibilities, ranging from turning small businesses into bigger ones, writing for newspapers, publishing 'ghosted' autobiographies, advertising or doing public relations work for private companies. They trod a fine line between deference and ambition. Whilst accepting the status quo within the game and the social divisions built into it, they left their working-class accents and origins behind and headed for the leafy avenues of suburbia. Such ambiguous attitudes reflected the contradictory and multiple perceptions of class in Britain, which embraced both the notion of an ancient, seamless hierarchy and that of a more open, tiered structure.[25] Both visions were equally valid. The careers of the great cricketers affirmed the authority of the upper-class MCC, whilst also revealing the social opportunities on offer to the exceptional player.

Of the great English professional batsmen only Wally Hammond and Bill Edrich had fathers who were not directly involved in manual work. Hammond's father joined the army and rose from bombardier to officer rank in the First World War, marrying the daughter of a railway clerk and leaving just enough money to send his son as a boarder to Cirencester Grammar School. After the war, in which his father was killed, 'Walter R. Hammond', as he liked to style himself, had to make his own way in the world.[26] Bill Edrich came from an established family of substantial Norfolk tenant farmers and cricketers and was sent to Bracondale, a private school with a professional cricket coach. This 'yeoman of England' was in due course offered a job in the City that allowed him to play as an amateur. This was considered more appropriate for a war-time squadron leader.[27] Hammond and Edrich were the only two top 'players' to renounce their professional status to become 'gentlemen'. Why did others not do so? Loss of good wages was obviously a factor. But it was not the whole story. Hammond and Edrich with their private school background were perhaps more socially confident than Hobbs and Sutcliffe, who both had successful retail businesses during their playing careers. They could well have afforded

to become amateurs, especially given the generous expenses and perks that
the gentlemen got, including jobs as county secretaries or company direc-
tors. Yet both remained as professionals. Hobbs was the son of a Cambridge
college servant, who never lost his sense of admiration and respect for
the gentlemen. He could never cross the divide. Sutcliffe was made of
less deferential northern stuff. For all his emulation of the amateur, he
was less inclined to bow the knee than Hobbs, for whom paternalism was
a part of the natural scheme of things. Sutcliffe privately thought that
Hobbs should have asked for the England captaincy in the 1920s. But Hobbs
was disinclined to do so. 'Jack always called me, "sir"', the Surrey captain,
Monty Garland-Wells recalled, 'and it scared me to death.'[28] However,
'Herbert was the first of a new generation of professionals who made it
clear that their skill and social standing must be taken into account', Sidney
Hainsworth, a prominent Yorkshire businessman observed.[29] Sutcliffe was
less diffident than Hobbs but not really so different, withdrawing his candi-
dacy for the Yorkshire captaincy in 1927 to avoid controversy.

   Hendren and Woolley, born like Hobbs in the Home Counties in the
1880s, tended to have a similar view of the world to that of 'The Master'.
Hendren's father was an Irish plasterer, who had emigrated to London, and
'Patsy' was contented with his lot. He had done well; he was liked by the
amateurs and he liked them, retiring from the game after thirty years to
coach the young gentlemen of Harrow School before returning to Middlesex
as a scorer. For him Middlesex was like a family and the younger players
his children.[30] Frank Woolley, whose father had a small garage in Tonbridge,
thought about Kent in the same kind of way. These men were held in awe
wherever they played but they were careful never to use the power of public
affection to challenge the system. When they retired in the late 1930s,
Hendren recorded his satisfaction with the status quo in an article in
Wisden, whilst Woolley mourned the passing of 'the days when plenty of
amateurs could spare the time for cricket'.[31]

   Those whose careers began before the First World War and those who
came afterwards mixed deference with ambition in rather different proportions, the balance gradually shifting from the former to the latter. Hammond
was an 'arriviste', anxious to cultivate amateurs like the rich Gloucestershire
captain 'Bev' Lyon, who 'drove a Rolls, gave the best parties and always
had a stack of notes in his breast pocket'. Just as thousands of boys copied
Hammond's stance at the wicket, so Wally copied 'Bev's 'blue silk hand-
kerchief peeping out of the hip trouser pocket' and 'wore a flamboyant
trilby to be like him'.[32] Compton's father was a lorry driver. But Denis
'never felt nor minded the distinction' between amateurs and professionals,
mixing easily and adopting a comfortable middle-class way of life.[33]
Compton's rival as the post-war hero of English cricket, Len Hutton, was

the same. Hutton was brought up in a working-class home in the same Yorkshire village of Pudsey as Herbert Sutcliffe. Like his mentor, he was fiercely determined to distance himself from his humble origins and fully succeeded in doing so.

Accent was thought an extremely sensitive indicator of social class. The elite of professional cricketers cultivated the forms of speech of the southern middle class, though Sutcliffe and Hutton could resort to dialect when they wished. Sutcliffe surprised C. P. Snow with a speech in London at the Cricket Writers' dinner for the Australian team. 'One would never know you had not been to public school and Cambridge', remarked Snow. Sutcliffe replied that he had spoken in dialect with the Yorkshire team but 'it was when I became a member of the England team and mixed with amateurs that . . . I tried to speak to their standard'.[34] Hammond, too, worked at the refinement of his vowels as part of a deliberate strategy of self-advancement. Adopting a middle-class accent seemed to come as naturally to Compton, a suburban Londoner, as making runs. Hutton had to work harder to produce the 'polished tones' that were noted in his Oval speech on re-gaining the Ashes in 1953 and admitted he was 'a bit of an actor'.[35] The upper-class English of the huntin' and shootin' fraternity was being replaced by 'correct' BBC English. The linguistic gap between the gentleman and the player was closing. The 'best people' and the best players increasingly spoke in a similar way.

Looking and sounding solidly middle class, acquiring new manners and friends, prospering in business through sporting contacts, these men stood for a new kind of gentility, a comfortable, accessible, polite Englishness. This seemed within the grasp of an increasing proportion of the population as the number of those in non-manual employment rose from around nine million in 1921 to thirteen million in 1951. Falling prices and low interest rates made house purchase far more widely available. The top cricketers were earning over £1,000 a year and with money from elsewhere could well afford good homes as owner-occupiers. A rare domestic photo taken in 1925 shows Hobbs in a dark three-piece suit with trilby and furled umbrella, leaving his substantial semi-detached villa at 17 Englewood Road, Clapham Common for the Oval, waved off by his young daughter.[36] Hendren made less than Hobbs, but still had enough to buy a new house in metroland at Canon's Park in Edgware, whilst Woolley built a large bungalow in the comfortable Kentish village of Hildenborough.

The two Yorkshiremen, Sutcliffe and Hutton, did especially well financially. From his beginnings as a clerk in the mill office, Sutcliffe ran a successful sports shop in Leeds and acquired interests in a range of other companies, buying Woodlands, a mill owner's house on seven acres, and a Rolls Royce. He lived like the industrial squires of the textile industry, giving an annual garden party and sending his son to public school. This meant Billy Sutcliffe was able to captain Yorkshire when his more illustrious father had not. Len Hutton invested shrewdly with tips from star-struck stockbrokers and represented Fenners, a mining suppliers with interests in Australia, South Africa and India, where business and political contacts made through cricket proved invaluable.[37] He moved south to join suburbia, more or less cutting his links with Yorkshire, buying a substantial house in Kingston-upon-Thames, and playing golf at Wentworth with clients from the Surrey stockbroker belt. His sons went to Repton and Cambridge.

As this process of gentrification gathered pace, the old distinctions began to seem increasingly unrealistic and embarrassing. Geoffrey Green in *The Times* caught the flux and shifting mood of the cricket establishment. 'Though there are many who will look back with sorrow at the passing of an age, there are yet those who will welcome the ending of an anachronism.' 'In this age of so-called equal opportunity for all', he concluded, 'the professional player has at last attained his fullest stature.'[38] Hutton, however, was followed by several more amateur England captains, the most famous of whom was Peter May (Charterhouse and Cambridge), who had taken Hutton, the Yorkshire professional, as his model. The two streams that had fed English cricket separately for so long were finally coming together, though the formal distinction was not abolished until 1962. Social origins were ceasing to be as important as social achievement. The MCC decided to elect the most distinguished professional cricketers to honorary membership in 1949. Public honours were bestowed on the great players for the first time. Hobbs was knighted in 1953 – the first knighthood for a professional spotsman – and Hutton in 1956. Compton and Sutcliffe were awarded the CBE. The state had officially raised the greatest of the players to the rank of gentleman.

How did heroic players become national heroes? For the cricketer success on the field was a necessary, but not a sufficient condition of public acclaim. Heroism in England involved a relationship of affection between performer and public. Heroism was a gift, which the English bestowed on those whose 'character' appeared to be at one with their achievements. Given the random distribution of sporting excellence, it was inevitable that some of the best players would not be the best of men. Most of them, however, did conform to a canon of decent 'manliness' laid down by the Victorians. It is highly instructive to see how far the press would go to cover up for those who fell below accepted standards of behaviour. Courage, flair and tenacity were universal sporting virtues to which the English added modesty, humour and respectability. The inter-war professional was admired for his ordinary virtues. Far more than the Americans, who loved a winner and indulged the gargantuan appetites of Babe Ruth

– the great baseball hitter of the 1920s – the English sporting hero was supposed to be a nice man.

This was revealed in the deep and widespread reverence for Jack Hobbs, England's inter-war hero 'par excellence'. 'Despite all the fuss and adulation made of him he was surprisingly modest and with a great sense of humour', remarked his Surrey partner, Andrew Sandham, whilst the most famous of his county captains, Percy Fender, called him the 'most charming and modest man anyone could meet'.[39] 'The Master', as he was sometimes called, was quiet and dignified, respectable without being stuffy. He never swore and drank very little. When he passed Grace's record of 126 centuries – an event that attracted great public interest – he toasted his achievement with ginger beer. Hobbs was an Anglican and a regular churchgoer. A reader of E. W. Swanton's cricket journalism 'remembered how on Sunday mornings his parents used to take their family to church by a longer route from their Streatham home for the pleasure of seeing the Hobbses similarly on their way'.[40] Hobbs was devoted to his wife, Ada, whom he nursed later in life, and to his four children. 'It was his character and not the statistics' which gave Hobbs his 'wider dominion in national life', as one of his biographers, Ronald Mason, observed. Other students of Hobbs, including John Arlott, came to the same conclusion.[41]

Frank Woolley called Hobbs 'a good living fellow respected by everyone he met'.[42] The same could have been said of Woolley himself and their contemporary, 'Patsy' Hendren. They were uxorious men. All of them had long happy marriages to wives who were well-known in cricket circles. Sybil Woolley was a vet's daughter from Ashford, a life-long supporter of Kent cricket and a keen horsewoman.[43] This trio were not only good husbands, but apparently good fathers to their own children and paternal to the players under them. Yorkshire's batting heroes had similarly long marriages and placed great importance on public respectability. Sutcliffe bristled at the slightest suggestion that he was a 'ladies' man'. Hutton had met the sister of a Yorkshire professional at the Scarborough cricket festival 'and that was it. And I might tell you, that was it, literally it', as J. M. Kilburn recalled. 'I never saw Leonard, and I went all over the world with him, look at anybody else at all.'[44]

No one could have said that about Wally Hammond. 'Wally liked a shag', as Eddie Paynter, the earthy little Lancashire test player, put it.[45] He was a 'philanderer on a grand scale', divorcing his first wife after she had lost the money he married her for and betraying a string of other women. All of this was known to insiders but was kept from the public, just as the syphilis he had contracted in the West Indies was covered up as 'a mosquito bite in the groin'. Hammond was never exposed in the press, a remarkable reversal of present practice. Despite his sourness and condescension, journalists still contrived to present him as worthy of the captaincy. But you can't fool all of the people all of the time. Cricket was a public spectacle, and Hammond could be notoriously sullen in the field, often refusing to bowl, and rarely giving a word of encouragement to his own side. With his divorce and relative loss of form after the war, the critics and the public began to turn on him. England's greatest all-rounder left to start a new life in South Africa and passed into relative obscurity, a victim not of the nation's short memory but of its standards of good character.

Hammond was not the only one whose true character was kept from the public to preserve the respectability and prestige of the national game. The famous Middlesex partnership of Edrich and Compton were fond of drinking and womanising. Edrich, who was married four times, was seen by Bob Wyatt, the chairman of the selectors, coming back drunk in the middle of the night before a test match at Lord's in 1950, where as it happened the West Indies beat England for the first time. He was privately disciplined for letting the side down and presumably for undermining the MCC's sense of racial superiority in the process. But nothing was said publicly. He was simply dropped from the team for a long period without explanation.[46] Edrich thought Wyatt was 'a bloody Puritan – I'd done an indiscreet thing but it didn't warrant a punishment like that.'[47] Public confidence in the cricketer as hero had to be preserved.

Compton would occasionally turn up on tour dishevelled after a night on the town, once sporting a black eye, which was improbably attributed to a collision with a garden tap. When such stories did come out, excuses were found because Edrich and Compton were warm 'clubbable' chaps unlike Hammond. Nevertheless, it was Hutton, not Compton, who was chosen as the first professional captain of England and subsequently knighted. Compton was one kind of hero, carefree, instinctive, and gregarious, Hutton was another, more conventional, dedicated and respectable. Compton was probably the more popular, Hutton the more widely respected.

Valour, for so long a universal quality of heroism, was not a requirement of the inter-war English sporting hero. Amateurs such as Stanley Jackson had risen to the rank of Colonel in the Boer War, but few of the great professional players found their way to the Front. Hobbs did not enlist in 1914, citing his obligations to his widowed mother and young children. When he was finally conscripted, he became an aircraft mechanic in Bradford and played some league cricket. Woolley, who had stood up to the fastest bowling in the world, volunteered, but was turned down on 'the grounds of eyesight', and ended up flying an Admiral of the Fleet and future President of the MCC around the Firth of Forth.[48] Patsy Hendren worked as a mechanic before he was conscripted, but he never got beyond Dover and played plenty of cricket. These men did not lack patriotism, but they did refuse to play the role of the 'sacrificial warrior' in the manner of the young public school recruit. Yet having an easy war did not damage their reputations. Inter-war England witnessed a widespread reaction against the more strident forms of nationalism and militarism. Quiet men, who commuted from the suburbs, fitted the new national mood.

England used its sporting heroes to far greater effect in the Second World War to keep up service and civilian morale, through playing exhibition matches, making public appearances and working for charities. But they were not expected to risk their lives for their country. Hutton was a physical training instructor. Sutcliffe became a major in the Royal Ordnance Corps, and was retired early in 1942 without seeing action. Compton seemed to spend his time in the services playing football for Arsenal and plenty of cricket. Hammond was the most privileged of all, spending the war organising games at the Gezira Club in Cairo with trips to South Africa and England to visit his girlfriends. For this he was promoted to the rank of squadron leader and posted back to an office beside Lord's in 1944. Plenty of fine cricketers did brave things in the war, but the best-known batsmen were not among them.

Humour was more important than valour. Hammond was humourless and this eventually told against him. Hobbs was 'always a boyish chap at heart and a great leg puller' and Woolley had a dry, quizzical humour.[49] But it was Patsy Hendren's comic antics, mimicry and chatter with the crowd that was best known. When he died the Secretary of the MCC, wrote that 'apart from being a great cricketer . . . he brought a tremendous amount of fun and happiness to everything associated with the game'.[50] Similarly, both Edrich and Compton thought cricket should be entertaining and liked a joke. Like Hendren they played for Middlesex at Lord's where the presence of the MCC shored up the amateur spirit.

Northern culture was rather different and Yorkshire was a law unto itself.[51] Sutcliffe and Hutton were far from jovial. 'Give 'em nowt' and 'we don't play cricket in Yorkshire for fun, you know' were two of the favourite sayings of the folk hero of Yorkshire cricket, Wilfred Rhodes, who first played for England in 1899 and was called up for his last test in 1926. There was always a counter-current to the dominant gentlemanly values within the England side. This not only helped the team to achieve more on the field. It gave those who had little time for the airs and graces of the MCC a few gritty champions of their own such as Maurice Leyland or Arthur 'Ticker' Mitchell, who guarded traditional Yorkshire values with 'endearing severity'. His great moment came when he was called from his garden at the last minute to play against South Africa at Headingley in 1935 and made 58 and 72. Neville Cardus loved these Yorkshire characters but his affection was not necessarily returned. 'I don't like thy writing, Mester Cardus', complained Mitchell, 'it's too fancy'. 'Well, that's more than anybody could say about thy batting, Arthur', Leyland replied.[52] The veteran cricket correspondents of the *Yorkshire Post*, A. W. Pullin ('Old Ebor') and his successor J. M. Kilburn, spent a lifetime recording the lives and doings of men who were regional heroes rather than national icons.

Other counties had their own favourites with careers as long as the great test batsmen and locally they were as influential and as deeply admired. Though Hammond was the star of Gloucestershire, his opening partner, Charlie Barnett, a cricket professional and a country gentleman, whose father and uncle had both played for the county as amateurs, was more popular. So, too, was Barnett's successor, George Emmett, whilst the off-break bowler Tom Goddard's deep West Country 'How were it?' or 'How were that, then?' became part of the local oral tradition. Every Somerset supporter knew the story of how Harold Gimblett missed the bus to Frome for his first county match, and had to hitch a lift and borrow a bat before making his maiden century in sixty-three minutes.[53] The other counties were similar. They all had their 'characters' and mythologies.[54]

The ideal of English manhood, which the sporting hero was supposed to represent, was bound to vary from place to place, though common decency remained at its core. The northern worker tended to admire the tenacity which Compton dismissed as 'joyless concentration', whilst the suburban southerner preferred the cavalier 'Happy Warrior' approach. This is where the fact that cricket was played by pairs of batsmen comes into its own. Famous partnerships such as that of Hobbs and Sutcliffe opening for England in the 1920s were a perfect opportunity to show how apparently different cultural traditions could combine to strengthen the nation. There was always a 'pick and mix' dimension to national identity, with no strict definition of Englishness and no obligation to be rational or consistent. Englishness was a mixture of cultural traditions passed on in the family, at school, in church, at work and at play. It was a shifting and subjective business which defies simple generalisation.

For all that, a few general conclusions emerge which seem to hold good for most of the top players for most of the time. First, there was a general but not universal admiration for the amateur tradition and the system of upper-class rule that went with it. These batsmen half-consciously nurtured a myth of cohesion and hierarchy, of a paternalistic, ordered and pastoral England evoked by the likes of Stanley Baldwin. Second, through their material success and middle-class manners, they fed the myth of meritocracy and mobility, of an open, competitive England where a man could shape his destiny by natural talent. The instinctive combination of these different visions of the social order had a powerful appeal in a country that valued both its exclusive ancient traditions and its modern democratic freedoms. Third, binding this together was the ideal of good character, of the well-balanced, modest, self-disciplined man with a sense of humour and self-control, who looked after his family and respected established institutions. The Indian summer of amateurism, of May, Cowdrey, Sheppard and Dexter briefly re-invigorated the amateur ideal in the 1950s before it went into a swift decline. The 1960s not only saw the abolition of an invidious social distinction; the decade also marked the collapse of cricket as something culturally central to English identity. The great batsman – and there were far fewer of them – was now just another celebrity sportsman. The beauty had faded and the authority had gone.

Acknowledgement

I would like to express my gratitude to the editors for a very helpful reading of the first draft of this article.

Notes

1   V. Bonham-Carter, 'Childhood and education', in E. Barker (ed.), *The Character of England* (Oxford, 1947), p. 210.

2   *Ibid.*, p. 210.

3   The literature of cricket is very large but lacks critical histories. J. Williams, *Cricket and England: a Cultural and Social History of Cricket in the Inter-War Years* (London, 1999) is a valuable new addition to C. Brookes, *English Cricket* (London, 1978); R. Sissons, *The Players, a Social History of the Professional Cricketer* (London, 1988); and K. A. P. Sandiford, *Cricket and the Victorians* (Aldershot, 1994).

4   J. P. Coldham, *Lord Hawke: a Cricketing Biography* (Marlborough, 1990), p. 184.

5   On the amateur–professional division see the oral history by M. Marshall, *Gentlemen and Players: Conversations with Cricketers* (London, 1987).

6   H. de Selincourt, *The Cricket Match* (Oxford, 1980); A. G. Macdonell, *England Their England* (London, 1986); E. Blunden, *Cricket Country* (London, 1985).

7   M. Girouard, *The Return to Camelot: Chivalry and the English Gentleman* (London, 1981); on moral competition, see G. R. Searle, *Morality and the Market Place* (Oxford, 1999).

8   For a general view of amateurism, see R. Holt, *Sport and the British: a Modern History* (Oxford, 1989), pp. 74–116.

9   J. Williams, 'Churches, sport and identities in the North, 1900–1939', in J. Hill and J. Williams (eds), *Sport and Identity in the North of England* (Keele, 1986), p. 115.

10 For an expert summary, see 'E. W. Swanton', in P. Hayter (ed), *Cricket Heroes* (London, 1990), pp. 92–4; S. Rae, *W. G. Grace* (London, 1998) is the best biography of any cricketer to date.

11 D. Frith, *The Golden Age of Cricket, 1890–1914* (Ware, 1983) is one of the better nostalgic illustrated evocations available.

12 *Women's Cricket*, July 1932, p. 70; I am grateful to Liz Taplin for this reference.

13 R. McKibbin, *Classes and Cultures: England 1918–1951* (Oxford, 1998), p. 505.

14 C. Brookes, *His Own Man: the Life of Neville Cardus* (London, 1985), p. 84.

15 D. Birley, *The Willow Wand: Some Cricket Myths Explored* (London, 1989) provides a good historical account of cultural meanings.

16 J. Huntingdon-Whiteley and R. Holt (eds), *The Book of British Sporting Heroes* (London, The National Portrait Gallery, 1998), curator's introduction.

17 C. Martin-Jenkins, *Ball by Ball: the Story of Cricket Broadcasting* (London, 1990), p. 105.

18 J. M. Kilburn, *In Search of Cricket* (London, 1990), p. 9.

19 Cited in A. Lewis, *Double Century: The Story of the MCC and Cricket* (London, 1987), p. 205.

20 Birley, *The Willow Wand*, p. 167.

21 J. Hill, 'The Legend of Denis Compton', *The Sports Historian*, 18:2 (1998), 20.

22 L. Hutton, *Fifty Years in Cricket* (London, 1984), p. 21.

23 Cited in C. Martin-Jenkins, *The Complete Who's Who of Test Cricketers* (London, 1987), p. 62.

24 A. Hill, *Herbert Sutcliffe: Cricket Maestro* (London, 1991), pp. 97–8, one of the best recent cricket biographies with some nice social detail.

25 D. Cannadine, *Class in Britain* (New Haven, 1998).

26 D. Foot, *Wally Hammond: the Reasons Why* (London, 1998), pp. 59–72; Foot deals honestly with Hammond's private life and corrects G. Howat's otherwise valuable *Walter Hammond* (London, 1984).

27 R. Barker, *The Cricketing Family Edrich* (London, 1976), esp. p. 79.

28 Hill, *Herbert Sutcliffe*, p. 125.

29 *Ibid.*, p. 125.

30 I. Peebles, *'Patsy' Hendren: the Cricketer and his Times* (London, 1969), p. 157.

31 B. Green (ed.), *The Wisden Papers 1888–1946* (London, 1989); Woolley, cited in Lewis, *Double Century*, p. 205.

32 Foot, *Wally Hammond*, p. 6.

33 D. Compton, *End of an Innings* (London, 1988), p. 194.

34 Hill, *Herbert Sutcliffe*, p. 87.

35 G. Howat, *Len Hutton: the Biography* (London, 1988), p. 205.

36 J. L. Carr, *Carr's Illustrated Dictionary of Extra-Ordinary Cricketers* (London, 1983).

37 D. Trelford, *Len Hutton Remembered* (London, 1992), pp. 176–9.

38 Cited in D. Lemmon, *The Crisis of Captaincy: Servant and Master in English Cricket* (London, 1988), pp. 90–1.

39 B. Green (ed.), *The Wisden Papers of Neville Cardus* (London,1989), pp. 103–4.

40 Hayter, *Cricket Heroes*, p. 123.

41 R. Mason, *Jack Hobbs* (London, 1961), p. 4.

42 Green, *The Wisden Papers of Neville Cardus*, p. 104.

43 I. Peebles, *Woolley: The Pride of Kent* (London, 1969), p. 53.

44 Trelford, *Len Hutton Remembered*, p. 126.

45 Foot, *Wally Hammond*, p. 172.

46 Lemmon, *The Crisis of Captaincy*, pp. 85–6.

47 Barker, *The Cricketing Family Edrich*, p. 102.

48 Peebles, *Woolley: the Pride of Kent*, p. 53.

49 B. Green (comp.), *The Wisden Book of Cricketers' Lives* (London,1986), p. 436.

50 *Ibid.*, p. 416.

51 D. Russell, 'Sport and identity: the case of Yorkshire County Cricket Club, 1890–1939', *Twentieth Century British History*, 7:2 (1996), 206–30 gives an excellent account of regional culture expressed through sport.

52 Birley, *The Willow Wand*, p. 169.

53 Hayter, *Cricket Heroes*, p. 84.

54 S. Chalke, *Runs in the Memory: County Cricket in the 1950s* (Bath, 1997) is an evocative oral history.

PART V

THE CONTEMPORARY HERO

Nelson Mandela: political saint
for a new democracy

At the beginning of her book, Mary Benson, Nelson Mandela's first biographer, posed the question, 'How is it that a man imprisoned for more than twenty three years . . . has become the embodiment of the struggle for liberation . . . and is the vital symbol of a new society?'[1] Biography itself can supply only part of the answer; usually the processes which lead to certain men or women becoming venerated in popular political culture extend well beyond the concerns which inform the analysis of a particular life. Even so, biography represents an obvious starting point in the investigation of iconographies, especially in the case of Nelson Mandela's public life, which features so conspicuously the deliberate construction of emblematic attributes by himself and others.

To date, Mandela's own testimony supplies the most comprehensive biographical portrait of the man.[2] *Long Walk to Freedom* is not quite autobiography, though. Part of the text is based upon a manuscript written in prison in 1977 and the rest is assembled from interviews conducted in 1994 by an American journalist, Richard Stengel. Since its publication, an illustrated coffee table edition has appeared as well as an abridged edition in basic English, pointers to the heterodox social character of Mandela's devotees. Notwithstanding the participation of his ghost writer, it is a safe assumption that the book's eight hundred or so pages are a faithful reflection of Mandela's own conception of his life and personality, in Stengel's words, a mirror 'of the proud and graceful persona Mr Mandela has crafted for himself'.[3]

Even so, Mandela's autobiography reveals a complicated man. 'Nurture, rather than nature, is the primary moulder of personality', Mandela maintains, but in his case nurture included a childhood shaped by an inherited sense of destiny, 'groomed like my father before me, to counsel the rulers of the tribe'. Despite his father's death, as a boy Mandela 'defined myself' through him. Brought up under the guardianship of the Thembu regent, he acquired knowledge 'like all Xhosa children through observation, through imitation and emulation', developing 'notions of leadership' by watching the regent in his court. Here he found 'democracy in its purest form', a democracy in which 'everyone was heard, equal in their worth as citizens', in which meetings would continue until the attainment of consensus and 'majority rule was a foreign notion'. Only at the end of the meeting would the regent speak. 'As a leader', Mandela claims at this point in his narrative, 'I have always followed the principles I first saw demonstrated by the regent at the great palace.' 'A leader is like a shepherd', nudging and prodding his flock before him. But Mandela's birthname is Rolihlahla – he was only named Nelson later, on his first day at mission school – and Rolihlahla means 'troublemaker', or, more literally, one who pulls branches off a tree. Mandela's relationship with 'tradition' is by no means straightforward.

Today, Mandela likes to be called by his friends and political associates 'Madiba', his clan name, signifying both the intimacy of kinship and the respect of ascribed status, and the name has become popularised in the South African press. Certainly, he continues to be attracted to what he perceives to be traditional notions of leadership and community, but, as his history demonstrates, in his later career he was to exercise a completely different style of leadership – one in which personal initiatives had to usurp the imperative for consensus. 'Sometimes one must go public with an idea to nudge a reluctant organisation in the direction you want it to go', he observes with reference to his unauthorised public statement in 1961 that the days of non-violent struggle were over. Or, as he explains when discussing his decision to begin negotiations from prison, 'There are times when a leader must move ahead of the flock.' And though his autobiography does not quote it, Mandela's famous remark at a later stage of negotiations, his profession of faith in the 'ordinary democracy' of majority rule,[4] suggests that his understanding of African traditions supplies only one element, though an important one, in his political make-up. Traditions can be useful – Mandela's manipulation of custom suggests a shrewdly instrumental recognition of their role – but his narrative acknowledges that the past is another country. Returning to his Transkeien birthplace after his release from prison he finds a landscape littered with plastic bags and a community in which pride and self worth 'seemed to have vanished'. The argument is underlined in his discussion of his relationship with the new generation of Black Consciousness political activists who appeared on Robben Island from 1974; here he acknowledges the danger of clinging to ideas which 'had become frozen in time'. Mandela's empathy with rebellious youth is a frequent theme in his public utterances. In an angry speech delivered to a thousand amakhosi and indunas in Kwa Zulu Natal in 1996, Mandela reprimanded local chiefs who had helped to encourage political violence, warning them that 'they would be left behind by the real leaders emerging from the youth of the country'.[5] A few months before the 1994 election he created a furore by suggesting that the franchise should be extended to fourteen-year-olds, a proposal which his embarrassed ANC colleagues hurriedly repudiated.

The tensions between different facets of Mandela's personality remain unresolved in his autobiography. They are evident in the different voices which tell his story. One voice is magisterial and statesmanlike, the voice which emphasises the central themes of racial reconciliation and man's essential goodness ('all men have a core of decency') which run through the text. Another voice is the less measured one which expresses anguish and personal loss, experiences which are rendered most poignantly in the powerful recurrent image of a child putting on the clothing of his dead or absent father. This is a voice which can subvert the impersonal heroic collective political emotions which he attributes to his public self. On the day of the presidential inauguration, 'I felt that day, as I have on so many others, that I was simply the sum of all those African patriots who had gone before me'. But as he concedes one page later, 'every man has twin obligations' and in serving his people he was prevented from fulfilling his roles as 'a son, a brother, a father and a husband'. The pain which arises from the latter recognition is generally controlled and suppressed in the book; indeed learning to control and conceal pain and its accompaniment, fear, is one of the defining qualities of manhood he learns as a child; nevertheless it is frequently evident, nowhere more than in the curious mixture of the languages of bureaucratic rationality and private tribute with which he announces his separation from his wife, 'Comrade Nomzamo'.

The public emotions which Mandela professes are also carefully managed. The political Mandela is at least in part the product of artifice. The third section of the book is entitled 'The birth of a freedom fighter' and its occasional deliberate use of the third-person voice – 'it is important for a freedom fighter to remain in touch with his own roots' – is a significant indication of Mandela's own consciousness of inventing a public identity and acting out a heroic role. There are other kinds of acting too; at several points in the narrative Mandela assumes disguises and false identities. Clothing, costume and style are indispensable components in the different personas Mandela assumes, nowhere more obviously than in his choice of a leopard skin kaross to wear at his first appearance in court after his arrest in 1962. 'I had chosen traditional Xhosa dress to emphasise the symbolism that I was a black African walking into a white man's court ... I felt myself to be the embodiment of African nationalism.' Later, he refers to prison as 'a different and smaller arena' (compared with the court-room), 'an arena in which the only audience was ourselves and our oppressors'. This awareness of an audience and his conviction of the historic destiny are both indispensable accomplices in Mandela's own crafting of his exemplary life. The links between political leadership and theatrical performance are emphasised in a reference to his role as Creon in Sophocles' *Antigone*. Significantly, several commentaries have used the metaphors of masks and masking in their analysis of Mandela's personality,[6] a term Mandela himself used in describing the way in which in prison he concealed his anguished longing for his family.[7]

Mandela himself has an ambivalent attitude to his heroic status, recognising the merits of the ANC personalising the cause in the campaign for his release but often affecting disdain for 'the exaltation of the president and denigration of other ANC leaders (which) constitutes praise which I do not accept'.[8] In his speech after his release, as he suggests in his autobiography, he 'wanted first of all to tell the people that I was not a messiah, but an ordinary man who had become a leader because of extraordinary circumstances'. The address is carefully written in the idiom of the ANC's conventions of collective leadership,[9] prefaced with a long series of salutes to its various constituencies and organisational 'formations'.[10] In fact, though, the ANC's development during his political life allowed plenty of scope for the influence of strong prophetic personalities. When Mandela joined the African National Congress, in 1942, the organisation had only recently emerged from a decade of torpor and its small following was concentrated in three cities. From its foundation in 1912 its programme had only occasionally extended beyond an annual convention of African gentry and notables. With the exception of a few communists, its leadership had been mostly at best amateur politicians; Mandela and his fellow youth leaguers were the first substantial cohort of African middle-class professionals to make political activism the central focus in their lives, hence their extraordinarily rapid ascent in a movement whose following ballooned in their wake. From his first hesitant association with the organisation shortly after his arrival in Johannesburg, it took just ten years for Mandela to emerge as its second-ranking leader. The ANC's switch to militant forms of mass protest in the 1950s coincided with the development of a popular press directed at African readers and from the time of his appointment as 'National Volunteer-in-chief' in the 1952 Defiance Campaign – a civil disobedience programme which emphasised the sacrificial role of inspirational leadership – Mandela became one of South Africa's first black media personalities. Through the following decade of mobilisation politics, ANC leaders became increasingly aware of the potentialities of newspaper celebrity.[11] Mandela himself tells how in the first months of 1961 while he was hiding from the police and undertaking preparations for a national strike his 'outlaw existence caught the imagination of the press'. Journalists called him the 'Black Pimpernel' and he would foster 'the mythology . . . by taking a pocketful of tickeys (threepenny bits) and phoning individual newspaper reporters from telephone boxes and relaying stories of what we were planning or the ineptitude of the police'. Some of the myths which were generated during this period have enjoyed a long currency; in her biography of Winnie Mandela, Nancy Harrison describes Mandela's dramatic appearance at the 'all-in-conference' in Pietermaritzberg and reproduces the populist legend that he made his speech barefoot, as a man of the people. Unfortunately, the photograph taken of this occasion confirms that he was wearing well-polished shoes to match his characteristically elegant three-piece tweed suit.[12]

In the early 1960s there was an especial need for the ANC to develop a heroic pantheon of leaders. On the African continent its exiled representatives were encountering strong opposition from its offshoot rival, the Pan-Africanist Congress, which had been rather more successful in assuming an 'authentic' African identity roughly comparable to the popular nationalist movements presided over by the charismatic and messianic leaders which were spearheading African decolonisation at that time. When the Free Mandela Committee was established at the time of Mandela's 1962 trial its organisers distributed a lapel button, bearing a portrait of the imprisoned leader wrapped in the West African toga then favoured by the continent's emergent rulers. The ultimate success of such efforts to embody the ANC's cause in a saga of individual heroism probably exceeded any of the expectations among ANC strategists in the early 1960s. In the twenty-seven years of his confinement Nelson Mandela accumulated honorary degrees, freedoms of cities and awards from governments. In 1988 admirers in the Netherlands alone swamped the South African prison service with 170,000 letters and birthday cards.[13] In the same year, 250,000 people assembled in London's Hyde Park at the conclusion of the Free Mandela March to listen to thirty minutes of readings from Mandela's correspondence with his wife.[14] His face appeared on postage stamps and official sculpture and his deeds, mythical and real, were celebrated at rock concerts.

By the 1980s, Nelson Mandela could with justification claim to be 'the world's most famous political prisoner'.[15] Some of this fame arose from the popular attention which Mandela's own actions commanded: at the time of his well-publicised court appearances his story exemplified old-fashioned virtues: honour, courage, and chivalry. The explanation of this extraordinary international celebrity status cannot, though, be confined to Mandela's actions or the ANC's own efforts to foster cults of charismatic leadership, important as they were. Such endeavours were given ample assistance by the peculiar moral appeal of South African liberation and its resonance in the international politics of anti-racism and decolonisation; the emergence of a transnational anti-apartheid 'new social movement'; Mandela's cultural adaptability as a modern folk hero; and the immortality conferred upon him by seclusion. The internationalisation of South African political conflict is obviously attributable to the existence of a uniquely institutionalised system of racism in a relatively important and accessible country in a world climate shaped by the post-war reaction against Nazism and colonialism. Anti-apartheid as a social movement drew its strength from the same forces which helped to engender a range of new political identities in mature industrial societies. But Mandela's personal qualities which made him especially susceptible to international cult status and the effects of his compelled isolation from everyday life deserve more extended commentary.

'I confess to being something of an anglophile', Mandela tells us in his autobiography. The passage continues: 'When I thought of Western democracy and freedom, I thought of the British parliamentary system. In so many ways, the very model of the gentleman for me was an Englishman. . . . While I abhorred the notion of British imperialism, I never rejected the trappings of British style and manners.' On the eve of his departure from Johannesburg on a journey to address members of both houses of parliament at Westminster in 1993 he told journalists: 'I have not discarded the influence which Britain and British influence and culture exercised on us.'[16] As Richard Stengel has noticed, 'To him, the British audience is more important than either the American or the European.'[17] Relatively few Third World insurgencies managed to combine in their leaderships such an effective mixture of guerrilla glamour and reassuring metropolitan respectability.[18] Like many other ANC leaders of his generation, Mandela's Anglo-Methodist schooling and his liberal literary education equipped him with a familiarity with Anglo-American culture and a capacity, consciously or otherwise, to invoke its social codes. A particularly telling example of this attribute in his personality and life history is the tragic story of his second marriage; significantly one of his first acts of rebellion was to reject a customary union arranged by his guardian. During his imprisonment, his beautiful and personable wife played a substantial role in ensuring the durability of his political authority. Notwithstanding such gestures to African tradition as the payment of *lobola*, Nelson and Winnie Mandela's correspondence with each other employs the informal egalitarian idioms and expresses the sexual intimacies of modern Western domestic life. Mandela's very public subscription to an idyll of romantic love was a vital element in the narratives directed at Western audiences.[19] More generally, his and the ANC's role as representatives of an industrialised urban community made them especially culturally intelligible in Europe and North America, all the more so given the appearance in the 1950s of an unusually talented generation of black South African writers who began to find a significant readership outside South Africa.[20]

Mandela's incarceration and the official South African bans on the publication of his words and portraits as well as the authorities' refusal to allow photographs of him in prison ensured that public narratives were shaped by the words and images that were available from the epic struggle which stretched from the Defiance campaign to the Rivonia trial, a few timeless and ageless texts and pictures which, as Rob Nixon perceptively notes, kept 'circulating in a heraldic fashion perfect for the needs of an international political movement'.[21] The imprisonment and isolation from public view kept the narrative and the images which accompanied it pristine, invested with the glamour of martyrdom but reinforced by the apocalyptic possibilities of a second coming. Sipho Sepemla, a poet of the 1980s activist generation, expresses especially powerfully this vision of an assertive youthful Mandela striding his way out of prison, fist raised high in the straight-armed black power salute:

> I need today oh so very badly/Nelson Mandela/Out of the prison gates/ to walk broad-shouldered among counsel/down Commissioner/up West street/and lead us away from the shadow/of impotent word weavers/his clenched fist hoisted higher than hope/for all to see and follow.[22]

Government strategists told an American researcher at the beginning of the 1980s that they were aware that Mandela's removal from the political stage freed him from the requirement 'to make hard, human decisions'.[23] 'Mandela is not so much a political figure as a mythical one. For this reason', opined Professor Willie Breytenbach, a key government advisor in the 1980s, 'I believe that if he should be released the key problem would be surviving long enough to play any role at all.'[24] Credo Mutwa, a self-professed 'High Witchdoctor' and an authority on indigenous culture much favoured by the old South African authorities, predicted in 1986 that Mandela's release would replace a revered hero-saviour with 'a spent force like an arrow which has spent its passion'.[25] Public opinion polling since the aftermath of the Soweto uprising consistently suggested that Mandela's personal following exceeded that of the ANC,[26] an indication of the extent to which the alluring enigmas created by his absence from active politics had helped to transform the guerrilla convict into a patriotic icon. When Chief Buthelezi's differences with the ANC became public, he attempted to demonstrate his membership of a more legitimate patriotic community by publishing his private correspondence with Mandela.[27] And though freedom did not bring all the dividends for which his captors may have hoped it certainly detracted from the more millenarian dimensions of the myth. During protracted negotiations which followed Mandela's release, some South African urban legends inverted the logic of the second coming to explain why freedom was taking so long to arrive. A young black truck driver informed Jeremy Cronin, a Communist Party leader, that the real Nelson Mandela was killed in prison. 'Today's Mandela is a lookalike. He was trained for years by the Boers and finally presented to the public in 1990. The mission of this look-alike is to pretend to be against the system. But in reality he is working for it.'[28]

Mandela's captivity enhanced the omnibus appeal of his authority. Mandela biographies and hagiographies project quite different understandings of his personal greatness and its broader social meanings. Such projections have reflected the differing imperatives of various constituencies within the broad movement he represented during his imprisonment as well as its changing ideological predispositions. They also testify to the ways in which his life has become emblematic for people quite separate from the ANC's community and even outside South Africa.

Mandela's first biographer, Mary Benson, was secretary to the ANC president in the 1950s and was close to many of the events she describes. In 1963, by which time she was living in London, she wrote a richly textured popular history of the ANC. Her Mandela biography was first published in 1980 as a volume in the 'PanAf Great Lives' Series.[29] A second updated edition appeared in 1986.[30] Limited by its author's restricted access to sources, Benson's book concerns itself mainly with Mandela's political career, at least until his first meeting with Winnie (Evalyn, his first wife receives only the most perfunctory of references). The opening chapter supplies a bare outline of its subject's genealogy, childhood and education. For Benson, the important developments in the story begin after Mandela's arrival in Johannesburg. At this point, she believes, he had put his rural upbringing firmly behind him. His rejection of his guardian's plans for his marriage reflected a deeper political impulse: 'By this time he had realised he was being prepared for chieftainship and he had made up his mind never to rule over an oppressed people.' 'My guardian was no democrat', Mandela told Mary Benson many years earlier when she interviewed him, 'he did not think it worthwhile to consult me about a wife.' This view of Mandela as a rebel against tradition was widely shared. In 1988, *New Nation*, a weekly paper in Johannesburg edited by ANC sympathisers, referred to Mandela as 'by birth a Xhosa chief who at a young age resisted all tribal ties'.[31] Most of Benson's biography comprises a chronology of public events and references to Mandela's contribution to these. Its treatment is very general and its focus is mainly on the organisation, not the man. Long extracts from Mandela's polemical writings and his trial addresses occupy a large portion of Benson's text. They help to reinforce a rather impersonal tribute with the accent on Mandela's identity as a modern liberal democratic politician. This is the identity which was accentuated in those public commemorations of Mandela which were directed at Europeans and North Americans. In one volume of 'literary homage', Jacques Derrida writes of Mandela as the ultimate apostle and interpreter of the rational legal traditions associated with the Western Enlightenment.[32]

A fuller version of Mandela's political testament, a collection of his speeches and writings was published in London in 1965 in the Heinemann African Writers series, edited by Ruth First with an introduction by Oliver Tambo. In her foreword to the second edition (1973), First compares the author to the then fashionable American black power heroes, George Jackson, Soledad Brother and Angela Davis. A grainy picture of Mandela visiting an Algerian military facility adds visual confirmation to First's presentation of the ANC's 'underground political commander' as the personification of 'revolutionary power'.[33] The 'light editing' of the original material included the excision from an article first published in 1956 about the Freedom Charter of a passage describing the benefits the Charter would bring to a nascent African bourgeoisie. However, even without Ruth First's editorial tidying, Mandela's 1950s writings suggest a more intellectually radical figure than the pragmatic reformist projected in British and American analyses of the ANC's leadership. Mandela's initial political experience was gained from casual attendance at night schools organised by the Communist Party and though he subsequently for a while opposed communist influence within the ANC, he retained an affinity with the ideas of the Left. In a speech delivered to the ANC's Youth League in 1951 he reminded his listeners never to forget 'the advance guard of American penetration . . . the infinitely more dangerous enemy sustaining all those with loans, capital and arms'. Given the growing affinity between 'English, Jewish and Afrikaner financial and industrial interests', it was quite likely that all these 'found the fascist policy of Malan suitable'. 'The possibility of a liberal capitalist democracy in South Africa is extremely nil.' South Africa was rapidly becoming 'an openly fascist state', the creation of 'monopoly capitalism gone mad'. Political opposition required the talents 'of a professional revolutionary'. Certainly, such rhetoric incorporated many of the sentiments which were then normal in anti-colonialist or anti-imperialist discourses, but Mandela's deployment of them is strikingly logical and disciplined. His often reprinted articles first published in the left-wing journal *Liberation*, are especially impressive, with their carefully structured and conceptually systematic arguments. This is particularly evident in his well-known characterisation of the Freedom Charter as 'by no means a blueprint for a socialist state' but rather 'a programme for the unification of certain classes' engaged in 'a democratic struggle' of 'various classes and political groupings'. The language is remarkable as much for its cerebral dispassionateness as its sociological sophistication.

During the 1980s both the exiled ANC and internal political groups which stationed themselves in the Congress camp looked forward to a post-Apartheid 'National Democracy' in which 'monopoly capital' had been displaced, a transitional stage which would proceed a fully socialised society.[34] In this context, fresh meaning was discovered in Mandela's life history. For example, within the National Union of Mineworkers, according to one of its spokesmen, after the Union's election of Mandela as its honorary Life President, 'work was done to inform workers of Mandela's history and the struggles he waged as a mineworker in Crown Mines'.[35] Mandela did stay at Crown Mines for a very short period after his arrival in Johannesburg and, indeed, deploying his extensive family connections, managed to secure the relatively privileged post of a compound policeman until word arrived from the regent's court in the Transkei that he should be sent home. However, according to Mandela in his autobiography, he helped trade unionists to mobilise mining compounds during the 1946 mineworkers' strike.

Fatima Meer's 'authorised' seventieth birthday tribute to Nelson Mandela, initially in its first South African edition effusively sub-titled *Rolihlahla We Love You*,[36] reflects a rather different set of social priorities and political imperatives from the earlier depictions of a liberal democrat, revolutionary intellectual and working-class hero. Fatima Meer herself is a member of an important Indian political dynasty within the Congress movement and her book is written from the perspective of a social elite whose moral authority experienced growing challenge in the insurrectionary climate of the 1980s. This volume is, according to Winnie Mandela,[37] who supplied a supportive preface, the 'real family biography'. This is true in two senses. First, the portrayal is as much of Mandela the private man as it is of him as a public figure; it describes the unhappy course of his first marriage and is openly honest about Mandela's contribution to its breakdown ('Nelson was extremely attractive to women and he was easily attracted to them'); it takes as a central theme the preoccupations of its protagonist as a father and head of 'a large household of dependents'. But it is also about family as lineage, succession, dynasty, and inherited greatness. For this is a book about a royal leader, the descendant of kings who 'ruled all the Aba Tembu at a time when the land belonged to them and they were free.' It is about a man who learnt his patrimonial history in 'silent veneration' at the feet of his elders and who is inspired with a lifelong mission to recapture for all South Africans 'the ubuntu (humanity) of the African kings'. Without a father from the age of ten, he was brought up by 'a member of our clan' for whom 'according to our custom I was his child and his responsibility'. His second, more successful marriage is to another representative of aristocratic lineage, to the daughter of a line of 'marauding chieftains'. Winnie's upbringing owed much to the influence of her grandmother, a reluctant convert to Christianity. From her, she learnt 'things that my mother had taken care to see I'd never learn',

> She took me into the ways of our ancestors, she put the skins and the beads that had been hers when she was a young girl on me and taught me to sing and dance. I learnt to milk cows and ride horses and cook mealie porridge, mealie with meat, mealie with vegetables, and I learnt to make umphokoqo the way Makhulu made it.

In Fatima Meer's book, it is this world which defines the Mandelas' moral centre. For though Nelson learns to 'manage' and 'integrate' Johannesburg 'from the standpoint of Orlando', the city was never home, he remained 'intensely rural'; 'it was the first half of his life that really mattered when it came to roots'. Notwithstanding his wider political and social loyalties, 'there were deep-rooted historical identities that could not be denied ... the first experience of human solidarity ... in the family, in the clan, in the tribe ... constituted the real identities, the nurseries for larger solidarities'. His leadership is patrician and inborn, gifted with powers of 'breathtaking oratory', compassion 'for the poor', and above all the social empathy that enables him to assume a 'rough and ready disguise' and move unrecognised in the crowd ('it felt good to be one of the people'). His social universe is one which is organic, in which, to cite his early mentor, Anton Lembede, 'individual parts exist merely as interdependent aspects of one whole'. Political conflicts in this world can be intensely personal, involving as they do betrayals between kinsfolk, betrayals which recur dynastically: 'Sabata's great grandfather ... had been betrayed by his brother Sabata; now the grandson, K.D. Matanzima was betraying Sabata and would eventually depose him. They were all madibas, and should have stayed together at all times; but Madiba was split from Madiba.' Authority is also personal; in 1960, Nelson receives at his Orlando home deputations of Tembu and Mpondo tribesmen to report on the Mandelas' errant kinsfolk's terrorisation of an 'illiterate region ... not deemed worthy of literate recording'. For Mandela can listen to them with the sympathy and insight of a personality 'whose instincts were still rooted in rural politics'.

In this depiction of a rural notable and communal patriarch presiding over an organic inter-dependent society there seems little scope for either the liberal or the 'national democratic' conceptions of democracy which helped to shape the earlier discourses about Mandela, nor is there much room for the popular sovereignty favoured by modern trade unions and civic organisations in the messianic obeisance to the leader which was prescribed by spokesmen for the Release Mandela Campaign during the 1980s. For Audrey Mokoena, the RMC's Transvaal chairman, Mandela was 'the pivotal factor in the struggle for liberation. He has the stature and the charisma which derives from his contribution to the struggle.'[38] Mokoena's language was not atypical. Mewa Ramgobin told his audience at a Soweto RMC meeting in July 1984 that 'I want to make bold and say in clear language that the human race must remain grateful, that the human race must go down on its knees and say thank you for the gifts it has been endowed with in the lives of the Nelson Mandelas of this country.'[39] Peter Mokaba, the president at the time of the South African Youth Congress, chaired the rally held in a Soweto stadium on 24 February 1990 to celebrate Mandela's release. He had this to say: 'Comrade President, here are your people, gathered to pay tribute to their messiah, their saviour whom the Apartheid regime failed dismally to silence. These are the comrades and the combatants that fought tooth and nail in the wilderness ... they toiled in the valley of darkness, and now that their messiah and saviour is released, they want to be shown the way to freedom.'[40]

The attribution of Mandela with redemptive qualities of leadership reached its apogee during his visit to the United States in June 1990, four months after his release. Intended by the ANC as a fundraising trip (and most successful in this respect, with donations totalling $7 million), for his African-American hosts as well as many people in his various audiences the occasion served quite different needs. As a New York newspaper report put it: 'the Mandela visit has become perhaps the largest and most vivid symbol that after many years on the edges of New York city power and politics the black community has arrived.'[41] For *Village Voice*'s Harlem correspondent, 'The visit of the freedom fighter positioned us, for a minute, in the center of world politics. It made us the first family. And gave us, again, an accessible past, so that the African part of the equation suddenly had a lot more sense.'[42] The notion of familyhood featured frequently in the comments recorded from spectators: 'We are all from Africa. This is like family. He's a symbol of who we are.'[43] And there to welcome Mandela was the city's first black mayor, David Dinkins, there to organise his security was the city's second black police commissioner, and there to determine the events in his schedule were the legions of black community leaders in Brooklyn and Harlem 'who together with more than 500 black churches had turned New York's African Americans into the largest ethnic voting bloc in the city'.[44] So in an important respect, Mandela's American journey helped to consolidate the leadership credentials of an African American elite of municipal bosses, civil rights luminaries, and show business personalities.

But juxtaposed with the triumphalist language which accompanied Mandela's progress was the perception that the South African visitor supplied a missing moral dimension of authority, that his presence in

America could rekindle hope in ghetto communities affected by social pathologies and political decay. Benjamin Chavis, the influential former director of the United Church of Christ Mission, captured this feeling eloquently: 'We have a new Jerusalem. When he gets back on the 'plane, we have to keep that fire alive and thank God that Mandela has lit a fire that was extinguished in the 1960s. I think you're going to see a lot of African Americans break out of the cycle of hopelessness we've had.'[45] Veterans of the Civil Rights movement repeatedly confided to journalists their conviction that Mandela's coming 'had filled a void which had been left by the deaths of Dr Martin Luther King and Malcolm X'.[46] This perception was widely distributed. While waiting for Mandela's arrival, schoolteacher Mark Reeves and his class spent 'all week studying Mr Mandela and relating him to Martin Luther King and the Civil Rights movement'.[47] New Yorkers 'turned him into an instant American celebrity, a civil rights leader they could call their own'.[48] Winnie's presence evoked similar emotions. Brushing aside the troubling controversies then surrounding Mrs Mandela in South Africa, Mrs Julie Belafonte, one of the main organisers of the Mandela tour, told reporters: 'We don't know what happened over there . . . and in any case it's irrelevant in relation to the positive power she has displayed and the pressure she has been under. She's a wonderful role model for women.'[49]

Some 750,000 people lined the streets of New York to cheer Mandela's progress whilst, in many other cities outside the eleven stops of his tour, programmes of festive events were arranged.[50] Taraja Samuel, an administrator in the New York education department, 'felt a blessing from God that I could be a part of this'.[51] Malcolm X's widow, Betty Shabazz, introduced Winnie Mandela to the congregation of Harlem's House of the Lord Church by saying: 'This sister's presence in our midst is enough. She shouldn't have to speak. To have gone through what she has gone through, and to see her so present, so composed! There must be a God. There's got to be a God.'[52] At a meeting in Bedford Stuyvessant, Brooklyn, *Village Voice's* correspondent watched the sun shine through 'his silver Afro hair like a halo . . . this is a truly religious experience, a man back from the dead to lead the living, and an authentic African queen'.[53] Even the more measured official rhetoric which accompanied the tour resonated with chiliastic expectation. In his welcoming address, David Dinkins likened Mandela to a modern-day Moses 'leading the people of South Africa out of enslavement at the hands of the pharaoh'.[54]

Mandela deftly tapped into the historical well-springs of the emotions which greeted him with gracious acknowledgement of a pantheon of appropriate local heroes. Each of his speeches included a recitation of their names: Sojourner Truth, Paul Robeson, Rosa Parks, Marcus Garvey, Fanie

Lou Harries, Malcolm X and Harriet Tobias. However his protestations of being merely a representative of a greater collective entity, the ANC, like his self-deprecatory meditations on the evanescent quality of human genius – 'each shall, like a meteor, a mere brief passing moment in time and space, flit across the human stage'[55] – were drowned in the clamour arising from the procession of an American (sic) hero embodying American dreams.

In the perceptions of white South Africans, no strangers to millennial political traditions,[56] the incarnation of Nelson Mandela as national hero has signified the possibility of personal and communal salvation or baptism in a new 'rainbow' patriotism. Warder James Gregory's memoir, *Goodbye Bafana*, celebrates in its ingenuous fashion 'a cleansing process, one of ridding the anger'[57] which he experienced in his dealings with his famous prisoner. The book's title draws parallels between his relationship with Mandela and the lost innocence of a 'pre-apartheid' childhood friendship with a Zulu boy on his father's farm. As Mandela leaves prison, Gregory's mind 'returns to [his] boyhood and to the farm where [he] played with Bafana all those years ago'.[58] In a less intrusive fashion than Gregory's exploitative text, many others seek personally to appropriate a portion of Mandela's aura and in so doing lay to rest old demons:

> The icon of the 90s is a picture of yourself with President Mandela . . . In home where, during the apartheid era, the word 'struggle' was used loosely that it could mean your wife had broken a nail or the maid hadn't pitched, Mandela's benevolent face now gazes out of large silver frames placed on study desks. He watches you from the wood panelled libraries or from the walls of boardrooms. In those places the 'Me and Mandela' factor works as a talisman against the past, pushing it out of sight and into the dark recesses of time.[59]

Not content with donations to the ANC and undertaking the reconstruction of Mandela's old primary school, Bill Venter, chairman of Altron, an electronics firm which became an major industrial company in the 1980s as a consequence of winning defence contracts, has made the birthday poem he wrote for Nelson Mandela required reading for his employees, including it in a little red book, *Memos from the Chairman*, circulated to all staff. The poem reads: 'Your wisdom has woven a tapestry/ Much more lovely than any artist's hand/ With a vibrancy that only we can understand/ We, who are Africa's people/ And feel the heartbeat of this land.'[60] As the new 'father of the nation', Mandela can summon expressions of loyalty from the most unexpected sources. Rejoicing in South Africa's new-found international acceptability, the conservative *Citizen* newspaper noted 'the respect, almost awe' with which South Africa was now held, informing its readers that 'we take even greater pride in the recognition of President Mandela's stature in the world. He is a great man who towers above other leaders, both at home, in Africa, and abroad.'[61] The more traditionally liberal *Star* profitably tapped a similar vein of sentiment when it filled a 'commercial feature' on 18 July 1994, Mandela's birthday, with congratulatory advertisements from businesses and other organisations. Throughout his presidency, Nelson Mandela undertook a series of imaginative gestures of reconciliation and empathy with white South Africans, despite frequent expressions of displeasure by black journalists. These have included his professed recognition of Afrikaans as a 'truly African language', a 'language of liberation and hope',[62] his appearance at the Rugby World Cup Final dressed in a Springbok jersey and cap, his presiding over corporate fund-raising dinners in Robben Island, and, of course, a sequence of well-publicised social encounters with old adversaries including Mrs Betsie Verwoerd (whose grandchildren represent Mandela's party in parliament) and his prosecutor at the Rivonia trial, Dr Percy Yutar. The latter event moved one Johannesburg journalist to refer to Mandela's 'superhuman forgiveness' more or less seriously as 'holy magnanimity', a phrase adapted from the concept of 'holy disbelief' used by Elizer Berkovits to describe the loss of faith in concentration camps.[63]

What have been the political effects of this canonization of democratic South Africa's first president? In the 1960s, charismatic heroes represented a central focus in the interpretation of African politics. David Apter described how the legitimacy of new institutions was both strengthened and weakened by Kwame Nkrumah's charismatic authority, a sacred authority which remained 'an important device by which political institutional transfer'[64] was affected. Certainly, Mandela's moral and political authority performs some of the positive functions assigned to charismatic authority by the analysts of political modernisation thirty years ago. In a country in which liberal democratic institutions and procedures are not especially popular,[65] his identification with them may have endowed them with a degree of legitimacy they might otherwise have lacked. Mandela's moral endorsement of political compromise is generally perceived to have been an indispensable factor in the success of South Africa's 'pacted' political transition. Transition theory with its focus on the choices and decisions made by political elites is especially receptive to 'Great Men' readings of history.[66] Within the domain of foreign policy, Mandela's personal appeal has enabled South Africa to elicit special treatment. As Paul Neifert, a US AID representative, lamented to a House of Representatives hearing, 'Our relationship with the new South Africa has become overly personal, substituting a reckless form of hero worship for a sober analysis of long term national interest.'[67]

Mandela himself has made attempts to democratise his myth, to assert his secular authority over the more sacred dimensions of his appeal. In his speech on leaving prison he told his audience that he stood before them, 'not as a prophet ... but as a humble servant of you, the people'. In his autobiography he insists on his status as 'an ordinary man who became a leader because of extraordinary circumstances'. In this spirit during the ANC's election campaign, the organisation borrowed from American politics the device of a people's forum, in which members of the audience would direct questions at Mandela, standing on a podium so that they could confer with him as individualised equals, not anonymous voices from the floor. In explaining the break-up of his marriage he observes that his wife 'married a man who soon left her; that man became a myth, and then that myth returned home and proved to be just a man after all'. And though one should be wary of courtiers' tributes to their master's humility[68] – these have been so frequently a feature of modern autocracies – in Mandela's case his unwillingness to take his authority for granted is often very evident. He was 'never sure whether young people liked him or not' he confessed when announcing the donation of his Nobel prize money to children's charities.[69] He often tells interviewers an anecdote from a private visit he made to the Bahamas in October 1993:

> A couple approached him in the street and the man asked: Aren't you Nelson Mandela? – I am often confused with that chap – was Mandela's mischievous response. Unconvinced, the man whispered to his wife to inform her of their unexpected find – What is he famous for? – his wife inquired in a hushed tone. Unsatisfied with her husband's inaudible response the woman asked Mandela outright – What are you famous for?

He concludes the anecdote, 'I hope that when I step down no one is going to ask me: what are you famous for?'. Perhaps it is Mandela's vulnerability as an 'ordinary man' which has done most to reduce the sacred dimension of his appeal. His divorce hearing prompted the publication of his wife's letters to her lover, Dali Mpofu, in which she referred to her husband with the dismissive diminutive, 'Tata' (father). In Mandela's evidence in the trial he told the court this letter left him feeling 'the loneliest man'.[70] At the beginning of 1996, as was noted above, in trying to prepare the ground for his succession Mandela took the unusual step of publicly criticising 'the exaltation of the president, and denigration of other ANC leaders, (which) constitutes praise which I do not accept'.[71] In any case, Mandela acknowledged his own mortality: 'I don't want a country like ours to be led by an octogenarian ... I must step down while there are one or two people who admire me'.[72]

In all this modesty there is an ambiguity, though. His preference in many of his public statements for the impersonal 'we' rather than 'I' can be read as the testimony of democratic humility, in Jacques Derrida's phrase, the presentation of 'himself in his people'.[73] But another reading might suggest a different sense in which a leader perceives himself to be the totality of popular aspirations. The people's forums cited above did not just draw upon American electioneering; they also had a local historic resonance in the public assemblies in which chiefs customarily secured consensual popular sanction for decisions. Mandela's preoccupation with reconciliation may be just one facet of a deeper preoccupation with unity, and the politics of maintaining unity can be deeply authoritarian. Running alongside the admirable formal adherence by Mandela and his government to the tenets of liberal democracy – the ANC's respect for the independence of the constitutional court is an especially notable example of this – is a quite different discourse. Black journalists who criticise the ANC, according to Mandela, 'have been coopted by conservative elements to attack the democratic movement',[74] prominent individuals such as Desmond Tutu should not criticise the ANC publicly since this 'created the impression of division within the movement',[75] and South African politicians should emulate the example of Zimbabwe in fostering the politics of unity. The mood such rhetoric evokes is at its ugliest when Mandela uses his personal authority to defend the misdemeanours of his subordinates, in for example, the thunderous applause from ANC benches in parliament which followed his defence of his instructions to the security guards who fired into an Inkatha demonstration outside the ANC's headquarters.[76] The existence of such a discourse should surprise no one. In modern South Africa messianic politics has been employed to demobilise a popular insurrection in one of the world's most unequal societies, and in such a context the institutions of liberal democracy depend upon the protection afforded by highly authoritarian forms of charismatic authority.

Postscript

Two years after this chapter was written, few of its arguments require updating. Until his departure from public office in June 1999, Nelson Mandela's stature amongst the South African public remained undiminished, notwithstanding the wavering levels of popular approval for his government and his political organisation discerned by opinion polls. Just before the 1999 general election public satisfaction with his 'performance' as president stood at 80 per cent. This feeling was shared across racial boundaries; in a poll conducted in November 1998, 59 per cent of white South Africans believed Mandela 'was doing his job well', despite the general antipathy to the ANC shared by most whites.[77] Even after his retirement, South Africans continue to invest their hopes for national reconstruction in Mandela's iconic status: most recently a proposal to mint 'Mandelarands' in place of Krugerrands was motivated by the belief that such a venture will harness the savings of African-Americans in the cause of restoring the fortunes of the goldmining industry.[78]

The myths and narratives associated with Mandela's life undergo constant change, though. One important contributor to this process is his former wife, Winnie Madikizela-Mandela, as she now prefers to be called. In March 1999, she ceremonially presented her wedding ring to thirteen-year-old Candice Erasmus, the daughter of a retired security policeman who once spied on her and who has since joined the Madikizela-Mandela household. This, she said, was a 'symbol of reconciliation' with her former tormentors, but the occasion also marked the opening of a rhetorical offensive against her ex-husband. He was guilty, she informed journalists in April, 'of using Apartheid legislation which denied property rights to African women to eject Winnie and her daughters' from the home they once shared. Mrs Mandela had been administering the house as a museum, financing the enterprise through the sale of jars of soil from the garden. Mandela's lawyers responded to Winnie's protestations by noting that the 'property was sacred to the Mandela family', for in its vicinity were buried the umbilical cords of his first children, 'in accordance with African custom'.[79] In May, during the election campaign, Madikizela-Mandela travelled to America where she presented to television viewers a very different picture of her marriage to her previous testimony on the subject, one in which her one-time husband had been cold and neglectful throughout their union, interested only in his political ambitions. Returning to South Africa, she urged voters to support Mandela's successor, Thabo Mbeki, in the polls, for South Africa needed, she said, 'a young man' at its helm.[80]

The infirmities resulting from Mandela's age are a theme developed in the first full biography of Thabo Mbeki, in which an exhausted and querulous octogenarian president is depicted as visibly irked by the procedures 'of weaning (him) from authority ... taking place at a quicker pace than he would have liked'. Indeed, the book's authors maintain, many of the accomplishments of Mandela's administration are 'a reflection of Thabo's work'.[81] Such disparaging efforts by Mbeki's admirers are unlikely to find much official favour, however. Instead, the new ANC leadership seems more predisposed to emphasise Mandela's record as an 'Africanist' traditionalist, and as such, a guiding genius together with the new president, of a South African-led 'African Renaissance'. The ANC's preferred model of consensual democracy, 'cooperative governance', is very much in the 'organic' vein favoured by Mandela in his patriarchal meditative mode.[82] During the 1999 election, opposition hecklers at public meetings were exhorted to return 'home' to the 'family'[83] and Mandela's brief public appearances were mainly directed at securing the loyalty of chiefs in the former homelands, to whom he delivered a series of homilies on the merits of respecting age and custom, and amongst whom he celebrated his third wedding to Graca Machel, widow of the first Mozambican president. At these festivities, his old adversary and his cousin, ex-Transkeien politician, Paramount Chief Kaiser Matanzima, was in prominent attendance. Graca Machel's anointment as a 'full member of the Madiba clan' became the occasion for a final act of reconciliation, one in which the rift between Apartheid's African collaborators and 'progressive' nationalists was symbolically closed through the incantations of a praise singer: 'Hail Dalibunga! [Mandela's praise name] . . . Hail Daliwonga! [Matanzima's] . . . the bones of Dalinyebo, Sabatha, Ngangelizwe [Xhosa kings] are shaking now that the Thembu nation is united in this ritual'.[84]

For Nelson Mandela's cult is likely to long out-live its subject. As black South African notables close ranks, modernist and traditional, in South Africa's second bourgeois republic, Mandela's many personas as well as the myths surrounding them will remain the most powerful source of ideological legitimation at their disposal.

Notes

1   M. Benson, *Nelson Mandela* (London, 1986), p. 13.
2   N. Mandela, *Long Walk to Freedom* (London, 1995). Since this paper was first written, two new biographies have appeared, an unsolicited volume by M. Meredith, *Nelson Mandela: a Biography* (London, 1997) which draws heavily on the autobiography but which also contains additional information, mainly about recent events, and an 'official' narrative by Anthony Sampson, which though shorter than Mandela's massive text contains much that is new, A. Sampson, *Mandela: the Authorised Biography* (London, 1999). Sampson's book is at its most illuminating in its treatment of the prison years. Drawing upon hitherto classified government documentation as well as the memories of other prisoners, it emphasises the formative impact of his incarceration on Mandela's character and his politics, especially in engendering the skills and convictions he would deploy as an architect of negotiated compromise.
3   R. Stengel, 'Mandela: the man and the mask', *Sunday Times* (Johannesburg), 27 Nov. 1994.
4   C. Jung and I. Shapiro, 'South Africa's negotiated transition: Democracy, Opposition and the New Constitutional Order', *Politics and Society*, 23:3 (1995), 287.
5   S. Sole, 'Angry Mandela reads the riot act', *Sunday Independent* (Johannesburg), 17 Mar. 1996.
6   C. Braude, 'We need to share Mandela's hidden pain to lay past abuses to rest', *Sunday Independent*, 3 Mar. 1996.
7   F. Meer, *Higher than Hope: the Authorised Biography of Nelson Mandela* (New York, 1990), p. 334: 'I have been fairly successful in putting on a mask behind which I have pined for my family, alone, never rushing for the post until somebody calls out my name . . .'
8   K. Nyatsumbe, 'Mandela raps praise singers', *The Star* (Johannesburg), 28 Feb. 1996.

9 The address was drafted by Mandela in conjunction with two members of the 'National Reception Committee', Cyril Ramaphosa and Trevor Manuel, both representatives of the political movement which had developed during the 1980s out of trade unions and local voluntary associations, a movement which emphasised popular sovereignty and accorded leaders very limited authority.

10 E. S. Reddy, *Nelson Mandela: Symbol of Resistance and Hope for a Free South Africa* (New Delhi, 1990), pp. 1–6.

11 Winnie Mandela wrote:

> I have a sense of being commoditised by the press. My relationship with it began the moment I stepped off the train in Johannesburg on a morning in 1953, a late teenager in my school uniform, with an iron trunk on my head, a food basket in my hand and an ambition in my heart to become a social worker. It was such a momentous step for a rural girl to take. Yet I was not newsworthy in that respect. I had to become a smart city girl, acquire glamour, before I could begin to be processed into a personality. And I began to be processed thus because I made my entry into Egoli at a time when there was an emergent black bourgeoisie and magazines like *Zonk* and *Drum* to reflect that bourgeoisie . . . they were on the lookout for role models: they were like talent scouts, looking for people who could be converted into personalities, glamorised and projected larger than life. . . .

Nomazano Winifred Madikizela Mandela, 'A country girl reflects on the media that turned her into a commodity', *Sunday Independent*, 8 Sept. 1996.

12 N. Harrison, *Winnie Mandela: Mother of a Nation* (London, 1985). For photograph see A. Hagemann, *Nelson Mandela* (Johannesburg, 1996), p. 61.

13 F. Meer, *Higher than Hope: the Authorised Biography of Nelson Mandela* (New York, 1990), p. 317.

14 *South* (Cape Town), 21 July 1988.

15 As is suggested in the preface in S. Johns and R. Hunt Davis, *Mandela, Tambo and the African National Congress* (Oxford and New York, 1991), p. ix.

16 J. Carlin, 'Love affair with Britain', *The Star*, 1 May 1993.

17 R. Stengel, 'The Mandela I came to know', *The Spectator*, 19 Nov. 1994.

18 This respectability is retained despite the disapproval sometimes expressed by representatives of Western governments evoked by Mandela's insistence on retaining warm relations with such authorities as Fidel Castro, Muammar Qaddafi, and Gennaday Zyufanov of the Russian Communist Party. Such eccentric behaviour could reassuringly be explained in Mandela's case by the invocation of Anglo-Saxon patrician codes of honour and loyalty.

19 See especially Harrison, *Winnie Mandela*, p. 85, who describes Mandela returning home from his mission abroad to obtain foreign support for Umkhonto we Sizwe, carrying a suitcase filled with national costumes for his wife. Mandela's 'fairytale' marriage featured prominently in a television soap opera broadcast starring Danny Glover and Alfre Woodward in more than eighty countries in 1988 (*Sunday Times*, 11 Feb. 1990). Ronald Harwood's screenplay was intended to emphasise 'the remarkable qualities of Winnie Mandela . . . (and) the extraordinary bond between the man and the woman', R. Harwood, *Mandela* (London, 1987), back cover.

20 And not only black writers. In 1948, Alan Paton's *Cry the Beloved Country* was the first South African fiction which introduced the moral drama of apartheid to an international best-seller audience. The book was subsequently filmed, inside South Africa, with a young Sidney Poitier in its leading role. Forty years later, Poitier returned to play the part of Mandela in a film made for American TV about South Africa's transition to democracy.

21 R. Nixon, *Homelands, Harlem and Hollywood: South African Culture and the World Beyond* (London, 1994), p. 178. A. Khumalo and E. Mphahlele's *Mandela: Echoes of an Era* (London, 1990) reproduces a good range of the press photographs of Mandela taken by Khumalo for South African newspapers in the 1950s and 1960s.

22 Sipho Sepemla, 'I Need', reprinted as the frontispiece of F. Meer, *Higher than Hope*.

23 S. Davis, *Apartheid's Rebels: Inside South Africa's Hidden War* (New Haven, 1987), p. 50.

24 C. Erasmus, 'Mandela: the Options', *Inside South Africa*, Sept. 1988.

25 C. Mutwa, *Let not my country die* (Pretoria, 1986), pp. 162–64.

26 Examples: a 1981 poll of black South Africans living on the Witwatersrand found 42 per cent of the sample choosing 'ANC leaders' as the 'real leaders of South Africa' as opposed to the 37 per cent who favoured the ANC as an organisation which 'will be important in their lives' (L. Schlemmer, 'The Report of the Attitude Surveys', *Buthelezi Commission* (Durban, 1982), I, pp. 244–45). Another 1981 poll of black South Africans in Johannesburg, Cape Town and Durban found 78 per cent endorsing Mandela as opposed to the 40 per cent of the respondents who favoured the ANC (C. Charney, 'Who are the black leaders?', *The Star*, 23 Sept. 1981). A 1985 national survey of black urban residents found 23 per cent acknowledging Mandela's leadership as opposed to 8 per cent favouring the organisation – in both cases the largest proportions of support for an individual or an organisation (M. Orkin, *The Struggle and the Future: What Black South Africans Really Think* (Johannesburg, 1986), pp. 35–36).

27 'Letters from Black South Africans to the President of Inkatha', *Inhlabamkhosi*, Bureau of Communication, Department of the Chief Minister, Government of Kwa Zulu (Ulundi, Feb. 1984), pp. 7–10.

28 S. Uys, 'The ANC generation gap that haunts Mandela', *The Guardian Weekly*, 23 Apr. 1993.

29 M. Benson, *Nelson Mandela* (London, 1980).

30 M. Benson, *Nelson Mandela* (London 1986).

31 'And that's why they won't release him', *New Nation*, 7 July 1988.

32 Though Derrida also suggests that in Mandela's future actions there will be represented 'the effective accomplishment, the filling out of the democratic form' when the 'seeds of African revolutionary democracy' infuse and fulfil the potential of Anglo-American forms. J. Derrida, 'The laws of reflection: Nelson Mandela, in admiration', J. Derrida and M. Tlili (eds), *For Nelson Mandela* (New York, 1987).

33 N. Mandela, *No Easy Walk to Freedom* (London, 1973), pp. v–vii.

34 For one version of this argument see R. Suttner and J. Cronin, *30 years of the Freedom Charter* (Johannesburg, 1986), pp. 179–80.

35 'The Charter on the Mines', *SASPU National*, Last Quarter, 1987, supplement on the Freedom Charter, p. 5.

36 F. Meer, *Higher than Hope: Rolihlahla We Love You* (Johannesburg, 1988).

37 F. Meer, *Higher than Hope: The Authorised Biography*, p. xi.

38 'Heed Free Mandela Movement, Government Urged', press cutting used as Exhibit D 30 in *State vs. Mewa Ramgobin*.

39 Speech at Release Mandela Committee meeting, Soweto, 8 July 1984, Schedule A, Indictment, p. 19, *State vs. Mewa Ramgobin*.

40 From transcript of rally reproduced in I. Saki Shabangu, *Madiba, The Folk Hero* (Giyani, 1995), p. 107.

41 M. Gottleib, 'Mandela's visit, New York's pride', *New York Times*, 25 June 1990.

42 L. Jones, 'Nelson and Winnie in the Black Metropolis', *Village Voice*, 3 July 1990.

43 'Waiting joyously for an African Godot', *New York Newsday*, 21 June 1990.

44 Gottleib, 'Mandela's visit'.
45 P. Applebone, 'American Blacks talk of change after Mandela', *New York Times*, 1 July 1990.
46 'Mandela takes his message to rally in the Yankee Stadium', *New York Times*, 22 June 1990.
47 *New York Newsday*, 21 June 1990.
48 A. Stanley, 'Pride and confusion mix in talk on education', *New York Times*, 21 June 1990.
49 J. Tierney, 'Meeting New York on her own', *New York Times*, 23 June 1990.
50 In certain centres preparations began months in advance, 'Rainbow coalition celebrates release of Nelson Mandela', *The Montclair Times* (NJ), 8 Feb. 1990.
51 Stanley, 'Pride and Confusion'.
52 Jones, 'Nelson and Winnie'.
53 *Ibid.*
54 Nixon, *Homelands, Harlem and Hollywood*, p. 187.
55 From his address to the joint session of the US House of Congress, 26 June 1990, in E. S. Reddy, *Nelson Mandela*, p. 83.
56 T. Dunbar Moodie, *The Rise of Afrikanerdom: Power, Apartheid, and the Afrikaner Civil Religion* (Berkeley, CA, 1975), pp. 18–21.
57 J. Gregory, *Goodbye Bafana: Nelson Mandela, My Prisoner, My Friend* (London, 1995), p. 434.
58 *Ibid.*, p. 489.
59 L. Sampson, 'Me and Mandela', *Sunday Life* (Cape Town), 19 Jan. 1997.
60 M. Gevisser, 'Grown fat on Total Onslaught Contracts, Bill Venter meets Mandela on the road to Damascus', *Sunday Independent*, 15 Dec. 1996.
61 Editorial, *The Citizen* (Johannesburg), 15 Jan. 1994.
62 S. Johnson, 'Allaying anxiety about Afrikaans', *The Star*, 19 Sept. 1991.
63 C. Braude, 'Yutar and holy disbelief', *Weekly Mail and Guardian*, 27 Mar. 1997.
64 D. Apter, *Ghana in Transition* (New Jersey, 1972), p. 323.
65 Recent market research suggests that 60 per cent of the population see no role for an opposition party and more than 25 per cent would prefer a one-party state (Editorial, *Weekly Mail*, 20 Mar. 1997). In 1994 pollsters found that 50 per cent of African respondents of a Witwatersrand sample would not allow members of the party they most opposed to live in their neighbourhood, and that 59 per cent of the same sample would try to stop such party members from canvassing support in their area (R. W. Johnson and L. Schlemmer, 'Political attitudes in South Africa's economic heartland', in R. W. Johnson and L. Schlemmer, *Launching Democracy in South Africa: The First Open Election, April 1994* (New Haven, 1996), p. 261.
66 For a very readable popular reflection of transition analysis with Mandela at its centre, see A. Sparks, *Tomorrow is Another Country* (London, 1995).
67 A. Russell, 'Mandela magic leaves the world lost for words', *Daily Telegraph*, 5 July 1996.
68 P. Krost, 'Focused spindoctor at Madiba's side', *The Star*, 11 Jan. 1997.
69 E. Waugh, 'Mandela gives Nobel money to children', *The Star*, 11 Mar. 1994.
70 'I won't be your bloody fool, Dali, wrote furious Winnie', *The Star*, 20 Mar. 1996.
71 *Sunday Times*, 25 Feb. 1996.
72 'Presidential accolades for nation-building citizens', *The Star*, 11 Nov. 1996.
73 Derrida, 'The laws of reflection', p. 26.
74 'Mandela fires newsmen', *The Star*, 14 Nov. 1996.
75 'Mandela hits out at Tutu, chief whip', *The Star*, 27 Sept. 1994.
76 H. W. Vilikazi, 'Leaders' moral quality must rise', *The Star*, 12 June 1995.

77   Findings from *Opinion 99*, a poll conducted by the Electoral Institute in conjunc-
     tion with the Institute for Democracy in South Africa (IDASA), the South African
     Broadcasting Corporation, and the survey agency, Markinor. Similar percentages
     emerged from a poll conducted in March 1999 by the Human Sciences Research
     Council through its *Democracy SA* project.
78   J. Rosenthal and F. Nxumalo, 'Mandelarand may oust Oom Paul', *Business Report*,
     Mar. 1999.
79   'Mandela using Nat laws to eject Winnie', *The Star*, 17 Apr. 1999.
80   Meanwhile Winnie Mandela's own status in public history is undergoing critical re-
     evaluation, her continuing popularity notwithstanding. A memorial stone
     commemorating the site of the plane crash in which Mozambique's Samora Machel
     met his death had its inscription worded so that the original message of condo-
     lence received by the Machel family from the Mandela family, reproduced on the
     stone, had Winnie's name excised (P. Fauvet, 'History remade as Winnie's name
     left off Machel plaque', *The Star*, 23 Jan. 1999).
81   A. Hadland and J. Rantao, *The Life and Times of Thabo Mbeki* (Rivonia, 1999),
     p. 98 and p. 149.
82   For a perceptive exposition of the democratic implications of Mandela's ideas about
     national consensus see A. Nash, 'Mandela's Democracy', *Monthly Review*, Apr. 1999,
     pp. 18–28.
83   R. Munusamy, 'Come Home, ANC tells UDM supporters', *Sunday Times*, 31 Jan.
     1999.
84   Xolesa Vapi, 'Hail Queen Graca', *The Star*, 10 Apr. 1999.

INDEX